A Pageant of Old Scandinavia

A Pageant
of Old Scandinavia

EDITED BY

HENRY GODDARD LEACH

1946

PRINCETON UNIVERSITY PRESS

PRINCETON

FOR THE AMERICAN-SCANDINAVIAN FOUNDATION

NEW YORK

PRINTED IN THE UNITED STATES OF AMERICA BY PRINCETON
UNIVERSITY PRESS AT PRINCETON, NEW JERSEY

TO
AGNES BROWN LEACH

PREFACE

Both reader and editor owe their thanks to the many scholars and librarians at home and abroad who, during the past forty years, have generously assisted in assembling this anthology. The passages selected are not always the most accurate. Rather, they show variety in the methods of translation as well as diversity in the original documents. Some translations are scrupulously exact, others are freely literary, and one departs from the text in order to reproduce the spirit of the original. Readers who require a literal rendering will consult the Scandinavian texts.

Extensive bibliographies have been omitted from this volume, as they already exist for Old Norse or West Scandinavian in the serial bibliographies prepared by Dr. Halldór Hermannsson beginning in 1908 and appearing at intervals in *Islandica,* where editions of the originals are recorded, together with critical commentary, and translations into various languages. For the East Scandinavian area of Denmark and Sweden there is no corresponding bibliography. In view of the vast literature of essays and commentary available in public libraries, the notes in the present book are made as brief as possible and placed at the back, with the acknowledgment to translators and publishers.

Many statements in this volume will seem to some scholars too categorical. Instead of quoting authorities or using the words, "perhaps," "possibly," "probably," or "some assert," it has seemed best to accept the weight of evidence to date, subject to future refutation.

Readers should not be troubled by the fact that the same proper name may be spelled in three ways on the same page: the original spelling, the editor's spelling, the translator's spelling.

Unless otherwise indicated the translations are from Old Norse or West Scandinavian, the language of Norway and Iceland and the Scandinavian colonies in Ireland, the British Isles, the Faeroes, and Greenland. In the introductory essay, not to repeat matter elsewhere available, inventories and catalogues of poems and sagas are omitted. Within a few years, The American-Scandinavian Foundation hopes to publish histories of the literature of each of the Scandinavian countries.

H. G. Leach

Widener Library
Harvard University
January 2, 1946

ACKNOWLEDGMENTS

THIS book, the popularization of research in many languages, is made possible by the collaboration of many scholars to whom the editor is deeply indebted. First, he gives grateful acknowledgment to the publishers and translators who have permitted quotation from their works and whose names are recorded in the note on sources at the end of the book. Second, he emphasizes his obligation to Princeton University Press and to the members of the Publication Council of The American-Scandinavian Foundation whose names appear at the end of this volume, who have encouraged him during the years of preparation and given unsparingly of their time and counsel. Of these especial thanks are due to William Witherle Lawrence, Professor of English in Columbia University, to Halldór Hermannsson, Professor of Scandinavian Languages in Cornell University, and to his pupil, John B. C. Watkins, Associate Professor of English in the University of Manitoba, all of whom have been consulted at various stages of the manuscript and the proof. Also the editor has enjoyed the personal criticisms and the scores of philological essays of an American scholar whose profound researches in recent years have explored nearly this entire territory, Kemp Malone, former Fellow of this Foundation to Iceland and Professor of English in The Johns Hopkins University.

The editor records with very warm thanks the help of the librarians and the staffs of several libraries, but especially the officers of Harvard College Library, where a room was allocated for this project, Cornell University Library, the University Libraries of Copenhagen, Oslo, Uppsala, the Royal Libraries of Copenhagen and Stockholm, the Library of Congress, and the British Museum. He acknowledges his debt to Dr. Carl F. Bayerschmidt of Columbia University; F. Stanton Cawley, Professor of German in Harvard University; Gustaf Cederschiöld, Professor of Northern Philology in Göteborg College; Professors Finnur Jónsson, Axel Olrik, Johannes C. H. R. Steenstrup, and Dr. Gudmund Schütte, of the University of Copenhagen; Sir William Craigie, Professor of English in Oxford University; Samuel Hazzard Cross, Editor of *Speculum*; Stefán Einarsson, Professor of Scandinavian Philology in The Johns Hopkins University; Harald Ingholt, Associate Professor of Archeology in

Yale University; Jess H. Jackson, former Foundation Fellow and Professor of English in The College of William and Mary; Walter S. Hinchman, author and instructor in English in Groton School, Haverford College, and Milton Academy; Sigurd Bernhard Hustvedt, Professor of English in the University of California; Dr. Kristian Kålund, Curator of the Arnamagnean Collection; George Lyman Kittredge, Professor of English in Harvard University; Dr. Sven Liljeblad, Instructor in Swedish in Harvard University; Roger S. Loomis, Associate Professor of English in Columbia University; Francis P. Magoun Jr., Professor of Comparative Literature in Harvard University; Professor Sigurthur Nordal of the University of Reykjavik; Professors Alexander Bugge, Moltke Moe, and Knut Liestöl of the University of Oslo; Fred N. Robinson, Professor of Celtic in Harvard University; Dr. A. N. Rygg, Editor of *Nordisk Tidende*; Professor Arthur F. J. Remy of Columbia University; Gertrude Schoepperle, Professor of English in Vassar College; William Henry Schofield, Professor of Comparative Literature in Harvard University; President Henrik Schück of Uppsala University; and Barrett Wendell, Professor of English in Harvard University.

The editor is profoundly grateful to all the translators and their publishers for generous permission to include here selections from their books. The precise collation is explained in the back of this book under the heading "Sources."

A final acknowledgment is due to a great editor, Dr. Hanna Astrup Larsen, who for thirty-five years has patiently urged the author to complete this work and insisted on some measure of literary style as well as authentic scholarship.

H.G.L.

CONTENTS

A Pageant of Old Scandinavia

On an Icelandic Skald

(Egill Skallagrimsson)

By Henry Adams Bellows

Singer and conqueror of battles vast
  With sea, and earth, and men in days of yore,
  Father of mighty sons, who on the shore
Of barren Iceland reared a house to last
The generations of an age long past,
  Now do thy kinsmen hear thy voice no more,
  Nor ever shall they see thy flame-tipped oar
Lash the white spray to meet the bending mast.

Ten centuries weigh down upon thy grave;
  Yet one still hears thy song, and sees thy face,
    Stern, battle-scarred, unyielding; for the wave
That thunders on to work the east wind's will
  Makes his heart sing with the old gladness still,
    And tells him we are of the selfsame race.

OLD SCANDINAVIAN LITERATURE

THE LITERATURE of ancient Scandinavia offers a striking contrast to the stream of consciousness and the symbolism that are popular in our contemporary fiction and poetry. The sagas and the eddas are exterior delineations of human conduct. The author does not himself interpret his character but he makes it easy for his reader or his listener to do so. Old Scandinavian writers habitually refrain from revealing the thoughts or analyzing the behavior of their heroes. Yet the action is not so important to them as character developing through action and conversation. American behaviorists could regard the Icelandic sagas as their model literature.

Ancient Scandinavian letters can easily be defined by stating what they are not. Like the Greek classics, Old Norse literature developed in comparative isolation, but little influenced by ideas from other civilizations. Unlike Greek literature, however, it did not produce a single epic poem, or bequeath to us a single drama. The Scandinavian past has left to us no *Odyssey,* no Sophocles. Its verse was broken into stanzas, and its dialogue was woven into prose narrative. Yet Old Norse was inherently both epic and dramatic. What Aristotle attributed in his *Poetics* to Homer is true of both the poetry and the prose of the North: "Homer, admirable in all respects, has the special merit of being the only poet who rightly appreciates the part he should take himself. The poet should speak as little as possible in his own person, for it is not this that makes him an imitator of character, emotion, and action. Other poets appear themselves upon the scene throughout, and imitate life but little and rarely. Homer, after a few prefatory words, at once brings in a man, or woman, or other personage: none of them wanting in characteristic qualities, but each with a character of his own."

If ancient Scandinavia did not produce an epic or a drama, neither did it bequeath to us an original romance or novel in the modern sense, a *Tristan* or *David Copperfield.* For all that, Old Norse remains a vast, original, and indigenous contribution to the imitation of human conduct in art.

NATIONAL INSTINCT has always proved more productive for Scandinavians than have models or criticisms from abroad. In saying that their literature is indigenous we must, however, make reservations. While the literature of Iceland was, like that of Athens, chiefly native, it was stimulated by contact with two European centers, Ath-Cliath in Ireland, which the Scandinavians called Dublin (*Dyflin*), and Constantinople or Byzantium, which they called The Great City (*Miklagarth*). The practical Scandinavian was impressed by the imaginative, almost magical quality of the Irish mind, and the glamor of Irish women and slaves. The Bardic Schools of elaborate metrics in Ireland influenced the Icelandic development of skaldic poetry. The Icelanders did not establish training schools for poets, as did the Irish, but they did achieve similar results in complicated versification, through tutors and self-training.

At the other end of Europe, Byzantium was a university of culture and learning for the Scandinavians, and, on every possible occasion, vikings, traders, and tourists made long voyages to the Bosporus and resided there, enjoying the luxury and learning and sophistication of the city that perpetuated Greek and Roman civilization for one thousand years after the fall of Rome. The Byzantine emperors liked the Norsemen and employed them in their select bodyguard. For six hundred years, until the fall of Constantinople spread its culture to the Renaissance of western Europe, the Scandinavians drew from that source of intellectual discipline.

Also, a stream of oriental folk tales reached Sweden, Denmark, and Norway through Russia.

The Danish historian Saxo Grammaticus paid a tribute to the cosmopolitan curiosity of the Icelanders at the turn of the twelfth century that is always worth quoting: "Nor may the pains of the men of Thule be blotted in oblivion; for though they lack all that can foster luxury (so naturally barren is the soil) yet they make up for their neediness by their wit, by keeping continually every observance of soberness, and devoting every instant of their lives to perfecting our knowledge of the deeds of foreigners. Indeed, they account it a delight to learn and to consign to remembrance the history of all nations, deeming it as great a glory to set forth the excellence of others as to display their own."

ABOUT 13,000 B.C. the ice of the last glacial period began to recede from the southern tip of the Scandinavian peninsula. Swedish geologists have traced this recession exactly year by year. As fertile fields became tillable, the Gothonic peoples—Goths and Scandinavians—began, year after year, to occupy the freed soil of the Jutland peninsula, the Danish islands, and what is now Sweden and Norway, pushing north and east a Turanian stock, the Finns and the Lapps. Eventually the Finns settled the present Finland and Estonia and the Lapps roamed the Arctic wastes of Norway, Sweden, and Finland.

The Goths settled in what is now southern Sweden. In later centuries their colonies emigrated in large measure to southern Europe. But they left behind them their names in the Götland provinces of Sweden and the island of Gotland in the Baltic. The Goths of Sweden maintained their own kingdom, which was, at long last, absorbed by the Swedes of Uppsala, to the north, who were aware of themselves as a state before the time of Tacitus.

The archeological remains of those prehistoric times are numerous. In historic times the coins and the gold vessels and ornaments of Rome reached the North or were imitated by the Scandinavian smiths. Mediterranean peoples were conscious of the existence of the Scandinavians in antiquity, but had no direct contact until the Cimbri and other nations from the peninsula of Jutland, in the second century before Christ, invaded Gaul and Italy in search of better farms.

It was Pytheas of Marseilles who made the first recorded visit to the Scandinavian North, in the fourth century before the Christian era. Although his own account is lost, we know that he visited Britain and from Britain set out across the sea toward "the ultimate realms of the pole." He landed in "Thule." Now Thule was the Mediterranean term for farthest north. In the case of Pytheas very likely Thule was the coast of Norway, as he was impressed by the darkness. In later times Latin writers extended the name to Iceland.

In their confused accounts of Scandinavian countries classical writers blended fact and fancy. Perhaps the Greeks had the Scandinavians in mind when they described those ultimate peoples the Cimmerians and the Hyperboreans. In the *Odyssey* we read: "She came to the limits of the world, to the deep flowing Oceanus. There is the land and the city of the Cimmerians, shrouded in mist and cloud, and never does the shining sun look down on them with his rays, neither when he climbs up the starry heaven, nor when again he turns earthward from the firmament, but deadly night is outspread over miserable mortals."

Less gloomy, true and tender but not dark, was Pindar's description of the Hyperboreans: "The muse is no stranger to their manors. The dances of girls, and the sweet melody of the lyre and pipe, resound on every side, and twining their hair with the glittering bay, they feast joyously. There is no doom of sickness or disease for this sacred race: but they live apart from toil and battles, undisturbed by exacting Nemesis."

Greek and Roman writers of the early centuries of the Christian era gave brief descriptions of the Scandinavians, and Augustus Caesar recorded a visit of his fleet to Jutland. The Swedes were the first of the Northern peoples to set up a centralized kingdom and they were the last to adopt Christianity. About A.D. 400 the so-called Gold Period was ushered in with a central authority in Denmark on the island of Sjælland, whose kings of a century later were celebrated in the English epic *Bēowulf*. The more individualistic Norwegians, however, preferred small kingdoms and jarldoms, and it was not until the ninth century that Norway was united. The two centuries from 400 to 600 produced many heroic characters who came, centuries later, to figure in legendary literature. From 600 to 800 Scandinavia relaxed behind an historical mist until, about 800, the North emerged into the fierce light of history with the viking raids and the far-flung settlements that ended with the Norman conquest of England in 1066.

Norwegians occupied the Orkneys, the Shetlands, the Hebrides and Man, and large sections of northern France, England, Scotland, and Ireland. The Danes for a time ruled England and planted colonies in Normandy and Sicily. In 870 Norwegians began the settlement of Iceland, and in the following centuries Icelanders set up two colonies in Greenland who attempted also to colonize the American mainland.

Meanwhile, the Swedes, the "Russ," turning toward the east and south, founded the Russian state and engaged in trade with the Arabs and the Greeks, and almost succeeded in military operations against Byzantium.

It was in Iceland that the literary genius of old Scandinavia was concentrated. Iceland became the Athens of the North. The age of settlement from 870 to 930 was completed by the establishment of the central assembly of the Icelandic republic, the Althing, in 930. Thereafter for 333 years, Iceland was a republic unique in the history of nations in having no executive, no legislature, no police or military, in our sense, governed only by a legislating court of law. The hundred years from 930 to 1030 is sometimes called the Saga Age of Iceland. It was the period of local history in the making, recorded in oral tradition and recitation, to be written down in the following centuries in the sheepskin manuscripts of the Icelandic sagas.

THE VERBAL record of Scandinavia begins with the loan words preserved in Finnish from the beginning of the Christian era. As these words were not subjected to the same changes as those which took place in Scandinavian languages, they remain somewhat as mummies of early Scandinavian. They can, of course, hardly be called literature.

Old Scandinavian literature begins with the runic inscriptions in the older futhork of twenty-four letters, about A.D. 200. About A.D. 600 these began to be replaced by a shorter futhork of sixteen letters, at which time the common Scandinavian language began gradually to split into dialects. The runes are adaptations of Greek and Roman letters, probably fashioned by the Goths in southern Europe whence their use spread over northern Europe.

The Latin alphabet was introduced into the Scandinavian countries along with Christianity and replaced the more unwieldy runic characters, but it was not until the twelfth century that the Icelanders wrote down their own verse and prose on sheepskins in the vernacular, instead of in Latin, by means of the new alphabet. The production of manuscripts recording literature previously transmitted by oral recitation continued throughout the thirteenth and fourteenth centuries, and was followed by transcripts on paper well into the age of printing.

Our knowledge of Scandinavian mythology is derived chiefly from the eddas, using that term for the poetry and the poetics that describe the gods and the mythical heroes. The Poetic Edda is a collection of anonymous poems about gods and heroes. The Prose Edda is a manual of poetics compiled by Snorri Sturluson about A.D. 1222. This *Snorra Edda* contains three sections: the first, stories about the gods; the second, legendary lore required by poets; the third, instruction in the art of skaldic verse. The best explanation of the word *edda* is that it is derived from *Oddi*, meaning "Book of Oddi," the name of the manor owned by Sæmund the Wise (1056-1133). In his youth Snorri was foster-son there during the residence of the great landlord Jón Loptsson (1124-1197). In the library of that estate Snorri must have had access to the mythological poems.

The poems of the Poetic or Elder or Sæmundar Edda are anonymous and without date or place of origin. They have been assigned to almost as many places as laid claim to Homer. Norway claims some of them and the British Isles as well as Iceland, but we are sure only that one was composed in Greenland. Probably none of them assumed their present form before A.D. 800.

The verse of the Poetic Edda is not rhymed. It is alliterative like Anglo-Saxon poetry, but, unlike the Anglo-Saxon, is stanzaic instead of stichic. Scandinavian art was more dramatic and realistic, English more epic and reflective. Eddic poems are simple in structure and easily translatable into alliterating English verse. There are three types: eddic-meter, speech-meter, chant-meter. Two of the poems are dramatic monologues; the rest contain some narrative, but are chiefly cast in dialogue. Thus we are free to believe that originally they were oral folk drama performed at religious ceremonies and lay festivals. They are interspersed with numerous passages of explanatory prose which resemble stage directions.

A FEW PARAGRAPHS will suffice to introduce the deities of the Scandinavian pantheon. To this day we still invoke four heathen English equivalents of Norse gods on four days of every week: Tuesday, Wednesday, Thursday, Friday. The lives and the adventures of the high Northern divinities, as recorded in the early literature of the North and systematized by the Icelandic author Snorri Sturluson in the thirteenth century, are quite as elaborate as the stories of the Greek age of fable and mythology. Othin enjoyed as numerous offspring born out of wedlock as did Zeus. Indeed, a patient scholar could devote a year with profit as well as pleasure to tracing but one of the thousand tales of the Norse divinities in edda and saga and in related Indo-European literature.

War between two races of gods, Æsir and Vanir, was wisely settled by an exchange of hostages. One of Othin's three brothers went over to the Vanir, and three of the Vanir—Njorth and his two children— were adopted into the Æsir.

The origin of life recorded in Northern myth is not unlike the theory advanced by some living scientists that life arose from the action of carbon monoxide on sea water. In the profound abyss of Ginnunga-gap, heat playing with the frost mist first produced not seaweed or jellyfish but a giant, as well as a cow to sustain him. The cow kept licking the frozen salt until another being emerged who became the progenitor of Othin and his brothers Vili and Ve, forbears of the Æsir. The Æsir made order out of chaos and out of two trees created man and woman. The Æsir appointed separate domains for the gods, the giants, the elves, the dwarfs, and for men, and abodes also for the dead. The gods dwelt in Asgarth. In Asgarth there were many mansions and among them Valhall, the glorious hall where the Valkyries waited upon those who were slain in battle. Beings so unfortunate as to die a natural death spent a less exciting hereafter in Hel.

Othin, supreme deity, was god of battle and of wisdom. He presided over the assemblies of all the gods at the ash Yggdrasil ("horse of the awful one"), the tree of the universe. At sacrifices men were dedicated to Othin by being hanged on a tree and pierced with a spear. A whole hostile army could be consecrated to Othin by hurling a spear high over their heads. Othin once performed this rite upon himself on the ash Yggdrasil: "I ween that I hung on the windy tree, hung there for nights full nine; with the spear I was wounded, and offered I was to Othin, myself to myself." In Valhall Othin received the slain into a perpetual communion of combat, resurrection, mead, and bliss.

Of the greater Æsir there were twelve in addition to Othin, who constituted the daily council, not the occasional assembly, of the gods. Chief of these was Thor, the Thunderer, god of strength, who held sway over the elements and the harvests, and defended with his hammer, Mjollnir, the gods and men against the overweening race of giants. He was the favorite god of the farmer, while the warrior worshipped Othin. Baldr the beautiful was god of light. Njorth and Freyr shared with Thor the disciplines of vegetable and human propagation. Tyr was a more ancient but still honored god of war. The fact that his name is synonymous with Zeus, Jove, and *divus* and in the plural meant "gods" indicated his primordial importance. Heimdall was watchman for the gods, Bragi their god of poetry, Forseti of justice, while the remaining four—Hoth, Vali, Vithar, and Ull—had each his special assignment.

Among other deities Loki the troublemaker must not be overlooked. This creature of evil was a giant adopted by the Æsir. His giant sons, the Fenris Wolf and the Mithgarth Serpent, as well as his daughter Hel, who presided over the realm of the unslain dead, were destined to play unpleasant parts in Ragnarok, the Doom of the Gods.

Chief of the goddesses were Frigg (Othin's wife), Jorth, and Freyja of the Vanir, owner of the greatest jewel of Asgarth, the Brisingamen, a necklace made by the dwarfs. As to the Scandinavian fates, the Norns, they were, of course, as effective in their sterner duties as were the battle maidens, the glamorous Valkyries.

Mythology is one thing, religion something else. Thanks to Icelandic scholarship we have a systematic account of the gods as revealed to the patrician members of old Scandinavian society. But a manual of religious observance like that of the Hebrews no medieval Icelandic prophet thought worth compiling. The proletarians of Scandinavia, the plain folk who caught the fish and ploughed the rye fields, knew very little about Othin; nor did they expect beautiful Valkyries at death to take them to abodes in blessed Valhall. Although immortality was a general Scandinavian belief, the farmhand, fisherman, servant, or thrall awaited nothing better in the hereafter than a quiet existence in the subterranean regions of Hel. That Thor was more real to them than Othin was attested by the frequency of his name in the place-names and the person-names of the North. In some future time, a group of scholars working in collaboration—too much for any one mind—may, from a thousand hints in the sagas, construct an account of old Scandinavian religious life to supplement Snorri's history of the gods.

Consistent with their religious respect for the laws of nature was a sense of social law and order, with established codes of honor that governed even the technique of physical combat.

The worship of Othin was confined chiefly to the fighting front and to the poets who depended on him for the gift of metrical skill. Thor was the most popular god, as he was largely responsible for good crops, thunder, and all sorts of weather, as well as fruitful marriage. There were temples to Thor all over Scandinavia. These temples were not copies of the marble structures of the ancient Greeks. They were simple wooden affairs, with pillars inside instead of out on the portico, with a shrine and a hall for feasting. Next to Thor, Freyr was most revered, as he also controlled crops and childbearing. There were many temples to Freyr, and some temples contained images or carved reliefs of several gods. The people regarded the gods as their warm personal friends. After the ceremony of sacrificing animals, they ate the flesh, but dedicated the blood to the gods. Occasionally they sacrificed human beings, usually prisoners or slaves. There was no priesthood or caste of priests. Religion was democratic. They chose for priest the most influential man in the community, who was probably also the lawyer. He maintained the temple on his own property at his own expense, assisted by the offerings of the community.

HALF of the poems of the Poetic Edda are concerned not with the gods but with legendary heroes from the time when men were not surprised to meet and talk with friendly supernatural beings. Most of these heroes were suggested by historical men and women who actually lived, not in the settlements of the west but back in the homelands of Sweden and Denmark or among the kindred Goths on the continent. Other repositories of mythical tradition are the Sagas of Antiquity (*fornaldar sögur*), collected in Iceland in the fourteenth century, and in Denmark the Latin history of the Danes (*Gesta Danorum*) by the Danish monk Saxo Grammaticus (1150-1220). Both these collections are full of accretions of centuries of folk tales, attached now to one hero now to another. Saxo greatly confused the problem of future historians by his arrangement of legends from different periods as historical chronicle. He did not, however, telescope and rationalize old legends as much as the more imaginative Snorri Sturluson. The less accurate Saxo's history, the greater his contribution to Danish folklore. At a recent historical convention in Copenhagen an eminent Danish folklorist became indignant when an historian tried to prove that a certain famous supposedly legendary fiction recorded by Saxo was actually an historic fact!

Although the Scandinavians were rather late in writing down the stories of their old heroes from behind the historical curtain and, in fact, first developed the stories of heroes nearer their own time, the earlier themes became the more popular in the later Middle Ages. Some of these heroes doubtless belong to pure folklore that can never be dated. Such is Wayland the Smith and that King Frothi whose millstone ground gold and peace. One of the earliest of the heroes of legend is Helgi Hundingsbane, who probably lived in the second century of the Christian era. Both Sweden and Denmark claim him, as well might the peoples of the south shore of the Baltic, the "nest" of the Hreith-Goths. Of heroes who lived before Offa of the Eider and Hrolf of Hleithra, Helgi was the noblest character of Scandinavian antiquity. A normal man, objective, a statesman, a fearless warrior, and a generous personality, it is small wonder that Helgi was loved by an immortal woman, a Valkyrie who combined the athleticism of Diana with the ardor of Venus. Their loyalty and affection provided Scandinavia with one of the most passionate love stories and the most erotic verse of Northern Europe. Their friendship transcended the grave, and both hero and Valkyrie were twice born again!

To about A.D. 360 we can date the hero Offa of south Jutland. This dumb youth who gained his speech to save his people was celebrated in preserved Anglo-Saxon legends as well as in lost Danish songs translated into Latin by Saxo Grammaticus.

To A.D. 400 we may assign the Danish king Sigehere of Sigersted, last of the dynasty of S-kings or Siklings, who left treasures in the soil for the pleasure of modern archeologists. Instead of denoting their descent by suffixing "-son" or "-daughter" to the father's name, royalty in that era indicated their lineage by alliteration. Thus we have Sigar, Sigrith, Sigvaldi, Signy. When, in the fifth century, the seat of royalty was moved to the neighborhood of Leire, also on Sjælland, by the Skjoldungs or Scyldings, members of that family were distinguished by the initial H: Halfdan, Hroar, Halga, Hrolf, Heoroweard, Hroerik, Harald, Hring. When a queen appears in this dynasty whose name does not begin with H she is probably foreign born. Meanwhile the Swedish royal house of Uppsala preferred an initial vowel to denote their illustrious parentage: Aun, Egil, Ottar, Athils. They borrowed from the Danes the legendary Ing and even claimed Othin for an ancestor. Hamlet—Amlothi, "mad Ole"—was a scion of this Swedish "vowel house" transplanted in Jutland and by Shakespeare to Elsinore in Sjælland, where his father's ghost still walks the ramparts on eerie moonlit nights!

We are on historical ground for a time with the Danish kings who adopted the royal H and resided in the Hall of Heorot, "The Hart," at Hleithargarth, celebrated in Anglo-Saxon epic and in Danish histories.

More popular even than native legend was the Cycle of the Volsungs, dealing with Franks, Burgundians, Goths, and Huns, which probably was not crystallized before the end of the sixth century.

As an epilogue to legendary history Sigurth Hring may be mentioned. Here we have the last vestige of the royal H of the House of Heorot. After the destruction of Heorot and an intermission of civil war, another great king of the H's arose in Denmark in Harald Hildetand. He gave his nephew Hring dominion over southern Sweden. Growing old, the uncle challenged the nephew to battle at Bravalla, where the hosts of the Scandinavian North met for slaughter. Harald was slain and dedicated to Othin and burned with his equipment in magnificent state. Hring succeeded him to both Sweden and Denmark. In his old age, instead of dying in battle, Hring ended his days like early heroes of the S dynasty, by sailing seaward on a burning ship. Thus ended the heroic age, the gold age of costly ornaments and magnificent utensils and inscriptions in the early runes.

THE TWO CENTURIES following, Vendel-time, were comparatively undramatic, preparing for the age of viking enterprise. In that period of relative calm the poems of the Poetic Edda were conceived. It became questionable good taste to attach folklore or the supernatural to historical characters of later periods. For that reason we may omit discussion of the picturesque but rather maudlin experiences attributed to Ragnar Lothbrok and his intrepid sons, though an exception can be made of the alleged encounters of the troll folk of Iceland with Grettir the Strong, who lived as late as the eleventh century.

OLD SCANDINAVIAN LITERATURE achieved its greatest triumphs in the historical saga-writing of Iceland. From the days of the settlements in the ninth century the history of each family was recorded in oral recitation, often beginning with its origin in Norway. The prose transmission was, for the most part, trustworthy, especially when accompanied by alliterating poems. In the twelfth, and still more in the thirteenth century, the sagas were written down on sheepskin in the vernacular in the new Latin lettering. Extroverted as they are, the Icelandic sagas are unsurpassed in the action of their characters and the tragedy of their social plots.

The typical Icelandic saga is the story of a family, and its plot the fate of one generation. There are five longer Icelandic family sagas: *Eyrbyggja, Egils, Laxdæla, Grettis*, and—last written, longest, and best—*Njáls saga*. All five have been well translated into English and other languages.

Possibly a third of the shorter family sagas have also been translated. Their number is almost legion. Most of them are models of character development through action and of ironical understatement by the narrator and the scribe. All are anonymous. Most of them are masculine in mood and dwell upon deeds of violence rather than domestic bliss. There are, among them, however, several good love stories, tales of farm life, lawsuits, and sea adventures.

The plots of the sagas are often developments of conflict between personal choice and social code. A wife must bring herself to sacrifice her husband in order to accomplish the prescribed revenge for her brother. Cousin must avenge cousin upon a sworn friend. A maiden should seek death rather than suffer seduction. Family revenge is the outstanding theme of the sagas. Insult must be atoned by manslaughter and manslaughter by revenge according to a code as strict as that imputed to our southern mountaineers today. The Icelandic code is so severe that in the Saga of Gisli the Outlaw the hero has to subdue his personal feelings and kill his sister's husband in order to avenge his wife's brother. Thus his sister is bound to bring about the death of her own dear brother. When at last the noble Gisli is killed, it becomes his sister's duty to see that he also is avenged.

Manhood is valued above virtue, for the good is a variable and incommensurable quality, while manhood is an instinctive ethic. The pragmatic science of life is more to be praised than metaphysics.

One of the most perfect of the shorter Icelandic sagas is the Story of the Confederates (*Bandamanna saga*). A great-hearted, enterprising youth who amassed wealth speedily but was naïve in the defensive techniques of criticism and petty malice is brought to court by a group of shrewd scoundrels who conspire to strip him of his well-earned possessions. His aged father, impecunious but versed in law and wily in stratagems, undertakes his son's defense. In a series of witty dialogues and speeches he outwits the conspirators and puts them to shame and derision. The humor of this tale is sustained from beginning to end. The narrative is pregnant with the salty sophistication of the *Hávamál* and the ironical understatement in which saga-men delighted. *Bandamanna saga* is material out of which an Aristophanes or a Molière or a Holberg could construct a farce.

The sagas of the Bishops of Iceland, as well as the laws, the annals, and the extensive literature of instruction and popular science contain many lay passages that deserve the title of literature.

OUT OF THE ANONYMITY of saga-writing in Iceland emerge the names of four great historians: Sæmund Sigfusson of Oddi (1056-1133), Ari Thorgilsson (1067-1148), Snorri Sturluson (1178-1241), and Sturla Thortharson (1215-1284). The work of Sæmund the Wise is lost, but his library and the verbal tradition of Oddi were sources of writing that survives. Ari the Learned wrote three important works: the Book of the Kings of Norway (*Konunga-bók*), the Book of the Settlements of Iceland (*Landnáma-bók*), and the Book of the Icelanders (*Íslendinga-bók*). The first of these works is lost, and the last is preserved in an abridgment made by Ari himself.

Snorri Sturluson spent his boyhood from the age of three till nineteen as foster-son in the household of Oddi, then owned by Jón Loptsson, the leading law-man of Iceland, and absorbed the knowledge of that seat of learning. Snorri was himself several times lawspeaker of Iceland. Twice he visited King Hakon in Norway. About 1222 he completed his manual of Norse poetry, the so-called Younger Edda, and about 1230 his history of the kings of Norway down to 1177, the so-called *Heimskringla*. Snorri made history as well as wrote it. He championed Icelandic independence against the ambitions of Norway until, in 1241, by order of the king, he was assassinated. In 1263 Iceland became a province of Norway, later passing to Denmark, and did not again acquire complete independence until 1944.

Snorri was not a man of high moral rectitude. But he was a great artist and a shrewd politician. He belonged to the distinguished line of Herodotus and Gibbon and was one of the greatest historians of the Middle Ages. For his era he was scientific. He preferred the petrified records of skaldic verse to fluid oral prose tradition. He used folklore to color his narrative more sparingly than did his Latin contemporaries in Continental Europe. The imaginative faculties that made his recording art were employed in his selection of material, his dramatization of narrative, his continuity of cause and effect, and his mastery of a language that flowed with clearness, force, easy imagery, and elegance.

Although Norway had several native historians, Icelanders were the classic chroniclers of Norway. Other Icelanders wrote other Norwegian histories, of which many are preserved and several available in English translations.

Sturla, Snorri's nephew, was also an able historian, but his narratives of the contemporary reigns of Hakon and of Magnus are merely good reading compared with the brilliant style of his uncle. He is sometimes more lively in his long compilation of Icelandic family feuds from 1117 to 1264, the *Sturlunga saga,* part of which he wrote himself. Some of the intimate domestic scenes are recorded with the skill of a modern novelist.

THE NORSE SETTLEMENTS in other islands of the west had their literature, although it did not compare in excellence with the production of Iceland. We have a saga of the Orkneys and a saga of the Faeroes. The accounts of the settlements in Greenland and the voyages to Vinland were written down in Iceland. Possibly many of the eddic and skaldic poems were composed in the western isles.

In Denmark most of the songs and sagas in the vernacular have been lost. Even the Icelandic history of the dynasty of Heorot, the *Skjöldunga saga,* exists only in fragments and Latin epitomes. The *Hrólfs saga kraka* is late and exaggerated. Danish folklore, poetry, and story are, however, paraphrased in the *Gesta Danorum* of Saxo Grammaticus. For Danish history we must resort to the scattered episodes in Icelandic saga and skaldic verse, to Anglo-Saxon poems, and continental Latin chroniclers. Nevertheless, the Danes were an imaginative and artistic people who continued to preserve their record in the arts and crafts and, in the later Middle Ages, contributed to world literature beautiful popular ballads.

For the expression of the Swedish imagination, likewise, we must consult the art of the carver, the miner, and the molder, as well as foreign sources. The annals of the Latin chroniclers and the literatures of the Slavs, the Byzantines, and the Arabs are rich in still unpublished accounts of the Swedes, of their voyages on the Russian rivers and the search for gold and fine raiment and glamorous design, as well as their visits to the Caspian and the Bosporus and the Mediterranean and Saracenic civilizations. In foreign sources we read also of their magnificent pagan ritual which survived the acceptance of Christianity by other Scandinavian countries for a century and a half.

Every year at the present time Sweden publishes great monographs by her archeologists and historians dealing with those long millennia from the recession of the ice to the well-recorded historical times of Gustaf Vasa and the Lutheran Reformation. These books are fascinating reading, but much is still hypothesis. Accounts of the Swedes, Europe's oldest kingdom, excited Tacitus in the first century of the Christian era. Today each new discovery from the Stone Age, the Bronze Age, and the era of runic inscriptions stimulates our curiosity. The standard history of ancient Swedish art has still to be written. Swedish literature did not come into its own until the eighteenth century.

IN NORWAY already in the ninth century poets began to eschew the simpler eddic forms of verse and to compose in the more elaborate skaldic meters. These required not only alliteration but internal rhymes and assonances. To make such difficult constructions possible the poets had the use of a large vocabulary of synonyms or poetic diction based on mythology and history, called *kennings*, by which metaphors or condensed similes or learned allusions could be substituted for a given word. Instead of "gold" one could use "the meal of Frothi" or "the seed of Fyris plain" or "the fire of the Rhine." Thus the court-meters and flowing-meters of the skalds can hardly, in a literal sense, be translated.

To the Norsemen poetry was not only an inspiration but also a technical craft. Profound passion is often concealed beneath the scintillating veneer of elaborate expression. It required years of study to be able to compose such verse spontaneously when called upon at a festival or to exhort the troops in the heat of battle. Today students are skeptical that such an intellectual miracle was possible, but many Norwegian and Icelandic skalds actually performed it. Skaldic verse was, in fact, no more intricate than the construction and control of an airplane today.

Icelandic historians used the skaldic poems as source material. Obviously such rigid compositions would remain unchanged in memory for many centuries and were more reliable than prose recitation. It is because they were quoted in the histories of Norway and Iceland that much of the skaldic verse has been preserved.

The early skalds were Norwegians, but, in the tenth century, the Icelanders took over that craft. Icelandic skalds attached themselves to the Norwegian royal bodyguard, accompanied the king in battle, and recited his achievements on the spot. Some Icelandic skalds were themselves intrepid vikings and as nimble with their axes as with their wits, and not too shy to praise their own deeds in "bound" language.

Saga had its master in Snorri Sturluson, and skaldic poetry had a master in Egil Skallagrimsson (910-990). Like Snorri, this genius was not a charming personality. He was a swarthy giant of a fellow, with gray hair and fierce black eyes. He was a mercenary landlord and an impulsive fighter who killed his man on the flash of an eyelid. His selfishness was colossal. He carried with him on his voyages the chests of silver that King Athelstan of England gave him, and, rather than let his heirs inherit them, buried his treasures before his death. But Egil was a great artist, and song was his gift from Othin. His three important odes—intense, passionate, and as elaborate as Pindar—defy exact translation.

DURING THE REIGN of Hakon Hakonarson the Old (1217-1263) Norway threw off its isolation and took a responsible place in the European society of nations. Hakon sent his envoys with presents of keen Icelandic falcons to the courts of England, Germany, and Morocco. France invited him to be the admiral of the next crusade. By strategy, without a military mission, he succeeded in uniting Iceland and Greenland under the Norwegian crown. He died in the Orkneys as admiral of a great naval expedition, designed to obtain the sovereignty over Scotland and Ireland. At home he established a fashionable court which astonished elite foreign envoys. He had prepared in Norwegian a manual for Norwegian gentlemen, *The King's Mirror*. In 1226 he authorized an Anglo-Norman monk in Norway to translate into Norwegian the most popular romance of medieval Europe: *Tristan*. Other romances were translated by his order, and the Lays of Marie de France.

Continental literature also reached Iceland and appeared in many translations there, as well as in domestic adaptations, covering the Arthurian metrical romances and the Carolingian epics and the Matter of Antiquity. Native poems, *rímur* and *kvæði*, also, were composed on these themes. The romances of chivalry in Iceland were called *riddarasögur*.

Many of the romances with foreign settings that appeared in Icelandic in the fourteenth and fifteenth centuries have no ascertainable foreign source. They are called lying sagas (*lýgisögur*). Only a few of these have, as yet, been printed. Some of them seem to be translations; others are collections of folk-tales threaded with fiction. Their themes are chiefly oriental, derived by the trade routes over Russia and from Icelandic pilgrims to Byzantium. To folklorists the lying sagas are mines of exciting episodes, to literary critics they are a degenerate art of decadence, the sere and yellow leaves of Icelandic fiction.

In the fourteenth century Scandinavian literature as well as political life went into a decline. The three calamities of German commerce, the Black Death, and a long period of intense cold were too much for initiative. Icelandic did not emerge again as a creative world literature until the present century.

OLD SCANDINAVIAN LITERATURE has another background, a different imagery from that of Christian Europe. Through the screen of Christian thought gleam the glory that was Greece and the grandeur that was Rome and the glamor that was Hebrew mysticism. In medieval Scandinavia, at a time when British, French, and Italian writers were compiling commentaries on the classics and lives of the saints, a pagan literature that knew not Homer or Aristotle, and neither the law nor the prophets, was producing a poetry and a prose dedicated to Othin or to Thor. While the eddas and sagas have not the placidity of the Greek classics, or the exaltation of the Hebrew scriptures, they hold their own in command of passionate intensity, graphic brevity, and objectivity.

The ultimate source of much Scandinavian literature, whether in ancient or modern times, is folklore. From time immemorial, in the homes of the North, the long winter evenings around the firesides were enlivened by oral recitation. Often folk tales were repeated and added to, generation after generation, before they found their way to pen or to print. Snorri in Iceland drew for saga material from that storehouse, as did Andersen in Denmark, Ibsen in Norway, and Lagerlöf in Sweden. From the folk tale Northern literature has derived its directness and vividness.

From the folk tale, also, the literature of the North has inherited its dramatic quality. The inherent power to analyze character swiftly and accurately, peculiar to the Dane and the Icelander, gives dramatic zest both to their conversation and to their letter-writing. In their literature story-tellers as different as Snorri and Hans Christian Andersen intersperse their prose with dramatic dialogue. Even a darning needle speaks its way through one of Andersen's fairy tales. In literature it is not the action that delights the Northern mind so much as the unfolding of personality through action.

Antiquity is in the background of Scandinavian behavior today, in the subconscious of every Scandinavian mind, and must always be studied if we are to understand their modern laboratories of social conduct and ethical principles devoted to the future progress of mankind.

It was a Scandinavian born in Iceland who realized that England had hidden in manuscript an English epic, *Bēowulf,* composed nearly a thousand years before *Paradise Lost* and brought about, at long last, its publication. It was therefore appropriate, in return, for English scholarship in the nineteenth century to introduce the Icelandic eddas and sagas to the literary heritage of Europe.

The concentrated metrical testimony of runic inscriptions, the lyric and dramatic passages of the Poetic Edda, the passionate intensity and elaborate metrical skill of untranslatable skaldic verse, the lucid and selective histories of Snorri Sturluson, and the dramatic records of fact in the sagas of Iceland—wherein the imaginative faculty appears in a technique of selection and arrangement that converts dry statistics into captivating art—make the production of ancient Scandinavia highly important in the golden treasury of letters.

H.G.L.

I. THE GODS

Nerthus

A.D. 98

Tacitus

From the Latin

In the year A.D. 98 Tacitus described the ritual of Nerthus, a goddess of fertility who was worshipped by the *Ingvæones*. The Ingvæones included the then inhabitants of Denmark. In Scandinavian myth Ing was a supernatural progenitor of the East Scandinavians; "Ingwine" was one of the Anglo-Saxon names for the Danes; the ancient Swedish kings were "Ynglings." The Norse mythology of the Eddas gives us, in place of Nerthus, the masculine god Njorth who, with his son Freyr and his daughter Freyja, was a deity of fruitfulness. Njorth had begotten his offspring by a former spouse, his sister Ingun, and their son was sometimes called Ingunar-Freyr.

◈§THERE is nothing noteworthy about any one of these tribes (Ingvæones) except that in common they worship Nerthus, that is, Mother Earth, and believe that she intervenes in human affairs and visits the peoples. On an island in the ocean there is an unviolated grove, and within it a consecrated car protected by a covering, which but one priest is permitted to touch. He knows when the goddess is present in her sanctuary, and walks beside her with great reverence as she is drawn along by cows. It is a season of rejoicing, and every place which the goddess deigns to visit is a scene of festivity. No wars are undertaken, no arms are touched; every weapon is shut up; then only are peace and quiet to be observed, then only loved, until at length the same priest restores the goddess, weary of mortal intercourse, to her temple. Afterwards the car and its coverings, and if you are willing to believe it, the divinity herself, are washed in a secret lake. Slaves perform this office, whom the same lake instantly swallows up. Hence arises a mysterious dread and a holy ignorance concerning what that may be which only those witness who are about to perish.

The Beginning and the End

Völuspá

A prophetess recites at Othin's bidding the history of the universe.

Hearing I ask   from the holy races,
From Heimdall's sons,   both high and low;
Thou wilt, Valfather,   that well I relate
Old tales I remember   of men long ago.

I remember yet   the giants of yore,
Who gave me bread   in the days gone by;
Nine worlds I knew,   the nine in the tree
With mighty roots   beneath the mold.

Of old was the age   when Ymir lived;
Sea nor cool waves   nor sand there were;
Earth had not been,   nor heaven above,
But a yawning gap,   and grass nowhere.

Then Bur's sons lifted   the level land,
Mithgarth the mighty   there they made;
The sun from the south   warmed the stones of earth,
And green was the ground   with growing leeks.

The sun, the sister   of the moon, from the south
Her right hand cast   over heaven's rim;
No knowledge she had   where her home should be,
The moon knew not   what might was his,
The stars knew not   where their stations were.

Then sought the gods   their assembly-seats,
The holy ones,   and council held;
Names then gave they   to noon and twilight,
Morning they named,   and the waning moon,
Night and evening,   the years to number.

At Ithavoll met   the mighty gods,
Shrines and temples   they timbered high;
Forges they set,   and they smithied ore,
Tongs they wrought,   and tools they fashioned.

In their dwellings at peace　　they played at tables,
Of gold no lack　　did the gods then know,—
Till thither came up　　giant-maids three,
Huge of might,　　out of Jotunheim.

Then sought the gods　　their assembly-seats,
The holy ones,　　and council held,
To find who should raise　　the race of dwarfs
Out of Brimir's blood　　and the legs of Blain.

* * *

Then from the throng　　did three come forth,
From the home of the gods,　　the mighty and gracious;
Two without fate　　on the land they found,
Ask and Embla,　　empty of might.

Soul they had not,　　sense they had not,
Heat nor motion,　　nor goodly hue;
Soul gave Othin,　　sense gave Hönir,
Heat gave Lothur　　and goodly hue.

An ash I know,　　Yggdrasil its name,
With water white　　is the great tree wet;
Thence come the dews　　that fall in the dales,
Green by Urth's well　　does it ever grow.

Thence come the maidens　　mighty in wisdom,
Three from the dwelling　　down 'neath the tree;
Urth is one named,　　Verthandi the next,—
On the wood they scored,—　　and Skuld the third.
Laws they made there,　　and life allotted
To the sons of men,　　and set their fates.

The war I remember,　　the first in the world,
When the gods with spears　　had smitten Gollveig,
And in the hall　　of Hor had burned her,—
Three times burned,　　and three times born,
Oft and again,　　yet ever she lives.

Heith they named her　　who sought their home,
The wide-seeing witch,　　in magic wise;
Minds she bewitched　　that were moved by her magic,
To evil women　　a joy she was.

On the host his spear　　did Othin hurl,
Then in the world　　did war first come;
The wall that girdled　　the gods was broken,
And the field by the warlike　　Wanes was trodden.

Then sought the gods　　their assembly-seats,
The holy ones,　　and council held,
Whether the gods　　should tribute give,
Or to all alike　　should worship belong.

Then sought the gods　　their assembly-seats,
The holy ones,　　and council held,
To find who with venom　　the air had filled,
Or had given Oth's bride　　to the giants' brood.

In swelling rage　　then rose up Thor,—
Seldom he sits　　when he such things hears,—
And the oaths were broken,　　the words and bonds,
The mighty pledges　　between them made.

I know of the horn　　of Heimdall, hidden
Under the high-reaching　　holy tree;
On it there pours　　from Valfather's pledge
A mighty stream:　　would you know yet more?

Alone I sat　　when the Old One sought me,
The terror of gods,　　and gazed in mine eyes:
"What hast thou to ask?　　why comest thou hither?
Othin, I know　　where thine eye is hidden."

I know where Othin's　　eye is hidden,
Deep in the wide-famed　　well of Mimir;
Mead from the pledge　　of Othin each morn
Does Mimir drink:　　would you know yet more?

Necklaces had I　　and rings from Heerfather,
Wise was my speech　　and my magic wisdom;
. 　. 　. 　. 　. 　. 　. 　. 　. 　. 　. 　.

Widely I saw　　over all the worlds.

On all sides saw I　　Valkyries assemble,
Ready to ride　　to the ranks of the gods;
Skuld bore the shield,　　and Skogul rode next,

Guth, Hild, Gondul,   and Geirskogul.
Of Herjan's maidens   the list have ye heard,
Valkyries ready   to ride o'er the earth.

I saw for Baldr,   the bleeding god,
The son of Othin,   his destiny set:
Famous and fair   in the lofty fields,
Full grown in strength   the mistletoe stood.

From the branch which seemed   so slender and fair
Came a harmful shaft   that Hoth should hurl;
But the brother of Baldr   was born ere long,
And one night old   fought Othin's son.

His hands he washed not,   his hair he combed not,
Till he bore to the bale-blaze   Baldr's foe.
But in Fensalir   did Frigg weep sore
For Valhall's need: would you know yet more?

One did I see   in the wet woods bound,
A lover of ill,   and to Loki like;
By his side does Sigyn   sit, nor is glad
To see her mate: would you know yet more?

* * *

The giantess old   in Ironwood sat,
In the east, and bore   the brood of Fenrir;
Among these one   in monster's guise
Was soon to steal   the sun from the sky.

There feeds he full   on the flesh of the dead,
And the home of the gods   he reddens with gore;
Dark grows the sun,   and in summer soon
Come mighty storms: would you know yet more?

On a hill there sat,   and smote on his harp,
Eggther the joyous,   the giants' warder;
Above him the cock   in the bird-wood crowed,
Fair and red   did Fjalar stand.

Then to the gods   crowed Gollinkambi,
He wakes the heroes   in Othin's hall;
And beneath the earth   does another crow,
The rust-red bird   at the bars of Hel.

Now Garm howls loud　　　before Gnipahellir,
The fetters will burst,　　　and the wolf run free;
Much do I know,　　　and more can see
Of the fate of the gods,　　　the mighty in fight.

Brothers shall fight　　　and fell each other,
And sisters' sons　　　shall kinship stain;
Hard is it on earth,　　　with mighty whoredom;
Axe-time, sword-time,　　　shields are sundered,
Wind-time, wolf-time,　　　ere the world falls;
Nor ever shall men　　　each other spare.

Fast move the sons　　　of Mim, and fate
Is heard in the note　　　of the Gjallarhorn;
Loud blows Heimdall,　　　the horn is aloft,
In fear quake all　　　who on Hel-roads are.

Yggdrasil shakes,　　　and shiver on high
The ancient limbs,　　　and the giant is loose;
To the head of Mim　　　does Othin give heed,
But the kinsman of Surt　　　shall slay him soon.

How fare the gods?　　　how fare the elves?
All Jotunheim groans,　　　the gods are at council;
Loud roar the dwarfs　　　by the doors of stone,
The masters of the rocks:　　　would you know yet more?

Now Garm howls loud　　　before Gnipahellir,
The fetters will burst,　　　and the wolf run free;
Much do I know,　　　and more can see
Of the fate of the gods,　　　the mighty in fight.

From the east comes Hrym　　　with shield held high;
In giant-wrath　　　does the serpent writhe;
O'er the waves he twists,　　　and the tawny eagle
Gnaws corpses screaming;　　　Naglfar is loose.

O'er the sea from the north　　　there sails a ship
With the people of Hel,　　　at the helm stands Loki;
After the wolf　　　do wild men follow,
And with them the brother　　　of Byleist goes.

Surt fares from the south with the scourge of branches,
The sun of the battle-gods shone from his sword;
The crags are sundered, the giant-women sink,
The dead throng Hel-way, and heaven is cloven.

Now comes to Hlin yet another hurt,
When Othin fares to fight with the wolf,
And Beli's fair slayer seeks out Surt,
For there must fall the joy of Frigg.

Then comes Sigfather's mighty son,
Vithar, to fight with the foaming wolf;
In the giant's son does he thrust his sword
Full to the heart: his father is avenged.

Hither there comes the son of Hlothyn,
The bright snake gapes to heaven above;

.   .   .   .

Against the serpent goes Othin's son.

In anger smites the warder of earth,—
Forth from their homes must all men flee;—
Nine paces fares the son of Fjorgyn,
And, slain by the serpent, fearless he sinks.

The sun turns black, earth sinks in the sea,
The hot stars down from heaven are whirled;
Fierce grows the steam and the life-feeding flame,
Till fire leaps high about heaven itself.

Now Garm howls loud before Gnipahellir,
The fetters will burst, and the wolf run free;
Much do I know, and more can see
Of the fate of the gods, the mighty in fight.

Now do I see the earth anew
Rise all green from the waves again;
The cataracts fall, and the eagle flies,
And fish he catches beneath the cliffs.

The gods in Ithavoll meet together,
Of the terrible girdler of earth they talk,
And the mighty past they call to mind,
And the ancient runes of the Ruler of Gods.

In wondrous beauty   once again
Shall the golden tables   stand mid the grass,
Which the gods had owned   in the days of old,

.   .   .   .

Then fields unsowed   bear ripened fruit,
All ills grow better,   and Baldr comes back;
Baldr and Hoth dwell   in Hropt's battle-hall,
And the mighty gods: would you know yet more?

*   *   *

More fair than the sun,   a hall I see,
Roofed with gold,   on Gimle it stands;
There shall the righteous   rulers dwell,
And happiness ever   there shall they have.

*   *   *

The Sayings of the High One

Hávamál

THE wisdom of Othin is not as kindly as the wisdom of Solomon. These
are the salty and sophisticated proverbs of Norse antiquity.

Within the gates   ere a man shall go,
(Full warily let him watch,)
Full long let him look about him;
For little he knows   where a foe may lurk,
And sit in the seats within.

Hail to the giver!   a guest has come;
Where shall the stranger sit?
Swift shall he be   who with swords shall try
The proof of his might to make.

Fire he needs   who with frozen knees
Has come from the cold without;
Food and clothes   must the farer have,
The man from the mountains come.

Water and towels   and welcoming speech
Should he find who comes to the feast;
If renown he would get,   and again be greeted,
Wisely and well must he act.

Wits must he have   who wanders wide,
  But all is easy at home;
At the witless man   the wise shall wink
  When among such men he sits.

A man shall not boast   of his keenness of mind,
  But keep it close in his breast;
To the silent and wise   does ill come seldom
  When he goes as guest to a house;
(For a faster friend   one never finds
  Than wisdom tried and true.)

The knowing guest   who goes to the feast,
  In silent attention sits;
With his ears he hears,   with his eyes he watches,
  Thus wary are wise men all.

Happy the one   who wins for himself
  Favor and praises fair;
Less safe by far   is the wisdom found
  That is hid in another's heart.

Happy the man   who has while he lives
  Wisdom and praise as well,
For evil counsel   a man full oft
  Has from another's heart.

A better burden   may no man bear
  For wanderings wide than wisdom;
It is better than wealth   on unknown ways,
  And in grief a refuge it gives.

A better burden   may no man bear
  For wanderings wide than wisdom;
Worse food for the journey   he brings not afield
  Than an over-drinking of ale.

Less good there lies   than most believe
  In ale for mortal men;
For the more he drinks   the less does man
  Of his mind the mastery hold.

Over beer the bird   of forgetfulness broods,
  And steals the minds of men;
With the heron's feathers   fettered I lay
  And in Gunnloth's house was held.

Drunk I was,   I was dead-drunk,
  When with Fjalar wise I was;
'Tis the best of drinking   if back one brings
  His wisdom with him home.

The son of a king   shall be silent and wise,
  And bold in battle as well;
Bravely and gladly   a man shall go,
  Till the day of his death is come.

The sluggard believes   he shall live forever,
  If the fight he faces not;
But age shall not grant him   the gift of peace,
  Though spears may spare his life.

The fool is agape   when he comes to the feast,
  He stammers or else is still;
But soon if he gets   a drink is it seen
  What the mind of the man is like.

He alone is aware   who has wandered wide,
  And far abroad has fared,
How great a mind   is guided by him
  That wealth of wisdom has.

Shun not the mead,   but drink in measure;
  Speak to the point or be still;
For rudeness none   shall rightly blame thee
  If soon thy bed thou seekest.

The greedy man,   if his mind be vague,
  Will eat till sick he is;
The vulgar man,   when among the wise,
  To scorn by his belly is brought.

The herds know well   when home they shall fare,
  And then from the grass they go;
But the foolish man   his belly's measure
  Shall never know aright.

A paltry man   and poor of mind
  At all things ever mocks;
For never he knows,   what he ought to know,
  That he is not free from faults.

The witless man   is awake all night,
  Thinking of many things;
Care-worn he is   when the morning comes,
  And his woe is just as it was.

The foolish man   for friends all those
  Who laugh at him will hold;
When among the wise   he marks it not
  Though hatred of him they speak.

The foolish man   for friends all those
  Who laugh at him will hold;
But the truth when he comes   to the council he learns,
  That few in his favor will speak.

An ignorant man   thinks that all he knows,
  When he sits by himself in a corner;
But never what answer   to make he knows,
  When others with questions come.

A witless man,   when he meets with men,
  Had best in silence abide;
For no one shall find   that nothing he knows,
  If his mouth is not open too much.
(But a man knows not,   if nothing he knows,
  When his mouth has been open too much.)

Wise shall he seem   who well can question,
  And also answer well;
Nought is concealed   that men may say
  Among the sons of men.

Often he speaks   who never is still
  With words that win no faith;
The babbling tongue,   if a bridle it find not,
  Oft for itself sings ill.

In mockery no one   a man shall hold,
  Although he fare to the feast;

Wise seems one oft,   if nought he is asked,
  And safely he sits dry-skinned.

Wise a guest holds it   to take to his heels,
  When mock of another he makes;
But little he knows   who laughs at the feast,
  Though he mocks in the midst of his foes.

Friendly of mind   are many men,
  Till feasting they mock at their friends;
To mankind a bane   must it ever be
  When guests together strive.

Oft should one make   an early meal,
  Nor fasting come to the feast;
Else he sits and chews   as if he would choke,
  And little is able to ask.

Crooked and far   is the road to a foe,
  Though his house on the highway be;
But wide and straight   is the way to a friend,
  Though far away he fare.

Forth shall one go,   nor stay as a guest
  In a single spot forever;
Love becomes loathing   if long one sits
  By the hearth in another's home.

Better a house,   though a hut it be,
  A man is master at home;
A pair of goats   and a patched-up roof
  Are better far than begging.

Better a house,   though a hut it be,
  A man is master at home;
His heart is bleeding   who needs must beg
  When food he fain would have.

Away from his arms   in the open field
  A man should fare not a foot;
For never he knows   when the need for a spear
  Shall arise on the distant road.

If wealth a man   has won for himself,
  Let him never suffer in need;
Oft he saves for a foe   what he plans for a friend,
  For much goes worse than we wish.

None so free with gifts   or food have I found
  That gladly he took not a gift,
Nor one who so widely   scattered his wealth
  That of recompense hatred he had.

Friends shall gladden each other   with arms and garments,
  As each for himself can see;
Gift-givers' friendships   are longest found,
  If fair their fates may be.

To his friend a man   a friend shall prove,
  And gifts with gifts requite;
But men shall mocking   with mockery answer,
  And fraud with falsehood meet.

To his friend a man   a friend shall prove,
  To him and the friend of his friend;
But never a man   shall friendship make
  With one of his foeman's friends.

If a friend thou hast   whom thou fully wilt trust,
  And good from him wouldst get,
Thy thoughts with his mingle,   and gifts shalt thou make,
  And fare to find him oft.

If another thou hast   whom thou hardly wilt trust,
  Yet good from him wouldst get,
Thou shalt speak him fair,   but falsely think,
  And fraud with falsehood requite.

So is it with him   whom thou hardly wilt trust,
  And whose mind thou mayst not know;
Laugh with him mayst thou,   but speak not thy mind,
  Like gifts to his shalt thou give.

Young was I once,   and wandered alone,
  And nought of the road I knew;
Rich did I feel   when a comrade I found,
  For man is man's delight.

The lives of the brave   and noble are best,
  Sorrows they seldom feed;
But the coward fear   of all things feels,
  And not gladly the niggard gives.

My garments once   in a field I gave
  To a pair of carven poles;
Heroes they seemed   when clothes they had,
  But the naked man is nought.

On the hillside drear   the fir-tree dies,
  All bootless its needles and bark;
It is like a man   whom no one loves,—
  Why should his life be long?

Hotter than fire   between false friends
  Does friendship five days burn;
When the sixth day comes   the fire cools,
  And ended is all the love.

No great thing needs   a man to give,
  Oft little will purchase praise;
With half a loaf   and a half-filled cup
  A friend full fast I made.

A little sand   has a little sea,
  And small are the minds of men;
Though all men are not   equal in wisdom,
  Yet half-wise only are all.

A measure of wisdom   each man shall have,
  But never too much let him know;
The fairest lives   do those men live
  Whose wisdom wide has grown.

A measure of wisdom   each man shall have,
  But never too much let him know;
For the wise man's heart   is seldom happy,
  If wisdom too great he has won.

A measure of wisdom   each man shall have,
  But never too much let him know;
Let no man the fate   before him see,
  For so is he freest from sorrow.

A brand from a brand   is kindled and burned,
  And fire from fire begotten;
And man by his speech   is known to men,
  And the stupid by their stillness.

He must early go forth   who fain the blood
  Or the goods of another would get;
The wolf that lies idle   shall win little meat,
  Or the sleeping man success.

He must early go forth   whose workers are few,
  Himself his work to seek;
Much remains undone   for the morning-sleeper,
  For the swift is wealth half won.

Of seasoned shingles   and strips of bark
  For the thatch let one know his need,
And how much of wood   he must have for a month,
  Or in half a year he will use.

Washed and fed   to the council fare,
  But care not too much for thy clothes;
Let none be ashamed   of his shoes and hose,
  Less still of the steed he rides,
  (Though poor be the horse he has.)

When the eagle comes   to the ancient sea,
  He snaps and hangs his head;
So is a man   in the midst of a throng,
  Who few to speak for him finds.

*   *   *

Fire for men   is the fairest gift,
  And power to see the sun;
Health as well,   if a man may have it,
  And a life not stained with sin.

All wretched is no man,   though never so sick;
  Some from their sons have joy,
Some win it from kinsmen,   and some from their wealth,
  And some from worthy works.

It is better to live   than to lie a corpse,
  The live man catches the cow;

I saw flames rise   for the rich man's pyre,
  And before his door he lay dead.

The lame rides a horse,   the handless is herdsman,
  The deaf in battle is bold;
The blind man is better   than one that is burned,
  No good can come of a corpse.

A son is better,   though late he be born,
  And his father to death have fared;
Memory-stones   seldom stand by the road
  Save when kinsman honors his kin.

*   *   *

Cattle die,   and kinsmen die,
  And so one dies one's self;
But a noble name   will never die,
  If good renown one gets.

Cattle die,   and kinsmen die,
  And so one dies one's self;
One thing I know   that never dies,
  The fame of a dead man's deeds.

*   *   *

Give praise to the day at evening,   to a woman on her pyre,
To a weapon which is tried,   to a maid at wedlock,
To ice when it is crossed,   to ale that is drunk.

When the gale blows hew wood,   in fair winds seek the
    water;
Sport with maidens at dusk,   for day's eyes are many;
From the ship seek swiftness,   from the shield protection,
Cuts from the sword,   from the maiden kisses.

By the fire drink ale,   over ice go on skates;
Buy a steed that is lean,   and a sword when tarnished,
The horse at home fatten,   the hound in thy dwelling.

*   *   *

A man shall trust not   the oath of a maid,
  Nor the word a woman speaks;
For their hearts on a whirling   wheel were fashioned,
  And fickle their breasts were formed.

The love of women   fickle of will
Is like starting o'er ice   with a steed unshod,
A two-year-old restive   and little tamed,
Or steering a rudderless   ship in a storm,
Or, lame, hunting reindeer   on slippery rocks.

       *   *   *

I ween that I hung   on the windy tree,
   Hung there for nights full nine;
With the spear I was wounded,   and offered I was
   To Othin, myself to myself,
On the tree that none   may ever know
   What root beneath it runs.

Freyr's Courtship

Skírnismál

THE Old Norsemen were a passionate race. Even their gods could fall in love.

FREYR, the son of Njorth, had sat one day in Hlithskjolf, and looked over all the worlds. He looked into Jotunheim, and saw there a fair maiden, as she went from her father's house to her bower. Forthwith he felt a mighty love-sickness. Skirnir was the name of Freyr's servant; Njorth bade him ask speech of Freyr. He said:

"Go now, Skirnir!   and seek to gain
   Speech from my son;
And answer to win,   for whom the wise one
   Is mightily moved."

     Skirnir spake:
"Ill words do I now   await from thy son,
   If I seek to get speech with him,
And answer to win,   for whom the wise one
   Is mightily moved."

     Skirnir spake:
"Speak prithee, Freyr,   foremost of the gods,
   For now I fain would know;
Why sittest thou here   in the wide halls,
   Days long, my prince, alone?"

Freyr spake:
"How shall I tell thee,   thou hero young,
  Of all my grief so great?
Though every day   the elfbeam dawns,
  It lights my longing never."

Skirnir spake:
"Thy longings, methinks,   are not so large
  That thou mayst not tell them to me;
Since in days of yore   we were young together,
  We two might each other trust."

Freyr spake:
"From Gymir's house   I beheld go forth
  A maiden dear to me;
Her arms glittered,   and from their gleam
  Shone all the sea and sky.

"To me more dear   than in days of old
  Was ever maiden to man;
But no one of gods   or elves will grant
  That we both together should be."

Skirnir spake:
"Then give me the horse   that goes through the dark
  And magic flickering flames;
And the sword as well   that fights of itself
  Against the giants grim."

Freyr spake:
"The horse will I give thee   that goes through the dark
  And magic flickering flames,
And the sword as well   that will fight of itself
  If a worthy hero wields it."

Skirnir spake to the horse:
"Dark is it without,   and I deem it time
  To fare through the wild fells,
  (To fare through the giants' fastness;)
We shall both come back,   or us both together
  The terrible giant will take."

Skirnir rode into Jotunheim to Gymir's house. There were fierce dogs bound before the gate of the fence which was around Gerth's hall. He rode to where a herdsman sat on a hill, and said:

"Tell me, herdsman,   sitting on the hill,
  And watching all the ways,
How may I win   a word with the maid
  Past the hounds of Gymir here?"

The herdsman spake:
"Art thou doomed to die   or already dead,
  Thou horseman that ridest hither?
Barred from speech   shalt thou ever be
  With Gymir's daughter good."

Skirnir spake:
"Boldness is better   than plaints can be
  For him whose feet must fare;
To a destined day   has mine age been doomed,
  And my life's span thereto laid."

Gerth spake:
"What noise is that   which now so loud
  I hear within our house?
The ground shakes,   and the home of Gymir
  Around me trembles too."

The Serving-Maid spake:
"One stands without   who has leapt from his steed,
  And lets his horse loose to graze;"

. . . .
. . . .

Gerth spake:
"Bid the man come in,   and drink good mead
  Here within our hall;
Though this I fear,   that there without
  My brother's slayer stands.

"Art thou of the elves   or the offspring of gods,
  Or of the wise Wanes?

How camst thou alone through the leaping flame
Thus to behold our home?"

Skirnir spake:

"I am not of the elves, nor the offspring of gods,
Nor of the wise Wanes;
Though I came alone through the leaping flame
Thus to behold thy home.

"Eleven apples, all of gold,
Here will I give thee, Gerth,
To buy thy troth that Freyr shall be
Deemed to be dearest to you."

Gerth spake:

"I will not take at any man's wish
These eleven apples ever;
Nor shall Freyr and I one dwelling find
So long as we two live."

Skirnir spake:

"Then do I bring thee the ring that was burned
Of old with Othin's son;
From it do eight of like weight fall
On every ninth night."

Gerth spake:

"The ring I wish not, though burned it was
Of old with Othin's son;
In Gymir's home is no lack of gold
In the wealth my father wields."

Skirnir spake:

"Seest thou, maiden, this keen, bright sword
That I hold here in my hand?
Thy head from thy neck shall I straightway hew,
If thou wilt not do my will."

Gerth spake:

"For no man's sake will I ever suffer
To be thus moved by might;
But gladly, methinks, will Gymir seek
To fight if he finds thee here."

Skirnir spake:

"Seest thou, maiden,   this keen, bright sword
　That I hold here in my hand?
Before its blade   the old giant bends,—
　Thy father is doomed to die.

"I strike thee, maid,   with my magic staff,
　To tame thee to work my will;
There shalt thou go   where never again
　The sons of men shall see thee.

"On the eagle's hill   shalt thou ever sit,
　And gaze on the gates of Hel;
More loathsome to thee   than the light-hued snake
　To men, shall thy meat become.

"Fearful to see,   if thou comest forth,
　Hrimnir will stand and stare,
　(Men will marvel at thee;)
More famed shalt thou grow   than the watchman of the
　　gods!
　Peer forth, then, from thy prison.

"Rage and longing,   fetters and wrath,
　Tears and torment are thine;
Where thou sittest down   my doom is on thee
　Of heavy heart
　And double dole.

"In the giants' home   shall vile things harm thee
　Each day with evil deeds;
Grief shalt thou get   instead of gladness,
　And sorrow to suffer with tears.

"With three-headed giants   thou shalt dwell ever,
　Or never know a husband;
(Let longing grip thee,   let wasting waste thee,—)
Be like to the thistle   that in the loft
　Was cast and there was crushed.

"I go to the wood,   and to the wet forest,
　To win a magic wand;

. . . .

　I won a magic wand.

"Othin grows angry, angered is the best of the gods,
 Freyr shall be thy foe,
Most evil maid, who the magic wrath
 Of gods hast got for thyself.

"Give heed, frost-rulers, hear it, giants,
 Sons of Suttung,
 And gods, ye too,
How I forbid and how I ban
 The meeting of men with the maid,
 (The joy of men with the maid.)

"Hrimgrimnir is he, the giant who shall have thee
 In the depth by the doors of Hel;
To the frost-giants' halls each day shalt thou fare,
 Crawling and craving in vain,
 (Crawling and having no hope.)

"Base wretches there by the root of the tree
 Will hold for thee horns of filth;
A fairer drink shalt thou never find,
 Maid, to meet thy wish,
 (Maid, to meet my wish.)

"I write thee a charm and three runes therewith,
 Longing and madness and lust;
But what I have writ I may yet unwrite
 If I find a need therefor."

 Gerth spake:
"Find welcome rather, and with it take
 The frost-cup filled with mead;
Though I did not believe that I should so love
 Ever one of the Wanes."

 Skirnir spake:
"My tidings all must I truly learn
 Ere homeward hence I ride:
How soon thou wilt with the mighty son
 Of Njorth a meeting make."

Gerth spake:

"Barri there is,   which we both know well,
   A forest fair and still;
And nine nights hence   to the son of Njorth
   Will Gerth there grant delight."

Then Skirnir rode home. Freyr stood without, and spoke to him, and asked for tidings:

"Tell me, Skirnir,   ere thou take off the saddle,
   Or farest forward a step:
What hast thou done   in the giants' dwelling
   To make glad thee or me?"

Skirnir spake:

"Barri there is,   which we both know well,
   A forest fair and still;
And nine nights hence   to the son of Njorth
   Will Gerth there grant delight."

Freyr spake:

"Long is one night,   longer are two;
   How then shall I bear three?
Often to me   has a month seemed less
   Than now half a night of desire."

Thor Gets Back His Hammer

Þrymskviða

OTHIN was a shrewd god, skilled in stratagem and war and the art of poetry. Thor, who announced his coming with thunder, was a naïve and friendly and athletic god. His hammer Mjollnir was used to consecrate crops and weddings. In tests of cunning Thor was outwitted by Othin, but in tests of strength he was more than a match for the mighty but stupid giants. *Þrymskviða* describes one of Thor's adventures with the giants. This ballad is the most popular of the poems in the Poetic Edda; its theme has survived into modern times in folk ballads, in which the actors are human beings, in Denmark, Norway, and Sweden.

Wrath was Ving-Thor   when he awakened
and found his hammer   not at hand.
He shook his beard   and tossed his locks,
the son of Earth   groped about him.

And of words this   was the first he spake:
"Hearken, Loki,   hear what I tell:
It is not known   on all the earth
nor yet in high heaven: Thor is reft of his hammer!"

They went to the fair   dwellings of Freyja
and of words this   was the first he spake:
"Wilt thou, Freyja,   lend me thy feather-coat
that I perchance   may find my hammer?"

Freyja said:
"I would give it thee   tho' 'twere of gold,
and grant it   tho' 'twere of silver."

Flew Loki then   the feather-coat resounded
until he came outside   the Aesir's dwellings
and came within   the lands of the giants.

Thrym sat on a howe   the lord of giants
for his hounds   he plaited golden leashes
and of his steeds   he smoothed the manes.

Thrym said:
"How goes it with Aesir   how with the elves?
Why art thou come alone   into Jötunheim?"

Loki said:
"Ill goes it with the Aesir   ill with the elves:
hast thou hidden   the hammer of Hlórriði?"

Thrym said:
"I have hidden   the hammer of Hlórriði
eight leagues   below the earth:
It no man shall   win back again
Unless he bring me   Freyja to wife."

Flew Loki then   the feather-coat rustled
until he came outside   the lands of the giants
and came within   the Aesir's dwellings:
Thor he met   midway in the court
and of words this   was the first he spake:

"Hast thou tidings   to equal thy toil?
Say thy long tale   here in the open

oft he who speaks sitting   tells a stumbling tale
and he who speaks recumbent   oft utters a lie."

Loki said:
"I have had toil   and also good tidings:
Thrym has thy hammer,   the lord of giants,
It no man shall   win back again
Unless he bring him   Freyja to wife."

They go to seek   the fair Freyja
and of words this   was the first he spake:
"Gird thyself, Freyja,   in bridal linen,
we two shall drive   into Giant-land."

Wrath was Freyja   she snorted
the whole hall of the Aesir   trembled thereat:
the great Brísing torque   burst asunder.
"Thou shalt know me   most wanton of women,
If I drive with thee   into Giant-land."

Straightway the Aesir   met all in council
And the goddesses   all in parley
And took counsel together   the mighty powers
How they might win   the hammer of Hlórriði.

Then said Heimdall   the whitest of Aesir
—Well could he foretell   like other Vanir—
"Let us gird on Thor then   the bridal linen,
let him wear   the great Brísing torque!

"Let us from him   hang the jingling keys,
And women's weeds   let fall round his knees
on his breast   the broad stones
and with skill the wimple   let us bind round his head!"

Then said Thor   the valiant god:
"Womanish they   will call me, the Aesir,
If I let myself be girt   in bridal linen."

Then said Loki,   Laufey's son:
"Utter not, Thor   such words as these:
straightway will the giants   come dwell in Ásgard
Unless thou fetchest   thy hammer to thee."

They girt on Thor then   the bridal linen,
and the great   Brísing torque;
they hung from him   the jingling keys,
and women's weeds   let fall round his knees;
on his breast   the broad stones,
and with skill the wimple   they bound round his head.

Then said Loki   Laufey's son:
"I also with thee   will be thy wench;
we two maids will drive   into Giant-land."

At once the goats   were driven home,
harnessed to the poles   well should they run:
Rent were the mountains   earth was aflame
Odin's son drove   into Giant-land.

Thus spake Thrym   the lord of giants:
"Rise up, ye giants,   and strew the benches;
Now ye bring me   Freyja to wife,
Njörd's daughter   from Nóatún.

"There wander in my yard   gold horned kine
Oxen all swart   to pleasure the giant,
Much store have I of treasure,   much store of jewels;
Meseems I lack   nought but Freyja."

Swiftly drew   the day to evening,
and ale was borne   before the giants:
Alone he ate an ox   eight salmon,
all the dainties   set for the women;
The husband of Sif   drank three tuns of mead.

Then spake Thrym   the lord of giants:
"Where saw ye a bride   more sharply set?
Ne'er saw I wenches   eat more heartily,
nor a maiden quaff   so deeply of mead."

The crafty maid   sat beside,
who found an answer   to the giant's speech:
"No whit ate Freyja   for eight nights
So eager was she   for Giant-land."

He bent under the wimple,   he longed to kiss
but started back   the length of the hall:
"Why is so fierce   the glance of Freyja?
Meseemed from her eyes   flames are darting!"

The crafty maid   sat beside,
who found an answer   to the giant's speech:
"No whit slept Freyja   for eight nights,
so eager was she   for Giant-land."

In came the wretched   sister of giants,
who dared to ask   for a bridal gift.
"Take from thine arms   the ruddy rings
if thou would'st win   my love,
my love   and all favours."

Then spake Thrym   the lord of giants:
"Bear in the hammer   to hallow the bride.
Lay Mjöllnir   on the maiden's knee;
let Vár hallow   our clasped hands!"

The heart of Hlórriði   laughed in his breast,
when the doughty one   knew his hammer once more;
first he slew Thrym   the lord of giants
and lamed all   the race of the giant.

He slew the ancient   sister of giants
she who had begged   for a bridal gift;
cuffs she gained   in place of coins
and blows of the hammer   for wealth of rings:
So came Odin's son   by his hammer again.

Thor's Exploits

Snorra Edda

THIS is another of the humorous adventures of Thor recorded in the eddas.

◆§IT is not unknown, though one be not a scholar, that Thor took redress for this journey of which the tale has but now been told; and he did not tarry at home long before he made ready for his journey so hastily that he had with him no chariot and no he-goats and no retinue. He went out over Midgard in the guise of a young lad, and came one evening at twilight to a certain giant's, who was called Hymir. Thor abode as guest there overnight; but at dawn Hymir arose and clothed himself and made ready to row to sea a-fishing. Then Thor sprang up and was speedily ready, and asked Hymir to let him row to sea with him. But Hymir said that Thor would be of little help to him, being so small and a youth, "And thou wilt freeze, if I stay so long and so far out as I am wont." But Thor said that he would be able to row far out from land, for the reason that it was not certain whether he would be the first to ask to row back. Thor became so enraged at the giant that he was forthwith ready to let his hammer crash against him; but he forced himself to forbear, since he purposed to try his strength in another quarter. He asked Hymir what they should have for bait, but Hymir bade him get bait for himself. Then Thor turned away thither where he saw a certain herd of oxen, which Hymir owned; he took the largest ox, called Himin-brjotr, and cut off its head and went therewith to the sea. By that time Hymir had shoved out the boat.

Thor went aboard the skiff and sat down in the stern-seat, took two oars and rowed; and it seemed to Hymir that swift progress came of his rowing. Hymir rowed forward in the bow, and the row-ing proceeded rapidly; then Hymir said that they had arrived at those fishing-banks where he was wont to anchor and angle for flat-fish. But Thor said that he desired to row much farther, and they took a sharp pull; then Hymir said that they had come so far that it was perilous to abide out farther because of the Midgard Serpent. Thor replied that they would row a while yet, and so he did; but Hymir was then sore afraid. Now as soon as Thor had laid by the oars, he made ready a very strong fishing-line, and the hook was no less large and strong. Then Thor put the ox-head on the hook and cast it overboard, and the hook went to the bottom; and it is telling thee the truth to say that then Thor beguiled the Midgard Serpent no less than Útgarda-Loki had mocked Thor, at the time when he lifted up the Serpent in his hand.

The Midgard Serpent snapped at the ox-head, and the hook caught in its jaw; but when the Serpent was aware of this, it dashed away so fiercely that both Thor's fists crashed against the gunwale. Then Thor was angered, and took upon him his divine strength, braced his feet so strongly that he plunged through the ship with both feet, and dashed his feet against the bottom; then he drew the Serpent up to the gunwale. And it may be said that no one has seen very fearful sights who might not see that: how Thor flashed fiery glances at the Serpent, and the Serpent in turn stared up toward him from below and blew venom. Then, it is said, the giant Hymir grew pale, became yellow, and was sore afraid, when he saw the Serpent, and how the sea rushed out and in through the boat. In the very moment when Thor clutched his hammer and raised it on high, then the giant fumbled for his fish-knife and hacked off Thor's line at the gunwale, and the Serpent sank down into the sea. Thor hurled his hammer after it; and men say that he struck off its head against the bottom; but I think it were true to tell thee that the Midgard Serpent yet lives and lies in the encompassing sea. But Thor swung his fist and brought it against Hymir's ear, so that he plunged overboard, and Thor saw the soles of his feet. And Thor waded to land.

The Horse Sleipnir

Snorra Edda

OTHIN'S eight-legged horse, which apparently had the speed of light, served as decoration on ancient monuments and is still one of the designs in modern Scandinavian weaving.

❧§IT was early in the first days of the gods' dwelling here, when the gods had established the Midgard and made Valhall; there came at that time a certain wright and offered to build them a citadel in three seasons, so good that it should be staunch and proof against the Hill-Giants and the Rime-Giants, though they should come in over Midgard. But he demanded as wages that he should have possession of Freyja, and would fain have had the sun and the moon. Then the Æsir held parley and took counsel together; and a bargain was made with the wright, that he should have that which he demanded, if he should succeed in completing the citadel in one winter. On the first day of summer, if any part of the citadel were left unfinished, he should lose his reward; and he was to receive help from no man in the work. When they told him these conditions, he asked that they would give him leave to have the help of his stallion, which was called Svadilfari; and Loki advised it, so that the wright's petition was granted. He set to work the first day of winter to make the citadel, and by night he hauled stones with the stallion's aid; and it seemed very marvellous to the Æsir what great rocks that horse drew, for the horse did more rough work by half than did the wright. But there were strong witnesses to their bargain, and many oaths, since it seemed unsafe to the giant to be among the Æsir without truce, if Thor should come home. But Thor had then gone away into the eastern region to fight trolls.

Now when the winter drew nigh unto its end, the building of the citadel was far advanced; and it was so high and strong that it could not be taken. When it lacked three days of summer, the work had almost reached the gate of the stronghold. Then the gods sat down in their judgment seats, and sought means of evasion, and asked one another who had advised giving Freyja into Jötunheim, or so destroying the air and the heaven as to take thence the sun and the moon and give them to the giants. The gods agreed that he must have counselled this who is wont to give evil advice, Loki Laufeyarson, and they declared him deserving of an ill death, if he could not hit upon a way of losing the wright his wages; and they threatened Loki with violence. But when he became frightened, then he swore oaths, that he would so contrive that the wright should lose his wages, cost him what it might.

That same evening, when the wright drove out after stone with the stallion Svadilfari, a mare bounded forth from a certain wood and whinnied to him. The stallion, perceiving what manner of horse this was, straightway became frantic, and snapped the traces asunder, and leaped over to the mare, and she away to the wood, and the wright after, striving to seize the stallion. These horses ran all night, and the wright stopped there that night; and afterward, at day, the work was not done as it had been before. When the wright saw that the work could not be brought to an end, he fell into giant's fury. Now that the Æsir saw surely that the hill-giant was come thither, they did not regard their oaths reverently, but called on Thor, who came as quickly. And straightway the hammer Mjöllnir was raised aloft; he paid the wright's wage, and not with the sun and the moon. Nay, he even denied him dwelling in Jötunheim, and struck but the one first blow, so that his skull was burst into small crumbs, and sent him down below under Niflhel. But Loki had such dealings with Svadilfari, that somewhat later he gave birth to a foal, which was gray and had eight feet; and this horse is the best among gods and men.

Wolves or Seagulls?

Snorra Edda

HIS wife preferred the mountain, but Njorth loved the sea.

⌘§THE third among the Æsir is he that is called Njördr: he dwells in heaven, in the abode called Nóatún. He rules the course of the wind, and stills sea and fire; on him shall men call for voyages and for hunting. He is so prosperous and abounding in wealth, that he may give them great plenty of lands or of gear; and him shall men invoke for such things. Njördr is not of the race of the Æsir: he was reared in the land of the Vanir, but the Vanir delivered him as hostage to the gods, and took for hostage in exchange him that men call Hœnir; he became an atonement between the gods and the Vanir. Njördr has to wife the woman called Skadi, daughter of Thjazi the giant. Skadi would fain dwell in the abode which her father had had, which is on certain mountains, in the place called Thrymheimr; but Njördr would be near the sea. They made a compact on these terms: they should be nine nights in Thrymheimr, but the second nine at Nóatún. But when Njördr came down from the mountain back to Nóatún, he sang this lay:

"Loath were the hills to me,   I was not long in them,
    Nights only nine;
To me the wailing of   wolves seemed ill,
    After the song of swans."

Then Skadi sang this:

"Sleep could I never   on the sea-beds,
    For the wailing of waterfowl;
He wakens me,   who comes from the deep—
    The sea-mew every morn."

Then Skadi went up onto the mountain, and dwelt in Thrymheimr. And she goes for the more part on snowshoes and with a bow and arrow, and shoots beasts; she is called Snowshoe-Goddess or Lady of the Snowshoes. So it is said:

"Thrymheimr 't is called,   where Thjazi dwelt,
   He the hideous giant;
But now Skadi abides,   pure bride of the gods,
   In her father's ancient freehold."

Freyr and Freyja

Snorra Edda

NJORTH and his kindly son and daughter, gods of fertility, were originally Vanir, but were adopted by the Æsir.

⅋§NJÖRDR in Nóatún begot afterward two children: the son was called Freyr, and the daughter Freyja; they were fair of face and mighty. Freyr is the most renowned of the Æsir; he rules over the rain and the shining of the sun, and therewithal the fruit of the earth; and it is good to call on him for fruitful seasons and peace. He governs also the prosperity of men. But Freyja is the most renowned of the goddesses; she has in heaven the dwelling called Fólkvangr, and wheresoever she rides to the strife, she has one-half of the kill, and Odin half, as is here said:

"Fólkvangr 't is called,   where Freyja rules
   Degrees of seats in the hall;
Half the kill   she keepeth each day,
   And half Odin hath."

Her hall Sessrúmnir is great and fair. When she goes forth, she drives her cats and sits in a chariot; she is most conformable to man's prayers, and from her name comes the name of honor, Frú, by which noblewomen are called. Songs of love are well-pleasing to her; it is good to call on her for furtherance in love.

Baldr the Beautiful

Snorra Edda

THE story of Baldr and his death by the mistletoe is one of the most sublime legends of Old Norse mythology.

⅋§THE beginning of the story is this, that Baldr the Good dreamed great and perilous dreams touching his life. When he told these dreams to the Æsir, then they took counsel together: and this was their decision: to ask safety for Baldr from all kinds of dangers. And Frigg took oaths to this purport, that fire and water should spare Baldr, likewise iron and metal of all kinds, stones, earth, trees, sicknesses, beasts, birds, venom, serpents. And when that was done and made known, then it was a diversion of Baldr's and the Æsir, that he should stand up in the Thing, and all the others should some shoot at him, some hew at him, some beat him with stones; but whatsoever was done hurt him not at all, and that seemed to them all a very worshipful thing.

But when Loki Laufeyarson saw this, it pleased him ill that Baldr took no hurt. He went to Fensalir to Frigg, and made himself into the likeness of a woman. Then Frigg asked if that woman knew what the Æsir did at the Thing. She said that all were shooting at Baldr, and moreover, that he took no hurt. Then said Frigg: "Neither weapons nor trees may hurt Baldr: I have taken oaths of them all." Then the woman asked: "Have all things taken oaths to spare Baldr?" and Frigg answered: "There grows a tree-sprout alone westward of Valhall: it is called Mistletoe; I thought it too young to ask the oath of." Then straightway the woman turned away; but Loki took Mistletoe and pulled it up and went to the Thing.

Hödr stood outside the ring of men, because he was blind. Then spake Loki to him: "Why dost thou not shoot at Baldr?" He answered: "Because I see not where Baldr is; and for this also, that I am weaponless." Then said Loki: "Do thou also after the manner of other men, and show Baldr honor as the other men do. I will direct thee where he stands; shoot at him with this wand." Hödr took Mistletoe and shot at Baldr, being guided by Loki: the shaft flew through Baldr, and he fell dead to the earth; and that was the greatest mischance that has ever befallen among gods and men.

Then, when Baldr was fallen, words failed all the Æsir, and their hands likewise to lay hold of him; each looked at the other, and all were of one mind as to him who had wrought the work, but none might take vengeance, so great a sanctuary was in that place. But when the Æsir tried to speak, then it befell first that weeping broke out, so that none might speak to the others with words concerning his grief. But Odin bore that misfortune by so much the worst, as he had most perception of how great harm and loss for the Æsir were in the death of Baldr.

Now when the gods had come to themselves, Frigg spake, and

asked who there might be among the Æsir who would fain have for his own all her love and favor: let him ride the road to Hel, and seek if he may find Baldr, and offer Hel a ransom if she will let Baldr come home to Ásgard. And he is named Hermódr the Bold, Odin's son, who undertook that embassy. Then Sleipnir was taken, Odin's steed, and led forward; and Hermódr mounted on that horse and galloped off.

The Æsir took the body of Baldr and brought it to the sea. Hringhorni is the name of Baldr's ship: it was greatest of all ships; the gods would have launched it and made Baldr's pyre thereon, but the ship stirred not forward. Then word was sent to Jötunheim after that giantess who is called Hyrrokkin. When she had come, riding a wolf and having a viper for bridle, then she leaped off the steed; and Odin called to four berserks to tend the steed; but they were not able to hold it until they had felled it. Then Hyrrokkin went to the prow of the boat and thrust it out at the first push, so that fire burst from the rollers, and all lands trembled. Thor became angry and clutched his hammer, and would straightway have broken her head, had not the gods prayed for peace for her.

Then was the body of Baldr borne out on shipboard; and when his wife, Nanna the daughter of Nep, saw that, straightway her heart burst with grief, and she died; she was borne to the pyre, and fire was kindled. Then Thor stood by and hallowed the pyre with Mjöllnir; and before his feet ran a certain dwarf which was named Litr; Thor kicked at him with his foot and thrust him into the fire, and he burned. People of many races visited this burning: First is to be told of Odin, how Frigg and the Valkyrs went with him, and his ravens; but Freyr drove in his chariot with the boar called Gold-Mane, or Fearful-Tusk, and Heimdallr rode the horse called Gold-Top, and Freyja drove her cats. Thither came also much people of the Rime-Giants and the Hill-Giants. Odin laid on the pyre that gold ring which is called Draupnir; this quality attended it, that every ninth night there dropped from it eight gold rings of equal weight. Baldr's horse was led to the bale-fire with all his trappings.

Now this is to be told concerning Hermódr, that he rode nine nights through dark dales and deep, so that he saw not before he was come to the river Gjöll and rode onto the Gjöll-Bridge; which bridge is thatched with glittering gold. Módgudr is the maiden called who guards the bridge; she asked him his name and race, saying that the day before there had ridden over the bridge five companies of dead men; "but the bridge thunders no less under thee alone, and thou hast not the color of dead men. Why ridest thou hither on Hel-way?" He answered: "I am appointed to ride to Hel to seek out Baldr. Hast thou perchance seen Baldr on Hel-way?" She said that Baldr had ridden there over Gjöll's Bridge,—"but down and north lieth Hel-way."

Then Hermódr rode on till he came to Hel-gate; he dismounted from his steed and made his girths fast, mounted and pricked him with his spurs; and the steed leaped so hard over the gate that he came nowise near to it. Then Hermódr rode home to the hall and dismounted from his steed, went into the hall, and saw sitting there in the high-seat Baldr, his brother; and Hermódr tarried there overnight. At morn Hermódr prayed Hel that Baldr might ride home with him, and told her how great weeping was among the Æsir. But Hel said that in this wise it should be put to the test, whether Baldr were so all-beloved as had been said: "If all things in the world, quick and dead, weep for him, then he shall go back to the Æsir; but he shall remain with Hel if any gainsay it or will not weep." Then Hermódr arose; but Baldr led him out of the hall, and took the ring Draupnir and sent it to Odin for a remembrance. And Nanna sent Frigg a linen smock, and yet more gifts, and to Fulla a golden finger-ring.

Then Hermódr rode his way back, and came into Ásgard, and told all those tidings which he had seen and heard. Thereupon the Æsir sent over all the world messengers to pray that Baldr be wept out of Hel; and all men did this, and quick things, and the earth, and stones, and trees, and all metals,—even as thou must have seen that these things weep when they come out of frost and into the heat. Then, when the messengers went home, having well wrought their errand, they found, in a certain cave, where a giantess sat: she called herself Thökk. They prayed her to weep Baldr out of Hel; she answered:

> "Thökk will weep   waterless tears
>   For Baldr's bale-fare;
> Living or dead,   I loved not the churl's son;
>   Let Hel hold to that she hath!"

And men deem that she who was there was Loki Laufeyarson, who hath wrought most ill among the Æsir.

II. LEGENDARY HEROES

The Lay of Wayland

Date uncertain
Völundarkviða

WAYLAND the Smith may not have been a native of Scandinavia, but an Old Norse poet made an important contribution to the widespread literature about this popular hero of European folklore.

THERE was a king in Sweden named Nithuth. He had two sons and one daughter; her name was Bothvild. There were three brothers, sons of a king of the Finns: one was called Slagfith, another Egil, the third Völund. They went on snowshoes and hunted wild beasts. They came into Ulfdalir and there they built themselves a house; there was a lake there which is called Ulfsjar. Early one morning they found on the shore of the lake three women, who were spinning flax. Near them were their swan-garments, for they were Valkyries. Two of them were daughters of King Hlothver, Hlathguth the Swan-White and Hervor the All-Wise, and the third was Olrun, daughter of Kjar from Valland. These did they bring home to their hall with them. Egil took Olrun, and Slagfith Swan-White, and Völund All-Wise. There they dwelt seven winters; but then they flew away to find battles, and came back no more. Then Egil set forth on his snowshoes to follow Olrun, and Slagfith followed Swan-White, but Völund stayed in Ulfdalir. He was a most skillful man, as men know from old tales. King Nithuth had him taken by force, as the poem here tells.

Maids from the south   through Myrkwood flew,
Fair and young   their fate to follow;
On the shore of the sea   to rest them they sat,
The maids of the south,   and flax they spun.

. . . .

Hlathguth and Hervor,   Hlothver's children,
And Olrun the Wise   Kjar's daughter was.

. . . .

One in her arms   took Egil then
To her bosom white,   the woman fair.

Swan-White second,—   swan-feathers she wore,

. . . .

And her arms the third   of the sisters threw
Next round Völund's   neck so white.

There did they sit   for seven winters,
In the eighth at last   came their longing again,
(And in the ninth   did need divide them).
The maidens yearned   for the murky wood,
The fair young maids,   their fate to follow.

Völund home   from his hunting came,
From a weary way,   the weather-wise bowman,
Slagfith and Egil   the hall found empty,
Out and in went they,   everywhere seeking.

East fared Egil   after Olrun,
And Slagfith south   to seek for Swan-White;
Völund alone   in Ulfdalir lay,

. . . .

Red gold he fashioned   with fairest gems,
And rings he strung   on ropes of bast;
So for his wife   he waited long,
If the fair one home   might come to him.

This Nithuth learned,   the lord of the Njars,
That Völund alone   in Ulfdalir lay;
By night went his men,   their mail-coats were studded,
Their shields in the waning   moonlight shone.

From their saddles the gable   wall they sought,
And in they went   at the end of the hall;
Rings they saw there   on ropes of bast,
Seven hundred   the hero had.

Off they took them,   but all they left
Save one alone   which they bore away.

. . . .

. . . .

Völund home   from his hunting came,
From a weary way,   the weather-wise bowman;
A brown bear's flesh   would he roast with fire;
Soon the wood so dry   was burning well,
(The wind-dried wood   that Völund's was).

On the bearskin he rested,   and counted the rings,
The master of elves,   but one he missed;
That Hlothver's daughter   had it he thought,
And the all-wise maid   had come once more.

So long he sat   that he fell asleep,
His waking empty   of gladness was;
Heavy chains   he saw on his hands,
And fetters bound   his feet together.

Völund spake:

"What men are they   who thus have laid
Ropes of bast   to bind me now?"

Then Nithuth called,   the lord of the Njars:
"How gottest thou, Völund,   greatest of elves,
These treasures of ours   in Ulfdalir?"

Völund spake:

"The gold was not   on Grani's way,
Far, methinks, is our realm   from the hills of the Rhine;
I mind me that treasures   more we had
When happy together   at home we were."

Without stood the wife   of Nithuth wise,
And in she came   from the end of the hall;
On the floor she stood,   and softly spoke:
"Not kind does he look   who comes from the wood."

King Nithuth gave to his daughter Bothvild the gold ring that he had taken from the bast rope in Völund's house, and he himself wore the sword that Völund had had. The queen spake:

"The glow of his eyes   is like gleaming snakes,
His teeth he gnashes   if now is shown
The sword, or Bothvild's   ring he sees;

Let them straightway cut   his sinews of strength,
And set him then   in Sævarstath."

So was it done: the sinews in his knee-joints were cut, and he was
set in an island which was near the mainland, and was called Sævarstath. There he smithied for the king all kinds of precious things. No
man dared to go to him, save only the king himself. Völund spake:

"At Nithuth's girdle   gleams the sword
That I sharpened keen   with cunningest craft,
(And hardened the steel   with highest skill;)
The bright blade far   forever is borne,
(Nor back shall I see it   borne to my smithy;)
Now Bothvild gets   the golden ring
(That was once my bride's,—   ne'er well shall it be.)"

He sat, nor slept,   and smote with his hammer,
Fast for Nithuth   wonders he fashioned;
Two boys did go   in his door to gaze,
Nithuth's sons,   into Sævarstath.

They came to the chest,   and they craved the keys,
The evil was open   when in they looked;
To the boys it seemed   that gems they saw,
Gold in plenty   and precious stones.

    Völund spake:

"Come ye alone,   the next day come,
Gold to you both   shall then be given;
Tell not the maids   or the men of the hall,
To no one say   that me you have sought."

.   .   .   .

Early did brother   to brother call:
"Swift let us go   the rings to see."

They came to the chest,   and they craved the keys,
The evil was open   when in they looked;
He smote off their heads,   and their feet he hid
Under the sooty   straps of the bellows.

Their skulls, once hid   by their hair, he took,
Set them in silver   and sent them to Nithuth;

Gems full fair   from their eyes he fashioned,
To Nithuth's wife   so wise he gave them.

And from the teeth   of the twain he wrought
A brooch for the breast,   to Bothvild he sent it;

.   .   .   .

Bothvild then   of her ring did boast,

.   .   .   .
.   .   .   .   .   "The ring I have broken,
I dare not say it   save to thee."

Völund spake:

"I shall weld the break   in the gold so well
That fairer than ever   thy father shall find it,
And better much   thy mother shall think it,
And thou no worse   than ever it was."

Beer he brought,   he was better in cunning,
Until in her seat   full soon she slept.

Völund spake:

"Now vengeance I have   for all my hurts,
Save one alone,   on the evil woman."

.   .   .   .
.   .   .   .

Quoth Völund: "Would   that well were the sinews
Maimed in my feet   by Nithuth's men."

Laughing Völund   rose aloft,
Weeping Bothvild   went from the isle,
For her lover's flight   and her father's wrath.

Without stood the wife   of Nithuth wise,
And in she came   from the end of the hall;
But he by the wall   in weariness sat:
"Wakest thou, Nithuth,   lord of the Njars?"

Nithuth spake:

"Always I wake,   and ever joyless,
Little I sleep   since my sons were slain;

Cold is my head,   cold was thy counsel,
One thing, with Völund   to speak, I wish.

.   .   .   .

"Answer me, Völund,   greatest of elves,
What happened with my boys   that hale once were?"

    Völund spake:

"First shalt thou all   the oaths now swear,
By the rail of ship,   and the rim of shield,
By the shoulder of steed,   and the edge of sword,
That to Völund's wife   thou wilt work no ill,
Nor yet my bride   to her death wilt bring,
Though a wife I should have   that well thou knowest,
And a child I should have   within thy hall.

"Seek the smithy   that thou didst set,
Thou shalt find the bellows   sprinkled with blood;
I smote off the heads   of both thy sons,
And their feet 'neath the sooty   straps I hid.

"Their skulls, once hid   by their hair, I took,
Set them in silver   and sent them to Nithuth;
Gems full fair   from their eyes I fashioned,
To Nithuth's wife   so wise I gave them.

"And from the teeth   of the twain I wrought
A brooch for the breast,   to Bothvild I gave it;
Now big with child   does Bothvild go,
The only daughter   ye two had ever."

    Nithuth spake:

"Never spakest thou word   that worse could hurt me,
Nor that made me, Völund,   more bitter for vengeance;
There is no man so high   from thy horse to take thee,
Or so doughty an archer   as down to shoot thee,
While high in the clouds   thy course thou takest."

Laughing Völund   rose aloft,
But left in sadness   Nithuth sat.

.   .   .   .

Then spake Nithuth,   lord of the Njars:
"Rise up, Thakkrath,   best of my thralls,
Bid Bothvild come,   the bright-browed maid,
Bedecked so fair,   with her father to speak."

.   .   .   .

.   .   .   .

"Is it true, Bothvild,   that which was told me;
Once in the isle   with Völund wert thou?"

Bothvild spake:

"True is it, Nithuth,   that which was told thee,
Once in the isle   with Völund was I,
An hour of lust,   alas it should be!
Nought was my might   with such a man,
Nor from his strength   could I save myself."

Frothi's Meal

Date uncertain

Snorra Edda

WHY is gold called Fródi's Meal? This is the tale thereof: One of Odin's sons, named Skjöldr,—from whom the Skjöldungs are come,—had his abode and ruled in the realm which now is called Denmark, but then was known as Gotland. Skjöldr's son, who ruled the land after him, was named Fridleifr. Fridleifr's son was Fródi: he succeeded to the kingdom after his father, in the time when Augustus Caesar imposed peace on all the world; at that time Christ was born. But because Fródi was mightiest of all kings in the Northern lands, the peace was called by his name wherever the Danish tongue was spoken; and men call it the Peace of Fródi. No man injured any other, even though he met face to face his father's slayer or his brother's, loose or bound. Neither was there any thief nor robber then, so that a gold ring lay long on Jalangr's Heath. King Fródi went to a feast in Sweden at the court of the king who was called Fjölnir, and there he bought two maid-servants, Fenja and Menja: they were huge and strong. In that time two mill-stones were found in Denmark, so great that no one was so strong that he could turn them: the nature of the mill was such that whatsoever he who turned asked for, was ground out by the mill-stones. This mill was called Grótti. He who gave King Fródi the mill was named Hengikjöptr. King Fródi had the maid-servants led to the mill, and bade them grind gold; and they did so. First they ground gold and peace and happiness for Fródi; then he would grant them rest or sleep no longer than the cuckoo held its peace or a song might be sung. It is said that they sang the song which is called the Lay of Grótti, and this is its beginning:

> Now are we come
> To the king's house,
> The two fore-knowing,
> Fenja and Menja:
> These are with Fródi
> Son of Fridleifr,
> The Mighty Maidens,
> As maid-thralls held.

And before they ceased their singing, they ground out a host against Fródi, so that the sea-king called Mýsingr came there that same night and slew Fródi, taking much plunder. Then the Peace of Fródi was ended. Mýsingr took Grótti with him, and Fenja and Menja also, and bade them grind salt. And at midnight they asked whether Mýsingr were not weary of salt. He bade them grind longer. They had ground but a little while, when down sank the ship; and from that time there has been a whirlpool in the sea where the water falls through the hole in the mill-stone. It was then that the sea became salt.

[The lay of Grótti:

> They to the flour-mill
> Were led, those maidens,
> And bidden tirelessly
> To turn the gray mill-stone:
> He promised to neither
> Peace nor surcease
> Till he had heard
> The handmaids' singing.
>
> They chanted the song
> Of the ceaseless mill-stone:

> "Lay we the bins right,
> Lift we the stones!"
> He urged the maidens
> To grind on ever.
>
> They sung and slung
> The whirling stone
> Till the men of Fródi
> For the most part slept;
> Then spake Menja,
> To the mill coming:

"Wealth grind we for Fródi,
We grind it in plenty,
Fullness of fee
At the mill of fortune:
Let him sit on riches
And sleep on down;
Let him wake in weal:
Then well 't is ground.

"Here may no one
Harm another,
Contrive evil,
Nor cast wiles for slaying,
Nor slaughter any
With sword well sharpened,
Though his brother's slayer
In bonds he find."

But he spake no word
Save only this:
"Sleep ye no longer
Than the hall-cuckoo's silence,
Nor longer than so,
While one song is sung."

"Thou wast not, Fródi,
Full in wisdom,
Thou friend of men,
When thou boughtest the maid-
ens
Didst choose for strength
And outward seeming;
But of their kindred
Didst not inquire.

"Hardy was Hrungnir,
And his father;
Yet was Thjazi
Than they more mighty:
Idi and Aurnir
Of us twain are kinsmen,—

Brothers of Hill-Giants,
Of them were we born.

"Grótti had not come
From the gray mountain,
Nor the hard boulder
From the earth's bosom,
Nor thus would grind
The Hill-Giants' Maiden,
If any had known
The news of her.

"We nine winters
Were playmates together,
Mighty of stature,
'Neath the earth's surface,
The maids had part
In mighty works:
Ourselves we moved
Mighty rocks from their place.

"We rolled the rock
O'er the Giants' roof-stead,
So that the ground,
Quaking, gave before us;
So slung we
The whirling stone,
The mighty boulder,
Till men took it.

"And soon after
In Sweden's realm,
We twain fore-knowing
Strode to the fighting;
Bears we hunted,
And shields we broke;
We strode through
The gray-mailed spear-host.

"We cast down a king,
We crowned another;
To Gotthormr good

We gave assistance;
No quiet was there
Ere Knúi fell.

"This course we held
Those years continuous,
That we were known
For warriors mighty;
There with sharp spears
Wounds we scored,
Let blood from wounds,
And reddened the brand.

"Now are we come
To the king's abode
Of mercy bereft
And held as bond-maids;
Clay eats our foot-soles,
Cold chills us above;
We turn the Peace-Grinder:
'T is gloomy at Fródi's.

"Hands must rest,
The stone must halt;
Enough have I turned,
My toil ceases:
Now may the hands
Have no remission
Till Fródi hold
The meal ground fully.

"The hands should hold
The hard shafts,
The weapons gore-stained,—
Wake thou, Fródi!
Wake thou, Fródi,
If thou wouldst hearken
To the songs of us twain
And to ancient stories.

"Fire I see burning
East of the burg,

War-tidings waken,
A beacon of warning:
A host shall come
Hither, with swiftness,
And fire the dwellings
Above King Fródi.

"Thou shalt not hold
The stead of Hleidr,
The red gold rings
Nor the gods' holy altar;
We grasp the handle,
Maiden, more hardly,—
We were not warmer
In the wound-gore of corpses.

"My father's maid
Mightily ground
For she saw the feyness
Of men full many;
The sturdy posts
From the flour-box started,
Made staunch with iron.
Grind we yet swifter.

"Grind we yet swifter!
The son of Yrsa,
Hálfdanr's kinsman,
Shall come with vengeance
On Fródi's head:
Him shall men call
Yrsa's son and brother.
We both know that."

The maidens ground,
Their might they tested,
Young and fresh
In giant-frenzy:
The bin-poles trembled,
And burst the flour-box;
In sunder burst
The heavy boulder.

And the sturdy bride
Of Hill-Giants spake:
"We have ground, O Fródi!

Soon we cease from grinding;
The women have labored
O'er long at the grist."

Thus sang Einarr Skúlason:

"I have heard that Fródi's hand-maids
Ground in the mill full gladly
The Serpent's Couch; with gold-meal
The king lets peace be broken:
The fair cheeks of my axe-head,
Fitted with maple, show forth
Fenja's Grist; exalted
Is the skald with the good king's riches."

So sang Egill:

"Glad are full many men
In Fródi's meal."]

Helgi Thrice Born

Second Century A.D.

Sæmundar Edda

MUSIC lovers have expressed their regret that Wagner did not use the cycle of eddic poems about the hero Helgi, with its romantic material available for tragedy or grand opera. Helgi was not a Burgundian, Goth, or Hun but a native Scandinavian. Danish historians claim him for Denmark, but Swedish archeologists point to the foundations of his castle in Sweden. Certainly he was as ardent as a lover as he was brave as a warrior and noble in his conduct toward his rivals. Some sceptics claim that his reincarnation was arranged by poets in order to rationalize the accounts of his deaths in three different encounters. But the fact that Valkyries chose him for their lover indicates his superphysical powers. William Henry Schofield preferred to translate Seva Fjoll, mountains that appear in the Helgi legend, as The Mountains of Passion. The following lyrics are taken from the translations of Helgi lays in The Poetic Edda by Henry Adams Bellows.

I

Hjorvarth and Sigrlin had a son, mighty and of noble stature; he was a silent man, and no name stuck fast to him. He sat on a hill, and saw nine Valkyries riding; one of them was the fairest of all. She spake:

"Late wilt thou, Helgi,   have hoard of rings,
Thou battle-tree fierce,   or of shining fields,—
The eagle screams soon,—   if never thou speakest,
Though, hero, hard   thy heart may cry."

Helgi spake:
"What gift shall I have   with Helgi's name,
Glorious maid,   for the giving is thine?
All thy words   shall I think on well,
But I want them not   if I win not thee."

*   *   *

Eylimi was the name of a king, whose daughter was Svava; she was a Valkyrie, and rode air and sea. She gave Helgi this name, and shielded him oft thereafter in battle.

*   *   *

King Helgi was a mighty warrior. He came to King Eylimi and sought the hand of his daughter, Svava. Then Helgi and Svava exchanged vows, and greatly they loved each other. Svava was at home with her father, while Helgi was in the field; Svava was still a Valkyrie as before.

*   *   *

There was a great battle, and there Helgi got a mortal wound.

Sigar riding   did Helgi send
To seek out Eylimi's   only daughter:
"Bid her swiftly   ready to be,
If her lover   alive she would find."

Sigar spake:
"Hither now   has Helgi sent me,
With thee, Svava,   thyself to speak;
The hero said   he fain would see thee
Ere life the nobly   born should leave."

Svava spake:
"What chanced with Helgi,   Hjorvarth's son?
Hard to me   is harm now come;
If the sea smote him,   or sword bit him,
Ill shall I bring   to all his foes."

Sigar spake:

"In the morn he fell   at Frekastein,
The king who was noblest   beneath the sun;
Alf has the joy   of victory all,
Though need therefor   is never his."

Helgi spake:

"Hail to thee, Svava!   thy sorrow rule,
Our meeting last   in life is this;
Hard the wounds   of the hero bleed,
And close to my heart   the sword has come.

"I bid thee, Svava,—   weep not, bride,—
If thou wilt hearken   to these my words,
The bed for Hethin   have thou ready,
And yield thy love   to the hero young."

Svava spake:

"A vow I had   in my dear-loved home,
When Helgi sought   with rings to have me,
That not of my will,   if the warrior died,
Would I fold in my arms   a man unfamed."

Hethin spake:

"Kiss me, Svava,   I come not back,
Rogheim to see,   or Rothulsfjoll,
Till vengeance I have   for the son of Hjorvarth,
The king who was noblest   beneath the sun."

II

In olden days,   when eagles screamed,
And holy streams   from heaven's crags fell,
Was Helgi then,   the hero-hearted,
Borghild's son,   in Bralund born.

'Twas night in the dwelling,   and Norns there came,
Who shaped the life   of the lofty one;
They bade him most famed   of fighters all
And best of princes   ever to be.

Mightily wove they   the web of fate,
While Bralund's towns   were trembling all;

And there the golden   threads they wove,
And in the moon's hall   fast they made them.

East and west   the ends they hid,
In the middle the hero   should have his land;
And Neri's kinswoman   northward cast
A chain, and bade it   firm ever to be.

* * *

Mighty he grew   in the midst of his friends,
The fair-born elm,   in fortune's glow;
To his comrades gold   he gladly gave,
The hero spared not   the blood-flecked hoard.

Short time for war   the chieftain waited,
When fifteen winters   old he was;
Hunding he slew,   the hardy wight
Who long had ruled   o'er lands and men.

* * *

Helgi bade higher   hoist the sails,
Nor did the ships'-folk   shun the waves,
Though dreadfully   did Ægir's daughters
Seek the steeds   of the sea to sink.

But from above   did Sigrun brave
Aid the men   and all their faring;

* * *

Swift as a storm   there smote together
The flashing blades   at Frekastein;
Ever was Helgi,   Hunding's slayer,
First in the throng   where warriors fought;
(Fierce in battle,   slow to fly,
Hard the heart   of the hero was.)

From heaven there came   the maidens helmed,—
The weapon-clang grew,—   who watched o'er the king;
Spake Sigrun fair,—   the wound-givers flew,
And the horse of the giantess   raven's-food had:—

"Hail to thee, hero!   full happy with men,
Offspring of Yngvi,   shalt ever live,
For thou the fearless   foe hast slain
Who to many the dread   of death had brought.

"Warrior, well   for thyself hast won
Red rings bright   and the noble bride;
Both now, warrior,   thine shall be,
Hogni's daughter   and Hringstathir,
Wealth and triumph;   the battle wanes."

* * *

Sigrun the joyful   chieftain sought,
Forthwith Helgi's   hand she took;
She greeted the hero   helmed and kissed him,
The warrior's heart   to the woman turned.

From her heart the daughter   of Hogni spake,
Dear was Helgi,   she said, to her;
"Long with all   my heart I loved
Sigmund's son   ere ever I saw him.

"At the meeting to Hothbrodd   mated I was,
But another hero   I fain would have;
Though, king, the wrath   of my kin I fear,
Since I broke my father's   fairest wish."

* * *

"Never shall Sigrun   from Sevafjoll,
Hothbrodd king,   be held in thine arms;
Granmar's sons   full cold have grown,
And the giant-steeds gray   on corpses gorge."

Then she sought out Helgi, and was full of joy. He said:

"Maid, not fair   is all thy fortune,
The Norns I blame   that this should be;
This morn there fell   at Frekastein
Bragi and Hogni   beneath my hand.

"At Hlebjorg fell   the sons of Hrollaug,
Starkath the king   at Styrkleifar;
Fighters more noble   saw I never,
The body fought   when the head had fallen.

"On the ground full low   the slain are lying,
Most are there   of the men of thy race;
Nought hast thou won,   for thy fate it was
Brave men to bring   to the battle-field."

Then Sigrun wept.   Helgi said:

"Grieve not, Sigrun,   the battle is gained,
The fighter can shun not his fate."

Sigrun spake:
"To life would I call   them who slaughtered lie,
If safe on thy breast I might be."

* * *

Helgi took Sigrun to wife, and they had sons. Helgi did not reach
old age. Dag, the son of Hogni, offered sacrifice to Othin to be
avenged for his father's death; Othin gave Dag his spear. Dag found
Helgi, his brother-in-law, at a place which is called Fjoturlund. He
thrust the spear through Helgi's body. Then Helgi fell, and Dag
rode to Sevafjoll and told Sigrun the tidings:

"Sad am I, sister,   sorrow to tell thee,
Woe to my kin   unwilling I worked;
In the morn there fell   at Fjoturlund
The noblest prince   the world has known,
(And his heel he set   on the heroes' necks.)"

Sigrun spake:
"Now may every   oath thee bite
That with Helgi   sworn thou hast,
By the water   bright of Leipt,
And the ice-cold   stone of Uth.

"The ship shall sail not   in which thou sailest,
Though a favoring wind   shall follow after;
The horse shall run not   whereon thou ridest,
Though fain thou art   thy foe to flee.

. . . .

. . . .

"The sword shall bite not   which thou bearest,
Till thy head itself   it sings about.

"Vengeance were mine   for Helgi's murder,
Wert thou a wolf   in the woods without,
Possessing nought   and knowing no joy,
Having no food   save corpses to feed on."

Dag spake:

"Mad art thou, sister,   and wild of mind,
Such a curse   on thy brother to cast;
Othin is ruler   of every ill,
Who sunders kin   with runes of spite.

"Thy brother rings   so red will give thee,
All Vandilsve   and Vigdalir;
Take half my land   to pay the harm,
Ring-decked maid,   and as meed for thy sons."

Sigrun spake:

"I shall sit not happy   at Sevafjoll,
Early or late,   my life to love,
If the light cannot show,   in the leader's band,
Vigblær bearing him   back to his home,
(The golden-bitted;   I shall greet him never.)

"Such the fear   that Helgi's foes
Ever felt,   and all their kin,
As makes the goats   with terror mad
Run from the wolf   among the rocks.

"Helgi rose   above heroes all
Like the lofty ash   above lowly thorns,
Or the noble stag,   with dew besprinkled,
Bearing his head   above all beasts,
(And his horns gleam bright   to heaven itself.)"

A hill was made in Helgi's memory. And when he came to Valhall, then Othin bade him rule over everything with himself.

* * *

One of Sigrun's maidens went one evening to Helgi's hill, and saw that Helgi rode to the hill with many men. The maiden said:

"Is this a dream   that methinks I see,
Or the doom of the gods,   that dead men ride,
And hither spurring   urge your steeds,
Or is home-coming now   to the heroes granted?"

Helgi spake:

"No dream is this   that thou thinkest to see,
Nor the end of the world,   though us thou beholdest,

And hither spurring   we urge our steeds,
Nor is home-coming now   to the heroes granted."

The maiden went home and said to Sigrun:

"Go forth, Sigrun,   from Sevafjoll,
If fain the lord   of the folk wouldst find;
(The hill is open,   Helgi is come;)
The sword-tracks bleed;   the monarch bade
That thou his wounds   shouldst now make well."

Sigrun went in the hill to Helgi, and said:

"Now am I glad   of our meeting together,
As Othin's hawks,   so eager for prey,
When slaughter and flesh   all warm they scent,
Or dew-wet see   the red of day.

"First will I kiss   the lifeless king,
Ere off the bloody   byrnie thou cast;
With frost thy hair   is heavy, Helgi,
And damp thou art   with the dew of death;
(Ice-cold hands   has Hogni's kinsman,
What, prince, can I   to bring thee ease?)"

Helgi spake:
"Thou alone, Sigrun   of Sevafjoll,
Art cause that Helgi   with dew is heavy;
Gold-decked maid,   thy tears are grievous,
(Sun-bright south-maid,   ere thou sleepest;)
Each falls like blood   on the hero's breast,
(Burned-out, cold,   and crushed with care.)

"Well shall we drink   a noble draught,
Though love and lands   are lost to me;
No man a song   of sorrow shall sing,
Though bleeding wounds   are on my breast;
Now in the hill   our brides we hold,
The heroes' loves,   by their husbands dead."

Sigrun made ready a bed in the hill.

"Here a bed   I have made for thee, Helgi,
To rest thee from care,   thou kin of the Ylfings;

I will make thee sink　　to sleep in my arms,
As once I lay　　with the living king."

Helgi spake:

"Now do I say　　that in Sevafjoll
Aught may happen,　　early or late,
Since thou sleepest clasped　　in a corpse's arms,
So fair in the hill,　　the daughter of Hogni!
(Living thou comest,　　a daughter of kings.)

"Now must I ride　　the reddened ways,
And my bay steed set　　to tread the sky;
Westward I go　　to wind-helm's bridges,
Ere Salgofnir wakes　　the warrior throng."

Then Helgi and his followers rode on their way, and the women went home to the dwelling. Another evening Sigrun bade the maiden keep watch at the hill. And at sunset when Sigrun came to the hill she said:

"Now were he come,　　if come he might,
Sigmund's son,　　from Othin's seat;
Hope grows dim　　of the hero's return
When eagles sit　　on the ash-tree boughs,
And men are seeking　　the meeting of dreams."

The Maiden said:
"Mad thou wouldst seem　　alone to seek,
Daughter of heroes,　　the house of the dead;
For mightier now　　at night are all
The ghosts of the dead　　than when day is bright."

III

Sigrun was early dead of sorrow and grief. It was believed in olden times that people were born again, but that is now called old wives' folly. Of Helgi and Sigrun it is said that they were born again; he became Helgi Haddingjaskati, and she Kara the daughter of Half-dan, as is told in the Lay of Kara, and she was a Valkyrie.

Offa

c. 360

Saxo Grammaticus

Gesta Danorum

From the Latin

OFFA was king of the Angles in Jutland before they came to England. English literature preserves his legend in several versions. Offa was dumb until his thirtieth year, when, in his people's crisis, he suddenly found his speech and took up arms. His date may be computed approximately from Anglo-Saxon genealogies. According to *Bēowulf* (1954 ff.) Offa was "the leader of heroes, of all mankind in my knowledge the best, between the seas, of the race of man."

◄§ THE LONG and leisurely tranquillity of a most prosperous and quiet time flowed by, and Wermund in undisturbed security maintained a prolonged and steady peace at home. He had no children during the prime of his life, but in his old age, by a belated gift of fortune, he begat a son, Uffe, though all the years which had glided by had raised him up no offspring. This Uffe surpassed all of his age in stature, but in his early youth was supposed to have so dull and foolish a spirit as to be useless for all affairs public or private. For from his first years he never used to play or make merry, but was so void of all human pleasure that he kept his lips sealed in a perennial silence, and utterly restrained his austere visage from the business of laughter. But though through the years of his youth he was reputed for an utter fool, he afterwards left that despised estate and became famous, turning out as great a pattern of wisdom and hardihood as he had been a picture of stagnation.

* * *

When Wermund was losing his sight by infirmity of age, the King of Saxony, thinking that Denmark lacked a leader, sent envoys ordering him to surrender to his charge the kingdom which he held beyond the due term of life; lest, if he thirsted to hold sway too long, he should strip his country of laws and defense. For how could he be reckoned a king, whose spirit was darkened with age, and his eyes with blindness not less black and awful? If he refused, but yet had a son who would dare to accept a challenge and fight with his son, let

him agree that the victor should possess the realm. But if he approved
neither offer, let him learn that he must be dealt with by weapons
and not by warnings; and in the end he must unwillingly surrender
what he was too proud at first to yield uncompelled. Wermund, shaken
by deep sighs, answered that it was too insolent to sting him with
these taunts upon his years; for he had passed no timorous youth, nor
shrunk from battle, that age should bring him to this extreme misery.
It was equally unfitting to cast in his teeth the infirmity of his blindness: for it was common for a loss of this kind to accompany such a
time of life as his, and it seemed a calamity fitter for sympathy than
for taunts. It were juster to fix the blame on the impatience of the
King of Saxony, whom it would have beseemed to wait for the old
man's death, and not demand his throne; for it was somewhat better
to succeed to the dead than to rob the living. Yet, that he might not
be thought to make over the honours of his ancient freedom, like a
madman, to the possession of another, he would accept the challenge
with his own hand. The envoys answered that they knew that their
king would shrink from the mockery of fighting a blind man, for
such an absurd mode of combat was thought more shameful than
honourable. It would surely be better to settle the affair by means of
their offspring on either side. The Danes were in consternation, and at
a sudden loss for a reply: but Uffe, who happened to be there with
the rest, craved his father's leave to answer; and suddenly the dumb
as it were spake. When Wermund asked who had thus begged leave
to speak, and the attendants said that it was Uffe, he declared that it
was enough that the insolent foreigner should jeer at the pangs of his
misery, without those of his own household vexing him with the
same wanton effrontery. But the courtiers persistently averred that
this man was Uffe; and the king said: "He is free, whosoever he be,
to say out what he thinks." Then said Uffe, "that it was idle for their
king to covet a realm which could rely not only on the service of its
own ruler, but also on the arms and wisdom of most valiant nobles.
Moreover, the king did not lack a son nor the kingdom an heir; and
they were to know that he had made up his mind to fight not only
the son of their king, but also, at the same time, whatsoever man the
prince should elect as his comrade out of the bravest of their nation."

The envoys laughed when they heard this, thinking it idle lip-
courage. Instantly the ground for the battle was agreed on, and a fixed
time appointed. But the bystanders were so amazed by the strange-

ness of Uffe's speaking and challenging, that one can scarce say if they were more astonished at his words or at his assurance.

But on the departure of the envoys Wermund praised him who had made the answer, because he had proved his confidence in his own valour by challenging not one only, but two; and said that he would sooner quit his kingdom for him, whoever he was, than for an insolent foe. But when one and all testified that he who with lofty self-confidence had spurned the arrogance of the envoys was his own son, he bade him come nearer to him, wishing to test with his hands what he could not find with his eyes. Then he carefully felt his body, and found by the size of his limbs and by his features that he was his son; and then began to believe their assertions, and to ask him why he had taken pains to hide so sweet an eloquence with such careful dissembling, and had borne to live through so long a span of life without utterance or any intercourse of talk, so as to let men think him utterly incapable of speech, and a born mute. He replied that he had been hitherto satisfied with the protection of his father, that he had not needed the use of his own voice, until he saw the wisdom of his own land hard pressed by the glibness of a foreigner. The king also asked him why he had chosen to challenge two rather than one. He said he had desired this mode of combat in order that the death of King Athisl, which, having been caused by two men, was a standing reproach to the Danes, might be balanced by the exploit of one, and that a new ensample of valour might erase the ancient record of their disgrace. Fresh honour, he said, would thus obliterate the guilt of their old dishonour.

Wermund said that his son had judged all things rightly, and bade him first learn the use of arms, since he had been little accustomed to them. When they were offered to Uffe, he split the narrow links of the mail-coats by the mighty girth of his chest, nor could any be found large enough to hold him properly. For he was too hugely built to be able to use the arms of any other man. At last, when he was bursting even his father's coat of mail by the violent compression of his body, Wermund ordered it to be cut away on the left side and patched with a buckle; thinking it mattered little if the side guarded by the shield were exposed to the sword. He also told him to be most careful in fixing on a sword which he could use safely. Several were offered him; but Uffe, grasping the hilt, shattered them one after the other into flinders by shaking them, and not a single blade was of so hard a temper but at the first blow he broke it into many pieces. But the king had a sword of extraordinary sharpness, called "Skrep," which at a single blow of the smiter struck straight through and cleft asunder any obstacle whatsoever; nor would aught be hard enough to check its edge when driven home. The king, loth to leave this for the benefit of posterity, and greatly grudging others the use of it, had buried it deep in the earth, meaning, since he had no hopes of his son's improvement, to debar everyone else from using it. But when he was now asked whether he had a sword worthy of the strength of Uffe, he said that he had one which, if he could recognize the lie of the ground and find what he had consigned long ago to earth, he could offer him as worthy of his bodily strength. Then he bade them lead him into a field, and kept questioning his companions over all the ground. At last he recognised the tokens, found the spot where he had buried the sword, drew it out of its hole, and handed it to his son. Uffe saw it was frail with great age and rusted away; and, not daring to strike with it, asked if he must prove this one also like the rest, declaring that he must try its temper before the battle ought to be fought. Wermund replied that if this sword were shattered by mere brandishing, there was nothing left which could serve for such strength as his. He must, therefore, forbear from the act, whose issue remained so doubtful.

So they repaired to the field of battle as agreed. It is fast encompassed by the waters of the river Eider, which roll between, and forbid any approach save by ship. Hither Uffe went unattended, while the Prince of Saxony was followed by a champion famous for his strength. Dense crowds on either side, eager to see, thronged each winding bank, and all bent their eyes upon this scene. Wermund planted himself on the end of the bridge, determined to perish in the waters if defeat were the lot of his son: he would rather share the fall of his own flesh and blood than behold, with heart full of anguish, the destruction of his own country. Both the warriors assaulted Uffe; but, distrusting his sword, he parried the blows of both with his shield, being determined to wait patiently and see which of the two he must beware of most heedfully, so that he might reach that one at all events with a single stroke of his blade. Wermund, thinking that his feebleness was at fault, that he took the blows so patiently, dragged himself little by little, in his longing for death, forward to the western edge of the bridge, meaning to fling himself down and perish, should all be over with his son.

Fortune shielded the old father who loved so passionately, for Uffe told the prince to engage with him more briskly, and to do some deed of prowess worthy of his famous race; lest the lowborn squire should seem braver than the prince. Then, in order to try the bravery of the champion, he bade him not skulk timorously at his master's heels, but requite by noble deeds of combat the trust placed in him by his prince, who had chosen him to be his single partner in the battle. The other complied, and when shame drove him to fight at close quarters, Uffe clove him through with the first stroke of his blade. The sound revived Wermund, who said that he heard the sword of his son, and asked "on what particular part he had dealt the blow?" Then the retainers answered that he had gone through no one limb, but the man's whole frame; whereat he drew back from the precipice and came again on the bridge, longing now as passionately to live as he had just wished to die. Then Uffe, wishing to destroy his remaining foe after the fashion of the first, incited the prince with vehement words to offer some sacrifice by way of requital to the shade of the servant slain in his cause. Drawing him by those appeals, and warily noting the right spot to plant his blow, he turned the other edge of his sword to the front, fearing that the thin side of his blade was too frail for his strength, and smote with a piercing stroke through the prince's body. When Wermund heard it, he said that the sound of his sword "Skrep" had reached his ear for the second time. Then, when the judges announced that his son had killed both enemies, he burst into tears from excess of joy. Thus gladness bedewed the cheeks which sorrow could not moisten. So while the Saxons, sad and shame-faced, bore their champions to burial with bitter shame, the Danes welcomed Uffe and bounded for joy. Then no more was heard of the disgrace of the murder of Athisl, and there was an end of the taunts of the Saxons.

Thus the realm of Saxony was transferred to the Danes, and Uffe, after his father, undertook its government; and he, who had not been thought equal to administering a single kingdom properly, was now appointed to manage both.

Tragedy at Sigersted

c. 400

Saxo Grammaticus

Gesta Danorum

From the Latin

NEAR the town of Sigersted in Danish Sjælland jewels and drinking vessels of the third and fourth centuries recovered by archeologists indicate the seat of a dynasty of kings whose names began with "Sig," the so-called Siklings. In the fifth century the seat of Danish authority was moved to the vicinity of Leire on the same island, and the new dynasty adopted names beginning with the letter "H."

Last of the Sig-kings was Sigar (or Sigehere). According to *Wīdsīð* "Sigehere longest ruled the Sea-Danes." According to Saxo his daughter Signy was the heroine of one of the most poignant legends of primitive passion.

❧ AFTERWARDS Hagbard dressed himself in woman's attire, and, as though he had not wronged Sigar's daughter by slaying her brothers, went back to her alone, trusting in the promise he had from her, and feeling more safe in her loyalty than alarmed by reason of his own misdeed. Thus does lust despise peril. And, not to lack a pretext for his journey, he gave himself out as a fighting-maid of Hakon, saying that he took an embassy from him to Sigar. And when he was taken to bed at night among the handmaids, and the women who washed his feet were wiping them, they asked him why he had such hairy legs, and why his hands were not at all soft to touch, he answered:

"What wonder that the soft hollow of my foot should harden, and that long hairs should stay on my shaggy leg, when the sand has so often smitten my soles beneath, and the briars have caught me in mid-step?

"Now I scour the forest with leaping, now the waters with running. Now the sea, now the earth, now the wave is my path.

"Nor could my breast, shut in bonds of steel, and wont to be beaten with lance and missile, ever have been soft to the touch, as with you who are covered by the mantle or the smooth gown.

"Not the distaff or the wool-frails, but spears dripping from the slaughter, have served for our handling."

Signe did not hesitate to back up his words with like dissembling, and replied that it was natural that hands which dealt more in wounds than wools, and in battle than in tasks of the house should show the hardness that befitted their service; and that, unenfeebled with the pliable softness of women, they should not feel smooth to the touch of others. For they were hardened partly by the toils of war, partly by the habit of seafaring. For, said she, the warlike hand-maid of Hakon did not deal in woman's business, but had been wont to bring her right hand blood-stained with hurling spears and flinging missiles. It was no wonder, therefore, if her soles were hardened by the immense journeys she had gone; and that, when the shores she had scoured so often had bruised them with their rough and broken shingle, they should toughen in a horny stiffness, and should not feel soft to the touch like theirs, whose steps never strayed, but who were forever cooped within the confines of the palace. Hagbard received her as his bedfellow, under plea that he was to have the couch of honour; and, amid their converse of mutual delight, he addressed her slowly in such words as these:

"If thy father takes me and gives me to bitter death, wilt thou ever, when I am dead, forget so strong a troth, and again seek the marriage-plight?

"For if the chance should fall that way, I can hope for no room for pardon; nor will the father who is to avenge his sons spare or have pity.

"For I stripped thy brothers of their power on the sea and slew them; and now, unknown to thy father, as though I had done naught before counter to his will, I hold thee in the couch we share.

"Say, then, my one love, what manner of wish wilt thou show when thou lackest the accustomed embrace?"

Signe answered:

"Trust me, dear; I wish to die with thee, if fate brings thy turn to perish first, and not to prolong my span of life at all, when once dismal death has cast thee to the tomb.

"For if thou chance to close thy eyes for ever, a victim to the maddened attack of the men-at-arms;—by whatsoever doom thy breath be cut off, by sword or disease, by sea or soil, I forswear every wanton and corrupt flame, and vow myself to a death like thine; that they who were bound by one marriage-union may be embraced in one and the same punishment. Nor will I quit this man, though I am to feel the pains of death; I have resolved he is worthy of my love who gathered the first kisses of my mouth, and had the first fruits of my delicate youth. I think that no vow will be surer than this, if speech of woman have any loyalty at all."

This speech so quickened the spirit of Hagbard, that he found more pleasure in her promise than peril in his own going away. The serving-women betrayed him; and when Sigar's men-at-arms attacked him, he defended himself long and stubbornly, and slew many of them in the doorway. But at last he was taken, and brought before the assembly, and found the voices of the people divided over him. For very many said that he should be punished for so great an offence; but Bilwis, the brother of Bolwis, and others, conceived a better judgment, and advised that it would be better to use his stout service than to deal with him too ruthlessly.

Then Bolwis came forward and declared that it was evil advice which urged the king to pardon when he ought to take vengeance, and to soften with unworthy compassion his righteous impulse to anger. For how could Sigar, in the case of this man, feel any desire to spare or pity him, when he had not only robbed him of the double comfort of his sons, but had also bestained him with the insult of deflowering his daughter? The greater part of the assembly voted for this opinion; Hagbard was condemned, and a gallows-tree planted to receive him. Hence it came about that he who at first had hardly one sinister voice against him was punished with general harshness. Soon after the queen handed him a cup, and, bidding him assuage his thirst, vexed him with threats after this manner:

"Now, insolent Hagbard, whom the whole assembly has pronounced worthy of death, now to quench thy thirst thou shalt give thy lips liquor to drink in a cup of horn.

"Wherefore cast away fear, and, at this last hour of thy life, taste with bold lips the deadly goblet;

"That, having drunk it, thou mayst presently land by the dwellings of those below, passing into the sequestered palace of stern Dis, giving thy body to the gibbet and thy spirit to Orcus."

Then the young man took the cup offered him, and is said to have made answer as follows:

"With this hand, wherewith I cut off thy twin sons, I will take my last taste, yea the draught of the last drink.

"Now not unavenged shall I go to the Elysian regions, not unchastising to the stern ghosts. For these men have first been shut in the dens of Tartarus by a slaughter wrought by my endeavours. This right hand was wet with blood that was yours; this hand robbed thy children of the years of their youth, children whom thy womb brought to light; but the deadly sword spared it not then. Infamous woman, raving in spirit, hapless, childless mother, no years shall restore to thee the lost, no time and no day whatsoever shall save thy child from the starkness of death, or redeem him!"

Thus he avenged the queen's threats of death by taunting her with the youths whom he had slain; and, flinging back the cup at her, drenched her face with the sprinkled wine.

Meantime Signe asked her weeping women whether they could endure to bear her company in the things which she purposed. They promised that they would carry out and perform themselves whatsoever their mistress should come to wish, and their promise was loyally kept. Then, drowned in tears, she said that she wished to follow in death the only partner of her bed that she had ever had; and ordered that, as soon as the signal had been given from a place of watch, torches should be put to the room, then that halters should be made out of their robes; and to these they should proffer their throats to be strangled, thrusting away the support to the feet. They agreed; and that they might blench the less at death, she gave them a draught of wine. After this Hagbard was led to the hill, which afterwards took its name from him, to be hanged. Then, to test the loyalty of his true love, he told the executioners to hang up his mantle, saying that it would be a pleasure to him if he could see the likeness of his approaching death rehearsed in some way. The request was granted; and the watcher on the outlook, thinking that the thing was being done to Hagbard, reported what she saw to the maidens who were shut within the palace. They quickly fired the house, and thrusting away the wooden support under their feet, gave their necks to the noose to be writhen. So Hagbard, when he saw the palace wrapped in fire, and the familiar chamber blazing, said that he felt more joy from the loyalty of his mistress than sorrow at his approaching death. He also charged the bystanders to do him to death, witnessing how little he made of his doom by a song like this:

"Swiftly, O warriors! let me be caught and lifted into the air. Sweet, O my bride! is it for me to die when thou hast gone.

"I perceive the crackling and the house ruddy with flames; and the love, long-promised, declares our troth.

"Behold, thy covenant is fulfilled with no doubtful vows, since thou sharest my life and my destruction.

"We shall have one end, one bond after our troth, and somewhere our first love will live on.

"Happy am I, that have deserved to have joy of such a consort, and not to go basely alone to the gods of Tartarus!

"Then let the knot gripe the midst of the throat; nought but pleasure the last doom shall bring,

"Since there remains a sure hope of the renewal of love, and a death which will soon have joys of its own.

"Either country is sweet; in both worlds shall be held in honour the repose of our souls together, our equal troth in love,

"For, see now, I welcome the doom before me; since not even among the shades does very love suffer the embrace of its partner to perish." And as he spoke the executioners strangled him. And, that none may think that all traces of antiquity have utterly disappeared, a proof of the aforesaid event is afforded by local marks yet existing; for the killing of Hagbard gave his name to the stead; and not far from the town of Sigar there is a place to be seen, where a mound a little above the level, with the appearance of a swelling in the ground, looks like an ancient homestead.

The Waking of Angantyr

Fifth century

Hervarar saga ok Heiðreks konungs

"From the saga we learn that after the battle with Hiálmar and Orvar Odd on Sáms-isle, the latter interred Angantýr and his brothers in a barrow with all their weapons. Before his death Angantýr had begotten a daughter. She wore armor like a man and joined a band of vikings whose chief she soon became. She lays her course to Sáms-isle to win Tyrfing, the wondrous sword. Alone she goes on land."—L.M.H.

The Shepherd said:
"Who by himself   hath come hither on isle?
Go thou straightway,   get thee shelter!"

Hervor said:
"I care not go   and get me shelter:
not any one know I   of the island's men.

Ere hence thou hiest,   in haste tell me:
where are the howes   for Hiorvarth named?"

The Shepherd said:
"Ask not of such,   if sage thou art,
friend-of-vikings: thou 'rt on ferly ways;
let us fare hence so fast   as feet will carry!
Without now is it   awful for men."

Hervor said:
"This trinket's thine   if thou tell me this:
't were hard to hold back   the heroes'-friend."

The Shepherd said:
"Thou canst not give   such golden trinkets,
such fair-shining rings,   that I fare with thee.

" 'Tis folly, in faith,   to fare thither
for a man alone   in this murky dark:
is fire abroad,   the barrows open,
burn field and fen: let us flee in haste."

Hervor said:
"I scorn to dread   a din like this,
though fires do burn   all about the isle!
Let not men who are dead   unman us, shepherd,
with fear so swiftly,   but say thou on!"

The Shepherd said:
"Is Hel's gate lifted,   the howes do ope,
the edge of the isle   is all afire—
awful is it   to be without:
to thy ships hie thee   in haste, oh maiden!"

Hervor said:
"Such nightly blaze   ye cannot build
that of their fires   afraid I grow:
will Hervor's heart   not be horror-struck,
e'en though a ghost   in grave-door stood.

"Awake, Angantýr!   Wakes thee Hervor,
thy only bairn,   born to Sváva;
the bitter brand   from thy belt gird thou,
which swinking dwarfs   for Sváfrlami wrought.

"Hervarth, Hiorvarth,   Hrani, Angantýr!
I awake you all,   ye wights neath mold
with helmets and byrnies   and bitter swords,
with gory spears   and all gear of war.

"Have Arngrím's sons,   the evil men's,
their corpses become   to clay and mold,
seeing that none   of the sons of Eyfura
with me will speak   in Munar Bay.

"May all of you feel   within your ribs
as though in ant-hill   your ill bones rotted,
but the sword ye fetch me   forged by Dvalin:
it befits not ghosts   to guard prized arms."

Angantýr said:

"Hervor, daughter,   why doest call me
with cold curses?   They will cost thee dear!
Bereft of reason   and raving art thou,
that with wildered thought   thou wak'st the dead.

"Neither father me buried   nor fellow kinsmen:
(thy brothers' banesmen   this barrow raised.)
The twain who lived   did Tyrfing win—
now one of the victors   wields it at last."

Hervor said:

"Thou say'st not sooth!   May so the gods
leave thee whole in howe   as thou hast not
Tyrfing with thee: unwilling art
to give thy daughter   her dearest wish."

Angantýr said:

"Hardly human   I hold thee, maiden,
about barrows who   hoverest at night,
with graven spear   and Gothic iron,
with helmet and byrnie,   the hall's gate before."

Hervor said:

"Howbeit, human   was I held to be
ere hither I hied me,   your hall to seek:
out of howe hand me   the hater-of-byrnies,
the dwarfs' handiwork: 't will not do to hide it!"

Angantýr said:
"Under my shoulders hidden   lies Hiálmar's bane,
about its blade   blazes fire:
in this wide world know I   no woman born
who would dare to wield   the dreaded sword."

Hervor said:
"Would I hold in hand—   if have it I might—
the bitter brand,   and in battle wield it.
Not a whit fear I   the fire blazing:
it swiftly sinks   as I seek it with eye."

Angantýr said:
"I tell thee, Hervor—   heed my warning!—
what will happen,   thou heroes' daughter!
I say but sooth: will this sword become
the slayer of all   thy sib and kin."

Hervor said:
"Thus shall I deal   with you dead men's bones
that in your graves   ye get no rest:
hand me, Angantýr,   out of the howe
the sword wherewith   thou slewest Hiálmar!"

Angantýr said:
"Witless art thou,   and of wanton mind,
like a fool to fling thee   into fire blazing!
Out of howe, rather,   shall I hand the sword,
hardy maiden,   nor withhold it from thee."

Hervor said:
"Well then doest thou,   warriors'-offspring,
out of the howe   to hand Tyrfing
which liefer to me,   thou lord-of-battle,
than now to have   all Norroway."

Angantýr said:
"Thou little knowest,   luckless woman,
what ill thou 'st wrought   with reckless speech:
I say but sooth: will this sword become
the slayer of all   thy sib and kin."

Hervor said:

"To my ships on shore   now shall I hie me:
is the hero's daughter   happy in mind.
Little reck I,   ruler of men,
whether my sons   will slay each other."

Angantýr said:

"Thou 'lt have it through life   and long joy in it;
but keep thou hidden,   Hiálmar's-slayer,
nor touch its edges: on the twain is poison.
Is that bitter brand   baneful to all.

"Thou'lt have a son   who hereafter
will wield Tyrfing   and trust his strength;
Heithrek will he   be hight of men,
and mightiest grow   of men under heaven.

"Farewell, daughter!   I would fain give thee
the thews of twelve men   if thou 'ldst but heed me—
their lives and strength,   the stored-up wealth
which Arngrím's sons   left after them."

Hervor said:

"Shall I hie me hence.   Happily may ye—
I long to be gone—   live in your howe.
But lately I lingered   'twixt life and death,
when all about me   blazed the fires."

HEROES OF HEOROT

A.D. 500-550

In Danish legendary history the most illustrious dynasty was that of the H-kings, the so-called Skyldings or Skjoldungs, whose seat was at Ut-Leire (Hleithargarth) in Sjælland. Their fame crossed the sea with the Angles from Jutland to England where, probably in the seventh century, the Anglo-Saxon epic *Bēowulf* was composed. In Scandinavia, the poems and sagas about the Skjoldungs were written down centuries later. The visiting hero, Beowulf the Geat, is in Scandinavia replaced by Bothvar Bjarki from Norway, and the nephew is now the distinguished monarch of the dynasty instead of the uncle who flourished in *Bēowulf*.

While the H-Dynasty was historical, the visiting heroes Beowulf and Bjarki were creatures of folklore or poetry. The European folk-tale of

"The Bear's Son," about a hero who slays supernatural beings dwelling underground, was attached to Beowulf and, in various forms, to several other characters in Old Scandinavian literature. The "Bear's Son" exploits of the historical Grettir and the romantic Samson are recorded later in these selections. Beowulf's name has been interpreted as "Bee-wolf," that is "Bear." As for Bothvar, his father was a bear, and his nickname "Bjarki" means "Little Bear."

The Anglo-Saxon name Heorot, the "Hart Hall" of the H-Kings, is not preserved in the Scandinavian accounts of the fortress of Hleithargarth. An American scholar has located its site at Hiort, a farm lying near Outer Leire, in Vixö Parish, several miles nearer the sea than the present village of Leire, but the identification is uncertain.

The Anglian Tradition

From the Anglo-Saxon

there towered the hall,
high, gabled wide, the hot surge waiting
of furious flame.

—Bēowulf 81-83

the hall they saw,
broad of gable and bright with gold.

—Bēowulf 307-8

Hrothwulf and Hrothgar held the longest
peace between them uncle and nephew
after they banished the band of the pirates,
bowed Ingeld's attack,
hewed down at Heorot the Heathobards' host.

—Wīdsīð 45-49

Kraki's Seed

Snorra Edda

WHY is gold called Kraki's Seed? In Denmark there was a king called Hrólfr Kraki: he was most renowned of all ancient kings for munificence, valor, and graciousness. One evidence of his graciousness which is often brought into stories is this: A little lad and poor, Vöggr by name, came into the hall of King Hrólfr. At that time the king was young, and of slender stature. Vöggr came into his presence and looked up at him; and the king said: "What wouldst thou say, lad, for thou lookest at me?" Vöggr answered: "When I was at home, I heard say that Hrólfr the king at Hleidr was the greatest man in the northern lands; but now there sitteth in the high seat a little pole, and he is called King." Then the king made answer: "Thou, boy, hast given me a name, so that I shall be called Hrólfr the Pole (Kraki); and it is the custom that the giving of a name be accompanied by a gift. Now I see that with the name which thou has fastened on me, thou hast no gift such as would be acceptable to me, wherefore he that has wherewith to give shall give to the other." And he took from his hand a gold ring and gave it to him. Then Vöggr said: "Above all kings be thou most blessed of givers! Now I swear an oath that I shall be that man's slayer who slays thee." Then spake the king, laughing loudly: "Vöggr is pleased with a small thing."

Another example is the tale told concerning the valor of Hrólfr Kraki: That king whom men call Adils ruled over Uppsala; he had to wife Yrsa, mother of Hrólfr Kraki. He was at strife with the king who ruled over Norway, whose name was Áli; the two joined battle on the ice of the lake called Vaeni. King Adils sent an embassy to Hrólfr Kraki, his stepson, praying him to come to his aid, and promised wages to all his host so long as they should be away; King Hrólfr himself should have three precious gifts, whatsoever three he might choose from all Sweden. King Hrólfr could not make the journey in person, owing to the strife in which he was engaged with the Saxons; but he sent to Adils his twelve berserks: Bödvar-Bjarki was there for one, and Hjalti the Stout-Hearted, Hvítserkr the Stern, Vöttr Véseti, and the brethren Svipdagr and Beigudr. In that battle King Áli fell, and the great part of his host with him; and King

Adils took from him in death the helm Battle-Swine and his horse
Raven. Then the berserks of Hrólfr Kraki demanded for their hire
three pounds of gold for each man of them; and in addition they
required that they might bear to Hrólfr Kraki those gifts of price
which they had chosen for him: which were the helm Battle-Boar
and the birnie Finn's Heritage,—on neither of which iron would
take hold,—and the gold ring which was called Pig of the Swedes,
which Adils' forefathers had had. But the king denied them all these
things, nor did he so much as pay their hire: the berserks went away
ill-pleased with their share, and told the state of things to Hrólfr
Kraki.

Straightway he began his journey to Uppsala; and when he had
brought his ships into the river Fýri, he rode at once to Uppsala,
and his twelve berserks with him, all without safe-conduct. Yrsa, his
mother, welcomed him and led him to lodgings, but not to the king's
hall: fires were made there before them, and ale was given them to
drink. Then men of King Adils came in and heaped firewood onto
the fire, and made it so great that the clothes were burnt off Hrólfr
and his men. And the fellows spake: "Is it true that Hrólfr Kraki and
his berserks shun neither fire nor iron?" Then Hrólfr Kraki leapt
up, and all they that were with him; and he said:

> "Add we to the fire
> In Adils' dwelling!"

took his shield and cast it onto the fire, and leapt over the flames,
while the shield burnt; and he spake again:

> "He flees not the flames
> Who o'er the fire leapeth!"

Even so did his men, one after another; and they laid hands on
those fellows who had heaped up the fire, and cast them into the
flames. Then Yrsa came and gave Hrólfr Kraki a deer's horn full
of gold; and she bade them ride away to the host. They vaulted onto
their horses and rode down into the Plain of the Fýri; and soon
they saw King Adils riding after them with his host all in armor,
hoping to slay them. Then Hrólfr Kraki plunged his right hand down
into the horn, grasped the gold, and strewed it all about the road.
When the Swedes saw that, they leapt down out of their saddles,
and each took up as much as he could lay hold of; but King Adils

bade them ride on, and himself rode furiously. His horse was called
Slöngvir, swiftest of all horses. Then Hrólfr Kraki saw that King
Adils was drawing close up to him, took the ring, Pig of the Swedes,
and threw it toward him, and bade him receive it as a gift. King
Adils rode at the ring and thrust at it with his spear-point, and let
it slide down over the shaft-socket. Then Hrólfr Kraki turned back
and saw how he bent down, and spake: "Now I have made him who
is mightiest of Swedes stoop as a swine stoops." Thus they parted.
For his cause gold is called Seed of Kraki or of Fýri's Plain. Thus
sang Eyvindr Skald-Despoiler:

> God of the blade of battle,
> We bear through Hákon's life-days
> The Seed of Fýri's valley
> On our arms, where sits the falcon.

Even as Thjódólfr sang:

> The king sows the bright seed-corn
> Of knuckle-splendid gold rings,
> With the crop of Yrsa's offspring,
> In his company's glad hand-grasp;
> The guileless Land-Director
> With Kraki's gleaming barley
> Sprinkles my arms, the flesh-grown
> Seat of the hooded falcon.

Bjarki and the Beast

Hrólfs saga kraka

ICELANDIC saga written in the fourteenth century.

❧ THEN Bothvar went on his way to Leire, and came to the king's
dwelling.

Bothvar stabled his horse by the king's best horses, without asking
leave; and then he went into the hall, and there were few men there.
He took a seat near the door, and when he had been there a little time
he heard a rummaging in a corner. Bothvar looked that way and
saw that a man's hand came up out of a great heap of bones which
lay there, and the hand was very black. Bothvar went thither and
asked who was there in the heap of bones.

Then an answer came, in a very weak voice, "Hott is my name, good fellow."

"Why art thou here?" said Bothvar, "and what art thou doing?"

Hott said, "I am making a shield-wall for myself, good fellow."

Bothvar said, "Out on thee and thy shield-wall!" and gripped him and jerked him up out of the heap of bones.

Then Hott cried out and said, "Now thou wilt be the death of me: do not do so. I had made it all so snug, and now thou hast scattered in pieces my shield-wall; and I had built it so high all round myself that it has protected me against all your blows, so that for long no blows have come upon me, and yet it was not so arranged as I meant it should be."

Then Bothvar said, "Thou wilt not build thy shield-wall any longer."

Hott said, weeping, "Wilt thou be the death of me, good fellow?" Bothvar told him not to make a noise, and then took him up and bore him out of the hall to some water which was close by, and washed him from head to foot. Few paid any heed to this.

Then Bothvar went to the place which he had taken before, and led Hott with him, and set Hott by his side. But Hott was so afraid that he was trembling in every limb, and yet he seemed to know that this man would help him.

After that it grew to evening, and men crowded into the hall: and Rolf's warriors saw that Hott was seated upon the bench. And it seemed to them that the man must be bold enough who had taken upon himself to put him there. Hott had an ill countenance when he saw his acquaintances, for he had received naught but evil from them. He wished to save his life and go back to his bone-heap, but Bothvar held him tightly so that he could not go away. For Hott thought that, if he could get back into his bone-heap, he would not be as much exposed to their blows as he was.

Now the retainers did as before; and first of all they tossed small bones across the floor towards Bothvar and Hott. Bothvar pretended not to see this. Hott was so afraid that he neither ate nor drank; and every moment he thought he would be smitten.

And now Hott said to Bothvar, "Good fellow, now a great knuckle bone is coming towards thee, aimed so as to do us sore injury." Bothvar told him to hold his tongue, and put up the hollow of his palm against the knuckle bone and caught it, and the leg bone was joined on to the knuckle bone. Then Bothvar sent the knuckle bone back, and hurled it straight at the man who had thrown it, with such a swift blow that it was the death of him. Then great fear came over the retainers.

Now news came to King Rolf and his men up in the castle that a stately man had come to the hall and killed a retainer, and that the retainers wished to kill the man. King Rolf asked whether the retainer who had been killed had given any offence. "Next to none," they said: then all the truth of the matter came up before King Rolf.

King Rolf said that it should be far from them to kill the man: "You have taken up an evil custom here in pelting men with bones without quarrel. It is a dishonour to me and a great shame to you to do so. I have spoken about it before, and you have paid no attention. I think that this man whom you have assailed must be a man of no small valour. Call him to me, so that I may know who he is."

Bothvar went before the king and greeted him courteously. The king asked him his name. "Your retainers call me Hott's protector, but my name is Bothvar."

The king said, "What compensation wilt thou offer me for my retainer?"

Bothvar said, "He only got what he asked for."

The king said, "Wilt thou become my man and fill his place?"

Bothvar said, "I do not refuse to be your man, but Hott and I must not part so. And we must sit nearer to thee than this man whom I have slain has sat; otherwise we will both depart together." The king said, "I do not see much credit in Hott, but I will not grudge him meat." Then Bothvar went to the seat that seemed good to him, and would not fill that which the other had before. He pulled up three men in one place, and then he and Hott sat down there higher in the hall than the place which had been given to them. The men thought Bothvar overbearing, and there was the greatest ill will among them concerning him.

And when it drew near to Christmas, men became gloomy. Both-var asked Hott the reason of this. Hott said to him that for two win-ters together a wild beast had come, great and awful, "And it has wings on its back, and flies. For two autumns it has attacked us here and done much damage. No weapon will wound it: and the champions of the king, those who are the greatest, come not back."

Bothvar said, "This hall is not so well arrayed as I thought, if one beast can lay waste the kingdom and the cattle of the king." Hott said, "It is no beast: it is the greatest troll."

Now Christmas-eve came; then said the king, "Now my will is that men to-night be still and quiet, and I forbid all my men to run into any peril with this beast. It must be with the cattle as fate will have it: but I do not wish to lose my men." All men promised to do as the king commanded. But Bothvar went out in secret that night; he caused Hott to go with him, but Hott did that only under compulsion, and said that it would be the death of him. Bothvar said that he hoped that it would be better than that. They went away from the hall, and Bothvar had to carry Hott, so frightened was he. Now they saw the beast; and thereupon Hott cried out as loud as he could, and said that the beast would swallow him. Bothvar said, "Be silent, thou dog," and threw him down in the mire. And there he lay in no small fear; but he did not dare to go home, any the more.

Now Bothvar went against the beast, and it happened that his sword was fast in his sheath when he wished to draw it. Bothvar now tugged at his sword, it moved, he wrenched the scabbard so that the sword came out. And at once he plunged it into the beast's shoulder so mightily that it pierced him to the heart, and the beast fell down dead to the earth. After that Bothvar went where Hott lay. Bothvar took him up and bore him to where the beast lay dead. Hott was trembling all over. Bothvar said, "Now must thou drink the blood of the beast." For long Hott was unwilling, and yet he did not dare to do anything else. Bothvar made him drink two great sups; also he made him eat somewhat of the heart of the beast.

After that Bothvar turned to Hott, and they fought a long time.

Bothvar said, "Thou hast now become very strong, and I do not believe that thou wilt now fear the retainers of King Rolf."

Hott said, "I shall not fear them, nor thee either, from now on."

"That is good, fellow Hott. Let us now go and raise up the beast, and so array him that others may think that he is still alive." And they did so. After that they went home, and were quiet, and no man knew what they had achieved.

In the morning the king asked what news there was of the beast, and whether it had made any attack upon them in the night. And answer was made to the king, that all the cattle were safe and uninjured in their folds. The king bade his men examine whether any trace could be seen of the beast having visited them. The watchers did so, and came quickly back to the king with the news that the beast was making for the castle, and in great fury. The king bade his retainers be brave, and each play the man according as he had spirit, and do away with this monster. And they did as the king bade, and made them ready.

Then the king faced towards the beast and said, "I see no sign of movement in the beast. Who now will undertake to go against it?"

Bothvar said, "That would be an enterprise for a man of true valour. Fellow Hott, now clear thyself of that ill-repute, in that men hold that there is no spirit or valour in thee. Go now and do thou kill the beast; thou canst see that there is no one else who is forward to do it."

"Yea," said Hott, "I will undertake this."

The king said, "I do not know whence this valour has come upon thee, Hott; and much has changed in thee in a short time."

Hott said, "Give me the sword Goldenboss [Gullinhjalti], which thou dost wield, and I will fell the beast or take my death." Rolf the king said, "That sword cannot be borne except by a man who is both a good warrior and valiant." Hott said, "So shalt thou ween that I am a man of that kind." The king said, "How can one know that more has not changed in thy temper than can be seen? Few men would know thee for the same man. Now take the sword and have joy of it, if this deed is accomplished." Then Hott went boldly to the beast and smote at it when he came within reach, and the beast fell down dead. Bothvar said, "See now, my lord, what he has achieved." The king said, "Verily, he has altered much, but Hott has not killed the beast alone, rather hast thou done it." Bothvar said, "It may be that it is so." The king said, "I knew when thou didst come here that few would be thine equals. But this seems to me nevertheless thy most honourable work, that thou hast made here another warrior of Hott, who did not seem shaped for much luck. And now I will that he shall be called no longer Hott, but Hjalti from this time; thou shalt be called after the sword Gullinhjalti [Goldenboss]."

The Destruction of Leire

c. 550

Biarkamál

THE Exhortation of the Housecarls, the famous poem composed about the destruction of Leire, is lost except for fragments, a Latin paraphrase by Saxo, and an Icelandic account in *Hrólfs saga kraka*. From these the Danish folklorist Axel Olrik reconstructed the lay. King Hrolf Kraki is attacked at night by his vassal Hiorvarth and his daughter Skuld, Hiorvarth's wife. Hrolf is slain but his men fight on. Hialti awakens the hero Bothvar Biarki, married to Hrolf's sister Hrut, from a deep slumber.

Hialti:

"Awake, arise,   rally, friends!
All ye foremost   athelings of Hrólf!
Awake not to wine   nor to your wives' converse,
but rather to Gondul's   game of war."

Biarki:

drowsily responds, calling out to a thrall:

"Bring a fardel of fagots   to kindle the fire!
Brush thou the hearth   and blow in the embers!
Let the kindling crackle   to kindle the logs:
'Tis winsome, with warm hand   to welcome friends."

He relapses into sleep; but Hialti exhorts the housecarls and plunges into battle with his king:

Hialti:

"Our great-hearted king   gave to his housecarls
rings, helms, short-swords,   and shining mail-coats;
his gifts in peace   must be gained in war;
in war is proved   what was pledged over ale.

"The ruler of Danes   chose him the doughty;
courage is known   when the craven flee;
in the tumult of battle   he needs trusty fighters:
conquest follows king   who may count on his men.

"Hold firm your hilts,   ye chosen housecarls,
shield flung on shoulder,   to show ye are men;

breast open 'gainst breast   offer we to our foemen:
beak against beak,   so shall battle the eagles.

"Foremost among fighters   bold Hiorvarth fares,
glorying in swordplay,   in gold-helm dight;
after him are marching   martial hosts of Gauts,
with ring-laid helms   and rattling spears.

"Skuld him egged on,   the Skioldung queen,
to his kin to be false,   his king to betray;
raving she is   and bereft of reason,
by evil norns   for ill created."

The tide of battle turns against Hrólf and he falls. Hialti continues:

"Now their last cup   for kingsmen is poured,
after his liege-lord   shall no one live
but he show him fearful   and shrink from blows,
or be too listless   his lord to avenge.

"Our byrnies are slit   and sundered our limbs;
blows of the bill   have broken the king's shield;
wide gapes the gate,   and the gallant flee,
the baleful battle-axe   gnaws men's brows.

"Lift thou now, Hrút,   thy light-haired brow,
leave thy bower,   for battle is nigh.

       *   *   *

the towers are tumbling,   the castle-gates tremble."

Hialti and his men fire the castle. They discover Biarki in profound sleep:

Hialti:
"Bidest thou yet, Biarki?   Do sleep-runes bind thee?
Come forth now with me   ere thee fire assail!
We fend off our foes   as we do bears—with firebrands:
the castle crumbles,   the king's hall flames."

As Biarki still tarries, Hialti once more rallies his warriors:

Hialti:
"Let us rally our ranks   as Hrólf us taught,
the hero who hewed down   the ring-hoarder.

Wretched was Hrœrek   though he riches owned:
but gold he gathered,   not gallant men.

"Hrólf harried on Hrœrek.   He ransom offered—
before the gates disgorged   his purse its gold:
he strewed before stronghold   stores of treasure.
Then was lavished on foe   what on friends was saved.

"Though our liege him slew: he allotted the hoard
among faithful followers,   refused it himself.
Nothing him gladdened   but he gave it to them:
to award it to warriors   naught was too welcome.

"The most large-hearted lord   lifeless has sunk;
lost is the life   men will longest remember:
he ran to the sword-play   as river toward sea,
fared against foe   like the fleet-footed stag.

"A burn of blood   from the battle-field flows,
as Hiorvarth among hosts   Hild's-play speedeth.
But the sword-giver smiles   in his sleep of death,
as at bountiful banquet   he beakers emptied.

"Fróthi's kinsman   on the Fýri Plains
his gold rings sowed,   glad in his mind;
him we joyfully follow   on his journey to Hel,
manly of speech   and firm of mettle.

"Blows of our brands   shall back our faith,
the glory of great deeds   never is forgotten.
Latched and locked   the hall still is left.
A third time, Biarki,   I bid thee come forth!"

Biarki:
"Eagerly doest thou, Hialti,   egg on Hrólf's kinsman;
but to vaunting words   fit valiant deeds.
Bide thou whilst Biarki   his byrnie fastens;
little he lists   to be burned alive.

"On an isle was I born,   barren and little;
twelve demesnes gave me   Hrólf to master,
realms to rule,   and ruddy gold, too—
his sister to wife;   here's worth to requite.

He plunges into battle:

"Shields on your shoulders,   if ye shun not death!
Only the craven   covers him now.
Bare your breasts!   Your bucklers fling down!
Gold-weighted arm   the glaive best wields.

"With my steel erst I struck   the 'wild stag' in battle,
with my short-sword slew him   which Snirtir is named.
Hero's name got I   when its hilt I gripped—
when Agnar Ingialdsson's   life I ended.

" 'Gainst my head he hewed,   but Hœking broke,
On Biarki's brow   his blade was shattered.
Then raised I Snirtir,   through his ribs thrust him,
his left hand and right leg   I lopped with one blow.

"Never was there, I ween, a   more warlike hero
than when, sword-hewn, sank   the son of Ingiald:
lifeless he lay   and laughed toward death;
to Valhall's gates   he gleefully hied him.

"To his heart I hewed   the hero but now,
young in years   but unyielding in spirit;
through his buckler I battered,   naught booted him
    his hauberk:
my Snirtir but seldom   slackens its blow.

"Guard you now, ye gallant   Gautish chieftains!
Athelings only   enter this battle!

*   *   *

"His loved son now loses   many a lord;
but for barons, not bondmen   Hel's bars will be
    lowered.
More closely comes   the clash of battle,
three blows I get   for one I give.

"Alone in the strife   I stand amongst the slain.
A bulwark I build me   of fallen bodies.
Where is now he   who whetted me before,
And tempted me sore,   as though twelve lives he had?"

Hialti:

"Few are the followers,   but far I am not.
Strong is now need   of stout-hearted men;
battered is my buckler,   broken and shattered—
yourself may see it: sight goes before hearsay.
Doest battle now, Biarki,   as thou bidedst before?"

Biarki:

"Thy spiteful speech   spurs me no longer:
not I am the cause   that tardy I came.
Now a Swedish sword   sorely has struck me;
through my war-weeds it went   as though water
     it cleft."

Biarki's wife Hrút has found her mortally wounded husband on the
battle field, where the conflict is now dying down.

"But where is Óthin,   the one-eyed grey-beard?
Say now, Hrút, swiftly: Seest thou him nowhere?"

Hrút:

"Lower thy eye   and look through my arm,
sign then thy view   with victory-runes:
unscathed shalt thou, Biarki,   then scan with thy glance
and fasten thy eyes   on the father of victory."

Biarki:

"Could I fasten my eyes   on Frigg's husband now,
the swift shield-swinger   and Sleipnir's rider,
his life would lose   the war-god at Leire—
blood for blood then   would Biarki crave.

"Here by my chieftain's   head I shall sink now,
thou by his feet   shalt find thee a rest.
Booty-seekers on battle field   shall bear me out:
the great-souled king's gifts   even the dead forget not.

"Soon greedy eagles   will gorge on our bodies,
ramping ravens   will rend our limbs.
To high-minded, hardy   hero it is seeming
dying to dwell   by his king rich in deeds."

HAMLET PRINCE OF DENMARK

Sixth century?

ACCORDING to SAXO, Hamlet, which may mean "mad Ole," did not live at Elsinore in Sjælland where Shakespeare placed him, but was a ruler under Danish sovereignty in Jutland. The quotations are from Skaldic verse, Icelandic saga, and Saxo Grammaticus.

"Here the Sea Is Called Hamlet's Churn"

Snorra Edda

෴ " 'TIS said," sang Snæbjörn, "that far out, off yonder ness, the Nine Maids of the Island Mill stir amain the host-cruel skerry-quern —they who in ages past ground Hamlet's meal. The good Chieftain furrows the hull's lair with his ship's beaked prow."

Hamlet the Fool

Ambales Saga

෴ Now when Amlode came in to the kitchen-stead he found his mother there, and Queen Ceta and her maids sat beside the gleeds on chairs, but the cauldrons were not then a-boiling, and Ambales seized aloft his mother on her chair and placed her on the cauldron-hearth, so that her clothes began to singe. Then Queen Ceta together with her maidens rushed thither and caught up Queen Amba, and bore her to the door, but all the stool was burnt. And now they rushed in great terror to the king's hall, and told of Ambales' doings, all as it had befallen, and they all said he was the wretchedest fool, and would never come to the wit of man, or to any breeding, and no one need fear vengeance from him. And then all there agreed that he should live to be the sport of men.

Now the king was most stern in his rule, and not the least so with lazy folk and evil-doers; he made slaves of them for the most part, but those that would not bestir themselves he had slain. Once he spake with his courtiers and said:—"It seemeth wrong that Ambales with skill and prowess to achieve whatso he lists yet doeth naught of any profit. Wherefore I would try whether he cannot stay with the herdsmen and guard the herds." Gamaliel and the other counsellors said it might well be tried. So the herdsmen were told to take him with them. They went to the kitchen-stead where Ambales was whit-tling at his spits, as was his wont, and they asked him of what use they were. "For father-revenge and not for father-revenge," he said. They bade him go with them, and told him the king's bidding and his pleasure. He rose swiftly, and went with them; but such was the speed of his walking that they soon lost sight of him; yet he took his course in the right direction toward a certain mountain where the herds were to be sought; when they reached the mountain noonday was passed, and the weather was very hot, with a gentle breeze. There was a water on one side of the mountain, bottomless and very dark. Ambales awaited there his comrades, and there they found him. Swiftly then he went down to the water, and lay flat beside it, turning his ears now here now there, as he listened for something; then he stood up and said to his comrades:—"Into water wind has come, out of water wind will go"; but these words they deemed were madness.

Hamlet's Shield

Saxo Grammaticus

Gesta Danorum

From the Latin

He also had a shield made for him, whereon the whole series of his exploits, beginning with his earliest youth, was painted in exquisite designs. This he bore as a record of his deeds of prowess, and gained great increase of fame thereby. Here were to be seen depicted the slaying of Horwendil; the fratricide and incest of Feng; the infamous uncle, the whimsical nephew; the shapes of the hooked stakes; the stepfather suspecting, the stepson dissembling; the various temptations offered, and the woman brought to beguile him; the gaping wolf; the finding of the rudder; the passing of the sand; the entering of the wood; the putting of the straw through the gadfly; the warning of the youth by the tokens; and the privy dealings with the maiden after the escort was eluded. And likewise could be seen the picture of the palace; the queen there with her son; the slaying of the eavesdropper; and how, after being killed, he was boiled down, and so dropped into the sewer, and so thrown out to the swine; how his limbs were strewn in the mud, and so left for the beasts to finish. Also it could be seen how Amleth surprised the secret of his sleeping attendants, how he erased the letters, and put new characters in their places; how he disdained the banquet and scorned the drink; how he condemned the face of the king and taxed the queen with faulty behaviour. There was also represented the hanging of the envoys, and the young man's wedding; then the voyage back to Denmark; the festive celebration of the funeral rites; Amleth, in answer to questions, pointing to the sticks in place of his attendants, acting as cup-bearer, and purposely drawing his sword and pricking his fingers; the sword riveted through, the swelling cheers of the banquet, the dance growing fast and furious; the hangings flung upon the sleepers, then fastened with the interlacing crooks, and wrapped tightly round them as they slumbered; the brand set to the mansion, the burning of the guests, the royal palace consumed with fire and tottering down; the visit to the sleeping-room of Feng, the theft of his sword, the useless one set in its place; and the king slain with his own sword's point by his stepson's hand. All this was there, painted upon Amleth's battle-shield by a careful craftsman in the choicest of handiwork; he copied truth in his figures, and embodied real deeds in his outlines.

THE VOLSUNGS

AMONG the historical events behind the legends of the Volsungs are the facts that Ermanaric died A.D. 376, the Huns slaughtered the Burgundians in 437, Attila died in 453, Sigebert died in 575, Guntram died in 592, and Queen Brunhilda died in 613.

The historical prototypes of the characters of the Volsung Cycle were not Scandinavians, although the supernatural beings and folklore were native, but their legends were preserved in the North in a more primitive state than in the *Niebelungenlied*. Sigurth was a Frank, Gunnar and his kin were Burgundians, Ermanaric a Goth, Attila a Hun. This rich literature is represented here by a few examples from The Poetic Edda, Snorri, The Volsung Saga, and the ballads of the Faeroe Islands.

The Otter's Wergild

Snorra Edda

⚬§ FOR what reason is gold called Otter's Wergild? It is related that when certain of the Æsir, Odin and Loki and Hœnir, went forth to explore the earth, they came to a certain river, and proceeded along the river to a waterfall. And beside the fall was an otter, which had taken a salmon from the fall and was eating, blinking his eyes the while. Then Loki took up a stone and cast it at the otter, and struck its head. And Loki boasted in his catch, that he had got otter and salmon with one blow. Then they took up the salmon and the otter and bore them along with them, and coming to the buildings of a certain farm, they went in. Now the husbandman who dwelt there was named Hreidmarr: he was a man of much substance, and very skilled in black magic. The Æsir asked him for a night's lodging, saying that they had sufficient food with them, and showed him their catch. But when Hreidmarr saw the otter, straightway he called to him his sons, Fáfnir and Reginn, and told them that the otter their brother was slain, and who had done that deed.

Now father and sons went up to the Æsir, seized them, bound them, and told them about the otter, how he was Hreidmarr's son. The Æsir offered a ransom for their lives, as much wealth as Hreidmarr himself desired to appoint; and a covenant was made between them on those terms, and confirmed with oaths. Then the otter was flayed, and Hreidmarr, taking the otter-skin, bade them fill the skin with red gold and also cover it altogether; and that should be the condition of the covenant between them. Thereupon Odin sent Loki into the Land of the Black Elves, and he came to the dwarf who is called Andvari, who was as a fish in the water. Loki caught him in his hands and required of him in ransom of his life all the gold that he had in his rock; and when they came within the rock, the dwarf brought forth all the gold he had, and it was very much wealth. Then the dwarf quickly swept under his hand one little gold ring, but Loki saw it and commanded him to give over the ring. The dwarf prayed him not to take the ring from him, saying that from this ring he could multiply wealth for himself if he might keep it. Loki answered that he should not have one penny left, and took the ring from him and went out; but the dwarf declared that that ring should be the ruin of every one who should come into possession of it. Loki replied that this seemed well enough to him, and that this condition should hold good provided that he himself brought it to the ears of them that should receive the ring and the curse. He went his way and came to Hreidmarr's dwelling, and showed the gold to Odin; but when Odin saw the ring, it seemed fair to him, and he took it away from the treasure, and paid the gold to Hreidmarr. Then Hreidmarr filled the otter-skin as much as he could, and set it up when it was full. Next Odin went up, having the skin to cover with gold, and he bade Hreidmarr look whether the skin were yet altogether hidden. But Hreidmarr looked at it searchingly, and saw one of the hairs of the snout, and commanded that this be covered, else their covenant should be at an end. Then Odin drew out the ring, and covered the hair, saying that they were now delivered from their debt for the slaying of the otter. But when Odin had taken his spear, and Loki his shoes, and they had no longer any need to be afraid, then Loki declared that the curse which Andvari had uttered should be fulfilled: that this ring and this gold should be the destruction of him who received it; and that was fulfilled afterward. Now it has been told wherefore gold is called Otter's Wergild, or Forced Payment of the Æsir, or Metal of Strife.

What more is to be said of the gold? Hreidmarr took the gold for his son's wergild, but Fáfnir and Reginn claimed some part of their brother's blood-money for themselves. Hreidmarr would not grant them one penny of the gold. This was the wicked purpose of those brethren: they slew their father for the gold. Then Reginn demanded that Fáfnir share the gold with him, half for half. Fáfnir answered that there was little chance of his sharing it with his brother, seeing that he had slain his father for its sake; and he bade Reginn go hence, else he should fare even as Hreidmarr. Fáfnir had taken the helmet which Hreidmarr had posssessed, and set it upon his head (this helmet was called the Helm of Terror, of which all living creatures that see it are afraid), and the sword called Hrotti. Reginn had that sword which was named Refill. So he fled away, and Fáfnir went up to Gnita Heath, and made himself a lair, and turned himself into a serpent, and laid him down upon the gold.

Then Reginn went to King Hjálprekr at Thjód, and there he became his smith; and he took into his fostering Sigurdr, son of Sigmundr, Völsungr's son, and of Hjördís, daughter of Eylimi. Sigurdr was most illustrious of all Host-Kings in race, in prowess, and in mind. Reginn declared to him where Fáfnir lay on the gold, and incited him to seek the gold. Then Reginn fashioned the sword Gramr, which was so sharp that Sigurdr, bringing it down into running water, cut asunder a flock of wool which drifted down-stream onto

the sword's edge. Next Sigurdr clove Reginn's anvil down to the
stock with the sword. After that they went, Sigurdr and Reginn, to
Gnita Heath, and there Sigurdr dug a pit in Fáfnir's way and laid
himself in ambush therein. And when Fáfnir glided toward the water
and came above the pit, Sigurdr straightway thrust his sword through
him, and that was his end.

Then Reginn came forward, saying that Sigurdr had slain his
brother, and demanded as a condition of reconciliation that he take
Fáfnir's heart and roast it with fire; and Reginn laid him down and
drank the blood of Fáfnir, and settled himself to sleep. But when
Sigurdr was roasting the heart, and thought that it must be quite
roasted, he touched it with his finger to see how hard it was; and
then the juice ran out from the heart onto his finger, so that he was
burned and put his finger to his mouth. As soon as the heart's blood
came upon his tongue, straightway he knew the speech of birds, and
he understood what the nuthatches were saying which were sitting in
the trees. Then one spake:

> "There sits Sigurdr
> Blood-besprinkled,
> Fáfnir's heart
> With flame he roasteth:
> Wise seemed to me
> The Spoiler of Rings
> If the gleaming
> Life-fibre he ate.

> "There lies Reginn—sang another—
> Rede he ponders,
> Would betray the youth
> Who trusteth in him:
> In his wrath he plots
> Wrong accusation;
> The smith of bale
> Would avenge his brother."

Then Sigurdr went over to Reginn and slew him, and thence to his
horse, which was named Grani, and rode till he came to Fáfnir's lair.
He took up the gold, trussed it up in his saddle-bags, laid it upon
Grani's back, mounted up himself, and then rode his ways. Now the

tale is told why gold is called Lair or Abode of Fáfnir, or Metal of Gnita Heath, or Grani's Burden.

Then Sigurdr rode on till he found a house on the mountain, wherein a woman in helm and birnie lay sleeping. He drew his sword and cut the birnie from her: she awoke then, and gave her name as Hildr: she is called Brynhildr, and was a Valkyr. Sigurdr rode away and came to the king who was named Gjúki, whose wife was Grímhildr; their children were Gunnarr, Högni, Gudrún, Gudný; Gotthormr was Gjúki's stepson. Sigurdr tarried there a long time, and then he obtained the hand of Gudrún, daughter of Gjúki, and Gunnarr and Högni swore oaths of blood-brotherhood with Sigurdr. Thereafter Sigurdr and the sons of Gjúki went unto Atli, Budli's son, to sue for the hand of Brynhildr his sister in marriage to Gunnarr. Brynhildr abode on Hinda-Fell, and about her hall there was a flaring fire; and she had made a solemn vow to take none but that man who should dare to ride through the flaring fire.

Then Sigurdr and the sons of Gjúki (who were also called Niflungs) rode up onto the mountain, and Gunnarr should have ridden through the flaring fire: but he had the horse named Goti, and that horse dared not leap into the fire. So they exchanged shapes, Sigurdr and Gunnarr, and names likewise; for Grani would go under no man but Sigurdr. Then Sigurdr leapt onto Grani and rode through the flaring fire. That eve he was wedded with Brynhildr. But when they came to bed, he drew the sword Gramr from its sheath and laid it between them. In the morning when he arose and clothed himself, he gave Brynhildr as linen-fee the same gold ring which Loki had taken from Andvari, and took another ring from her hand for remembrance. Then Sigurdr mounted his horse and rode to his fellows, and he and Gunnarr changed shapes again and went home to Gjúki with Brynhildr. Sigurdr and Gudrún had two children, Sigmundr and Svanhildr.

It befell on a time that Brynhildr and Gudrún went to the water to wash their hair. And when they came to the river, Brynhildr waded out from the bank well into the river, saying that she would not touch to her head the water which ran out of the hair of Gudrún, since herself had the more valorous husband. Then Gudrún went into the river after her and said that it was her right to wash her hair higher upstream, for the reason that she had to husband such a man as neither Gunnarr nor any other in the world matched in valor, seeing that he had slain Fáfnir and Reginn and succeeded to the heritage of both. And Brynhildr made answer: "It was a matter of greater worth that Gunnarr rode through the flaring fire and Sigurdr durst not." Then Gudrún laughed, and said: "Dost thou think that Gunnarr rode through the flaring fire? Now I think that he who went into the bride-bed with thee was the same that gave me this gold ring; and the gold ring which thou bearest on thine hand and didst receive for linen-fee is called Andvari's Yield, and I believe that it was not Gunnarr who got that ring on Gnita Heath." Then Brynhildr was silent, and went home.

After that she egged on Gunnarr and Högni to slay Sigurdr; but because they were Sigurdr's sworn blood-brothers, they stirred up Gotthormr their brother to slay him. He thrust his sword through Sigurdr as he slept; but when Sigurdr felt the wound, he hurled his sword Gramr after Gotthormr, so that it cut the man asunder at the middle. There fell Sigurdr and Sigmundr, his son of three winters, whom they slew. Then Brynhildr stabbed herself with a sword, and she was burned with Sigurdr; but Gunnarr and Högni took Fáfnir's heritage and Andvari's Yield, and ruled the lands thereafter.

King Atli, Budli's son, and brother to Brynhildr, then wedded Gudrún, whom Sigurdr had had to wife; and they had children. King Atli invited to him Gunnarr and Högni, and they came at his invitation. Yet before they departed from their land, they hid the gold, Fáfnir's heritage, in the Rhine, and that gold has never since been found. Now King Atli had a host in readiness, and fought with Gunnarr and Högni; and they were made captive. King Atli bade the heart be cut out of Högni alive, and that was his end. Gunnarr he caused to be cast into a den of serpents. But a harp was brought secretly to Gunnarr, and he struck it with his toes, his hands being bound; he played the harp so that all the serpents fell asleep, saving only one adder, which glided over to him and gnawed into the cartilage of his breast-bone so far that her head sank within the wound, and she clove to his liver till he died. Gunnarr and Högni were called Niflungs and Gjúkungs, for which reason gold is called Treasure, or Heritage, of the Niflungs.

Sigurth in Faeroëse

Siúrð kvæði. annar táttur: Brinhild

Then up spake Sigurd Sigmundarson:
(So do they tell the tale)
"Because of the sign my shield doth bear
I'll leap the burning bale."

Grane bore the golden hoard,
Wroth did Sigurd swing his sword,
There he slew the Dragon grim,
Wroth did Sigurd swing his sword.

Was ne'er a one but Sigmund's son
That entered in Hildar-hall,
For Grane the steed so good at need
He leapt the fiery wall.

So lightly leapt Grane
The barrier o'er,
That the clash of his fore-feet
Rang hard on the door.

So swiftly sprang Grane
As bird in its flight,
That scarce a spire of burning fire
On Sigurd's loins did bite

Sigurd alone the fortress won
Where all had turned the rein;
With one blow of his sword-blade
He clave the door in twain.

With one blow of his sword-blade
He lopped the lock away,
& there beheld the maiden
In coat of mail that lay.

She slept, the noble maiden,
In warrior's byrnie blue;
With one blow of his sword-blade
He clave the mail in two.

Up spake Budli's daughter
All betwixt sweven & sleep:
"What warrior-hand doth wield the brand
That dares to bite so deep?"

Up spake Budli's daughter
All betwixt sleep & sweven:
"What warrior bold the brand doth hold
My byrnie blue hath riven?"

"Sigurd shalt thou name me,
Of Sigmund the son;
Hjørdis she that bore
After his days were done."

Up sat the lady Brynhild
A-smiling secretly:
"Now welcome, thou that comest
Hither from far countrie!

"But harken, Sigurd Sigmundarson,
Who told thee how to seek
& find my bower thro' the leaping flame,
& thro' the driving reek?"

"That tidings I heard from the wildwood bird
Sitting on linden-tree:
So fair is Brynhild Budli's daughter,
Hath laid her love on thee."

"Now harken, Sigurd Sigmundarson,
& to my words give heed,
Go, get thee forth to my father's garth,
& rule thee by his rede."

Oh, wise was Sigurd Sigmundarson,
That spake this word straightway;
"But little heed to thy father's rede
Hast thou been wont to pay!"

"O'er-long, I trow, hast tarried
Thy fortune to fulfil,

& I will not forth to thy father's garth,
Nor seek to learn his will."

Right gladly Sigurd laid his arms
About her neck so white;
Ásla, the daughter of Sigurd,
Was gotten that self-same night.

Right gladly Sigurd laid his arms
Her snow-white neck around;
"I swear to thee that ne'er in me
Shall aught of false be found!"

Twelve rings of red, red gold
He laid her arms between,
& set above them all
The great ring of the Queen.

All on her lily hand
He set twelve rings of gold:
"Of our true love the token
Here shalt thou have & hold."

It was Sigurd Sigmundarson
That would no splendour spare;
Three rings of ruddy gold he twined
All in her braided hair.

A Valkyrie Awakens

Sigrdrífumál

⇜§SIGURTH rode up on Hindarfjoll and turned southward toward the land of the Franks. On the mountain he saw a great light, as if fire were burning, and the glow reached up to heaven. And when he came thither, there stood a tower of shields, and above it was a banner. Sigurth went into the shield-tower, and saw that a man lay there sleeping with all his war-weapons. First he took the helm from his head, and then he saw that it was a woman. The mail-coat was as fast as if it had grown to the flesh. Then he cut the mail-coat from the head-opening downward, and out to both the arm-holes. Then he took the mail-coat from her, and she awoke, and sat up and saw Sigurth, and said:

"What bit through the byrnie?   how was broken my sleep?
Who made me free   of the fetters pale?"

He answered:

"Sigmund's son,   with Sigurth's sword,
That late with flesh   hath fed the ravens."

Sigurth sat beside her and asked her name. She took a horn full of mead and gave him a memory-draught.

"Hail, day!   Hail, sons of day!
And night and her daughter now!
Look on us here   with loving eyes,
That waiting we victory win.

"Hail to the gods!   Ye goddesses, hail,
And all the generous earth!
Give to us wisdom   and goodly speech,
And healing hands, life-long.

"Long did I sleep,   my slumber was long,
And long are the griefs of life;
Othin decreed   that I could not break
The heavy spells of sleep."

Brynhild's Complaint

Völsunga saga

ONE day Brynhild and Gudrun went to the river Rhine to bathe, and Brynhild waded farther out into the water. Gudrun asked what that meant; Brynhild said,

"Why should I make myself equal to thee in this rather than aught else? Methinks that my father is richer than thine, and my husband has wrought many a glorious deed, and he rode through the flaming fire; but thy husband, forsooth, was a vassal of King Hjalprek." Gudrun answered angrily,

"Thou wouldst be wiser to hold thy tongue than to speak ill of my husband, for all men say that none has ever been his like in the whole

world. It ill befits thee to speak ill of him, for he was thy first husband, and he slew Fafnir and rode through the flaming fire when thou
thoughtest he was Gunnar; and he it was who lay by thee and took
from thee Andvari's ring. Behold, thou mayest know it again!"

Brynhild saw the ring and knew it, and she turned pale as though
she were dead. She went home again and spoke not a word that evening. And when Sigurd went to bed Gudrun asked him,

"Why is Brynhild so sad?" Sigurd answered,

"I do not yet clearly know, but I suspect that soon we shall all
know more fully."

* * *

The next day when Sigurd came home from the hunt he met
Gudrun and said,

"It seems to me that Brynhild's fever is very heavy, and she will
die of it." Gudrun answered,

"My lord, it is a great wonder; she has now slept seven days, and
no one has dared to awaken her." Sigurd answered,

"She is not asleep, but is planning fearful things against me." Then
Gudrun spoke, weeping,

"It is a great woe to know of thy death; go to her rather and speak
to her and see if her anger may not be lessened. Give her gold and
soften her wrath with it."

Sigurd went out and found her hall door open; he thought she was
asleep, and he lifted the covers from her and said,

"Awake, Brynhild! The sun is shining over all the town, and thou
has slept long enough; cast off thy sorrow and be glad!" She said,

"How is it thou darest to come and see me? None deceived me
worse than thou." Sigurd asked,

"Why wilt thou not speak with those about thee? What vexes
thee?" Brynhild answered,

"I shall tell thee the cause of my wrath!" Sigurd said,

"Thou art bespelled if thou thinkest me grimly disposed towards
thee. And thy husband was of thy choosing."

"Nay," said she, "Gunnar did not ride through the fire to me, and
he did not give me my price of slaughters. I wondered at the man who
came into my hall, and I thought I recognized thine eyes, and yet
I could not see clearly because of the shroud that lay over my fate."
Sigurd said,

"I am no nobler than the sons of Gjuki; they slew the Danish king and a great prince, the brother of King Budli." Brynhild answered,

"I have many wrongs to pay them for: do not call these griefs to my mind. Thou, Sigurd, didst slay the dragon and ride through the fire for my sake, and the sons of Gjuki were not there then." Sigurd answered,

"I was not thy husband and thou wert not my wife, but a noble king paid for thy dower." Brynhild answered,

"Never were my thoughts mirthful towards Gunnar, but they are grim towards him now, though I conceal it from the others."

"It is a strange thing," said Sigurd, "to have no love for such a king. But what is it that vexes thee most? Methinks his love should be dearer to thee than gold." Brynhild answered,

"Most bitter of all my woes it is that I might not contrive to stain a sharp sword with thy blood." Sigurd replied,

"Have no fear; in a short time from now a sharp sword will indeed stand in my heart, and thou mayest pray for no worse for thyself, for thou shalt not live after me; but few days are left to us hereafter." Brynhild answered,

"Thy words are portents of peril; since the time ye betrayed the whole of my joy, I care not a whit for my life." Sigurd answered,

"Live thou and love King Gunnar and me; I shall give all my wealth if thou die not." She said,

"Little dost thou know my mood. Thou dost surpass all men, and yet no woman is more hateful to thee than I." Sigurd answered,

"The truth is otherwise: I love thee better than myself, though I was betrayed therein. And now it may not be changed; ever, since I could heed my wits again, have I had pain in my heart because thou wert not my wife, but I bore it as I might since I dwelt in a king's hall. And still I was well pleased that we were together. It may also come to pass as was foretold before, and I shall mind it little." Brynhild replied,

"Too late thou comest to tell me that my suffering distresses thee, and now I have no comfort of it." Sigurd answered,

"It is my wish that we might enter one bed together, and that thou shouldst become my wife." Brynhild answered,

"Such a thing may not be said. I will not have two kings mine in the same hall, and I shall sooner lose my life than deceive King Gunnar." Then she reminded him how they met on the mountain and pledged their faith together, "but that is all changed now, and I will live no longer."

"I had forgotten thy name," said Sigurd, "and I knew thee not again until thou wert married, and that is the greatest woe of all." Then said Brynhild,

"I swore an oath to have only that man who rode through my flaming fire. That oath I shall keep, or die."

"Rather than thou shouldst die, I will take thee and leave Gudrun," cried Sigurd; and so greatly were his sides swollen with grief that the rings of his byrnie burst.

"I desire thee not," said Brynhild; "thee, nor any other."

Sigurd went away, even as is told in the Lay of Sigurd:

> When their speech was done, bold Sigurd went forth,
> Grieving and heavy of heart;
> So great was his woe that the rings of steel
> On his byrnie were broken apart.

And when he came into the hall, Gunnar asked him if he knew now the cause of her grief, and whether she had recovered her speech. Sigurd said she could talk. Then Gunnar went to see her again, and asked her what ailed her, and whether there was any cure.

"I do not wish to live," said Brynhild, "for Sigurd has betrayed me, and thee no less, when thou gavest him leave to come into my bed. But I shall not have two husbands in one hall, and that must be Sigurd's bane or thine or mine, for he has told Gudrun all about it, and she mocks me."

"Home They Brought Her Warrior Dead"

Guðrúnarkviða

GUTHRUN sat by the dead Sigurth; she did not weep as other women, but her heart was near to bursting with grief. The men and women came to her to console her, but that was not easy to do. It is told of men that Guthrun had eaten of Fafnir's heart, and that she understood the speech of birds. This is a poem about Guthrun.

> Then did Guthrun   think to die,
> When she by Sigurth   sorrowing sat;
> Tears she had not,   nor wrung her hands,
> Nor ever wailed,   as other women.

To her the warriors   wise there came,
Longing her heavy   woe to lighten;
Grieving could not   Guthrun weep,
So sad her heart,   it seemed, would break.

Then the wives   of the warriors came,
Gold-adorned,   and Guthrun sought;
Each one then   of her own grief spoke,
The bitterest pain   she had ever borne.

Then spake Gjaflaug,   Gjuki's sister:
"Most joyless of all   on earth am I;
Husbands five   were from me taken,
(Two daughters then,   and sisters three,)
Brothers eight,   yet I have lived."

Grieving could not   Guthrun weep,
Such grief she had   for her husband dead,
And so grim her heart   by the hero's body.

Then Herborg spake,   the queen of the Huns:
"I have a greater   grief to tell;
My seven sons   in the southern land,
And my husband, fell   in fight all eight.
(Father and mother   and brothers four
Amid the waves   the wind once smote,
And the seas crashed through   the sides of the ship.)

"The bodies all   with my own hands then
I decked for the grave,   and the dead I buried;
A half-year brought me   this to bear;
And no one came   to comfort me.

"Then bound I was,   and taken in war,
A sorrow yet   in the same half-year;
They bade me deck   and bind the shoes
Of the wife of the monarch   every morn.

"In jealous rage   her wrath she spake,
And beat me oft   with heavy blows;
Never a better   lord I knew,
And never a woman   worse I found."

Grieving could not   Guthrun weep,
Such grief she had   for her husband dead,
And so grim her heart   by the hero's body.

Then spake Gollrond,   Gjuki's daughter:
"Thy wisdom finds not,   my foster-mother,
The way to comfort   the wife so young."
She bade them uncover   the warrior's corpse.

The shroud she lifted   from Sigurth, laying
His well-loved head   on the knees of his wife:
"Look on thy loved one,   and lay thy lips
To his as if yet   the hero lived."

Once alone   did Guthrun look;
His hair all clotted   with blood beheld,
The blinded eyes   that once shone bright,
The hero's breast   that the blade had pierced.

Then Guthrun bent,   on her pillow bowed,
Her hair was loosened,   her cheek was hot,
And the tears like raindrops   downward ran.

Then Guthrun, daughter   of Gjuki, wept,
And through her tresses   flowed the tears;
And from the court   came the cry of geese,
The birds so fair   of the hero's bride.

Then Gollrond spake,   the daughter of Gjuki:
"Never a greater   love I knew
Than yours among   all men on earth;
Nowhere wast happy,   at home or abroad,
Sister mine,   with Sigurth away."

Guthrun spake:

"So was my Sigurth   o'er Gjuki's sons
As the spear-leek grown   above the grass,
Or the jewel bright   borne on the band,
The precious stone   that princes wear.

"To the leader of men   I loftier seemed
And higher than all   of Herjan's maids;

As little now   as the leaf I am
On the willow hanging;   my hero is dead.

"In his seat, in his bed,   I see no more
My heart's true friend;   the fault is theirs,
The sons of Gjuki,   for all my grief,
That so their sister   sorely weeps.

"So shall your land   its people lose
As ye have kept   your oaths of yore;
Gunnar, no joy   the gold shall give thee,
(The rings shall soon   thy slayers be,)
Who swarest oaths   with Sigurth once.

"In the court was greater   gladness then
The day my Sigurth   Grani saddled,
And went forth Brynhild's   hand to win,
That woman ill,   in an evil hour."

Then Brynhild spake,   the daughter of Buthli:
"May the witch now husband   and children want
Who, Guthrun, loosed   thy tears at last,
And with magic today   hath made thee speak."

Then Gollrond, daughter   of Gjuki, spake:
"Speak not such words,   thou hated woman;
Bane of the noble   thou e'er hast been,
(Borne thou art   on an evil wave,
Sorrow hast brought   to seven kings,)
And many a woman   hast loveless made."

Then Brynhild, daughter   of Buthli, spake:
"Atli is guilty   of all the sorrow,
(Son of Buthli   and brother of mine,)
When we saw in the hall   of the Hunnish race
The flame of the snake's bed   flash round the hero;
(For the journey since   full sore have I paid,
And ever I seek   the sight to forget.)"

By the pillars she stood,   and gathered her strength,
From the eyes of Brynhild,   Buthli's daughter,
Fire there burned,   and venom she breathed,
When the wounds she saw   on Sigurth then.

Attila the Hun

Atlakviða

&§GUTHRUN, Gjuki's daughter, avenged her brothers, as has become well known. She slew first Atli's sons, and thereafter she slew Atli, and burned the hall with his whole company. Concerning this was the following poem made:

Atli sent   of old to Gunnar
A keen-witted rider,   Knefröth did men call him;
To Gjuki's home came he   and to Gunnar's dwelling,
With benches round the hearth,   and to the beer so sweet.

Then the followers, hiding   their falseness, all drank
Their wine in the war-hall,   of the Huns' wrath wary;
And Knefröth spake loudly,   his words were crafty,
The hero from the south,   on the high bench sitting:

"Now Atli has sent me   his errand to ride,
On my bit-champing steed   through Myrkwood the secret,
To bid you, Gunnar,   to his benches to come,
With helms round the hearth,   and Atli's home seek.

"Shields shall ye choose there,   and shafts made of ash-wood,
Gold-adorned helmets,   and slaves out of Hunland,
Silver-gilt saddle-cloths,   shirts of bright scarlet,
With lances and spears too,   and bit-champing steeds.

"The field shall be given you   of wide Gnitaheith,
With loud-ringing lances,   and stems gold-o'er-laid,
Treasures full huge,   and the home of Danp,
And the mighty forest   that Myrkwood is called."

His head turned Gunnar,   and to Hogni he said:
"What thy counsel, young hero,   when such things we hear?
No gold do I know   on Gnitaheith lying
So fair that other   its equal we have not.

"We have seven halls,   each of swords is full,
(And all of gold   is the hilt of each;)
My steed is the swiftest,   my sword is sharpest,
My bows adorn benches,   my byrnies are golden,

My helm is the brightest   that came from Kjar's hall,
(Mine own is better   than all the Huns' treasure.)"

Hogni spake:

"What seeks she to say,   that she sends us a ring,
Woven with a wolf's hair?   methinks it gives warning;
In the red ring a hair   of the heath-dweller found I,
Wolf-like shall our road be   if we ride on this journey."

Not eager were his comrades,   nor the men of his kin,
The wise nor the wary,   nor the warriors bold.
But Gunnar spake forth   as befitted a king,
Noble in the beer-hall,   and bitter his scorn:

Stand forth now, Fjornir!   and hither on the floor
The beakers all golden   shalt thou bring to the warriors.

.   .   .   .

.   .   .   .

"The wolves then shall rule   the wealth of the Niflungs,
Wolves aged and grey-hued,   if Gunnar is lost,
And black-coated bears   with rending teeth bite,
And make glad the dogs,   if Gunnar returns not."

A following gallant   fared forth with the ruler,
Yet they wept as their home   with the hero they left;
And the little heir   of Hogni called loudly:
"Go safe now, ye wise ones,   wherever ye will!"

Then let the bold heroes   their bit-champing horses
On the mountains gallop,   and through Myrkwood the secret;
All Hunland was shaken   where the hard-souled ones rode,
On the whip-fearers fared they   through fields that were
    green.

Then they saw Atli's halls,   and his watch-towers high,
On the walls so lofty   stood the warriors of Buthli;
The hall of the southrons   with seats was surrounded,
With targets bound   and shields full bright.

Mid weapons and lances   did Atli his wine
In the war-hall drink,   without were his watchmen,

For Gunnar they waited,   if forth he should go,
With their ringing spears   they would fight with the ruler.

This their sister saw,   as soon as her brothers
Had entered the hall,—   little ale had she drunk:
"Betrayed art thou, Gunnar!   what guard hast thou, hero,
'Gainst the plots of the Huns?   from the hall flee swiftly!

"Brother, 'twere far better   to have come in byrnie,
With thy household helmed,   to see Atli's home,
And to sit in the saddle   all day 'neath the sun,
(That the sword-norns might weep   for the death-pale
     warriors,
And the Hunnish shield-maids   might shun not the sword,)
And send Atli himself   to the den of the snakes;
(Now the den of the snakes   for thee is destined.)"

      Gunnar spake:

.   .   .   .
"Too late is it, sister,   to summon the Niflungs,
Long is it to come   to the throng of our comrades,
The heroes gallant,   from the hills of the Rhine."

                    *   *   *

Then Gunnar they seized,   and they set him in chains,
The Burgundians' king,   and fast they bound him.

Hogni slew seven   with sword so keen,
And an eighth he flung   in the fire hot;
A hero should fight   with his foemen thus,
As Hogni strove   in Gunnar's behalf.

.   .   .   .
.   .   .   .
The leader they asked   if his life he fain
With gold would buy,   the king of the Goths.

      Gunnar spake:

"First the heart of Hogni   shall ye lay in my hands,
All bloody from the breast   of the bold one cut
With keen-biting sword,   from the son of the king."

. . . .
They cut out the heart from the breast of Hjalli,
On a platter they bore it, and brought it to Gunnar.

Then Gunnar spake forth, the lord of the folk:
"Here have I the heart of Hjalli the craven,
Unlike to the heart of Hogni the valiant,
For it trembles still as it stands on the platter;
Twice more did it tremble in the breast of the man."

Then Hogni laughed when they cut out the heart
Of the living helm-hammerer; tears he had not.
. . . .
On a platter they bore it, and brought it to Gunnar.

Then Gunnar spake forth, the spear of the Niflungs:
"Here have I the heart of Hogni the valiant,
Unlike to the heart of Hjalli the craven,
Little it trembles as it lies on the platter,
Still less did it tremble when it lay in his breast.

"So distant, Atli, from all men's eyes,
Shalt thou be as thou . . . . from the gold.
. . . .
. . . .

"To no one save me is the secret known
Of the Niflungs' hoard, now Hogni is dead;
Of old there were two, while we twain were alive,
Now is none but I, for I only am living.

"The swift Rhine shall hold the strife-gold of heroes,
That once was the gods', the wealth of the Niflungs,
In the depths of the waters the death-rings shall glitter,
And not shine on the hands of the Hunnish men."

  Atli spake:
"Ye shall bring the wagon, for now is he bound."

   * * *

On the long-maned Glaum rode Atli the great,
About him were warriors . . . . .
But Guthrun, akin to the gods of slaughter,
Yielded not to her tears in the hall of tumult.

Guthrun spake:

"It shall go with thee, Atli,   as with Gunnar thou heldest
The oaths ofttimes sworn,   and of old made firm,
By the sun in the south,   by Sigtyr's mountain,
By the horse of the rest-bed,   and the ring of Ull."

Then the champer of bits   drew the chieftain great,
The gold-guarder, down   to the place of death.

.   .   .   .

By the warriors' host   was the living hero
Cast in the den   where crawling about
Within were serpents,   but soon did Gunnar
With his hand in wrath   on the harp-strings smite;
The strings resounded,—   so shall a hero,
A ring-breaker, gold   from his enemies guard.

Then Atli rode   on his earth-treading steed,
Seeking his home,   from the slaughter-place;
There was clatter of hoofs   of the steeds in the court,
And the clashing of arms   as they came from the field.

Out then came Guthrun   to meeting with Atli,
With a golden beaker   as gift to the monarch:
"Thou mayst eat now, chieftain,   within thy dwelling,
Blithely with Guthrun   young beasts fresh slaughtered."

The wine-heavy ale-cups   of Atli resounded,
When there in the hall   the Hunnish youths clamored,
And the warriors bearded,   the brave ones, entered.

Then in came the shining one, ...
.   .   .   .   .   .   and drink she bore them;
Unwilling and bitter   brought she food to the warrior,
Till in scorn to the white-faced   Atli did she speak:

"Thou giver of swords,   of thy sons the hearts
All heavy with blood   in honey thou hast eaten;
Thou shalt stomach, thou hero,   the flesh of the slain,
To eat at thy feast,   and to send to thy followers.

"Thou shalt never call to thy knees again
Erp or Eitil, when merry with ale;
Thou shalt never see in their seats again
The sharers of gold their lances shaping,
(Clipping the manes or minding their steeds.)"

There was clamor on the benches, and the cry of men,
The clashing of weapons, and weeping of the Huns,
Save for Guthrun only, she wept not ever
For her bear-fierce brothers, or the boys so dear,
So young and so unhappy, whom with Atli she had.

Gold did she scatter, the swan-white one,
And rings of red gold to the followers gave she;
The fate she let grow, and the shining wealth go,
Nor spared she the treasure of the temple itself.

Unwise then was Atli, he had drunk to wildness,
No weapon did he have, and of Guthrun bewared not;
Oft their play was better when both in gladness
Each other embraced among princes all.

With her sword she gave blood for the bed to drink,
With her death-dealing hand, and the hounds she loosed,
The thralls she awakened, and a firebrand threw
In the door of the hall; so vengeance she had.

To the flames she gave all who yet were within,
And from Myrkheim had come from the murder of Gunnar;
The timbers old fell, the temple was in flames,
The dwelling of the Buthlungs, and the shield-maids burned,
They were slain in the house, in the hot flames they sank.

Now the tale is all told, nor in later time
Will a woman in byrnie avenge so her brothers;
The fair one to three of the kings of the folk
Brought the doom of death ere herself she died.

The Last of the Volsungs

Völsunga saga

GUDRUN heard of the death of Swanhild, and she said to her sons,

"How can ye sit so content and speak so merrily when Jormunrek has slain your sister and shamefully caused her to be trampled to death by horses? Ye have no spirit like to Hogni's or Gunnar's; they would have avenged their kinswoman." Hamdir answered,

"Thou hadst little praise for Gunnar and Hogni when they killed Sigurd and thou wert stained with his blood; and ill was the revenge thou didst take for thy brothers when thou slewest thine own sons. But we may well put King Jormunrek to death, for we cannot resist the taunts with which we are pressed!" Gudrun now went about laughing aloud. She gave them wine to drink out of great goblets, and after that she chose them fine large byrnies and other war-weeds. Then said Hamdir,

"Now we part from thee for the last time; thou wilt hear news of us and thou shalt hold one funeral feast for us and for Swanhild."

Then they departed, but Gudrun went to her bower with heavier sorrow than ever before, and she said,

"To three men have I been wedded: first to Sigurd Fafnir's Bane, who was betrayed, and that was the greatest of my woes; then I was given to King Atli, but my heart was so fierce towards him that I slew our sons in my great grief. After that I went down to the sea, but the waves carried me ashore; and then I was wedded to this king. Since then I gave Swanhild in marriage and sent her to a foreign land with great treasures. It is the sorest of my woes next to Sigurd's death, that she was trampled under the hoofs of horses; the grimmest pain was when Gunnar was put in the snake-pit, and the sharpest, when the heart was cut out of Hogni. Better it would be if Sigurd fetched me and I might go with him. No son or daughter remains to comfort me now. Dost thou recall, Sigurd, what we said to each other when we went into one bed together, that thou wouldst come for me and seek me from Hel itself?"

And therewith she ended her lamentations.

The Last Voyage of Sigurth Hring

Early seventh century

From the Latin epitome of the lost Skjöldunga saga

THE grand finale of the heroic age of Scandinavia was the Battle of Bravalla in Sweden about A.D. 600. From the two following centuries traditions are obscure until history emerges with the Viking kings in the eight hundreds. King Harald Wartooth, of the H-dynasty of Denmark, appointed his nephew Sigurth Hring king in Swedish Götland. When Harald grew old he decided to anticipate death from old age by death in battle and to take as many warriors as possible with him to Othin in Valhall. So he challenged his nephew to battle. Each assembled a great host. Descriptions of the Battle of Bravalla and of the list of heroes who participated rival the annals of the embattled champions of the *Iliad*. So stupendous was this engagement that Othin himself and the Valkyries appeared on the scene of carnage. Hring was victorious over Harald, as the Norns decreed, and gave him a mighty funeral. He had his illustrious uncle burned in his chariot with his arms and jewels and a great mound heaped over him as a memorial to posterity. Hring then became king of both Sweden and Denmark.

Hring was married to Alfhild, a Norwegian princess. After her death, when he was growing old, he was once touring the courts in western Sweden when his wife's relatives came to seek his aid in their local wars in Norway. At the head of an army he marched into Norway. At that time a great sacrificial festival was being held at Skiringsal, and King Hring, who was very religious, participated. Here he saw a Norwegian princess, Alfsol, a girl of surpassing beauty, and fell in love with her charms.

ᴥᎶALFSOL had two brothers, Alf, named after his father, and Ingvi. Sigurth sought their consent to marry their sister, but they refused to give the very beautiful young girl to a wrinkled old man. Enraged that the sons of a petty king should refuse such a great ruler, the king threatened to wage a bloody war in the future, for at the time he was not permitted to decide the matter by the sword because of a religious celebration. A little later, therefore, he challenged the aforementioned brothers to battle. As far as the brothers were concerned, they were very ready in heart and hand. Realizing, nevertheless, the tremendous size of Sigurth's army, they administered poison to their sister before they departed to battle in order to deprive the victor of his spoils. In the very bitter contest in which Alf and Ingvi bravely met death, Sigurth also was badly wounded.

When Alfsol's death was reported to him, he embarked upon a large ship on which were piled the bodies of the slain warriors; he alone was alive. Placing himself and the body of Alfsol in the stern, he ordered the vessel to be smeared with pitch, bitumen, and sulphur and to be fired. The sails were raised and were filled with a strong wind blowing from the land. He turned the prow seaward and then killed himself. In a cheerful spirit he had previously told his comrades who were left behind on the beach that he, who had performed so many deeds and owned so many kingdoms, chose to visit King Othin in royal pomp in the manner of his ancestors rather than to endure the weakness of an inactive old age. Certain persons relate that Sigurth killed himself before he left the beach. Nevertheless he caused a mound to be raised on the shore according to the prevailing custom, which he ordered to be called Hringshaug. But he himself on a craft guided by the elements sailed over the waves to Valhall.

III. ICELAND

Ingolf

870

Ari Þorgilsson

Íslendingabók

ICELAND was early sighted by Norwegian mariners, but the first settlement was made by Ingolf. The present account is found in one of the first sagas actually written down—"The Book of the Icelanders" by Ari the Learned. Ari was born in 1067 and died November 9, 1148.

ICELAND was first settled from Norway in the days of Harald the Fairhaired, son of Halfdan the Black, at the time—according to the opinion and calculation of Teit my foster-father, the wisest man I have known, son of Bishop Isleif, and of my paternal uncle Thorkel Gellisson who remembered far back, and of Thurid daughter of Snorri Godi who was both learned in many things and trustworthy—when Ivar, son of Ragnar Lodbrok, caused Edmund the Saint, king of the English, to be slain; and that was 870 years after the birth of Christ.

A Norwegian called Ingolf, it is told for certain, first went from there to Iceland when Harald the Fairhaired was sixteen winters old, and for the second time a few winters later. He settled south in Reykjavik. Ingolf's Head, east of Munthakseyri, is the name given to the place where he first landed, but Ingolf's Fell, west of Ölfus River, is where he afterwards took possession of land.

At that time Iceland was covered with forests between mountains and seashore. Then Christian men whom the Norsemen call Popes were here; but afterwards they went away, because they did not wish to live here together with heathen men, and they left behind Irish books, bells, and crooks. From this could be seen that they were Irishmen.

And then a very great emigration started out hither from Norway until King Harald forbade it, because he thought that the country would be laid waste. Then they came to this agreement that every man who was not exempted and who went from there hither should pay the king five ounces.

The Thorsness Settlement

c. 880

Eyrbyggja saga

THE Saga of the Ere-dwellers is one of the five longer Icelandic family sagas. The settlement at Thorsness is typical of the colonies planted in Iceland by powerful Norwegians who protested Harald Fairhaired's determination to place all Norway under one king. It was usual for these emigrants to transport the pillars of the home temple of Thor, to cast them overboard on approaching Iceland, and to occupy the strip of coast to which they drifted.

AFTER that they explored the land, and upon the uttermost part of the point, that is on the north of the bay, they found that Thunder was come ashore with the pillars. It was afterwards called Thor's-ness. After that Thor-wolf bore the fire round his settlement, starting inward from Staff-water, and landward to the water which he called Thor's-water, and he gave settlements to his mariners there. He set up a great homestead on Temple-bay, which he called Temple-stead. He set up a temple there, and it was a big house.

Thor-wolf called [all] between Wigre-frith and Temple-bay Thor's-ness. On this ness there stands a hill. This hill Thor-wolf had in such great reverence that no man might look thereon [pray towards it] unwashen, and there might be no destruction of anything, man or beast, on this hill, save the creature come off it of its own accord. This hill he called Holy-fell, and he believed that he should go into it when he died and all his kinsmen on the ness.

King Athelstan's Silver

937-990

Egils saga

THE Saga of Egil Skallagrimsson, warrior and poet, is one of the five long family sagas of Iceland. On one of his many expeditions Egil fought in England at the battle of Brunanburgh on the side of King Athelstan. After the battle, Athelstan gave Egil a present of silver which he always treasured, and hid before his death.

Another selection from *Egils saga* is published in the present collection, as well as two of Egil's poems.

937 ·

THEN went Egil and those about him to seek king Athelstan, and at once went before the king, where he sat at the drinking. There was much noise of merriment. And when the king saw that Egil was come in, he bade the lower bench be cleared for them, and that Egil should sit in the high-seat facing the king. Egil sat down there, and cast his shield before his feet. He had his helm on his head, and laid his sword across his knees; and now and again he half drew it, then clashed it back into the sheath. He sat upright, but with head bent forward.

Egil was large-featured, broad of forehead, with large eye-brows, a nose not long but very thick, lips wide and long, chin exceeding broad, as was all about the jaws; thick-necked was he, and big-shouldered beyond other men, hard-featured, and grim when angry. He was well-made, more than commonly tall, had hair wolf-gray and thick, but became early bald. He was black-eyed and brown-skinned.

But as he sat (as was before written), he drew one eye-brow down towards the cheek, the other up to the roots of the hair. He would not drink now, though the horn was borne to him, but alternately twitched his brows up and down. King Athelstan sat in the upper high-seat. He too laid his sword across his knees. When they had sat there for a time, then the king drew his sword from the sheath, and took from his arm a gold ring large and good, and placing it upon the sword-point he stood up, and went across the floor, and reached it over the fire to Egil. Egil stood up and drew his sword, and went across the floor. He stuck the sword-point within the round of the ring, and drew it to him; then he went back to his place. The king sate him again in the high-seat. But when Egil was set down, he drew the ring on his arm, and then his brows went back to their place. He now laid down sword and helm, took the horn that they bare to him, and drank it off.

*   *   *

Thereafter Egil drank his share, and talked with others. Presently the king caused to be borne in two chests; two men bare each. Both were full of silver.

The king said: "These chests, Egil, thou shalt have, and, if thou comest to Iceland, shalt carry this money to thy father; as payment for a son I send it to him: but some of the money thou shalt divide among such kinsmen as thyself and Thorolf as thou thinkest most honourable. But thou shalt take here payment for a brother with me, land or chattels, which thou wilt. And if thou wilt abide with me long, then will I give thee honour and dignity such as thyself mayst name."

*   *   *

Then gave Athelstan further to Egil as poet's meed two gold rings, each weighing a mark, and therewith a costly cloak that the king himself had formerly worn.

990

In the later days of Hacon the Great Egil Skallagrim's son was in his ninth decade of years, and save for his blindness was a hale and hearty man. One summer, when men made ready to go to the Thing, Egil asked Grim that he might ride with him to the Thing. Grim was slow to grant this. And when Grim and Thordis talked together, Grim told her what Egil had asked. "I would like you," said he, "to find out what lies under this request." Thordis then went to talk with Egil her uncle: it was Egil's chief pleasure to talk to her. And when she met him she asked: "Is it true, uncle, that you wish to ride to the Thing? I want you to tell me what plan you have in this?" "I will tell you," said he, "what I have thought of. I mean to take with me to the Thing two chests that king Athelstan gave me, each of which is full of English silver. I mean to have these chests carried to the Hill of Laws just when it is most crowded. Then I mean to sow broadcast the silver, and I shall be surprized if all share it fairly between them. Kicks, I fancy, there will be and blows; nay, it may end in a general fight of all the assembled Thing." Thordis said: "A famous plan, methinks, is this, and it will be remembered so long as Iceland is inhabited."

After this Thordis went to speak with Grim and told him Egil's plan. "That shall never be," said he, "that he carry this out, such monstrous folly." And when Egil came to speak with Grim of their going to the Thing, Grim talked him out of it all; and Egil sat at home during the Thing. But he did not like it, and he wore a frowning look.

At Moss-fell were the summer-sheds of the milch kine, and during the Thing-time Thordis was at the sheds. It chanced one evening, when the household at Moss-fell were preparing to go to bed, that Egil called to him two thralls of Grim's. He bade them bring him a horse. "I will go to the warm bath, and you shall go with me," said he. And when Egil was ready, he went out, and he had with him his chests of silver. He mounted the horse. They then went down through the home paddock and under the slope there, as men saw afterwards. But in the morning, when men rose, they saw Egil wandering about in the holt east of the farm, and leading the horse after him. They went to him, and brought him home. But neither thralls nor chests ever came back again, and many are the guesses as to where Egil hid his money. East of the farm at Moss-fell is a gill coming down from the fell: and it is noteworthy that in rapid thaws there was a great rush of water there, but after the water has fallen there have been found in the gill English pennies. Some guess that Egil must have hidden his money there. Below the farm enclosure at Moss-fell are bogs wide and very deep. Many feel sure that 'tis there Egil hid his money. And south of the river are hot springs, and hard by these large earthholes, and some men guess that Egil must have hidden his money there, because out that way cairn-fires were often seen to hover. Egil said that he had slain Grim's thralls, also that he had hidden the chests, but where he had hidden them he told no man.

In the autumn following Egil fell sick of the sickness whereof he died. When he was dead, then Grim had Egil dressed in goodly raiment, and carried down to Tjaldaness; there a sepulchral mound was made, and in it was Egil laid with his weapons and his raiment.

Lawsuit Against Hrafnkel

c. 940

Hrafnkels saga Freysgoða

THIS is one of the more famous suits of law at the Althing in Iceland. Hrafnkel was a goði (priest) of the god Freyr in eastern Iceland, and owned a horse which he dedicated to Freyr.

SAM now had his horse fetched, and rode up along the valley to a farm and gave notice of the slaying against Hrafnkel. Hrafnkel heard of this, and thought it laughable that Sam had taken up the case against him. The summer passed and the next winter, but in the spring, when it came to the summons-days, Sam rode from home up to Manor and summoned Hrafnkel for the slaying of Einar. After that Sam rode down through the valley and summoned the neighbours to the Thing-ride, and afterwards stayed quiet till men made ready for the Thing.

Hrafnkel then sent down along Glacierdale and summoned men together. He went out of his Thing-district with seventy men. With that company he rode east across Fleetdale hundred, and so by the head of the lake, and across the pass to Screedale, up along Screedale, and south to Axheath to She-Bear Firth, and took the common road of the Thingmen to Side. South from Fleetdale it is seventeen days' journey to the Thingfield.

After he had ridden out of the district, Sam called men to him; mostly he got landlopers to ride with him, and then, when he had got them together, Sam furnished these men with weapons, clothes, and victuals. Sam turned another way out of the dales. He went north to the bridges, and so over the bridges, and thence across Madderdale-heath, and they were in Madderdale overnight. From there they rode to Broadsholder Tongue, and so up above Bluefell, thence to Crookdale, and so south to Sand, coming down to Sheepfell, and thence to the Thingfield, where Hrafnkel had not then arrived. He got along the slower because he had the longer road. Sam pitched a booth for his men nowhere near where the Eastfirthers are accustomed to pitch, and somewhat later Hrafnkel reached the Thing, to pitch his booth where he usually did. He heard that Sam was at the Thing, and that seemed laughable to him.

That Thing was very crowded. Most of the chieftains who were in Iceland were there. Sam met all the chieftains and asked for help and assistance, but all answered the one way, so that no one declared he was enough bound to Sam to get to grips with Hrafnkel Godi and so risk his reputation, adding too that it had gone one way with most of those that had Thing-dealings with Hrafnkel, in that he had driven all men from the lawsuits which they had against him. Sam went home to his booth, and the kinsmen were heavy of heart, fearing that their case would so fall through that they would get nothing out of it save shame and dishonour, and such great dismay had the kinsmen that they could neither sleep nor eat; because all the chieftains hung back from helping the kinsmen, including those whom they had expected to grant them aid.

Early one morning old Thorbjorn awoke. He roused Sam and bade him get up.

"I cannot sleep."

Sam stood up and got into his clothes. They went out and down to the Axwater below the bridges, where they washed themselves.

Thorbjorn said to Sam, "It is my advice that you have our horses driven in, and let us make ready for home. It is now easy to see that there is nothing for us save dishonour."

"That is all very well," Sam answered, "since you wished for nothing save to tackle Hrafnkel, and would not take the offer that many a man would have taken who had to see to it after his near kinsman. You greatly challenged our courage, and that of all those who were not willing to go into this lawsuit with you, and I shall never give up until I think it past hope that I get something done."

At that Thorbjorn was so moved that he wept.

Then they saw, westward over the river, a little lower than where they sat, how five men went together from a booth. He was a tall man and not stoutly built who was their leader, and went in front in a leafgreen kirtle, and had a drawn sword in his hand; a man regular of feature and ruddy, of good bearing, with chestnut hair and plenty of it. This man was easily known, for he had a light lock in his hair on the left side.

"Let us stand up," said Sam, "and go westward across the river to meet these men."

They now went down to the river; and the man who went in front greeted them first and asked who they might be. They told him. Sam asked the man his name, and he said that his name was Thorkel, adding that he was the son of Thjostar. Sam asked from whom he was come and where his home was. He declared himself a Westfirther by kin and upbringing, and said that he had a home in Codfirth.

"Are you a godi?" asked Sam.

He said that was far from the truth.

"Are you a bondi then?"

He answered that he was not.

"What kind of man are you then?"

"I am a man without ties," he answered. "I came out here the summer before last. I have been abroad seven winters, and went out to Micklegarth, and am a follower of the Emperor; but now I am lodging with my brother, whose name is Thorgeir."

"Is he a man with a godord?" asked Sam.

"Godi he is, to be sure, over Codfirth, and still wider throughout the Westfirths."

"Is he here at the Thing?"

"Here he is, nothing surer."

"How many men has he?" Sam asked.

"Seventy of them."

"Are there any more brothers?"

"There is a third," replied Thorkel.

"Who is he?"

"His name is Thormod, and he dwells at Garth in Swansness. He is married to Thordis, the daughter of Thorolf Skallagrim's son from Borg."

"Will you give us some help?" asked Sam.

"What do you need?"

"The help and might of chieftains," Sam answered; "for we have a lawsuit to thrash out with Hrafnkel Godi about the slaying of Einar Thorbjorn's son; but we may well trust to our pleading with your backing."

"It so happens," Thorkel pointed out, "that, as I said, I am no godi."

"Why are you so put aside," asked Sam, "since you are a chieftain's son even as your other brothers?"

"I did not say that I did not own one," Thorkel made answer, "but I handed over my authority to Thorgeir, my brother, before I went abroad. I have not taken it back since, for I think it in good hands while he looks after it. Go and meet him, and ask him for help. He is a good-hearted man, a splendid fellow, and in every way a man of mark, young and eager for fame. Such men are the most likely to grant you help."

"We shall get nothing from him," said Sam, "unless you are in the pleading with us."

"This I promise," Thorkel answered, "to be rather for you than against, for it seems to me sufficient cause to take up the bloodsuit for a near kinsman. Now, go along to the booth, and go on inside. The men are asleep. You will see where two skin-beds stand at the far side of the booth. I got up from the one, but in the other rests Thorgeir my brother. He has had a great boil on the foot since he came to the Thing, and so has had little sleep at night, but the foot broke overnight and the core is out of the boil. He has slept since, and has stretched out his foot from under the clothes on to the foot-board, because of the excessive heat which is in the foot. Let the old man go first, and so in along the booth; he seems to me very infirm both in sight and years. And when, old man," Thorkel went on, "you come to the skin-bed, you must stumble heavily, and fall on to the foot-board, catch hold of the toe which is tied up, wrench it towards you, and find out how he takes it."

"You want to give us wholesome advice," said Sam, "but this does not seem a good plan to me."

"Do one thing or the other," Thorkel answered. "Take what I give or seek no advice from me."

Sam spoke, and said, "What he advises shall be done."

Thorkel declared that he would go along later.—"For I am waiting for my men."

Sam and Thorbjorn now set off and came into the booth. All there were asleep. They soon saw where Thorgeir was lying. Old Thorbjorn went in front, stumbling heavily, and when he came to the skin-bed he fell across the footboard, snatched at the toe that was bad and wrenched it towards him, and with that Thorgeir awoke and leapt up in bed, demanding who went there so headlong as to jump on men's feet, which were bad enough before. But Sam and Thorbjorn had nothing to say for themselves.

Then Thorkel stepped into the booth and spoke to Thorgeir his brother. "Be not so hasty and headstrong in this, kinsman, for it will not harm you. Many a man does worse than he intends, and it happens that many a man cannot attend equally well to everything when there is much on his mind. But it is your excuse, kinsman, that your foot is sore, and, indeed, it has been a great affliction; and you yourself have felt it most. Now it may also be that to the old man the death of his son is no less painful, but he gets no redress, and is missing everything. He must feel this most himself, and it is to be looked for that the man who has much on his mind will not pay due heed to everything."

Thorgeir answered, "I had no idea he could blame me for this, for I did not slay his son, and therefore he cannot avenge it on me."

"He did not mean to avenge it on you," said Thorkel, "but he made at you harder than he intended, and paid for his failing sight. He looked for some aid from you. It would be a fine thing now, to help an old man and a needy. This is need for him, and not greed, though he takes up the bloodsuit for his son. But now all the chieftains hang back from aiding these men, and by that show great meanness."

"Of whom have they to complain?" asked Thorgeir.

"Hrafnkel Godi has slain Thorbjorn's son sackless," Thorkel explained. "He does one ill deed after another, and will pay no one for them."

"It will fare with me as with the others," said Thorgeir, "that I do not know I have so much good to repay these men that I wish to get to grips with Hrafnkel. It seems to me that he goes to work in such a way every summer with those men who have lawsuits to settle with him that most men get little honour or none before it ends, and I see that it fares one way with all. Therefore, I fancy, most men are backward about it, whom no need brings to the push."

"It may be," Thorkel replied, "that it would so fare with me if I were a chieftain, that it would appear to me a bad business to strive with Hrafnkel, but, as it is, I do not look at it in that light, for I should think it best to have to do with him from whom all came off badly before; and I fancy that mine or that chieftain's fame would wax greatly who could get some pull over Hrafnkel, but not grow less though it should go with me as with the others, because —'That may to me, that happens to others,' and 'Nothing venture, nothing gain.'"

"I see how you are bent," said Thorgeir. "You want to help these men. I am now going to hand over to you my godord and authority, and do you have what I have had before, and from now on let us both have even shares. Now, you help those you want to!"

"It appears to me," said Thorkel, "that the godord is in the best keeping the longer you have it. I should not care for anyone to have it so much as you, for you have many good parts beyond us brothers, and I am not settled about what I intend to do. You know, kinsman, how I have meddled with few things since I came to Iceland. But I can see now what my word is worth, and I have pleaded as much as I will for the present. Maybe Thorkel Lock shall come where his word has more weight!"

"I see now how it is shaping, kinsman," Thorgeir answered. "You are offended. I cannot have that, so we will help these men, whatever comes of it, if you want to."

"I ask you nothing," said Thorkel, "but what I think better granted."

"Of what do these men reckon themselves capable," asked Thorgeir, "so that their case may turn out well?"

"Even as I said today," said Sam, "we need the strength of chieftains, but I shall look after the pleading of the suit myself."

Thorgeir told him that that was worth much.—"And it is now necessary to prepare the case as well as can be. I fancy that Thorkel would like you to let him know before the judges fare out. You shall then have something for your pains, some comfort or shame even greater than before, and disgrace and affliction. Now, go home and be cheerful, for if you want to tackle Hrafnkel Godi you shall need to bear up well in the meantime. But tell no one that we have promised you aid."

They then went back to their booth and were in high fettle. All men wondered at this, why they had so quickly changed their mood, for they were downcast when they went from their booth.

They stayed there till the judges fared out. Then Sam called up his men and went to the Hill of Laws. The court was then set there. Sam went boldly to the court, forthwith began naming witnesses, and carried on his case according to the true law of the land against Hrafnkel Godi, without a slip and with goodly pleading. With that, along came the sons of Thjostar with a great band of men. All the men from the west country gave them aid, and it was clear that the sons of Thjostar were popular men. Sam carried on the case in court until Hrafnkel was called on for the defence, unless that man were there present who wished to bring forward a defence in law. The applause was great at Sam's case, and it was a question whether anyone would wish to bring forward a legal defence for Hrafnkel. Men hastened to Hrafnkel's booth and told him what was afoot. He stirred himself quickly, called up his men, and went to the court, reckoning that there would be little defence there. He had it in mind to put an end to the bringing of lawsuits against him by petty folk, and meant to wreck the court for Sam and drive him from his case. But of this there was now no chance. There was such a press in front of him that Hrafnkel could get nowhere near, and he was crowded away by sheer force, so that he could not hear their case against him, and was therefore unable to bring forward a legal defence for himself. But Sam carried his suit the full length of the law, until Hrafnkel was outlawed at this Thing.

Hrafnkel went straightway to his booth, had his horses taken, and rode away from the Thing, ill content with his end of the case because he had never experienced such a thing before. He then rode east to Heatherdaleheath, and so east to Side, and did not stop until he came to Hrafnkelsdale and settled at Manor, making as if nothing had happened. But Sam stayed behind at the Thing, and went about with a swagger. Many men thought it well although it had turned out that Hrafnkel had been put to shame, and they now called to mind that he had shown injustice to many.

Farms and Fences

c. 947

Víga-Glúms saga

THIS tale is included to show that Norsemen were good farmers as well as fishermen and fighters.

◆§ ONE of the best things about the estate at Thverá was a certain field known by the name of "the Sure-giver," which was never without a crop. It had been so arranged in the partition of the land that either party should have this field year and year about. Then Astrida said to Thorkel and Sigmund, "It is clear that you wish to push me hard, and you see that I have no one to manage for me, but rather than give up my serfs I will leave the affair to be settled on your own terms." They replied that was very prudent on her part, and after consulting together they decided that they must either declare the men guilty, or award what damages they thought proper. But Thorstein did not stir in the case, so as to take the award out of their hands, and they assigned the field to themselves, as sole owners, with the intention of getting hold of all her land, by thus depriving her of the main prop of her housekeeping. And that very summer which was coming on, she ought, if she had her rights, to have had the field.

Now, in the summer, when men were gone to the Thing, and when this suit had been thus settled, the herdsmen going round the pastures found the two heifers in a landslip, where the snow had drifted over them early in the winter, and thus the calumny against

Astrida's serfs was exposed. When Thorkel and Sigmund heard
that the heifers had been found, they offered money to pay for the
field, but they refused to renounce the conveyance which had been
made of it to them. Astrida however answered that it would not be
too great a compensation for the false charge which had been got
up, if she were allowed to have what was her own. "So," said she,
"I will either have what belongs to me, or I will submit to the loss;
and though there is no one here to set the matter straight, I will wait,
and I expect that Glum will come out and put it in the right way."
Sigmund replied, "It will be a long time before he ploughs for that
harvest. Why, there is that son of yours, who is a much fitter man
to help you, sitting by and doing nothing." "Pride and wrong," said
she, "often end badly, and this may happen in your case."

It was somewhat late in the summer when Glum came out; he
stayed a little while with the ship, and then went home with his goods.
His temper and character were the same as they had been. He gave
little sign of what he thought, and seemed as if he did not hear what
had happened whilst he was away. He slept every day till nine o'clock,
and took no thought about the management of the farm. If they had
had their right, the field would, as has been said, have been that summer in the hands of Glum and his mother. Sigmund's cattle moreover did them much injury, and were to be found every morning in
their home-field.

One morning Astrida waked Glum up, and told him that many of
Sigmund's cattle had got into their home-field, and wanted to break
in among the hay which was laid in heaps, "and I am not active
enough to drive them out, and the men are all at work." He answered,
"Well, you have not often asked me to work, and there shall be no
offence in your doing so now." So he jumped up, took his horse, and
a large stick in his hand, drove the cattle briskly off the farm, thrash-
ing them well till they came to the homestead of Thorkel and Sigmund, and then he let them do what mischief they pleased. Thorkel
was looking after the hay and the fences that morning, and Sigmund
was with the labourers. The former called out to Glum, "You may
be sure people will not stand this at your hands—that you should
damage their beasts in this way, though you may have got some
credit while you were abroad." Glum answered, "The beasts are not
injured yet, but if they come again and trespass upon us some of
them will be lamed, and you will have to make the best of it; it is

all you will get; we are not going to suffer damage by your cattle any longer." Sigmund cried out, "You talk big, Glum, but in our eyes you are now just as great a simpleton as when you went away, and we shall not regulate our affairs according to your nonsense." Glum went home, and then a fit of laughter came upon him, and affected him in such a manner that he turned quite pale, and tears burst from his eyes, just like large hailstones. He was often afterwards taken in this way when the appetite for killing some one came upon him.

A Poet Falls in Love

c. 950

Kormáks saga

CORMAC the Skald was a brave man's man and a good poet, but as a lover he was painfully shy. He failed to appear on the day set for his wedding to Steingerd. For years he kept writing verses about her but he allowed her to marry two other men. These selections are accounts of Cormac's first infatuation and of his duel with Steingerd's first husband.

❧ THERE was a man named Thorkel lived at Túnga [Tongue]. He was a wedded man, and had a daughter called Steingerd who was fostered in Gnúpsdal [Knipedale].

Now it was one autumn that a whale came ashore at Vatnsnes [Watsness], and it belonged to the brothers, Dalla's sons. Thorgils asked Cormac would he rather go shepherding on the fell, or work at the whale. He chose to fare on the fell with the house-carles.

Tósti, the foreman, it was should be master of the sheep-gathering: so he and Cormac went together until they came to Gnúpsdal. It was night: there was a great hall, and fires for men to sit at.

That evening Steingerd came out of her bower, and a maid with her. Said the maid, "Steingerd mine, let us look at the guests."

"Nay," she said, "no need"; and yet went to the door, and stepped on the threshold, and spied across the gate. Now there was a space between the wicket and the threshold, and her feet showed through. Cormac saw that, and made this song:

> "At the door of my soul she is standing,
> So sweet in the gleam of her garment:

Her footfall awakens a fury,
A fierceness of love that I knew not,
Those feet of a wench in her wimple,
Their weird is my sorrow and troubling,
—Or naught may my knowledge avail me—
Both now and for aye to endure."

Then Steingerd knew she was seen. She turned aside into a corner where the likeness of Hagbard was carved on the wall, and peeped under Hagbard's beard. Then the firelight shone upon her face.

"Cormac," said Tósti, "seest eyes out yonder by that head of Hagbard?"

Cormac answered in song:

"There breaks on me, burning upon me,
A blaze from the cheeks of a maiden,
—I laugh not to look on the vision—
In the light of the hall by the doorway.
So sweet and so slender I deem her,
Though I spy but a glimpse of an ankle
By the threshold:—and through me there flashes
A thrill that shall age never more."

And then he made another song:

"The moon of her brow, it is beaming
'Neath the bright-litten heaven of her forehead:
So she gleams in her white robe, and gazes
With a glance that is keen as the falcon's.
But the star that is shining upon me
What spell shall it work by its witchcraft?
Ah, that moon of her brow shall be mighty
With mischief to her—and to me!"

Said Tósti, "She is fairly staring at thee!" And he answered:

"She's a ring-bedight oak of the ale-cup,
And her eyes never left me unhaunted.
The strife in my heart I could hide not,
For I hold myself bound in her bondage.
O gay in her necklet, and gainer
In the game that wins hearts on her chessboard,—

> When she looked at me long from the doorway
> Where the likeness of Hagbard is carved."

Then the girls went into the hall, and sat down. He heard what they said about his looks,—the maid, that he was black and ugly, and Steingerd, that he was handsome and everyway as best could be,—"There is only one blemish," said she, "his hair is tufted on his forehead:"—and he said:

> "One flaw in my features she noted
> —With the flame of the wave she was gleaming
> All white in the wane of the twilight—
> And that one was no hideous blemish.
> So highborn, so haughty a lady
> —I should have such a dame to befriend me:
> But she trows me uncouth for a trifle,
> For a tuft in the hair on my brow!"

Said the maid, "Black are his eyes, sister, and that becomes him not." Cormac heard her, and said in verse:

> "Yea, black are the eyes that I bring ye,
> O brave in your jewels, and dainty.
> But a draggle-tail, dirty-foot slattern
> Would dub me ill-favoured and sallow.
> Nay, many a maiden has loved me,
> Thou may of the glittering armlet:
> For I've tricks of the tongue to beguile them
> And turn them from handsomer lads."

At this house they spent the night. In the morning when Cormac rose up, he went to a trough and washed himself; then he went into the ladies' bower and saw nobody there, but heard folk talking in the inner room, and he turned and entered. There was Steingerd, and women with her.

Said the maid to Steingerd, "There comes thy bonny man, Steingerd."

"Well, and a fine-looking lad he is," said she.

Now she was combing her hair, and Cormac asked her, "Wilt thou give me leave?"

She reached out her comb for him to handle it. She had the finest hair of any woman. Said the maid, "Ye would give a deal for a wife with hair like Steingerd's, or such eyes!"

He answered:

> "One eye of the fay of the ale-horn
> Looking out of a form so bewitching,
> Would a bridegroom count money to buy it
> He must bring for it ransom three hundred.
> The curls that she combs of a morning,
> White-clothed in fair linen and spotless,
> They enhance the bright hoard of her value,—
> Five hundred might barely redeem them!"

Said the maid, "It's give and take with the two of ye! But thou'lt put a big price upon the whole of her!" He answered:—

> "The tree of my treasure and longing,
> It would take this whole Iceland to win her:
> She is dearer than far-away Denmark,
> And the doughty domain of the Hun-folk.
> With the gold she is combing, I count her
> More costly than England could ransom:
> So witty, so wealthy, my lady
> Is worth them,—and Ireland beside!"

Then Tósti came in, and called Cormac out to some work or other; but he said:

> "Take my swift-footed steed for thy riding,
> Ay, and stint not the lash to him, Tósti:
> On the desolate downs ye may wander
> And drive him along till he weary.
> I care not o'er mountain and moorland
> The murrey-brown wethers to follow,—
> Far liefer I'd linger the morning
> In long, cosy chatter with Steingerd."

Tósti said he would find it a merrier game, and went off; so Cormac sat down to chess, and right gay he was. Steingerd said he talked better than folk told of; and he sat there all the day; and then he made this song:

" 'Tis the dart that adorneth her tresses,
The deep, dewy grass of her forehead.
So kind to my keeping she gave it,
That good comb I shall ever remember!
A stranger was I when I sought her
—Sweet stem with the dragon's hoard shining—
With gold like the sea-dazzle gleaming—
The girl I shall never forget."

Tósti came off the fell and they fared home. After that Cormac
used to go to Gnúpsdal often to see Steingerd: and he asked his
mother to make him good clothes, so that Steingerd might like him
the most that could be. Dalla said there was a mighty great difference
betwixt them, and it was far from certain to end happily if Thorkel
at Túnga got to know.

The Holmgang
(duel)

Well, the time wore on, and the day came. He rode away with
fifteen men; Bersi also rode to the holm with as many. Cormac came
there first, and told Thorgils that he would sit apart by himself. So
he sat down and ungirt the sword.

Now, he never heeded whether the sun shone upon the hilt, for
he had girt the sword on him outside his clothes. And when he tried
to draw it he could not, until he set his feet upon the hilts. Then the
little worm came, and was not rightly done by; and so the sword came
groaning and creaking out of the scabbard, and the good luck of it
was gone.

After that Cormac went to his men. Bersi and his party had come
by that time, and many more to see the fight.

Cormac took up Bersi's target and cut at it, and sparks flew out.

Then a hide was taken and spread for them to stand on. Bersi
spoke and said, "Thou, Cormac, hast challenged me to the holmgang;
instead of that, I offer thee to fight in simple sword-play. Thou art a
young man and little tried; the holmgang needs craft and cunning,
but sword-play, man to man, is an easy game."

Cormac answered, "I should fight no better even so. I will run the
risk, and stand on equal footing with thee, every way."

"As thou wilt," said Bersi.

It was the law of the holmgang that the hide should be five ells long, with loops at its corners. Into these should be driven certain pins with heads to them, called *tjösnur*. He who made it ready should go to the pins in such a manner that he could see sky between his legs, holding the lobes of his ears and speaking the forewords used in the rite called "The Sacrifice of the *tjösnur*." Three squares should be marked round the hide, each one foot broad. At the outermost corners of the squares should be four poles, called hazels; when this is done, it is a hazelled field. Each man should have three shields, and when they were cut up he must get upon the hide if he had given way from it before, and guard himself with his weapons alone thereafter. He who had been challenged should strike the first stroke. If one was wounded so that blood fell upon the hide, he should fight no longer. If either set one foot outside the hazel poles "he went on his heel," they said; but he "ran" if both feet were outside. His own man was to hold the shield before each of the fighters. The one who was wounded should pay three marks of silver to be set free.

So the hide was taken and spread under their feet. Thorgils held his brother's shield, and Thórd Arndísarson that of Bersi. Bersi struck the first blow, and cleft Cormac's shield; Cormac struck at Bersi to the like peril. Each of them cut up and spoilt three shields of the other's. Then it was Cormac's turn. He struck at Bersi, who parried with Whitting. Sköfnung cut the point off Whitting in front of the ridge. The sword-point flew upon Cormac's hand, and he was wounded in the thumb. The joint was cleft, and blood dropped upon the hide. Thereupon folk went between them and stayed the fight.

Then said Cormac, "This is a mean victory that Bersi has gained; it is only from my bad luck; and yet we must part."

He flung down his sword, and it met Bersi's target. A shard was broken out of Sköfnung, and fire flew out of Thorveig's gift.

Bersi asked the money for release, Cormac said it would be paid; and so they parted.

Father and Son

961

Egils saga

THE story of Egil's visit to King Athelstan in England in 937 and the ode which he composed to save his life on another visit to England in

948, as well as the poem about the loss of his two sons, appear elsewhere in this book.

◄§Bodvar, son of Egil, was then well grown. He was the best make of man, fair to look upon, big and strong, like as had been Egil or Thorolf at his age. Egil loved him greatly, and Bodvar withal was dearly fond of him.

That was one summer, that a ship was in Whitewater, and there was there a great cheaping-fair. Egil had there bought much wood and let flit it home ashipboard: his housecarles went, and had an eight-oared ship that belonged to Egil. That was then on a time, that Bodvar begged to fare with them, and they granted him that. Fared he then up to the Meads with the housecarles. They were six in company in the eight-oared ship, and when they should fare down again then was the flood-tide late in the day, and since they needs must bide for it, then fared they late in the evening. Then leapt up a raging south-wester, and there went against it the outfall of the tide. Then it made heavy seas in the firth, as there can oft-times befall there. Ended it so, that the ship foundered under them, and they were all lost.

But the day after were the bodies thrown up ashore. Bodvar's body came in by Einarsness, but some came on the south side of the firth, and thither drave the ship: that was found up by Reekhammer. That day learned Egil these tidings, and straightway rode he to look for the bodies. He found, washed ashore, the body of Bodvar. Took he that up, and set it on his knees, and rode with it out to Digraness, to Skallagrim's howe. He let then open the howe, and laid Bodvar down there beside Skallagrim. Thereafter was the howe shut again; and the work was not ended until about day-set time. After that, rode Egil home to Burg.

And when he came home, then went he straightway to that shut-bed that he was wont to sleep in. He laid him down and shot to the lock. None durst crave speech of him. Now so, it is said, was Egil arrayed, then when they set Bodvar down, that his hose were tied fast at the leg: he had a kirtle of red fustian, tight in the upper part, and laced at the sides. But that is the tale of men, that he was swollen so that the kirtle burst on him, and the hose likewise.

But the day after, Egil opened not the shut-bed. He had then, too, neither meat nor drink. Lay he there that day and the night after. Not a man durst to speak with him.

But the third morning, soon as it was light, Asgerd let set a man a-horseback: rode that one his hardest west to Herdholt, and let say to Thorgerd all these tidings at once. And that was about the time of nones when he came there. He said that withal, that Asgerd had sent word to her to come, first she might, south to Burg. Thorgerd let straightway saddle her a horse, and there followed her two men. Rode they that evening and through the night, until they came to Burg. Thorgerd walked straightway into the fire-house.

Asgerd hailed her, and asked whether they had eaten supper.

Thorgerd saith loudly: "Nought have I had of supper, nor nought will I, till it be at Freyja's. Know I no better rede for me than my father's. No will have I to live after my father and brother."

She went to the shut chamber and called, "Father, open up the door. I will that we two fare one way, both of us."

Egil sprang the lock. Thorgerd went up into the bed-chamber and locked the door behind her. She laid her down in another bed that was there. Then spake Egil: "Well doest thou, daughter, sith thou wilt follow thy father. Dear love hast thou shown unto me. What hope is there that I should have the will to live with this sorrow?"

And now held they their peace for a while.

Then spake Egil: "What is it now, daughter? Chewest thou now somewhat?"

"I chew dulse," saith she; "because I am minded that then will it be worse with me than before. I am minded that else will I be overlong alive."

"Is that bad for a man?" saith Egil.

"Exceeding bad," saith she. "Wilt thou eat?"

"What can it matter?" saith he.

But a while later called she and bade give her to drink. So now was given her water to drink.

Then spake Egil: "So worketh it with one that eateth dulse, thirsteth he aye the more for that."

"Wilt thou drink, father?" saith she.

He took it, and swallowed a big draught, and that was in a beast's horn.

Then spake Thorgerd: "Now are we cheated! This is milk."

Then bit Egil a shard out of the horn, all that his teeth took hold on, and therewith cast down the horn.

Then spake Thorgerd: "What rede shall we two now take to? 'Tis ended now with this plan. Now would I, father, that we two lengthen our life, so that thou mightest work a funeral song after Bodvar; and I will score it on a roller; and then let us two die if it seems us good. Slow methinks will thy son Thorstein be to work the song after Bodvar, and that would not do if there were no right funeral held for him. For I am not minded that we two shall be sitting at the drinking of his funeral feast."

Egil saith that that was then not to be looked for, that he would have might to work then though he sought to: "Yet try this I may," saith he. Egil had then had a son that was named Gunnar, and that one too had died a little before.

* * *

Egil began to be brisk as it went forward with working of the song. And when the song was ended, then said he it over to Asgerd and Thorgerd and them of his household. Rose he then up out of his bed, and sat him in his high seat. This song called he *Sons' Wreck*.

Thereafter let Egil hold funeral for his sons after the ancient manner. But when Thorgerd fared home, then Egil led her on her way with gifts.

Gisli the Outlaw

978

Gísla saga Súrssonar

GISLI, like Grettir, was a man of noble and generous nature who had the misfortune to be outlawed. He, too, remained in Iceland, sheltered by friends and fleeing from place to place, until he met his death in the manner related here.

GISLI was at home all that summer, and all was now quiet. Then came the last night of the summer season. It is said that Gisli could not sleep, nor anyone of the three, Gisli, Aud, and Gudrid. The weather had so passed that there was exceeding calm, and there fell a great hoar-frost. Gisli said that he wished to go from the house to his hiding place to the south under the cliffs to see if he might sleep better.

Thither they fared, all of them. The two women were wearing kirtles, and their tunics brushed the dew and left tracks behind. Gisli was carrying a stick and cut runes upon it, and the chips fell to the ground.

At last they came to the hiding place. Gisli lay down and would know whether he could sleep, and the two women watched wakeful beside him. There came upon him great heaviness of sleep, and he dreamed that birds flew into the house and struck at him very stealthily. They were larger than cock-ptarmigans. Awful and hideous was the sound they made, and from the looks of them it seemed as if they had wallowed in blood and gore.

Aud then asked him what he had dreamed: "Again these were not good dreams thou hast just had?"

Gisli answered in a strophe:

"To my ears came a sound in the house that was erstwhile
My home by the river, the blood of the earth,
Such time as we left, O Bil, goddess of weaving.
Then verses I made, wonted drink of the dwarfs
When I, stalwart tree of the sword-speaking battle,
Heard flutter of birds, two male-angered partridge.
The rain of the bow, the battle will be
Soon centered around me, who ne'er was found flinching."

When he had spoken this, they all heard voices of men. Eyjolf had come there and fourteen men with him. He had first gone to the house and saw the tracks in the dew as plainly as if someone had shown them the way. And when Gisli, Aud, and Gudrid became aware of the men, they went up on the cliff where was the best vantage ground. Each of the women had a great club in her hands. Eyjolf and his men came beneath them. He called up to Gisli on the cliff: "It is now my advice to thee that thou no longer refuse meeting and let thyself no more be chased about like a faint-hearted man, for thou art called a man the most fearless. Not short has been the time between our meetings, and it is our wish that this be the last."

Gisli made answer: "Come on like men because I shall no longer seek to avoid thee. Thy duty it is, Eyjolf, to come at me first thyself, because thou hast business with me greater than other men here in thy party."

"I shall not leave it to thy judgment," said Eyjolf, "how I shall divide my strength."

"This was also rather likely, thou cowardly bitch," said Gisli, "that thou wouldst not dare thyself to trade weapons with me."

Eyjolf then said to Spying Helgi: "Great renown would be thine if thou shouldst rush first up the cliff at Gisli. The deed would live long to thy fame."

"Oft have I this proven," replied Helgi, "that thou wilt have others ahead of thee oftenest where there is some trial of courage; but for this reason, that thou urgest me so eagerly, I shall take thy counsel. But see to it that thou follow me bravely and go next after me, if thou hast not entirely a woman's heart in thee."

Helgi then moved to the attack where it seemed most likely and favorable. He had a great ax in his hands.

Gisli was fitted out thus: he had an ax in his hands and was girded with a sword and a shield at his side; he was dressed in a gray, cowled cloak, which was tied tightly to him by a rope.

Helgi took a run and ran up the cliff toward Gisli. Gisli turned quickly toward him, and raising his sword in the air, drove it down to his loins, so that it cleft him apart in the middle, and he fell in two parts down over the cliff.

Eyjolf came up at another place. Aud went there against him and struck him on the hand with her club, so that his hand lost all its grip and power, and he reeled over backwards.

Then said Gisli: "This have I known a long time, that I was well married, but I knew not that I was so well mated as I am. But less help thou hast shown to me now than thou wishest or hast intended, though great was thy daring, because both Helgi and Eyjolf might have by now fared the same journey."

Two men now went to hold Aud and Gudrid fast, and they thought they had enough to do. The other twelve went after Gisli and came up the sides of the cliff, but he so warded himself both with stones and weapons that great was the fame of his deed thereafter.

A companion of Eyjolf ran forward alone and called to Gisli: "Give up to me thy weapons, the good ones thou art bearing, all of them together, and with them Aud, thy wife."

Gisli answered: "Come and get them undaunted, for by no means suit thee the weapons which I have owned, nor such a woman."

Eyjolf hurled a spear at Gisli, but Gisli in turn cleft the spear from the handle, and the blow was so great that the ax struck on a flat stone and the head broke. Then he threw away the ax and seized his sword and fought with it and warded himself with his shield. The men attacked with fury, but he defended himself well and with great valor. They came on hard and fast, and Gisli slew two more of them. That made four who had been killed.

Eyjolf now urged his men to press on their boldest. "Not easy are we getting off," said he, "and of little worth would it be to our fame, even if good ending were the reward of our labors."

When it was least expected, Gisli turned from them and leaped from the cliff up to a crag which is called Einhamar. There he turned at bay. This move came to them unawares. Now seemed their situation less comfortable to them—with four men slain and they, the rest, wounded and weary. So there was a lull in the attack. Afterwards Eyjolf urged them on hard and made them fair promises if they should lay hold of Gisli.

Eyjolf had a body of men with him picked for their valor and hardihood. There was one man named Svein. He was the first to run up the crag against Gisli. Gisli hewed at him and split him down to the shoulders and threw him over the precipice. Then seemed they not to know when the deaths at the hands of this man would come to an end.

Gisli then shouted to Eyjolf: "These three things would I have as my wish, that thou shalt have most dearly bought the three hundred silver which thou hast taken for my head; that thou wouldst be willing to add to it another three hundred that we two had never met; and that thou wilt carry away with thee disgrace and shame for the loss of life."

Eyjolf and the rest now took counsel and decided not to turn back even if it should cost them their lives. They set upon Gisli from two sides, and following foremost upon Eyjolf's heels were two kinsmen of his. One of them was called Thorir and the other, Thord. They were the most fearless of men. The onslaught grew hard and fierce, and they were able to bring upon him some wounds from spear-thrusts. Still he kept them off with great daring and valor, and they had such hard treatment from him with stones and mighty strokes that none was unwounded who came at him.

Eyjolf and his two kinsmen pressed on hard, for they saw that therein lay their honor and reputation. They set upon him with spears so that his bowels fell out, but he gathered them up in his kirtle and fastened it behind with rope. Then he said to them that they should abide a little—"Ye shall soon have to this the end ye have been seeking."

Then he spoke a verse:

My Fulla, fair faced, the goddess of stones
Who gladdens me much, shall hear of her friend
Standing straight, unafraid in the rain of the spears,
Calm courage showing. My mind is at rest
Though raised high aloft the sword edges bite me.
Such prowess my father gave to his son.

This was the last strophe by Gisli, and as soon as he had uttered it, he straightway leaped down from the crag and brought his sword down upon the head of Thord, Eyjolf's kinsman, so that he forthwith came by his death. There Gisli, too, fell on top of him and breathed his last. They were all sorely wounded, the companions of Eyjolf.

Gisli himself lost his life from so many deep gashes that it seemed a strange and wonderful thing he could have so long endured them. Thus did his enemies speak of him, that he took not a step backward; nor did they see that his strokes were weaker, the last than the first. Here closes the life of Gisli and it is commonly said that he was a most valiant man, though not in every way a lucky one.

They turned his body over and took his sword from him. Then they buried him there in the stones and went down to the sea. There at the water's edge a sixth man died of his wounds.

Eyjolf asked Aud to go away with him, but she would not. After that, he and the rest fared home to Otradale. And the same night a seventh man died of his wounds and the eighth lay ill twelve months, when death took him. The others became well again, those who had been wounded, though they lived not down the disgrace.

And it is spoken by all men that never had there been here in Iceland so famous a stand made by one man alone, so far as men know for truth.

Frustrated Lovers

984-1011

Gunnlaugs saga ormstungu

WHILE Gunnlaug the poet was abroad, Helga the Fair married his rival. The love of Gunnlaug and Helga was a lifelong passion.

§IN the summer Thorstein made ready to go to the Thing, and he said to his wife before he went away:

"It so happens," he says, "that thou art with child; and if thou

givest birth to a girl-child, she shall be borne out and exposed, but if
it is a boy, rear him up." For that was the custom, while the land was
pagan, that poor men with many children let bear their infants out;
and yet men thought that the thing was always ill-done. And when
Thorstein had said this, Jofrid answered:

"That speech is not fitting for thee," she says, "considering thy
position; and it will not seem right for thee to have this done, when
thou art so well-off." Thorstein made answer,

"Thou knowest my nature," he said; "and things go not well if it
is aroused."

Then he rode to the Thing. Jofrid gave birth to a very fair girl-
child. The women wished to carry it to her, but she said there was
little need of it; and she caused her herdsman to be summoned, who
was called Thorvard, and she said to him:

"Take thou my horse and saddle it, and bear this child westwards to
Thorgerda Egil's daughter in Hjardarholt, and bid her rear it up
in secret, so that Thorstein knows naught of it. So tenderly I regard
this babe that surely I can not bear to have it exposed. Here be three
silver marks that thou shalt have in payment. And then Thorgerda
shall give thee western passage and provisions for the sea."

Thorvard did as she said. He rode west to Hjardarholt with the
child and gave it into Thorgerda's hands. She had a tenant of hers,
who dwelt in on Leysingjastead on Hvamsfirth, rear up the child.
And she gave Thorvard passage north to Steingrimsfirth in Skeljavik,
and provisions for a sea voyage. And he journeyed thence; and so he
is out of the saga.

When Thorstein came home from the Thing, Jofrid told him that
the child was exposed, as he had said before, and that the herdsman
had run away and stolen her horse. Thorstein said she had done well,
and got him another herdsman.

Now six winters pass by, and nothing was known of the matter.
Then Thorstein rode west to a feast in Hjardarholt at the house of
Olaf the Peacock, his kinsman, son of Hauskuld, who was held to be
a man of the greatest esteem among all the great men there in the
west. Thorstein was well received, as was fitting. And it is said that
one day of the feast Thorgerda sat talking with Thorstein her brother
on the dais, for Olaf was holding speech with another man. Opposite
them on the benches sat three maidens. Then Thorgerda said,

"What dost thou think, brother, of the maids that sit there opposite us?" He answered,

"Very highly," he says, "and there is one of them by far the fairest, who has the good looks of Olaf, but the fairness and features of us Myramen." Thorgerda replies,

"True it is, brother, as thou hast said, that she has the fairness and the features of us Myramen, but not that she has the good looks of Olaf the Peacock, for she is not his daughter."

"How may that be?" says Thorstein; "is she not thy daughter?" She answers,

"To tell thee truth, kinsman," she says, "that fair maid is thy daughter, not mine"; and therewith she told him all that had chanced, and asked him to forgive her and his wife for this wrong. Thorstein said,

"I cannot reproach you two for this, for naught can escape its fate. Ye two have well outwitted my foolishness. It seems to me now that there is great happiness in having a child as fair as this maid. And how is she called?"

"She is hight Helga," says Thorgerda.

"Helga the Fair," says Thorstein. "Now thou shalt make ready her journey home with me." And she did so.

Thorstein was sent away with rich gifts, and Helga rode home with him; and she was reared up there with great love and esteem by her father and mother and all her kin.

* * *

Then Gunnlaug rode away, and about evening he came up at Borg; and Thorstein the Husbandman bade him stay there, and he accepted. Gunnlaug told Thorstein what had passed between him and his father. Thorstein bade him remain there for the time if he wished. So he abode there a year and received knowledge of the law from Thorstein, and all men thought well of him. He and Helga often entertained themselves at chess together: they were very quickly inclined to each other, as it turned out later. They were much the same age. Helga was so fair, that it was the saying of wise men that she was the fairest woman in Iceland. She had so much hair that it might cover her entirely, and it was as bright as gold; and there was no match like Helga the Fair in all Borgarfirth or anywhere beyond.

One day, while men were sitting in the dwelling room at Borg, Gunnlaug said to Thorstein,

"There is one case at law that thou hast not taught me; how to betroth me a wife." Thorstein said,

"That is but a small case"; and he made known to him the procedure. Then Gunnlaug said,

"Now thou shalt test whether I have understood: I shall take thy hand and make as if I were plighting troth with thy daughter Helga." Thorstein said,

"I think that is needless," quoth he. But Gunnlaug grasped his hand and said,

"Grant it me."

"Do as thou wilt," says Thorstein; "but these folk who stand by shall know that it shall be as if it had never been said, and there shall be no secret reservation to follow it."

Then Gunnlaug named his witnesses and betrothed Helga to himself, and he asked then whether that might be of some use. He said it might be so; and the men who were present had great game of it.

* * *

Now it is to be said of Hrafn that he is sitting at his wedding-feast in Borg; and it was told by many men that the bride was more heavy-hearted than not. For the saw is true that one longs for that which one had in his youth; and so it went with her.

* * *

There was little joyousness at the feast. And on the day when they were making ready to depart, the women were moving about and preparing to leave for home. Gunnlaug went up to Helga and they talked together a long time. Then Gunnlaug spoke a verse:

> "No day hath brought to the Snake-tongued joy
>> Under the heaven's span
> Since Helga the Fair is called by the name
>> Of Hrafn, and since the man
> Who is her father gave her for gold
>> And the promise-breaking began."

And again he spoke:

> "Goddess of wine, I have small thanks to yield
>> To thy mother, nor yet thy sire:
> Their daughter's fairness hath taken away
>> My joy in life entire;

> Yet true it is that they begot
>   Together the lovely maid:
> No fairer work of woman and man
>   Hath been in flesh arrayed."

Then Gunnlaug gave Helga the mantle which was Athelred's gift, a very great treasure. She thanked him well for the gift. After that Gunnlaug went out. A number of horses were come into the yard, and Gunnlaug leaped on the back of one of them and ran fiercely at the one before which Hrafn was standing, so that he had to back his horse.

"Why dost thou back, Hrafn," he said, "since now thou needest not fear me more; but thou knewest him thou hast dealt with." Then Hrafn spake a verse:

> "It fits us little, warrior
>   Who art so famed in strife,
> That we should fall a-quarreling
>   For the sake of any wife:
> Many women just as fair
>   The sun looks down upon:
> Bethink thee wisely, it were best
>   Thou doughty champion!"

Gunnlaug said,

"It may be that there are many such, but it does not seem so to me." Then Illugi and Thorstein sprang up, not wishing the two of them to fight. Then Gunnlaug spoke a verse:

> "The lovely gold-wearing woman hath been
>   Yielded to Hrafn for pay,
> Though I am esteemed his equal—no less,
>   As many speakers say;
> This chanced while Athelred held me back
>   From journeying home from him;
> Because he needed me in the fight
>   My joy in speech is dim."

After that the two rode home, and everything was peaceful and uneventful during the winter; and Hrafn had no good of his love towards Helga since she and Gunnlaug met.

Then the two of them, Hrafn and Gunnlaug, fought with great blows in fearless attack, each against the other, and smote each other fiercely, without break. Gunnlaug had the sword which was Athelred's gift with him, the best of weapons. Finally he struck Hrafn a mighty blow with the sword upon Hrafn's foot. Yet Hrafn did not fall, but retreated to a tree-stump and leaned upon it. Then said Gunnlaug,

"Now thou art out of the fight, and I will combat no longer with thee, a maimed man." Hrafn answered,

"It is true," quoth he, "that my fate hath played with me sorely; but it would help me much if I might have something to drink." Gunnlaug replied,

"Do me no treachery if I bring thee water in my helmet."

"I shall not betray thee," said Hrafn. Then Gunnlaug went to a spring and fetched some of it in his helmet and brought it to Hrafn. But he reached out for it with his left hand, and with the right he smote at Gunnlaug's head with his sword, and gave him a great wound. Then said Gunnlaug,

"Foully didst thou deceive me, and shamefully hast thou done when I trusted thee." Hrafn answered,

"It is true," he said, "but it came to this, that I could not let thee have the embrace of Helga the Fair." And again they fought fiercely. And finally it was so ended that Gunnlaug conquered Hrafn, and there he lost his life. Then the Earl's guides came forward and bound up the wound on Gunnlaug's head. He sat and spoke this verse:

"Brave was the warrior Hrafn when he
  Battled against a foe;
And in this combat none the less
  He hath fought truly so;
Many a blow was given this day
  That on Dingness laid us low."

Then they buried the dead men, and after that they bore Gunnlaug with them on his horse until they came up to Lifangr. And there he lay three nights and received the ministrations of a priest and thereafter he died and was buried by the church. And all men thought it great scathe about the two of them, Gunnlaug and Hrafn, and the ending of their lives.

Thorstein Egil's son gave his daughter Helga in marriage, after some time was past, to a man hight Thorkell Hallkell's son. He dwelt out in Hraundale, and Helga went to keep his house, but she loved him little, for she never forgot Gunnlaug, though he were dead. Yet Thorkell was a brave man of himself and wealthy, and a great skald. They had children together, not a few. Thorarin was the name of a son of theirs, and Thorstein; and they had many other children.

It was the greatest delight of Helga to unfold the cloak that was Gunnlaug's gift, and gaze long upon it. And one time there came a great sickness into the homestead of Thorkell and Helga, and many were afflicted for a long time. Helga too was taken ill, but she did not go to bed. One Saturday eve Helga sat in the fire-house and leaned her head on the knee of Thorkell her husband; and she sent for the cloak that was Gunnlaug's gift. And when it was brought to her, she sat up and unrolled it before her and gazed upon it for a time. Then she fell over in the lap of her husband and was dead.

Gunnar of Lithend

990

Njáls saga

NJÁLS SAGA is the last written and best of the five longer Icelandic family sagas. Fortunately it has been translated by a master of English prose, Sir George Webbe Dasent. Gunnar was one of the noblest characters of the saga age. The story of his glamorous but selfish wife is a classic.

◆§ NEXT autumn Mord Valgard's son sent word that Gunnar would be all alone at home, but all his people would be down in the isles to make an end of their haymaking. Then Gizur the white and Geir the priest rode east over the rivers as soon as ever they heard that, and so east across the sands to Hof. Then they sent word to Starkad under the Threecorner, and there they all met who were to fall on Gunnar, and took counsel how they might best bring it about.

Mord said that they could not come on Gunnar unawares, unless they seized the farmer who dwelt at the next homestead, whose name was Thorkell, and made him go against his will with them to lay hands on the hound Sam, and unless he went before them to the homestead to do this.

Then they set out east for Lithend, but sent to fetch Thorkell. They seized him and bound him, and gave him two choices—one that they would slay him, or else he must lay hands on the hound; but he chooses rather to save his life, and went with them.

There was a beaten sunk road, between fences, above the farmyard at Lithend, and there they halted with their band. Master Thorkell went up to the homestead, and the tyke lay on the top of the house, and he entices the dog away with him into a deep hollow in the path. Just then the hound sees that there are men before them, and he leaps on Thorkell and tears his belly open.

Aunund of Witchwood smote the hound on the head with his axe, so that the blade sunk into the brain. The hound gave such a great howl that they thought it passing strange, and he fell down dead.

Gunnar woke up in his hall and said—

"Thou hast been sorely treated, Sam, my fosterling, and this warning is so meant that our two deaths will not be far apart."

Gunnar's hall was made all of wood, and roofed with beams above, and there were window-slits under the beams that carried the roof, and they were fitted with shutters.

Gunnar slept in a loft above the hall, and so did Hallgerda and his mother.

Now when they were come near to the house they knew not whether Gunnar were at home, and bade that some one would go straight up to the house and see if he could find out. But the rest sat them down on the ground.

Thorgrim the Easterling went and began to climb up on the hall; Gunnar sees that a red kirtle passed before the windowslit, and thrusts out the bill, and smote him on the middle. Thorgrim's feet slipped from under him, and he dropped his shield, and down he toppled from the roof.

Then he goes to Gizur and his band as they sat on the ground.

Gizur looked at him and said—

"Well, is Gunnar at home?"

"Find out that for yourselves," said Thorgrim; "but this I am sure of, that his bill is at home," and with that he fell down dead.

Then they made for the buildings. Gunnar shot out arrows at them, and made a stout defence, and they could get nothing done. Then some of them got into the out houses and tried to attack him thence, but Gunnar found them out with his arrows there also, and still they could get nothing done.

So it went on for a while, then they took a rest, and made a second onslaught. Gunnar still shot out at them, and they could do nothing, and fell off the second time. Then Gizur the white said—

"Let us press on harder; nothing comes of our onslaught."

Then they made a third bout of it, and were long at it, and then they fell off again.

Gunnar said, "There lies an arrow outside on the wall, and it is one of their shafts; I will shoot at them with it, and it will be a shame to them if they get a hurt from their own weapons."

His mother said, "Do not so, my son; nor rouse them again when they have already fallen off from the attack."

But Gunnar caught up the arrow and shot it after them, and struck Eylif Aunund's son, and he got a great wound; he was standing all by himself, and they knew not that he was wounded.

"Out came an arm yonder," says Gizur, "and there was a gold ring on it, and took an arrow from the roof, and they would not look outside for shafts if there were enough in doors; and now ye shall make a fresh onslaught."

"Let us burn him house and all," said Mord.

"That shall never be," says Gizur, "though I knew that my life lay on it; but it is easy for thee to find out some plan, such a cunning man as thou art said to be."

Some ropes lay there on the ground, and they were often used to strengthen the roof. Then Mord said—"Let us take the ropes and throw one end over the end of the carrying beams, but let us fasten the other end to these rocks and twist them tight with levers, and so pull the roof off the hall."

So they took the ropes and all lent a hand to carry this out, and before Gunnar was aware of it, they had pulled the whole roof off the hall.

Then Gunnar still shoots with his bow so that they could never come nigh him. Then Mord said again that they must burn the house over Gunnar's head. But Gizur said—

"I know not why thou wilt speak of that which no one else wishes, and that shall never be."

Just then Thorbrand Thorleik's son sprang up on the roof, and cuts asunder Gunnar's bowstring. Gunnar clutches the bill with both hands, and turns on him quickly and drives it through him, and hurls him down on the ground.

Then up sprung Asbrand his brother. Gunnar thrusts at him with the bill, and he threw his shield before the blow, but the bill passed clean through the shield and broke both his arms, and down he fell from the wall.

Gunnar had already wounded eight men and slain those twain. By that time Gunnar had got two wounds, and all men said that he never once winced either at wounds or death.

Then Gunnar said to Hallgerda, "Give me two locks of thy hair, and ye two, my mother and thou, twist them together into a bow-string for me."

"Does aught lie on it?" she says.

"My life lies on it," he said; "for they will never come to close quarters with me if I can keep them off with my bow."

"Well!" she says, "Now I will call to thy mind that slap on the face which thou gavest me; and I care never a whit whether thou holdest out a long while or a short."

Then Gunnar sang a song—

"Each who hurls the gory javelin
Hath some honour of his own,
Now my helpmeet wimple-hooded
Hurries all my fame to earth.
No one owner of a war-ship
Often asks for little things,
Woman, fond of Frodi's flour,
Wends her hand as she is wont."

"Every one has something to boast of," says Gunnar, "and I will ask thee no more for this."

"Thou behavest ill," said Rannveig, "and this shame shall long be had in mind."

Gunnar made a stout and bold defence, and now wounds other eight men with such sore wounds that many lay at death's door. Gunnar keeps them all off until he fell worn out with toil. Then they wounded him with many and great wounds, but still he got away out of their hands, and held his own against them a while longer, but at last it came about that they slew him.

Of this defence of his, Thorkell the Skald of Gota-Elf sang in the verses which follow—

> "We have heard how south in Iceland
> Gunnar guarded well himself,
> Boldly battle's thunder wielding,
> Fiercest foeman on the wave;
> Hero of the golden collar,
> Sixteen with the sword he wounded;
> In the shock that Odin loveth,
> Two before him tasted death."

But this is what Thormod Olaf's son sang—

> "None that scattered sea's bright sunbeams,
> Won more glorious fame than Gunnar,
> So runs fame of old in Iceland,
> Fitting fame of heathen men;
> Lord of fight when helms were crashing,
> Lives of foeman twain he took,
> Wielding bitter steel he sorely
> Wounded twelve, and four besides."

Then Gizur spoke and said, "We have now laid low to earth a mighty chief, and hard work has it been, and the fame of this defence of his shall last as long as men live in this land."

After that he went to see Rannveig and said, "Wilt thou grant us earth here for two of our men who are dead, that they may lie in a cairn here?"

"All the more willingly for two," she says, "because I wish with all my heart I had to grant it to all of you."

"It must be forgiven thee," he says, to speak thus, "for thou hast had a great loss."

Then he gave orders that no man should spoil or rob anything there.

Conversion of Iceland

1000

Kristni saga

ICELAND was converted to Christianity not by the sword or by saints but by lawyers and logic. "At whom were the old gods angry when Mount

Hecla poured down the lava on which the Supreme Court of Iceland assembled?"

⋙ THEN came a man running and saying that *earth-fire* was come up in Aulfus, and that it would overrun the homestead of Thor-ord the gode. Then the heathen men began to say, "It is no wonder that the gods are wroth at such speeches." Then Snorre the gode spoke: "What were the gods wroth over then, when the lava on which we are now standing was burning here?"

After that men left the Rock of the Laws.

Then the Christian men prayed Hall o' Side to speak the law for them which should follow Christendom.

* * *

That summer the whole assembly of the Moot was baptized as men were riding home. Most of the Western-men were baptized in Reek-bath in South Reek-dale. Snorre gode had the greatest weight among the West-frith-men.

The summer when Christendom was taken into the laws of Iceland there were gone from the incarnation of our Lord Jesus Christ one thousand winters.

The Tale of Thorstein Staff-Smitten

c. 1000

Þórsteins þáttr stangarhöggs

THE son was manlier even than his noble father.

⋙ THERE was a man named Thorarin who lived in Sundale, an old man with poor eyesight. He had been a wild viking in his youth. He was not pleasant to deal with in spite of his years. He had one son, who was called Thorstein. The latter was a big man and strong and calm, and he labored so faithfully on his father's farm that the work of three men would not have been more useful. Thorarin was rather poor, but he had a large assortment of weapons. Father and son also owned a stud and made their living chiefly by selling horses, second to none for riding and horse-fighting. There was a man named Thord, a servant of Bjarni of Temple. He was in charge of Bjarni's riding horses and was therefore called Horse-Thord. Thord was an unjust man, and he let many people feel that he was a great man's servant; but he himself was no more worthy for that, and neither did it win him friends. Two other men stayed at Bjarni's, one named Thorhall, the other Thorvald. They were great gossips about everything they heard in the district.

Thorstein and Thord agreed on a horsefight with young stallions. And when they urged on the stallions, Thord's horse was slow to bite. When he saw his horse worsted, Thord gave Thorstein's horse a great blow on the muzzle, but Thorstein saw it and struck Thord's horse a still harder blow, whereupon Thord's horse ran off and there was great cheering. Then Thord struck Thorstein with the horse staff; it hit the eyebrow and tore it down over his eye. Thorstein ripped off a piece of his shirt, tied up the eyebrow, and acted as though nothing had happened. He asked that the matter be kept from his father, and no more was heard about it. Thorvald and Thorhall made sport of this and called him Thorstein Staff-Blow.

That winter a little before Christmas the women rose for work at Sundale. Thorstein rose also and carried in hay and afterwards lay down on a bench. Then his old father, Thorarin, came into the room and asked who was lying there. Thorstein said it was he. "Why are you up so early, son?" said old Thorarin. Thorstein answered and said: "I have few helpers to share the work here." "Aren't you suffering from headache, son?" asked old Thorarin. "Not so I can feel it," said Thorstein. "What can you tell me, son, about the horse-fight last summer? Weren't you knocked senseless, kinsman, like a dog?" "I find no honor," said Thorstein, "in calling it a blow rather than an accident." Thorarin retorted: "Never did I expect to have a cowardly son!" "Speak no more of this, father," said Thorstein, "lest you find you have said too much." "I shan't utter what I have a mind to say," returned Thorarin.

Now Thorstein got up and took his weapons and went from the house. He walked until he came to the stable in which Thord tended Bjarni's horses, and found Thord there. Thorstein approached him and said: "I should like to know, friend Thord, whether it was by accident that I caught a blow from you last summer at the horsefight —or was it on purpose? If so, you must make amends for it." Thord made answer: "If you have two cheeks, put your tongue into each in turn and call it first accident and then intent—and there you have all the amends you'll get from me." "Be prepared, then," said Thorstein, "if I don't claim them oftener." Then Thorstein ran at Thord and gave him his deathblow. After that he went to the house at Temple and met a woman outside and said to her: "Tell Bjarni that a bull has gored his groom, and that Thord will wait for him to come down to the stall." "Go on home, my man," said she; "I'll tell Bjarni when I get ready." Thorstein went home and the woman went about her work.

Bjarni got up that morning, and as he sat at breakfast he asked where Thord was. They answered that he must have gone to the horses. "But I think he would be home by now," said Bjarni, "if he were all right." Then up spoke the woman whom Thorstein had accosted earlier: "True it is, as they so often say of us women, that little understanding is to be found in us. Thorstein Staff-Blow came here this morning and said that a bull had injured Thord so that he couldn't help himself, but I didn't dare waken you then, and later it left my mind." Then Bjarni got up from table, went to the horse-stall, and found Thord slain there. Bjarni had him buried; presently he prosecuted and got Thorstein convicted for the slaying. But Thorstein sat at home in Sundale working for his father, and Bjarni left him in peace just the same.

In the fall the people of Temple sat around the singeing fires, while Bjarni lay outside along the wall of the kitchen and from there listened to the conversation. The brothers Thorhall and Thorvald began to talk: "We didn't suspect, when we hired out with Slayer-Bjarni, that we would sit here singeing lambs' heads while Thorstein, the outlaw, singes wethers. It would have been better for Bjarni to have spared somewhat his kinsmen in Bodvarsdale, for then no outlaw would be sitting as high as he in Sundale. But most men are forlorn when they themselves are wounded, and we don't know when he intends to wipe out this spot on his honor." A man spoke up: "Such things you had best be silent about—the trolls have fastened on to your tongue for sure. We think Bjarni is unwilling to take the only support from a blind father and the other helpless folk there in Sundale. But it will surprise me if you have many more chances to singe lambs' heads here or prattle about what took place in Bodvarsdale." Then they went to dinner and afterwards to bed, but Bjarni gave no sign of having heard the conversation.

The following morning Bjarni wakened Thorhall and Thorvald and ordered them to ride to Sundale and bring him Thorstein's severed head by breakfast time, saying: "I consider you best suited to remove the spot from my honor, in case I don't have the manhood to do it myself." Now they saw for certain that they had said too much, but they went nevertheless and arrived at Sundale. Thorstein stood in the doorway whetting a sword. When they got up to him he asked where they were going, and they said they were searching for stray horses. Thorstein said they'd not have far to seek, since there were some near the fence hard by. "We're not sure of finding the horses unless you point them out more closely." Thorstein accordingly went out with them. And when they got down in the yard Thorvald raised his ax and ran at him, but Thorstein gave him a shove so that he fell and then drove his sword through him. Then Thorhall tried to get at him and met the same fate as Thorvald. Afterwards Thorstein tied them both onto their horses and bound up the reins; he led the horses into the path and they went home to Temple. Some serving-men were outside at Temple, and they went in and told Bjarni that Thorvald and Thorhall had returned, adding that their journey hadn't been in vain. Bjarni now went out and saw at once how things stood, but said nothing further. He had the bodies buried.

All was quiet until after Christmas. Then Rannveig took to speech one evening after they had gone to bed, she and Bjarni: "What do you think is oftenest talked about here in the district?" she began. "I don't know," said Bjarni; "there are many whose chatter isn't worth notice." "The question people ask themselves most is what Thorstein Staff-Blow will have to do before you see any need to avenge yourself. He has now slain three of your men. Your followers will think they have small prospect of support from you, if this remains unavenged, and you foolishly content to rest your hands on your knees." Bjarni replied: "Now it comes about, as the proverb has it, that no man takes warning from his neighbor's misfortune, and I shall do as you demand. But not without cause has Thorstein committed slayings." They stopped talking and slept the rest of the night. In the morning Rannveig woke up as Bjarni was taking down his shield from the wall, and she asked where he was bound for. "I'm going to match my worth against that of Thorstein of Sundale," he replied. "How many men will you take with you?" she asked. "I'll not gather a throng to meet Thorstein," said he; "I'm going alone." "Don't venture alone against that fiend's weapons!" she urged. Bjarni rejoined: "Don't be like those women who bewail one moment what they urged the moment before. I have put up with many a jeer from you and others; but there's no use hindering me when I am resolved to go."

Bjarni then rode to Sundale. Thorstein stood in the doorway, and they exchanged a few words. Bjarni said: "You shall do single combat with me today, Thorstein, on this hillock here in the yard." "I'm lacking in all that's required for duelling with you," answered Thorstein, "but I shall sail abroad as soon as ships can travel, for I know your character and that you will give my father assistance, if I go away." "There is no use in trying to talk yourself out of it," said Bjarni. "Then let me speak with my father first," said Thorstein. "Willingly," said Bjarni. Thorstein went in and told his father that Bjarni had come and challenged him to single combat. Old man Thorarin answered: "Any man who contends with a more powerful man in the neighborhood and has done him some harm, may expect not to wear out many more shirts. I can't lament you, for I think you have given much offence. Now take your weapons and defend yourself boldly, for I recall that in my day I should not have yielded to the likes of Bjarni, though he is a first-class warrior. And I think it better to lose you than to have a cowardly son."

Now Thorstein went out, and the two men went up on the hillock. They took to fighting savagely and came near chopping each other's shields to bits. And when they had fought a long time Bjarni said to Thorstein: "I am thirsty, for I am less used to such work than you." "Go to the brook then and drink," said Thorstein. Bjarni did so and laid his sword down beside him. Thorstein picked it up, looked at it, and said: "It couldn't have been this sword you had in Bodvarsdale." Bjarni didn't answer. They went back up on the hillock and fought again for a while, and Bjarni found the man a good fighter and more firm in meeting blows than he had expected. "Much happens to me today," he said; "now my shoestring has come loose." "Tie it," said Thorstein. Now Bjarni bent down, and Thorstein went in and fetched out two shields and a sword. He went up to Bjarni on the hill and said to him: "Here is a shield and a sword that my father sends you, and this blade won't grow more dull from chopping than the one you've been using. And I don't intend to stand shieldless under your blows any longer; but I should like to cease this game, for I fear that your good fortune will outweigh my bad luck, and every man looks to his own life at all odds, if he has anything to say about it." "It will do no good to beg off," said Bjarni; "we shall go on fighting." "I'll not strike first," said Thorstein. Then Bjarni hewed down Thorstein's whole shield, and Thorstein promptly hewed Bjarni's shield. "That's stout fighting," said Bjarni. "Your blows are just as stout," answered Thorstein. Bjarni continued: "The sword you've been using right along bites harder now." Thorstein said: "I'd willingly save myself misfortune, if I could, and it is with trembling I fight you. I should like still to leave our quarrel in your hands for settlement." It was Bjarni's turn to strike, and the two of them stood there uncovered. Then Bjarni said: "An evil deed would be poor reward for good fortune. I'll hold myself well compensated for my three men with you alone, if you will be faithful to me." Thorstein said: "I've had chance enough today to play you foul, if my misfortune had been stronger than your luck; and neither shall I betray you henceforth." "I see that you are superior to other men," said Bjarni; "you must allow me to go in to your father and tell him what I choose." "You have my leave to do as you wish," said Thorstein, "but act with care."

Bjarni went to the chamber in which old Thorarin lay. Thorarin asked who it was, and Bjarni revealed himself. "What tidings do you bring, friend Bjarni?" asked Thorarin. "The slaying of your son Thorstein," replied Bjarni. "Did he give much account of himself?" said Thorarin. "I can think of no man more bold in the use of weapons than your son Thorstein." "It's not strange," said the old man, "that you were hard to deal with in Bodvarsdale, if you have overcome my son." Then Bjarni said: "I wish to invite you to Temple, and you shall sit in the high seat opposite me while you live, and I shall be as a son to you." "My case is that of one who is powerless," said old Thorarin, "and a foolish man rejoices at promises. But the promises of you chieftains, when you wish to comfort a man after an event like this, are such as to give a month's peace of mind; thereafter we are treated like any other pauper, and our grief is little diminished by that. Nevertheless, he who gets a handshake and a promise from such a man as you should envy his lot, whatever they say; and I shall accept this offer of yours. Therefore come in to me— you must step close, for the old man is trembling to his very feet from weakness and old age, and it's not to be denied that the death of my son has shaken me." Bjarni thereupon went into the bedroom and took old Thorarin's hand. He then saw that the latter was fingering a sword and was about to run it through him. He jerked back his hand and shouted: "You most miserable of wretches! Now you will get what you deserve: your son Thorstein is alive, and he will go home with me to Temple, while you shall have only thralls to do your work for you; but you shall want for nothing during your lifetime." Thorstein thereafter followed Bjarni back to Temple and stayed with him to his death, and he was thought almost without peer for manhood and courage.

Bonnet and Sword

1002

Laxdæla saga

THE Saga of the Men of Laxdale is one of the five longer family sagas of Iceland. Guthrun was a woman whose ability equalled her overwhelming beauty. If she had been placed within a larger horizon, she could have played the role of a Queen Elizabeth or an Empress Catherine the Great. She was four times a widow. In her old age her son asked which man she had loved the most, and she indicated Kjartan, the lover whom she did not marry and whose violent death she instigated: "I was the worst to him I loved the best."

⋖§ KALF ASGEIRSON had been in Norway over the winter, having returned from England the previous autumn with the ship and trade-goods belonging to Kjartan and himself. And so soon as Kjartan had got his leave for the Iceland-voyage, Kalf and he set about their preparations; and when their ship was ready for the sea, then Kjartan went to see the king's sister Ingibjörg. She received him cordially and made room for him to sit beside her and they fell to talking. Kjartan then told Ingibjörg that he was ready to set sail for Iceland. Then she answered him, "It is our belief, Kjartan, that you have decided on this more out of your own willfulness than because anyone has provoked you to leave Norway and go away to Iceland." And there were few words passed between them after this. Presently Ingibjörg put out her hand to a mead-tankard standing by her side and brought out of it a white gold-worked bonnet and gave it to Kjartan, and she told him this would be quite good enough for Gudrun Osvifs-daughter to wrap about her head, "and you are to give her the bonnet for a wedding gift. I want the Icelandish women to know that the woman is not slave-born that you have been talking with while in

Norway." There was also a satin poke for a covering for the bonnet.
It was altogether an ornament of the rarest value. "I shall not be
seeing you off at all," said Ingibjörg, "and now farewell, and good
luck." Then Kjartan stood up and kissed Ingibjörg, and the story
goes that they found it hard to part.

Kjartan then went his way to the king, and told the king that he
was then all ready to go. King Olaf saw Kjartan off to the ship, and
a large company went down with him. And when they got to the ship
where it lay afloat with a single gangplank ashore, then the king
spoke up and said, "Here is a sword, Kjartan, which I wish you to
take as a parting gift from me. Let this weapon ever keep you company; for I believe that point or edge shall not touch you so long
as you carry this sword." It was a noble weapon and richly orna-
mented. Kjartan thanked the king with many fair words for all the
honors and preferment he had shown him while he had been in Norway. Then said the king, "This will I beg of you, Kjartan, that you
keep the faith wholly." So then the king and Kjartan took leave of
one another with great affection and Kjartan went aboard the ship.
The king stood looking out after him and said, "Many things and
great are told and expected of Kjartan and his kindred, and yet it
will be unhandy to turn aside their destiny."

*　*　*

Olaf and Osvif held to their friendship as before, even though
there was some hard feeling between the younger folks. This year
Olaf gave a banquet at his home a fortnight before the coming of
winter. And Osvif at the same time had made preparations for a
feast at the Winter Nights. So each of them invited the other to
come to the feast with as large a company as either thought would
do him the most honor. It was Osvif's turn to come first to the feast
at Olaf's, and he came to Hjardarholt at the appointed time. In his
company were Bolli and Gudrun and Osvif's sons. Next morning
when the company were on their way down the length of the hall, one
of the serving-women raised the question, in what order the women
guests were to be seated at table. It so happened that Gudrun was
just then coming along opposite the closet-bed in which Kjartan
usually slept. At that time Kjartan was dressing and was just putting
on his red scarlet coat. And Kjartan then spoke to the woman who
asked about the order of seating, as no one else spoke up, and told
her, "Hrefna is to sit in the highseat. And she is to bear the honors

before them all, so long as I am alive." But up to this time Gudrun
had always sat in the highseat, at Hjardarholt and elsewhere. Gudrun heard what was said and looked up at Kjartan, and she changed
color but said nothing. Next day Gudrun talked with Hrefna and
asked her to put on the Bonnet and let the folks see this most notable
ornament that had ever come to Iceland. Kjartan was there, though
not right near, and had overheard what Gudrun was saying. He was
quicker to find an answer than Hrefna. "She will not deck herself
out with the Bonnet in this company. For it means more to me that
Hrefna has got the best there is than to make a spectacle of it for
the crowd of guests today." This autumn festival at Olaf's was to
last a week's time. On the next day following Gudrun talked again
with Hrefna privately and asked her to let her see the Bonnet. She
consented. Later in the day they went out to the storehouse where
valuable things were kept. Hrefna then opened a chest and brought
out a satin poke, and out of the poke she took out the headdress and
showed it to Gudrun. She spread it open and looked it over for a
while and said nothing, neither good nor bad. Presently Hrefna put
the Bonnet away and they went back to their places in the hall. And
so time passed in sport and merrymaking.

Now on the day when the guests were taking leave and riding
away, Kjartan was taken up with looking after horses and riding-
gear for such of them as had come a long ways and needed anything
of the kind. Kjartan had not been carrying his sword, the king's
gift, about with him while he was looking after these things; although it was his habit very rarely to leave it out of his reach.
Afterwards he went to his closet-bed, where he had left the sword,
and it was then gone. He went directly to his father and told him.
Olaf said, "We will go about this very quietly; and I will get men
to go along and keep watch of every crowd as they ride away." And
so he did.

Án the White was to ride along with Osvif's folks and keep watch
of anyone who might go off to the side or fall behind. They were
riding up country by way of Ljárskog, past the farmstead known as
In-the-Skog, and they made a stop here at Skog and dismounted.
Osvif's son Thorolf with several others went off to one side, away
from the farmstead. They disappeared into a clump of underbrush
while the halt was made at Skog. Án kept company with the riders
as far as the Laxá river, where it comes down out of the Sælingsdal,

and there he took leave of them to turn back. Thorolf let him know that it would have been quite all right even if he had not come with them at all. During the previous night a very light snow had fallen, so that it was easy trailing. Án rode back to the Ljárskog woods and followed Thorolf's trail down to a certain spring or marshy place. There he groped about under water and put his hand on the sword-hilts. Án wanted witnesses to this affair, and so he rode back to Thorarin, at the Sælingsdal Tunga, and he went back with Án to see him take up the sword. Án thereupon carried the sword to Kjartan. Kjartan wrapped it in cloth and laid it away in a chest. The place is known as the Sword-Well where Thorolf thrust the king's-gift into hiding. Nothing was done about this, but the scabbard was never found again. Kjartan was more careful of the sword after this than before. Kjartan took all this to heart and was not willing to let it pass. But Olaf told him, "Let not this thing trouble you. They have turned a mean trick; but it is really no matter. Let us not be made sport of for making a feud out of all this, in such a case where we have to do with our own friends and kinsfolk." And on Olaf's advice Kjartan let it pass.

Presently it was Olaf's turn to go as a guest to the Winter-Nights festival to be held at Laugar, and he spoke to Kjartan about it and asked him to come along. Kjartan held back, but still he agreed to go at his father's insistence. Hrefna was to go, too, and was for leaving the Bonnet at home. But her mother-in-law Thorgerd asked her the question, "When are you to make use of such a splendid ornament, if it is to be left locked up at home when you go visiting?" Hrefna answered, "There are those who say that I could quite easily go to places where there are fewer to envy me than at Laugar." Thorgerd said, "We need not believe much of what anyone says who carries tales of that kind between neighbors." And so, seeing that Thorgerd was obstinately set on it, Hrefna wore the Bonnet; and Kjartan made no objection when he saw that his mother would have it so.

So then they set out and reached Laugar by nightfall and there they were welcomed cordially. Thorgerd and Hrefna handed over their wraps to be taken care of. But next morning, when the women were dressing, Hrefna looked for the Bonnet and it was then gone from the place where she had left it for safe-keeping. Search was made for it all over the place but it was not found. Gudrun said it was most likely the Bonnet had been left at home, or she might have been careless about it and dropped it somewhere. Hrefna then told Kjartan that the Bonnet had disappeared. He gave her the answer that it was not easy to keep an eye on these folks and asked her to let it pass. Then he told his father how the game was going. Olaf told him, "Once more I would have you do as before. Let it lie. Put up with the trouble and say nothing. I will look into this thing on the quiet. There is nothing I would not do to keep the peace between Bolli and you. Prevention is easier than cure, my son," said he. Kjartan replied, "It is quite plain, Father, that you wish everybody well. And yet, I don't know if I am willing to stand out of the way for these Lauga-folks at every turn."

On the day when the guests were taking their leave after the feast, Kjartan spoke up and said, "I hereby call on you to take notice, Cousin Bolli, that I count on you to deal more honestly with us hereafter than hitherto. I may as well speak out about it. For there already are many who know about these things that have been disappearing hereabout, and that we have reason to believe have found their way into your keeping. This fall, when we gave a feast at Hjardarholt, a sword of mine was taken. That came back, but not the scabbard. And now here again another article has been lost which would be considered to have value. And now I want both of them returned." Then said Bolli, "We are not at fault in these things that you charge us with, Kjartan. We might have looked for anything else from you, but not that you should be charging us with stealing." Kjartan replied, "We have reason to believe that there have been those persons concerned in this affair, for whom it is for you to make amends if you are so inclined. You have been crowding us more than there is any call for. We have long been trying to keep out of trouble with you. But I am now telling you openly that it will not do." Then Gudrun spoke up in answer to him and said, "You are raking up a fire now, Kjartan, which had better not be smoking. And then, even if it is as you say, that there are certain persons here who have taken pains to have the Bonnet disappear, then I should consider that such persons have only come into their own. You may believe anything you like about what has become of the headdress; but for my part, I am not sorry if it has been taken care of in such fashion that the Bonnet will not beautify Hrefna any more from this time on." After this they parted, with some ill-will. The Hjardarholt folks rode back home. The banquetings fell off after this. Still there might be said to be peace. No trace of the Bonnet was ever found.

The Burning of Njal

Autumn, 1011

Njáls saga

NJAL was an able farmer and a leader in the affairs of Iceland. He was a good neighbor, a man of peace, and his counsel was sought from far and wide. In his old age he became a patriarch at his homestead of Bergthorshvol. But his aggressive sons made many enemies, who finally united to burn the great homestead and destroy its inmates.

◦§ Now they took fire, and made a great pile before the doors. Then Skarphedinn said—

"What, lads! are ye lighting a fire, or are ye taking to cooking?"

"So it shall be," answered Grani Gunnar's son; "and thou shalt not need to be better done."

"Thou repayest me," said Skarphedinn, "as one may look for from the man that thou art. I avenged thy father, and thou settest most store by that duty which is farthest from thee."

Then the women threw whey on the fire, and quenched it as fast as they lit it. Some, too, brought water, or slops.

Then Kol Thorstein's son said to Flosi—

"A plan comes into my mind; I have seen a loft over the hall among the crosstrees, and we will put the fire in there, and light it with the vetch-stack that stands just above the house."

Then they took the vetch-stack and set fire to it, and they who were inside were not aware of it till the whole hall was a-blaze over their heads.

Then Flosi and his men made a great pile before each of the doors, and then the women folk who were inside began to weep and to wail.

Njal spoke to them and said, "Keep up your hearts, nor utter shrieks, for this is but a passing storm, and it will be long before ye have another such; and put your faith in God, and believe that he is so merciful that he will not let us burn both in this world and the next."

Such words of comfort had he for them all, and others still more strong.

Now the whole house began to blaze. Then Njal went to the door and said—

"Is Flosi so near that he can hear my voice?"

Flosi said that he could hear it.

"Wilt thou," said Njal, "take an atonement from my sons, or allow any men to go out?"

"I will not," answers Flosi, "take any atonement from thy sons, and now our dealings shall come to an end once for all, and I will not stir from this spot till they are all dead; but I will allow the women and children and house-carles to go out."

Then Njal went into the house, and said to the folk—

"Now all those must go out to whom leave is given, and so go thou out Thorhalla Asgrim's daughter, and all the people also with thee who may."

Then Thorhalla said—

"This is another parting between me and Helgi than I thought of a while ago; but still I will egg on my father and brothers to avenge this manscathe which is wrought here."

"Go, and good go with thee," said Njal, "for thou art a brave woman."

After that she went out and much folk with her.

Then Astrid of Deepback said to Helgi Njal's son—

"Come thou out with me, and I will throw a woman's cloak over thee, and tie thy head with a kerchief."

He spoke against it at first, but at last he did so at the prayer of others.

So Astrid wrapped the kerchief round Helgi's head, but Thorhilda, Skarphedinn's wife, threw the cloak over him, and he went out between them, and then Thorgerda Njal's daughter, and Helga her sister, and many other folk went out too.

But when Helgi came out Flosi said—

"That is a tall woman and broad across the shoulders that went yonder, take her and hold her."

But when Helgi heard that, he cast away the cloak. He had got his sword under his arm, and hewed at a man, and the blow fell on his shield and cut off the point of it, and the man's leg as well. Then Flosi came up and hewed at Helgi's neck, and took off his head at a stroke.

Then Flosi went to the door and called out to Njal, and said he would speak with him and Bergthora.

Now Njal does so, and Flosi said—

"I will offer thee, master Njal, leave to go out, for it is unworthy that thou shouldst burn indoors."

"I will not go out," said Njal, "for I am an old man, and little fitted to avenge my sons, but I will not live in shame."

Then Flosi said to Bergthora—

"Come thou out, housewife, for I will for no sake burn thee indoors."

"I was given away to Njal young," said Bergthora, "and I have promised him this, that we would both share the same fate."

After that they both went back into the house.

"What counsel shall we now take?" said Bergthora.

"We will go to our bed," said Njal, "and lay us down; I have long been eager for rest."

Then she said to the boy Thord, Kari's son—

"Thee will I take out, and thou shalt not burn in here."

"Thou hast promised me this, grandmother," says the boy, "that we should never part so long as I wished to be with thee; but methinks it is much better to die with thee and Njal than to live after you."

Then she bore the boy to her bed, and Njal spoke to his steward and said—

"Now shalt thou see where we lay us down, and how I lay us out, for I mean not to stir an inch hence, whether reek or burning smart me, and so thou wilt be able to guess where to look for our bones."

He said he would do so.

There had been an ox slaughtered and the hide lay there. Njal told the steward to spread the hide over them, and he did so.

So there they lay down both of them in their bed, and put the boy between them. Then they signed themselves and the boy with the cross, and gave over their souls into God's hand, and that was the last word that men heard them utter.

Then the steward took the hide and spread it over them, and went out afterwards. Kettle of the Mark caught hold of him, and dragged him out, he asked carefully after his father-in-law Njal, but the steward told him the whole truth. Then Kettle said—

"Great grief hath been sent on us, when we have had to share such ill-luck together."

Skarphedinn saw how his father laid him down, and how he laid himself out, and then he said—

"Our father goes early to bed, and that is what was to be looked for, for he is an old man."

Then Skarphedinn, and Kari, and Grim, caught the brands as fast as they dropped down, and hurled them out at them, and so it went on a while. Then they hurled spears in at them, but they caught them all as they flew, and sent them back again.

Then Flosi bade them cease shooting, "for all feats of arms will go hard with us when we deal with them; ye may well wait till the fire overcomes them."

So they do that, and shoot no more.

Then the great beams out of the roof began to fall, and Skarphedinn said—

"Now must my father be dead, and I have neither heard groan nor cough from him."

Then they went to the end of the hall, and there had fallen down a cross-beam inside which was much burnt in the middle.

Kari spoke to Skarphedinn, and said— "Leap thou out here, and I will help thee to do so, and I will leap out after thee, and then we shall both get away if we set about it so, for hitherward blows all the smoke."

"Thou shalt leap first," said Skarphedinn; "but I will leap straightway on thy heels."

"That is not wise," says Kari, "for I can get out well enough elsewhere, though it does not come about here."

"I will not do that," says Skarphedinn; "leap thou out first, but I will leap after thee at once."

"It is bidden to every man," says Kari, "to seek to save his life while he has a choice, and I will do so now; but still this parting of ours will be in such wise that we shall never see one another more; for if I leap out of the fire, I shall have no mind to leap back into the fire to thee, and then each of us will have to fare his own way."

"It joys me, brother-in-law," says Skarphedinn, "to think that if thou gettest away thou wilt avenge me."

Then Kari took up a blazing bench in his hand, and runs up along the cross-beam, then he hurls the bench out at the roof, and it fell among those who were outside.

Then they ran away, and by that time all Kari's upper clothing and his hair were a-blaze, then he threw himself down the roof, and so crept along with the smoke.

Then one man said who was nearest—

"Was that a man that leapt out at the roof?"

"Far from it," says another; "more likely it was Skarphedinn who hurled a firebrand at us."

After that they had no more mistrust.

Kari ran till he came to a stream, and then he threw himself down into it, and so quenched the fire on him.

After that he ran along under shelter of the smoke into a hollow, and rested him there, and that has since been called Kari's Hollow.

Now it is to be told of Skarphedinn that he runs out on the cross-beam straight after Kari, but when he came to where the beam was most burnt, then it broke down under him. Skarphedinn came down on his feet, and tried again the second time, and climbs up the wall with a run, then down on him came the wall-plate, and he toppled down again inside.

Then Skarphedinn said— "Now one can see what will come"; and then he went along the side wall. Gunnar Lambi's son leapt up on the wall and sees Skarphedinn, he spoke thus—

"Weepest thou now, Skarphedinn?"

"Not so," says Skarphedinn; "but true it is that the smoke makes one's eyes smart, but it is as it seems to me, dost thou laugh?"

"So it is surely," says Gunnar, "and I have never laughed since thou slewest Thrain on Markfleet."

Then Skarphedinn said— "Here now is a keepsake for thee"; and with that he took out of his purse the jaw-tooth which he had hewn out of Thrain, and threw it at Gunnar, and struck him in the eye, so that it started out and lay on his cheek.

Then Gunnar fell down from the roof.

Skarphedinn then went to his brother Grim, and they held one another by the hand and trode the fire; but when they came to the middle of the hall Grim fell down dead.

Then Skarphedinn went to the end of the house, and then there was a great crash, and down fell the roof. Skarphedinn was then shut in between it and the gable, and so he could not stir a step hence.

Flosi and his band stayed by the fire until it was broad daylight; then came a man riding up to them. Flosi asked him for his name, but he said his name was Geirmund, and that he was a kinsman of the sons of Sigfus.

"Ye have done a mighty deed," he says.

"Men," said Flosi, "will call it both a mighty deed and an ill deed, but that can't be helped now."

The Ghost of Glam

1014-1015

Grettis saga

THE Saga of Grettir the Strong is included with the five great family sagas. Grettir is historical, but the "Bear's Son" adventures attached to him are folklore. After his outlawry, he preferred to live a hunted life in Iceland, doing good deeds, and protected by friends, until he was finally slain on his island refuge.

NORTH in Iceland, among the mountains, in Waterdale, lived a man named Thorhall. He was a rich farmer and had more sheep than any one else in the valley. But he had this great trouble; his farm was haunted.

Thorhall's farm was so much haunted that he could scarcely get a shepherd to stay out his time. He asked all his friends what to do to scare away the spirits, and he tried all sorts of advice, and nothing did any good. At last he heard about a big Swede name Glam, who had come to Iceland. People said Glam was a first-class shepherd and too strong and ugly to be afraid of ghosts.

One day Thorhall was walking upon a mountain, when he saw a man coming toward him out of the woods, carrying brushwood on a horse. They soon met, and Thorhall asked his name. He said he was called Glam.

This man was very big indeed, strange and uncouth; his eyes were grey and glaring, and his hair grey like a wolf. Thorhall shivered when he saw him, and then he realized that this was the Swede. So he asked, "At what sort of work are you best?"

Glam growled, and said he was good at watching sheep in winter.

"Then will you take care of mine next winter?" asked Thorhall.

"On one condition," said Glam, gruffly, "that I do very much as I please. I have an ugly temper if things don't suit me."

"I am not afraid of that," replied Thorhall pleasantly. "I should like you to come to me."

"I'll do so," Glam said, "but is anything wrong at your place?"

"It is thought to be haunted," Thorhall admitted.

At that, Glam leaned back, and laughed a horrible guffaw. "Ha! Ha! Such bug-a-boos won't scare me. They make life more lively!"

"You'll need to be brave," said Thorhall. "My farm is no place for a coward."

After that they struck a bargain, and Glam was to come at the beginning of winter.

Summer passed, and Thorhall heard nothing about his shepherd, but at the appointed time he came to Thorhall-stead. Though the farmer received him well, the other farm-folks could not endure him, and the good-wife least of all.

Glam took to tending the sheep. They gave him little trouble, for he had a big, husky voice, and all the flock scrambled together as soon as he whooped.

Glam was not a religious man. In Sweden, where he came from, the people were still heathen, and Iceland had been Christian only a few years. Though there was a church at Thorhall-stead, Glam never went in. He hated the church service. He was also cross-grained and surly and hard to get on with.

Now time went by until the day before Christmas. That morning Glam got up early and called for his breakfast.

The farmer's wife replied: "It is not the custom for Christians to eat today, for to-morrow is Christmas, and today we ought to fast."

He scowled and answered her in his surly way. "You have so many foolish fashions from which I see no good come, and I don't see that people are better off now than they were before when they paid no attention to such tom-foolery. I think things were better when we were all called heathens—and now I want my food, and no fooling!"

Then the good-wife said, "I know for sure, you'll come to grief today, if you act in this way."

Glam cursed and raged, bade her bring his food at once, and said that otherwise she would be sorry for it. She was so frightened that she dared not refuse him. So he ate his breakfast, and then went out to his sheep, still cursing.

The weather was bad that day, murky all over; snow flakes fluttered down; there were loud noises in the sky; and it grew worse during the day.

All the morning, men heard Glam whooping for his sheep, off on the mountain. They heard less and less of him as the day passed. It snowed hard in the afternoon, and toward evening the storm was very heavy. Then people went to church, and came out about dark, and Glam had not come back. There was some talk of going to search for him, but nothing came of it, because of the snow-storm and the pitch-darkness.

All that night Glam did not come home. Next morning, Christmas morning, the storm stopped. Still men waited until after church. Then they went out on a search for him. They found his sheep scattered far and wide over the moors, or strayed up on the mountains. After a long hunt, they came to a great trampled place, high up in the valley, and it seemed as though there had been some terrible struggle, for rocks were torn up all around, and even clods of frozen earth. They looked about carefully and saw Glam lying a short distance off; he was dead, and as blue as hell and swollen up as big as an ox.

It was so horrible to look at him, their very souls seemed to shudder. Yet they tried to carry the body to the church. It was so heavy, they got it only to the edge of a cliff, a little further down.

There they left it, and went back to the farm, and told Thorhall what had happened. He asked them what killed Glam. They said they had tracked steps as though a barrel-bottom had been stamped down in the snow, leading from the trampled place up to the steep cliffs at the head of the valley; and all along the track there were huge blood-stains. Men drew from this that the evil spirit which lived there before had killed Glam, and then died of the wounds it received from him, for nothing has ever been seen of that demon since.

The day after Christmas they tried again to carry Glam to church for burial. They yoked horses to him and tugged all day, but he was so heavy now that they could only move him down hill, and not an inch on level ground; he had to be left there.

The third day a priest went with them, but Glam's body could not be found, though they searched all day. Next day he refused to go again, and when the priest was not with them, they found the body at once. But they stopped trying to bring Glam to church, and buried him on the spot to which he had been brought.

A little time after, people became aware that Glam's dead body was not lying quiet. In fact it seemed to be walking all over the valley. People who saw it said the body was twice as tall and big and ugly as when Glam was alive, all bloated and blue, with a hideous gleam in its eyes. Many people fell into a trance when they saw it, and some went mad. Just after Christmas-week men thought they saw it home at the farm and became terribly frightened, and many ran away. Next the dead Glam took to riding on the roofs of the houses at night, and almost broke them in. Soon it was walking about in broad daylight. People hardly dared go up into the valley of Waterdale to see Thorhall and other farmers who lived there, and everyone in Waterdale thought things were in a bad way.

In spring, Thorhall got new farm-hands, and started farming again; the hauntings began to stop as the days grew longer; and so things went on till mid-summer.

That summer a ship from Norway landed on the firth north of the Thorhall-stead, and on board was a man named Thorgaut. He was a foreigner, big and muscular, with the strength of two ordinary men. He was unhired and unmarried, and looking for a job. Thorhall rode to the ship and found Thorgaut, asked if he would work for him. Thorgaut said he was willing to do any sort of work.

"But before you think of coming to me," said Thorhall, "you must know that my farm is no place for a coward, because of the hauntings which have been going on there for several years. I'll not persuade you to come by lying."

Thorgaut laughed. "I won't think all's over with me if I see a few ghosts. It will be a very hard matter for other people, if I am frightened. I'll not shirk my job on that account."

So they struck a bargain on the spot, and Thorgaut was to watch sheep in winter.

Summer passed, and Thorgaut started shepherding with the winter and all the farm hands liked him. Then the dead Glam began coming again to the farm-house, and rode the roofs. Thorgaut thought this great sport. He said the spook would have to come nearer before he would be afraid of it.

Thorhall told him not to brag. "It will be better if you have no trial of each other."

"Your courage has certainly been shaken out of you," said Thorgaut, "but I'm not going to drop dead in broad daylight for such talk."

So things went on till Christmas. The morning of Christmas-eve, Thorgaut was starting out to his sheep, when the house-wife said to him, "I hope that things will not go the old way."

"Don't worry, good-wife!" said he, "there will be something worth telling about if I do not come back."

After that he went to his sheep. The weather was quite cold, and there was much snow. Thorgaut usually came home when twilight set in; today he did not return at that time. People went to church without him, and things began to look as they did the year before; the farmer wanted to search for his shepherd, but the church-goers begged off, saying that they would not risk themselves in the hands of evil demons at night; Thorhall dared not go alone, and so no search was made.

Christmas-day, after breakfast, the farm-hands went out to look for Thorgaut. They first walked to the cairn, the stone-hut in which Glam was buried, because they thought he was somehow to blame for the shepherd's disappearance. When they came near the cairn they saw something terrible had happened, for there they found the shepherd, with his neck twisted round, and every bone in his body broken.

They brought him to church, and no harm came from Thorgaut afterwards.

Now Glam's body took to getting new strength. It did so much mischief, at last, that all the farm-hands fled from Thorhall-stead, leaving Thorhall and his wife, and a cattleman. This cattleman had been with Thorhall many years, and was very old, and did not want to leave, for he saw that everything his master had would go to rack and ruin, if there was no one to look after it.

Now one morning after mid-winter, Thorhall's wife went out to the barn to milk the cows; by this time it was broad daylight, for no one ventured outside earlier than that, except the cattleman, who always went out at dawn. She heard a great cracking in the barn, and fearful bellowing and ran back to the house again, crying out, and said she did not know what frightful things were going on in the cattle-shed.

Thorhall hurried out to the cows, and found them goring each other. He thought he had better not go in there, so he went to the hay-barn, and looking through into the cow-shed, he saw the cattleman lying on his back, hanging over the stone partition between two stalls. He hung like a rag with his feet dangling in one stall and his head in the other. The farmer went up to him, and felt him all over, and found he was dead, and his back broken. It had been broken over the stone barrier between the stalls.

Now the farmer thought there was no living longer at Thorhall-stead. So he fled away from his farm, taking what he could with him. But all the live-stock which was left behind, Glam killed, and then went down the valley of Waterdale and ruined half the farms. Thorhall stayed with friends the rest of the winter.

Now no one could go up into Waterdale with a horse or a hound, for it was killed at once; but when spring came, and the days grew longer, the ghost-visits became less frequent, and Thorhall decided to return to his own land. Though he had no easy task in getting servants, still he opened his house again at Thorhall-stead. And things went on the same way as before; for when autumn came the hauntings began again. Glam showed himself most often to the farmer's daughter, and terrified her more and more each time, until at last she died of fright. Many plans were tried, all in vain, and it seemed as though all Waterdale would be laid waste, if no remedy were found.

About the time winter set in a young man named Grettir Asmund-son came to visit his uncle, who lived on a farm at the other end of Waterdale. This Grettir was the strongest man in Iceland. When only fifteen he killed a man and was banished from Iceland for three years. He went to Norway, where he did many great deeds, and was just this year come back to Iceland, at the age of eighteen.

Grettir's uncle received him well, and he was there three nights. At that time people in Waterdale talked about nothing else so much as Glam's walkings, and Grettir asked closely about all that had happened at Thorhall-stead. Grettir's uncle told him that every word was the truth, "but perhaps you are intending to go to Thorhall-stead your-self, nephew?"

Grettir said he was.

"Don't think of such a thing!" cried his uncle. "It's a dangerous venture. Your relatives don't care to lose you, for we think there is not another like you among the young men of Iceland; and 'bad will come from bad,' as the proverb says, where Glam is. It is far better to deal with mortal men than with demons."

Grettir said he would go to Thorhall-stead and see what was happening now.

"I see," his uncle replied, "it's no use to hold you back, but the old saying is true, that 'good luck and good heart do not always go together.'"

Grettir answered him with another old proverb, "'Sorrow stands before one's own door, when it has entered a neighbor's house.' Glam may come to your farm, uncle, if something is not done soon."

"Maybe we both see the future," his uncle answered, "and yet neither of us can prevent it."

After this they parted, and neither liked the other's forebodings.

Grettir rode to Thorhall-stead, and the farmer welcomed him; he asked where Grettir was going, and Grettir said he would stay over night if it were convenient for the farmer. Thorhall said he thanked him for staying, "but few people think it a treat to be guests at my house for any time; you must have heard what is going on here, and I don't want to get you into any trouble on my account; even if you yourself escape safe and sound, I am certain you will lose your horse, for no one who comes here can keep his horse uninjured."

Grettir said there were plenty of horses, no matter what happened to this one.

Then Thorhall was delighted that Grettir really wished to stay, and shook both his hands. The horse was locked up securely in an out-house, and they went to sleep; and that night passed, and Glam did not come.

Then said Thorhall, "Your coming here has done wonders, for every night Glam is in the habit of riding our roofs, or breaking open our doors, as you can see for yourself," and he pointed to the great doorway. The door had been splintered by Glam, and Thorhall had filled up its place with benches and planks and any heavy timber he could find.

"Then one of two things will happen," said Grettir, "either Glam will not hold back long, or the hauntings will stop for more than one night. I will stay here another night and see what happens."

After this they went to Grettir's horse, and it had not been meddled with, so the farmer thought things looked brighter.

Grettir stayed another night, and still the fiend did not come back; the farmer thought that a very hopeful sign. But this time when he went out to feed Grettir's horse, he found the out-house broken into, and the horse dragged out to the door, with every bone smashed. He told Grettir what had happened, and bade him save himself, "for your death is sure, if you wait for Glam."

Grettir answered, "I must be paid for my horse by at least one sight of that creature."

The farmer said it was no fun to see him, "for he is unlike anything in the shape of man; but I am thankful for every hour you are willing to stay with us."

The day went by, and when bed-time came Grettir would not take off his clothes, but lay down on a bench against the farmer's bed-closet. He spread a thick cloak over himself, wrapping one end of it under his feet, and doubling the other under his head, while he looked out at the head-opening; there was a heavy plank at the foot of the bench, and against this he braced his feet. The fittings of the outside door had all been broken by Glam on previous visits, and the heavy timbers set up instead, were roughly fastened for the night. The panelling which had once stretched across the hall was all broken away, both above and below the cross beam; the beds had all been pulled out of their places, and everything was upside down.

A light was left burning in the hall through the night; and when a third of the night had passed Grettir heard loud noises outside. Then something went up on the house and rode above the hall, and drove its heels into the roof, so that every rafter creaked. This went on for some time; then it came down from the roof and went to the door; and as the door opened, Grettir saw the death-walker thrust in his head; frightfully big he seemed and his features huge and coarse. Glam advanced slowly, and raised himself up when he came inside the door, till he towered up high toward the roof. Then he turned, and looked down the hall, resting his arms on the cross-beam, and glared about.

Thorhall kept silent in his closet and lay shivering. Grettir did not move a muscle. Glam saw the bundle lying on the bench, and thereupon he stalked up the hall and gripped the cloak. Grettir braced his feet against the plank, and did not budge. Glam tugged again, much harder; still the cloak did not move. The third time he pulled with both hands so hard that he drew Grettir upright from the bench. The cloak tore in two between them. Glam stared at the piece he held, as though wondering who it could be, who had pulled so hard against him; and, in that instant, Grettir dove in under his hands and gripped him tight around the middle, and bent back his spine as far as he could, intending to make him fall backwards. But the monster pushed down on Grettir's arms so fiercely, that he had to give way before Glam's strength. Then Grettir backed off to some benches fastened to the floor, but those overturned, and everything they stumbled on was broken.

Glam wanted to get him outside, but Grettir braced himself against everything he could. Yet Glam dragged him to the hall-door. There they had a fierce wrestling, because the death-walker meant to bring him out of doors, while Grettir saw that bad as it was to fight with Glam in the house, it would be still worse outside; therefore he struggled with all his might and main against leaving the hall. When they came to the outer door, the demon put forth all his strength, and hauled Grettir close up to him; and when Grettir saw he could not get a purchase in the door-way with his feet, he suddenly changed his plan, and threw himself with all his might against the creature's breast, pushing back with both feet against the half sunken stone which served as threshold. Glam was not ready for this, as he had been dragging Grettir toward him, so he staggered backwards, crashing out through the door, and his shoulders caught against the beam over the door-way, and the roof burst in two, both rafters and frozen thatch, and he fell back out of the house, with his arms thrown out, and Grettir on top of him.

Outside broken clouds drifted over the moon. Just as Glam fell a cloud was driven from the moon, and the death-walker cast his eye sharp against it; and Grettir himself says that of all the hideous things he ever saw, this alone frightened him.

Then Grettir's heart sank so low from the weariness and from seeing Glam roll his eyes so hideously, that he could not draw his sword, and lay just between earth and hell.

For the first time, then, the death-walker spoke. "Grettir, you have been very eager to meet me, but you will get little good from our acquaintance. You are strong as it is, and you would have been stronger still, if you had never seen me. I lay this spell on you that everything shall go wrong with you after this. You shall be outlawed and live a solitary life. And in the dark you shall always see these eyes of mine staring into your own, and find it hard to be alone, and that terror shall drag you to your death."

When Glam's ghost had done speaking, Grettir's weakness left him immediately, and drawing his sword, he hewed off Glam's head, and—as should be done with all those who walk after death—he laid the head against the creature's thigh.

Then the farmer came out, having dressed while Glam was speaking his spells. He dared not come near until Glam had fallen. Thorhall praised God and thanked Grettir for having vanquished this unclean spirit. Then they burned Glam's body till the coals of his corpse were cold. After that they gathered his ashes into a sack and buried it where sheep were least likely to pasture or men to tread. This done, they walked home, and it was now near day-break.

Grettir lay down, for he was very stiff, while Thorhall sent to the nearest farm for the men, and showed them, and told them what had taken place. All men thought highly of the adventure, and it was commonly said that for strength and daring and all kinds of deeds, there was none in all Iceland like Grettir Asmundson.

Thorhall saw Grettir off handsomely and gave him a good horse and a fine suit of clothes in place of those which had been torn to pieces. Then they parted, lifelong friends.

But always afterwards Grettir said he had become afraid in the dark, and that he dared not go anywhere alone after night-fall, for then he saw all kinds of horrors. This fear was at last the cause of Grettir's death.

And it has been a saying in Iceland, ever since, when people imagine things very different from what they are, that Glam gives them his eyes, or gives them Glam-sight.

The Trolls of the Waterfall

1027-1028

Grettis saga

THIS adventure of Grettir is derived from the same folktale as the deeds of Beowulf at the court of Hrothgar in Denmark.

THERE was dwelling at Eyjardalsa in Bardardal a priest named Steinn, a good farmer and wealthy. His son Kjartan was grown up and was now a fine young man. Thorsteinn the White was a man who dwelt at Sandhaugar to the south of Eyjardalsa; his wife Steinvor was young and of a merry disposition. They had children who at this time were yet young. Their place was generally thought to be much haunted by trolls. Two winters before Grettir came North into those parts, Steinvor the mistress of Sandhaugar went as usual to spend Yule at Eyjardalsa, while her husband stayed at home. Men lay down to sleep in the evening, and in the night they heard a great noise in the room near the bondi's bed. No one dared to get up to see what was the matter because there were so few of them. The mistress of the house returned home the next morning, but her husband had disappeared and no one knew what had become of him. So the next season passed. The following winter the mistress wanted to go to mass, and told her servant to stay at home; he was very unwilling but said she should be obeyed. It happened just as before; this time the servant disappeared. People thought it very strange and found some drops of blood upon the outer door, so they supposed that some evil spirit must have carried off both the men. The story spread all through the district and came to the ears of Grettir, who being well accustomed to deal with ghosts and spectres turned his steps to Bardardal and arrived at Yule-eve at Sandhaugar. He retained his disguise and called himself Gest. The lady of the house saw that he was enormously tall, and the servants were terribly afraid of him. He asked for hospitality; the mistress told him that food was ready for him but that he must see after himself. He said he would, and added: "I will stay in the house while you go to mass if you would like it."

She said: "You must be a brave man to venture to stay in the house."

"I do not care for a monotonous life," he said.

Then she said: "I do not want to remain at home but I cannot get across the river."

"I will come with you," said Gest. Then she made ready to go to mass with her little daughter. It was thawing outside; the river was flooded and was covered with ice. She said: "It is impossible for either man or horse to cross the river."

"There must be fords," said Gest; "do not be afraid."

"First carry the maiden over," she said; "she is lighter."

"I don't want to make two journeys of it," said he; "I will carry you in my arms."

She crossed herself and said: "That is impossible; what will you do with the girl?"

"I will find a way," he said, taking them both up and setting the girl on her mother's knee as he bore them both on his left arm, keeping his right arm free. So he carried them across. They were too frightened to cry out. The river came up to his breast, and a great piece of ice drove against him, which he pushed off with the hand that was free. Then the stream became so deep that it broke over his shoulder, but he waded on vigorously till he reached the other bank and put them on shore. It was nearly dark by the time he got home to Sandhaugar and called for some food. When he had eaten something he told the servants to go to the other end of the hall. Then he got some boards and loose logs and laid them across the hall to make a great barricade so that none of the servants could get across. No one dared to oppose him or to object to anything. The entrance was in the side wall of the hall under the back gable, and near it was a cross bench upon which Grettir laid himself, keeping on his clothes, with a light burning in the room. So he lay till into the night.

The mistress reached Eyjardalsa for mass and every one wondered how she had crossed the river. She said she did not know whether it was a man or a troll who had carried her over. The priest said it was certainly a man though unlike other men. "Let us keep silence over it; may be that he means to help you in your difficulties."

She stayed there the night.

We return now to tell of Gest. Towards midnight he heard a loud noise outside, and very soon there walked a huge troll-wife into the room. She carried a trough in one hand and a rather large cutlass in the other. She looked round the room as she entered, and on seeing Gest lying there she rushed at him; he started up and attacked her furiously. They fought long together; she was the stronger but he evaded her skilfully. Everything near them and the panelling of the back wall were broken to pieces. She dragged him through the hall door out to the porch, where he resisted vigorously. She wanted to drag him out of the house, but before that was done they had broken up all the fittings of the outer door and borne them away on their shoulders. Then she strove to get to the river and among the rocks. Gest was terribly fatigued, but there was no choice but either to brace himself or be dragged down to the rocks. All night long they struggled together, and he thought he had never met with such a monster for strength. She gripped him so tightly to herself that he could do nothing with either hand but cling to her waist. When at last they reached a rock by the river he swung the monster round and got his right hand loose. Then he quickly seized the short sword which he was wearing, drew it and struck at the troll's right shoulder, cutting off her right arm and releasing himself. She sprang among the rocks and disappeared in the waterfall. Gest, very stiff and tired, lay long by the rock. At daylight he went home and lay down on his bed, blue and swollen all over.

When the lady of the house came home she found the place rather in disorder. She went to Gest and asked him what had happened, and why everything was broken to pieces. He told her everything just as it had happened. She thought it a matter of great moment and asked him who he was. He told her the truth, said that he wished to see a priest and asked her to send for one. She did so; Steinn came to Sandhaugar and soon learnt that it was Grettir the son of Asmund who had come there under the name of Gest. The priest asked him what he thought had become of the men who had disappeared; Grettir said he thought that they must have gone among the rocks. The priest said he could not believe his word unless he gave some evidence of it. Grettir said that later it would be known, and the priest went home. Grettir lay many days in his bed and the lady did all she could for him; thus Yuletide passed. Grettir himself declared that the troll-woman sprang among the rocks when she was wounded, but the men of Bardardal say that the day dawned upon her while they were wrestling; that when he cut off her arm she broke, and that she is still standing there on the mountain in the likeness of a woman. The dwellers in the valley kept Grettir there in hiding.

One day that winter after Yule Grettir went to Eyjardalsa and met the priest, to whom he said: "I see, priest, that you have little belief in what I say. Now I wish you to come with me to the river and to see what probability there is in it."

The priest did so. When they reached the falls they saw a cave up under the rock. The cliff was there so abrupt that no one could climb it, and nearly ten fathoms down to the water. They had a rope with them. The priest said: "It is quite impossible for any one to get down to that."

Grettir answered: "It is certainly possible; and men of high mettle are those who would feel themselves happiest there. I want to see what there is in the fall. Do you mind the rope."

The priest said he could do so if he chose. He drove a stake into the ground and laid stones against it.

Grettir now fastened a stone in a loop at the end of the rope, and lowered it from above into the water.

"Which way do you mean to go?" asked the priest.

"I don't mean to be bound when I come into the fall," Grettir said. "So my mind tells me."

Then he prepared to go; he had few clothes on and only a short sword; no other arms. He jumped from a rock and got down to the fall. The priest saw the soles of his feet but after that did not know what had become of him. Grettir dived beneath the fall. It was very difficult swimming because of the currents, and he had to dive to the bottom to get behind the fall. There was a rock where he came up, and a great cave under the fall in front of which the water poured. He went into the cave, where there was a large fire burning and a horrible great giant most fearful to behold sitting before it. On Grettir entering the giant sprang up, seized a pike and struck at him, for he could both strike and thrust with it. It had a wooden shaft and was of the kind called "heptisax." Grettir struck back with his sword and cut through the shaft. Then the giant tried to reach up backwards to a sword which was hanging in the cave, and at that moment Grettir struck at him and cut open his lower breast and stomach so that all his entrails fell out into the river and floated down the stream. The priest who was sitting by the rope saw some débris being carried down all covered with blood and lost his head, making sure that Grettir was killed. He left the rope and ran off home, where he arrived in the evening and told them for certain that Grettir was dead, and said it was a great misfortune to them to have lost such a man.

Grettir struck few more blows at the giant before he was dead. He then entered the cave, kindled a light and explored. It is not told how much treasure he found there, but there is supposed to have been some. He stayed there till late into the night and found the bones of two men, which he carried away in a skin. Then he came out of the cave, swam to the rope and shook it, thinking the priest was there; finding him gone he had to swarm up the rope and so reached the top. He went home to Eyjardalsa and carried the skin with the bones in it into the vestibule of the church together with the rune-staff, upon which were most beautifully carved the following lines:

"Into the fall of the torrent I went;
dank its maw towards me gaped.
The floods before the ogress' den
Mighty against my shoulder played";

and then:

"Hideous the friend of Mella came.
Hard were the blows I dealt upon her.
The shaft of Heptisax was severed.
My sword has pierced the monster's breast."

There too it was told how Grettir had brought the bones from the
cave. The priest when he came to the church on the next morning
found the staff and all that was with it and read the runes. Grettir
had then returned home to Sandhaugar.

Stuf's Saga

c. 1050

Stúfs saga

THERE was a man named Stuf, the son of Thorth Cat, and he was
son of Thorth Ingun's son and Guthrun Oswif's daughter. Stuf was
a tall man and handsome and very strong. He was a good skald and
bold of speech. He went abroad to claim an inheritance in the north
of Norway. They reached Norway at harvest time. Afterwards he
went east by the sound passage and got whatever transportation he
could.

It happened that one day he came to a certain farmer and took
lodgings there. He was well received and sat opposite the farmer.
And when they made ready for meal-time the farmer was told that
many men were riding toward the farm and that a standard was
borne in front of one of the men.

The farmer stood up and said, "Let us all go out, because King
Harald has arrived here."

All the men went out except Stuf, who sat behind alone, and when
they came out the standard advanced towards them and with it the
king himself. The farmer welcomed the king well and said, "Now
you will not be received, Sire, as would be proper. Had we known

beforehand of your coming we would have had little idea how to receive you. But as you come unexpectedly, things will be even less satisfactory."

The king replied: "I do not expect the same now when we are on a hurried trip, as when we are traveling in state to the feasts that men prepare for us. Now our men will be busy about their own business, but we will go inside, farmer."

They did so. Then the farmer said to Stuf: "Now, my fellow, you must give up your place to him who has come."

"I do not think it disgraceful," said Stuf, "to sit farther away and give place to the king or his men. And it seems to me unnecessary not to respect what you now said."

King Harald said: "Here is come an Icelandic man. That promises fun. Sit in your place, Icelander!"

Stuf answered: "That I will accept, and it seems to me a much greater honor to accept it from you than to accept it from a farmer."

The king said: "Now I will have the table set and people begin eating, but my own men shall come and sit down as they become ready."

Now things were carried out as the king wished. It turned out that the farmer had plenty of liquor, and men became merry.

The king asked: "What is the name of the man who is sitting opposite me?"

"I am called Stuf," he replied.

The king said: "A queer name! And whose son are you?"

"I am the son of Cat," Stuf replied.

The king asked: "Which was the cat that was your father, the tom-cat or the tabby-cat?"

Then Stuf clapped his hands and laughed and said nothing. The king asked: "What are you laughing at, Icelander?"

"You guess, Sire!" Stuf replied.

"So shall it be," said the king. "I must have seemed to you to have asked an ignorant question when I asked which cat was your father, the tom-cat or the tabby-cat, because your father could not be the one who was a female."

"You guess it right, Sire," said Stuf. Then the laughing set in again on Stuf.

The king said: "Why are you laughing now, Stuf?"

"Guess again, Sire!"

"So shall it be," said the king. "I guess that this would be your answer: that my father was not a swine, although he was called Sow; but that I had brought this matter up because I thought you would not have the boldness to give me this answer, since I must know that your father would not be a cat, although so he was called."

Stuf said that he guessed right.

Then the king said: "Sit pretty, Icelander!"

Stuf replied: "May you sit the prettiest of all kings!"

After that the king was drinking and talking with the men who sat on both sides of him. Later in the evening, the king said: "Are you a man of learning, Stuf?"

"Certainly, Sire," said he.

The king spoke: "That is excellent. I desire then, farmer, to go early to sleep and let the Icelander retire to the same lodge that I sleep in."

Now that was done. And when the king was undressed, he said, "Now you shall recite poems, Stuf, if you are a learned man."

Stuf recited a poem, and when it was done the king said: "Recite another."

So it went on for a long time that the king asked him to recite, as soon as he paused, until all the men there in the lodge were asleep except those two, and long afterwards.

Then the king asked: "Do you know how many poems you have recited, Stuf?"

"That is far from my mind," said Stuf, "for I expected you to count them, Sire."

"And that I have done," said the king. "You have recited sixty ballads. Can you not recite anything but ballads?"

Stuf replied: "It is not so, Sire. I have not recited half of my ballads, but I know twice as many odes as ballads."

The king asked: "For whom do you intend to recite odes, when for me you recite only ballads?"

Stuf replied: "To you, Sire, I intend to recite."

"When, then?" said the king.

"The next time we meet," said Stuf.

"Why then, rather than now?" said the king.

Stuf replied: "For this reason, Sire: I would have it so with this as with all else, that you should like me better the more you know me."

The king said: "Big words you manage to utter, whatever may come true. But now I want first to sleep."

And so he did. In the morning, when the king was dressed and went down the staircase, Stuf went to him and said: "May you have a good day, Sire!"

The king answered: "You speak well, Icelander, and you entertained well last evening."

Stuf said: "And you accepted well, Sire. I will ask a favor of you now, and I would have you grant it to me."

The king replied: "What do you wish to ask for?"

Stuf answered: "It seems to me it would be more favorable if you grant it beforehand."

The king answered: "I am not used to granting a request unless I know what is asked for."

Stuf said: "I will then have to tell what it shall be. I wish leave to compose a poem about yourself."

The king asked: "Are you a poet?"

Stuf replied: "I am a good poet."

The king asked: "Are any skalds related to you?"

Stuf answered: "Glum Geirason was my great-grandfather, and there have been many other good skalds in my family."

The king said: "If you are such a skald as Glum Geirason was, then I will permit you to compose a poem about me."

Stuf answered: "I compose much better than Glum."

The king said: "Then compose; or have you composed any poems before about high-born men?"

Stuf answered: "The reason why I have composed no songs about high-born men, is that I have never met any high-born men before yourself."

The king said: "Some men will say, that you will prove yourself enterprising for the work of a beginner, if you start with me."

"Nevertheless, I will run the risk," said Stuf, "but I wish to ask you for still other favors."

"What do you want to ask now?"

Stuf said: "I wish to ask you to make me your kings-man."

The king said: "This may not be done so quickly, because there I am bound to have the counsel and consent of my court. I will, however, promote your case."

Stuf said: "I wish to ask you for still more, Sire. Or do you now want to grant me what I am going to ask for?"

The king said: "What will you ask for?"

Stuf replied: "That you have a letter prepared under your seal, so that I can get my inheritance which I have up in the north."

The king enquired: "Why did you ask me last for what was most necessary for you to obtain? I will grant you this."

Stuf replied: "This seemed to me the least important."

Afterwards they parted, and the king went his way, and Stuf went on his errand. And it was not long before Stuf met the king north in the city of Kaupang. He entered a drinking room where King Harald sat inside, and many prominent men beside him.

Stuf greeted the king. He answered: "Has Stuf come here, our friend?"

"So it is, Sire," he said, "and now I have the poem to offer you, and I wish to have silence."

The king said: "So shall it be. But you may expect me not to be indifferent to your poem, because I know a poem when I hear one. You have already boasted much about your verse-making and have spoken boldly about it."

Stuf replied: "It looks promising to me, Sire, that you are ready to listen well."

Then he recited the poem. And when it was finished, the king said: "It is true that the poem is well composed, and I now discern the truth in your speech that you are a man of great wisdom. But you have been bent on fun in our talks. Now you shall have the rank of kings-man and be with us, if you wish."

Afterwards Stuf was made a kings-man of King Harald and was with him a long time, and he was considered to be a wise man and popular. This ode that Stuf recited and composed about the king was called Stuf's Drapa. And here ends this adventure.

An Icelandic Story-Teller

c. 1050

Íslendings þáttr sögufróða

IT happened one summer that an Icelander, a young and alert fellow, came to King Harald and asked him for help. The king enquired if he had any talents. He allowed that he knew some sagas. The king replied, "I will receive you so that you will be in my household this winter and always provide entertainment whenever people want it, whoever asks you."

And so he did: he quickly became popular at the court, and the king's men gave him clothes and the king himself provided him with good weapons to carry. Thus time passed until Yule; then the Icelander became unhappy. The king enquired what caused his gloom. He replied that it was just his change of mood.

"That's not what I think," said the king, "and I will make you a guess. It is my guess that now your stories are all told out. You have been amusing everyone who has asked you, this winter, and now it seems bad for you to run out of sagas at Yule."

"It is just as you have guessed," he said, "there is only one story left, and I do not dare to recite that one here because it is the story of your own travels abroad."

The king said, "That is exactly the story that I am most curious to hear. You shall not recite again until Yule while everybody is greatly occupied, but the first day of Yule you shall begin this story and tell a part of it. I will arrange it so for you that the story and Yule will be equally long. At Yule there will be heavy drinking, and there will be only short intervals for listening. And you will not find out from me, while you are telling the story, whether I like it or not."

So it came to pass that the Icelander began the story the first day of Yule and recited for a while. The king soon bade him leave off. People started drinking, and many said there was courage in this, that the Icelander told this story, and they wondered what the king thought about it. To some he seemed to recite well, and some thought less of it. Thus Yule-time passed. The king insisted that the story should be well listened to. It worked out by the king's management that the Yule feast came to an end and the story was finished.

On Epiphany Eve, after the story had been finished that day, the king said: "Have you no curiosity, Icelander," said he, "as to how I like your story?"

"I am frightened about it, Sire," he replied.

The king said: "It seems to me very well told and nowhere worse than facts warranted, but who taught it to you?"

He answered, "It was my custom out there in Iceland to go every summer to the Thing, and I learned every summer some of this saga when Halldor Snorrason told it."

"Then I do not wonder," said the king, "that you know it so well.

It will prove a benefit to you. You shall be welcome with me and whenever you wish."

The king gave him a good cargo. And he was afterwards a well-to-do man.

Brand the Open-Handed
c. 1050
Brands þáttr örva

THIS is the story of an Icelander, famous for his generosity, who was put to the test at Nitharos in Norway by King Harald Harthrathi. It was of course unusual for a king to ask for gifts instead of lavishing them on his guests.

❧Now the story relates that one summer Brand the Open-handed came to the city. He was the son of Vermund in Vatnsfjord. He was a man popular and generous. Thjotholf the Skald had told the king continually about Brand, what a great man he was and what a fine character. Thjotholf asserted that he did not know of another man in all Iceland better fitted to be a companion of the king, because of his munificence and dignity. He had told the king much about Brand's generosity.

But the king said, "I shall now put him to the test. You go to him now and ask if he will make for me a present of his mantle."

Thjotholf went and came to the chamber which Brand occupied. Brand was standing in the middle of the floor measuring linen by a yardstick. He had on a scarlet robe and over it he wore a scarlet mantle bound to his head. In his armpit he gripped an axe inlaid with gold.

Thjotholf said, "The king will accept your mantle."

Brand kept on with his work and did not answer, but he let the mantle slip down off his shoulders. Thjotholf gathered it up and took it to the king, who asked how matters had gone. Thjotholf told him that Brand had not uttered a word, and afterward he told what he had been doing and finally about his clothing.

The king said: "This is indeed a proud-minded man, and he must be a distinguished person, since he did not consider words necessary. Go once more and tell him that I will accept from him the golden axe."

Thjotholf said: "Sire, I am not keen to go. I do not know how well he will take it."

"You started the discussion about Brand, both now and on previous occasions. Therefore you will now go and say that I shall accept the golden axe. I do not consider him generous unless he gives it."

Thjotholf went then to see Brand and said that the king would accept the axe. Brand handed Thjotholf the axe and remained silent. Thjotholf took it to the king and told him what had happened. The king said: "It seems to me likely that this man is more generous than other men, which at present benefits me. Go once more and tell him that I shall accept the robe he wears."

Thjotholf said: "Sire, it is not proper that I go once more."

"Nevertheless, you shall go," said the king.

Thjotholf went and entered the chamber and said that the king would accept the robe. Brand interrupted his work and silently took off his robe. He then cut off one of the sleeves and cast the robe aside, keeping the sleeve. Thjotholf picked up the robe, took it to the king, and showed it to him. The king looked at it and then said: "This man is both wise and generous. It is obvious to me why he has cut off the sleeve. It seems to him that I have got only one hand, the one that always accepts but never grants anything. Go now and fetch him."

This was done and Brand came into the presence of the king. He received from the king great honor and precious gifts.

This was done to test him.

Authun and His Bear

c. 1050

Auðunar þáttr vestfirzka

How Authun bought a polar bear in Greenland and took it to the king of Denmark.

ê THERE was a man named Authun whose family was settled along the northwestern fjords of Iceland. He was a poor man. He sailed abroad from the west fjords under the patronage of Thorsteinn, a well-to-do franklin, and Thorir the helmsman, who had received food and lodging from Thorsteinn during the winter. Authun was also there, working for Thorir, and received from him as a reward the trip abroad and his maintenance.

Authun gave most of his property—what there was of it—to his mother before he embarked with Thorir. It was reckoned enough for her to live on for three winters. Authun and Thorir then departed. Their journey was a smooth one. The following winter Authun spent with Thorir, who owned an estate in the province of Mœrr in Norway. The next summer they sailed to Greenland and remained there over the winter.

Now it is told that Authun bought a bear—a great treasure—and gave all he possessed for it. When summer came Authun and Thorir journeyed to Norway and had a good passage. Authun had his bear with him. He intended to travel south to Denmark to meet King Sveinn and give him the animal. When Authun arrived in the south of Norway, where King Harald of Norway happened to be staying, he disembarked, leading the bear behind him, and hired a lodging.

King Harald was soon told that there had arrived a bear, a great treasure, owned by an Icelander. The King sent men after him. When Authun came before the King, he greeted the King courteously. The King accepted his greeting and then asked: "Do you own a great treasure in the form of a bear?"

Authun answered by saying that he did possess a certain animal. The King said: "Will you sell us the animal for the same amount you paid for it?"

Authun replied: "I will not, my lord."

"Will you have," said the King, "that I give you double its value? —and that would be more just if you gave all you possessed for it."

"I will not, my lord," replied Authun.

The King said: "Will you give it to me then?"

Authun replied: "No, my lord."

"What are you going to do with it, then?" asked the King.

"Go to Denmark," replied Authun, "and give it to King Sveinn."

King Harald said: "Is it possible that you are a man so poorly informed that you have not heard that there is a war between his land and mine, or do you consider your luck so great that you can get through to Denmark with treasures where others can not get through without injury although they needs must go?"

Authun replied: "My lord, that is for you to determine, but I shall agree to nothing else than my original plan."

Then the King said: "Why should you not travel on your way as you will? But come to me when you return and tell me how King Sveinn has rewarded you for the animal. It may be that you are a lucky man."

"I promise you that," said Authun.

Authun now journeyed southwards: east to Oslo Fjord and then to Denmark. By this time his money was used up and he had to beg food both for himself and for the bear. He met King Sveinn's steward, whose name was Aki, and requested of him some provisions both for himself and the animal. "I intend," said Authun, "to give King Sveinn the bear." Aki agreed to sell Authun provisions if Authun so desired. Authun declared that he had nothing to pay with. "But I should nevertheless like," he said, "to find some way of bringing the animal to the King."

"I shall get you the provisions you need in order to meet the King," said Aki, "but in compensation I shall want to become half-owner of the bear. You must consider that the animal may die on your hands, since you lack food for it and your money is at an end. Then you would not even have the bear." When Authun thought this over, it seemed to him that the steward was right, so he agreed to sell Aki half the animal, the value of which the King should later estimate. They now planned both to go and meet the King, and this they did. They came to him while he was at table. The King tried to decide who the strange man might be, but he could not recognize him. He then said to Authun: "Who are you?"

Authun answered: "I am an Icelander, my lord, and have come from Greenland by way of Norway, intending to bring you this bear. I purchased it for all my possessions. But a great misfortune has befallen me, for I now own only half the bear." And he told the King what had passed between him and the King's steward.

The King asked: "Is what he says true, Aki?"

"True it is," said Aki.

The King said: "And you thought it proper, after I had bestowed upon you an important position, to hinder or make difficulties for a man who takes the trouble to bring me a treasure for which he gave all he possessed? And when King Harald was willing to let him go in peace although he is our enemy? Consider how fair that was on your part! It would be fitting if you were put to death—but I shall not do that now; but you must leave this land at once and never come within my sight again. To you, Authun, I can give my thanks as if you had presented me with the entire animal. Remain here with me." For this Authun thanked the King, and he stayed with him for a time.

When some time had passed, Authun said to the King: "I should like to go away now, sir."

The King answered slowly. "What do you want to do," he said, "if you will not remain with us?"

Authun replied: "I want to travel south to Rome."

"If you had not taken such good counsel," said the King, "I should be displeased at your eagerness to leave." The King now gave Authun a great deal of silver, and Authun journeyed southward with other pilgrims on their way to Rome. The King furnished him with provisions for the journey and bade him come to see him when he returned.

He now started his journey and travelled south until he came to Rome. When he had stayed there as long as he desired, he departed. He was now taken seriously ill and became very thin. All the money which the King had given him for the journey was used up. He had to take to begging and ask for food. He became bald and was very wretched looking.

At Eastertime he arrived in Denmark and near where the King was staying. He did not dare show himself however. He stayed in a corner of the church intending to meet the King when he went to church in the evening, but when he saw the King and the beautifully attired retinue, he did not dare show himself. When the King went into the hall to drink, Authun ate outside as is the custom for pilgrims come from Rome as long as they have not discarded staff and wallet. Later in the evening, when the King went to vespers, Authun planned to meet him. But unwilling as he was before, he was now the more reluctant because the retainers were drunk. When they went in again, the King noticed the man, who seemed not to have the courage to approach him. And now when the retainers had gone in, the King remained outside and said: "Come forward now, whoever wishes to speak with me. I suspect that that must be the man over there." At this, Authun went forward and fell at the King's feet and the King hardly recognized him. And when the King knew who it was, he took Authun's hand and bade him welcome. "You are greatly changed," he said, "since last we met." The King led Authun in with him. When the retainers saw Authun they laughed at him. But the King said: "There is no need for you to laugh, for he has provided better for his soul than you." Then the King let Authun be bathed and thereafter gave him clothes; and Authun stayed with the King.

It is told that once in the following spring the King asked Authun to be with him permanently and promised to make him his page and grant him much honor. Authun said: "God bless you, sir, for all the honor you are willing to bestow upon me, but it is my intention to journey to Iceland."

The King said: "That seems to me to be a queer choice."

Authun replied: "I cannot bear knowing, sir, that I enjoy so much honor here with you while my mother must beg for her food in Iceland; for the means with which I provided her before I left Iceland have now come to an end."

The King answered: "That is well and manfully spoken, and no doubt you will be a lucky man. This is the only thing that would reconcile me to your going away. Stay with me until ships are ready to sail." Authun did this.

One day in late spring, King Sveinn went along the piers where men were working, loading ships for various countries—the Baltic lands or Saxony, Sweden or Norway. He and Authun came upon a beautiful ship which men were making ready. The King then enquired: "How do you like this ship, Authun?"

Authun answered: "Well, sir."

The King said: "This ship I will give you in reward for the bear." Authun thanked the King for the gift as best he could.

When some time had passed and the ship was fully prepared, King Sveinn said to Authun: "If you wish to leave now, I do not want to hinder you. But I have heard that there are few good harbors in your country and that the coast is open and dangerous for ships. If you should be shipwrecked and lose ship and cargo, there would be little to show that you had met King Sveinn and given him a treasure." Then the King gave him a purse full of silver and said: "And now you will not be entirely penniless even if your ship is destroyed, if you keep hold of this. But it could happen," continued the King, "that you lose this money. It would then be of little use that you had met King Sveinn and given him a treasure." Then the King drew a ring from his hand, gave it to Authun, and said: "Even if you are so unfortunate as to wreck your ship and lose your possessions, you will not be penniless if you reach land. Many men have gold with them in a shipwreck—but it can be seen that you have met King

Sveinn, if you keep the ring. I would advise you," said the King, "that you do not give the ring away unless you feel that you are greatly obligated to reward some noble man—then give him the ring, for it is fitting for men of high rank to receive gifts. And now farewell!"

Authun set off to sea and came to Norway. He unloaded his cargo, and there was more to unload than when he had been in Norway before. He then travelled to meet King Harald, intending to fulfill the promise he had made to him before he went to Denmark. He greeted the King. King Harald welcomed him. "Sit down," said the King, "and drink with us." This Authun did.

King Harald then asked: "How did King Sveinn reward you for the animal?"

Authun replied: "By accepting, sir."

The King said: "I would have rewarded you in that way too. How else did he reward you?"

Authun answered: "He gave me money for a pilgrimage to Rome."

Then King Harald said: "King Sveinn gives many men money for pilgrimages to Rome and for other purposes even if they do not bring him treasures. Was there anything else?"

"He offered," said Authun, "to make me his page and show me much honor."

"That was well said," replied the King, "and did he reward you still more?"

Authun said: "He gave me a ship with a cargo which is of the best that has come to Norway."

"That was very generous," said the King, "but I should have given you the same reward. Did he reward you any further?"

Authun said: "He gave me a leather purse full of silver and said that I would not be penniless if I kept hold of it even though my ship were wrecked off Iceland."

The King said: "That was nobly done, and I would not have done that. I would have felt that I had fulfilled my obligation if I had given you the ship. Did he reward you further?"

"To be sure," said Authun, "he did. He gave me this ring which I have on my hand and bade me wear it and said that if I should lose all my possessions I would not be penniless if I owned this ring. He commanded me not to part with it unless I was obligated to reward some man of high rank so well that I wanted to give it to him. Now

I have found that man, for you had the power of taking from me both the bear and my life but you let me travel on in peace, as others were not allowed to do."

The King received the gift with friendliness and gave Authun many fine gifts in return before they parted. Authun invested his money in goods to be taken back home and sailed that summer for Iceland.

He was thought to be the luckiest of men.

A Cure for Love-Sickness

c. 1120

Ívars þáttr Ingimundarsonar

KING Eystein Magnusson (1103-1123) was famous for his sense of justice and his kindness. He was said to have studied all the laws of Norway.

⟶§ IN the instance now to be related it can be observed what a wonderful man King Eystein was, how loyal to his friends, and how thoughtful and ingenious he was in finding out from them what grieved them. There was a man with him named Ivar, the son of Ingimund, an Icelander by race and well born by family, a wise man and a good poet. The king valued him highly and showed his affection, as will be seen.

Thorfin was the name of Ivar's brother. He went abroad to meet King Eystein and was well received on account of his brother. But Thorfin was displeased that he should not be considered his brother's equal, but have to depend upon his brother's position. He was therefore not happy at the court, but prepared to return to Iceland.

Before the brothers separated, Ivar asked Thorfin to take a message to Oddny Johanns-daughter that she wait for him and marry no other. He intimated that he was more interested in her than in any other woman.

Thorfin then went out to Iceland and had a good voyage. He took this course, to ask for Oddny for himself, and he married her.

A little later Ivar came out and learned of this and thought Thorfin had kept his faith badly. He did not like to stay and therefore went back to King Eystein and was in good favor with him as before.

He took now to great sorrow, and when the king found this out he fetched Ivar for a private talk with himself and asked why he was so unhappy. "Before, when you were with us, there was always great fun in your conversation, and I will not conceal that I do not know that we have done any worse to you. As wise a man as you will not draw suspicion of what is not. And now tell me what is the matter."

Ivar answered, "What the cause is, Sire, I must not speak about."

The king said: "I will then guess. Are there some men here whom you do not get on with?"

"It is not that, Sire," said Ivar.

The king said: "Do you think that you received from me less honor than you desire?"

He said it was not that.

The king asked: "Have you seen something here in this country that has troubled you so much?"

He allowed that it was not so.

"It now becomes difficult to guess," said the king. "Do you want to have the management of some estates?"

He denied that.

"Are there any women in your country," said the king, "whom you are longing after?"

He answered, "So it is, Sire."

The king said: "Do not be distressed on that account. Fare you out there as soon as it is spring. I will provide you both with money and with a letter carrying my seal to those men who manage this woman's affairs. I know of no likelihood of those men refusing, after our greetings or our threats, to marry the woman to you."

Ivar answered, "This cannot be."

The king spoke. "On no account," said the king; "I shall add that even though another man possess her, still I can get her, if I wish, for yourself."

Ivar said, "The case is more serious than that, Sire. My brother now has the woman."

Then the king said: "We will turn away from that. I see now a good plan; after Yule I will go on travels to gather the tributes, and you will go with me and you will see many gentle ladies, and, if they are not princesses, I will get you one of them."

Ivar answered, "Sire, what makes my case still more serious is that constantly, whenever I see beautiful women, I am reminded of that one woman. This always makes my grief greater."

The king said: "I will give you some management and an estate, as I offered you before, that you may have pleasure in looking after it."

He replied, "I would not enjoy it."

The king said: "Then I will get you merchandise and you can make trading trips to whatever land you wish."

He allowed that he did not want that.

Then the king said: "This is now becoming rather difficult for me. I have tried whatever I can think of. There is only one thing left and it is of very little consequence compared to those things that I have offered you. And I am no longer certain that I can guess what is most likely to benefit you. Come now to me every day when the tables are set, if I am not sitting over affairs of state, and I will gossip with you. We shall talk about this woman, in every way that you wish and may remember, and I will reserve leisure time for this, because it sometimes happens that men's grief becomes lighter if they can discuss it. And this shall also come to pass, that you shall never go from our meeting without a gift."

Ivar answered, "That I desire, Sire, and you have my sincere thanks for your inquiry."

And so they did. When the king was not sitting over affairs of state, then he talked often about this woman with Ivar, and matters improved greatly. Ivar's sorrow grew lighter in a short time, and, after a while, he was glad and happy. He came back to the same state of mind as he had been in before, as to entertainment and good cheer. And he remained at the court with King Eystein.

Jón Loptsson Defies the Hierarchy

1179

Þorláks saga helga hin yngri

AFTER the archbishopric of Nitharos was created in Norway, in 1154, and Icelandic bishops were consecrated there, the Church claimed ownership of religious property in Iceland. Bishop Thorlak of Skalholt, however, encountered the opposition of the "uncrowned king" of Iceland, Jón Loptsson, landlord of Oddi, "The Point," the estate where Snorri Sturluson received his education.

◆§ At that time Jón Loptsson ruled over Oddi. He was then the most influential man in Iceland. He was a magistrate and well versed in the clerical learning which he had acquired from his forebears. He was an ordained deacon and an excellent singer in holy church. He took great pains that the churches which he controlled were well administered in every respect. He was skilled in most of those accomplishments which were usual for men of that period. He was an ambitious man and so powerful and persistent that there was hardly his equal; for he would yield to no one or give up anything that he undertook.

Jón had a wife named Halldora, the daughter of Brand. Their son was Sæmund. Jón was very fond of women and had many other sons by several other women; Thorstein and Halldor, Sigurth and Einar. Paul, who later became bishop, and Orm, who afterwards lived at Breithabolstath, were his sons by Ragneith, daughter of Thorhall and sister of Bishop Thorlak. Jón and she had been in love since early childhood. Still she had children by other men. They were grown up, Paul and Orm, the sons of Jón and Ragneith, when Thorlak came back to Iceland with the rank of bishop. Paul was living at Ytra-skarth and Orm at Breithabolstath. For long periods Jón kept Ragneith at Oddi.

At that time Jón had come in possession of Hofthabrekka, which was considered one of the best properties until the Hoftha River destroyed the land. There, a southwesterly gale had demolished two churches, and now Jón had had a new church built, elaborate in workmanship. Bishop Saint Thorlak was to make his quarters there the same autumn that he came from Austfjorth, as was already told. It was intended that he should there consecrate the church. A magnificent feast had been prepared to entertain him. On the appointed day he arrived with his retinue.

Jón was there already and many other prominent men. In the morning the bishop prepared for the church consecration, but Jón and those men who were in counsel with him went to the bishop, and there was talk about what the church inventory should be. The Lord Bishop asked, in accordance with his right, whether Jón had heard the archbishop's ordinance about church property.

Jón replied, "I can listen to the archbishop's message, but I am resolved to hold it of no account. I do not think that he means any better or is wiser than my forefathers Sæmund the Learned and his sons. I am not willing to condemn the policy of our bishops here in the land who have recognized the custom of this country that laymen govern the churches which their ancestors dedicated to God and the ownership of which they reserved for themselves and their descendants."

The bishop answered, on such grounds as those advanced before, and gave many other reasons, saying, "Well you know this, Jón, if you wish to follow the truth: that the bishop is to govern the church property, and the tithes, according to the ordinances of the apostles and other holy fathers. And since laymen may not have control of these matters, it must never be justified on grounds of ancient customs. I believe that the rulers of the church, those who have been before us, were much to be excused, as they were not ordered by their superiors to call churches and tithes under their control; but those who now withhold the tithes and the properties of God with obstinacy against the bishops' wish and consent are liable for excommunication."

Jón answered, "You can call excommunicated whomever you please, but never shall I yield up my property into your power, be it a small church or a large, which I have authority over."

There was also another matter of disagreement between them. It arose over the floods in the Hoftha River. The river had taken many farms which lay under Hofthabrekka and two that the churches were on. Accordingly, there were less tithes and fewer buildings for divine service. Jón maintained, therefore, that there should be no more than one priest and one deacon at the church, whereas before there had been two priests and two deacons. The Lord Bishop was, however, willing to make concessions in this matter, for the same reason. But concerning the former contention, each held to his claim and delayed much of the day. Those who pretended to be friends of both sides bade the bishop modify his claim, and all the common people were of the same opinion, because of old bad customs.

When Bishop Thorlak saw that he might not, at present, promote his measure, then these words sprang from his lips: "Although it will be intolerable, if it comes before proper judges, that you drag the management of the church under you, according to the custom of the land, and away from the bishops, still it is much more intolerable that the bishops are not powerful enough to take away from you your concubines, whom you keep against all customs and law of the land.

Maybe you will have your own way in the greater issue if you have
it your own way in the minor one, even if your intentions are worse."

It is believed that Bishop Thorlak spoke those words because he
found that the common people followed Jón in the church matter.
He gave way this time because he saw there would be no use for him
to persist, but much harm, in many ways, and he expected that the
church would get its rights later, with the archbishop's help. But
from where he expected comfort, there came the news of grief,
because, a little later, Archbishop Eystein was driven from the land
on account of the church property question. Here in Iceland everybody thought that he could do as men have done before in Norway.

That day the bishop consecrated the church and sang the masses,
although his wish there was not fulfilled. He was not at all satisfied
with this outcome. And other people acted afterwards according to
the precedent set by Jón, and none would give the churches into the
power of the bishop. This issue was dropped during his days.

Shipwreck
1180
Guðmundar saga biskups Arasonar

GUTHMUND the Good was bishop of Holar in Iceland from 1201 to 1237,
but the shipwreck was an adventure of his youth.

⊷§ IN the spring of 1180 when Gudmund was nineteen, Priest Ingimund [his uncle] begins to think of a voyage to Norway, and
Gudmund, his ward, with him. They took passage at Gásir (Eyja-
firth) with Hallstein Hunchback, and sailed on Sunday the day
before Michaelmas. The wind took them East under the Noups to
the Foxes' plain [Melrakkaslétta]: then came a headwind and they
drove before it, and tumbled about for a week, and drifted to the
Hornstrands. One evening as they were at supper the awning tore
open at the edge. A man called Asmund, an Easterling [Norwegian],
looks out and suddenly cries:

"Whish! down with the awning, up boys and clear the decks! We
are on the breakers—never mind your supper this time!" Then they
all jump at once and get in the awning. Hallvard, the mate, calls out:

"Where is the ship's chaplain?"

"Not far to look for him," says Ingimund. "What do you want with him?"

"We want to confess," said they.

He answers: "It is no better time for confession than it was this autumn every Sunday, when I preached to you to come to confession in the name of God: and you would never hear. Now I must even pray to God to hear you; for I am no more at home on the sea than you are: be bold and keep a good heart."

They said: "Then you must make a vow along with us, a pilgrimage or some other large vow: nothing else will do."

"Nothing less," says Ingimund: "I will vow, if I may order what the vow shall be. Or else I will give my word for every Icelander on board that not a man of them will be with you in the vowing: for I will not be under your rule now any more than you were under mine in these last weeks on shore."

"What then wilt thou vow, Priest?" said the men from Norway.

"I will vow to Almighty God and Holy Cross, to our Lady St. Mary and All Saints, to give a tithe of all that comes safe on shore to churches or poor men as the bishop shall dispose."

They answered: "Thou shalt give the word, Priest, for we cannot do now without thy care." Now pledges are given all over the ship to keep this vow. And by this time they are well in among the breakers. Then there is a great dispute what is best to be done, and every man wants his own way. Some are for hoisting the sail, and they begin at this. Then Hallvard the mate asks Ingimund if he knows the highest name of God.

He answers: "I know some names of God; and I believe what the Apostle Paul says, that there is no name higher nor holier than the name of Jesus—but what thou callest the highest name I know not."

He answers: "I do not reckon such to be priests who do not know the name of God."

Then Ingimund calls to Hallvard: "Dost thou know the highest name?"

"God's truth," says Hallvard, "I scarcely think I can get my tongue to it now, and sorry for it. But Thord Crow (Kráka) will know. Thord Crow! canst thou name the high name?"

He says: "Worse luck, mate, it is slipped my mind, but some one else is sure to know. Thorbiorn Humla (Hops) will know."

"Aye aye! well well! Thorbiorn Humla, name the name if thou canst!"

He says: "I wish I could; but as far as I can tell, I never heard it: but I will show you a man that can, I think Einar Naepa (Neep, Turnip) knows."

Then they tried him, and he names the name. And when they had the sail up no more than the height of a man there comes a great beam sea breaking over the freight amidships and fore and aft as well. Every man was at a rope then, and Ingimund caught hold of a boathook, and tried to bring down the sail. Gudmund, his ward, had a berth in the ship's boat: he was standing between the boat and the sail, to see the sail clear. Then comes another heavy sea over the whole ship, and carries off the vane of the mast and both the bulwarks, and overboard everything loose amidships, except men; and the ship was much knocked about and the boat as well. Then they come through the breakers, and get a third sea, not so heavy as the others. Then they rushed to the bailing, fore and aft, and a piece of sail was hoisted.

Then they see land, and talk it over where they might have come: some said they must be at Malmey; but Thorarin Rosti, an Icelander, said that would be too short for all the time they had been driving. Then Mar Eyjolf's son speaks, and says he knows they are off the Hornstrands at Skjaldabjarnarvik, and said he had been there before, that summer. Then they asked him to lay them a course for a harbour, and wished to go North to Tharalatrs Fjord; for there was a safe harbour there.

Then they looked about to see what damage was done, and Ingimund comes to Gudmund, his nephew. Now the big sea had cast him into the boat, and his right leg hung over the gunwale of the boat and was caught in the sail. Ingimund asked why he did not get up. And he said there was such a weight on him that he could not stir nor stand. Then the loose sail was rolled off him; but still he did not rise. Ingimund asked why. He said his foot was so heavy he could not move it.

"The leg is broken," says Ingimund.

"I know not," says Gudmund. "I have no feeling in it."

Then they looked, and the leg was broken on the gunwale, the bones in shivers, and the toes pointing where the heels should be. So they put him to bed in the boat. Then Ingimund missed his trunk of books;

it had gone overboard. And he was hard hit, as he thought; for there was his pleasure where his books were; and the man crippled that he loved best. Yet he gave thanks to God; and thought there had been a quick fulfilment of his dream. For the night before he had dreamt of Archbishop Eystein, how he came to the Archbishop and was bidden welcome. He had told the dream to Gudmund, and Gudmund's reading of it was that there was some "arch business" ahead for them. And that same day, before they had come to rough water, Magnus Amundason had asked whether anyone knew of any breakers called "The Humps." And he was told that there were such, namely, off the Hornstrands.

"I dreamt," he says, "that we were near them." And a little after he had said that, they were aware of the breakers.

Now they are carried North, off Reykjafjord. Then they bring up, and lower the sail and cast anchor, and lie at anchor there all night. In the morning they get to land with planks from the ship, and cut down their mast and let it drive ashore, with a line fast to the ship. Then they debated what should be done with Gudmund. Then up speaks a man called Bersi, who went by the name of Corpselight—one of his cheeks was coal-black—and says:

"Why should we trouble about a sick man, and his leg broken, when we have enough to do to save ourselves? Send him overboard!"

Thorarin Rosti answered: "Hold the blasted tongue of thee! Send thee overboard thyself, and little loss! We must think of another way."

He jumps overboard at once, and Einar Neep along with him. The moving of the ship had brought her aground, and they let down Gudmund over the side in a web of wadmal, and Thorarin and Einar took him one on each side, and he sat on their arms with a hand about the neck of either man. And some men went behind to make some shelter from the seas. And so they made their way ashore, drawn backward by the downdraught of the sea, and sped onward as the new wave caught them. And they brought him to land. Then the ship canted seaward, and all that was in her went into the sea, and she broke up all to flinders, and little of her freight came to land.

At that place lived a man called Snorri, son of Arngeir; he was a leech. He takes Gudmund and brings him home with him, and treats him as well as he can; his house was not a rich one, but his will was good. Many men came to the place from the neighbouring homesteads to see what they could do for them or their goods. Then Ingimund made a vow and prayer that his book-trunk and his books might come to land. A few nights later news came that the box had come ashore at the Drongs, and everything in it that might be looked for; one hasp was holding and the other two were broken; and all the other chests that came ashore were broken and empty. Ingimund went there to dry his books; and was there till Martinmas. Then he came back to see his ward and learn how his leg was mending.

The Two Thoras
1196
Sturla Þórðarson
Sturlunga saga

THIS is a charming episode about two sisters and how they chose their husbands.

❧AT that time Gudmund Gris was living at Thingvellir. He was married to Jón Loptsson's daughter Solveig. They had two daughters, both named Thora, and to distinguish between them the one was called Thora the Younger and the other Thora the Elder. They were both very gifted and accomplished young ladies and were regarded as the best matches among the unmarried women.

They always went up into the Almanna Gorge with their linen, to the river that flows there. One day as they were amusing themselves beside the river, the elder Thora began to speak:

"How long do you think it will go on like this, sister, that no men come along and ask to marry us, and what do you suppose lies in store for us?"

"I don't give much thought to that," said Thora the Younger, "for I'm quite content with things as they are."

"To be sure," said Thora the Elder, "it's very pleasant and proper to be here with father and mother, but it's not particularly cheerful or amusing for all that."

"That's true," said Thora the Younger, "but it's by no means certain that you'll be any happier when things change."

"Well, anyway," said Thora the Elder, "let's have some fun out of it and test our wits. Tell me whom you would most like to have propose to you, for I don't suppose we'll sit at home unmarried all our lives."

"I see no point in that," said Thora the Younger, "since everything is foreordained, and it does no good to think about such things or talk nonsense about them."

"It's true, of course," said Thora the Elder, "that less important things than human destiny are foreordained. Nevertheless, I should like you to tell me what future you would choose."

"I suggest," said Thora the Younger, "that we let this conversation drop, for words once spoken travel fast."

"It seems to me no shame," said Thora the Elder, "if what we say is repeated. I'll tell you first what I should choose if you will tell me afterwards."

"You are the elder," said Thora the Younger, "so you must of course tell me first, since you're still determined not to stop this foolish chatter."

"What I should choose," said Thora the Elder, "is that Jon Sigmundsson should come riding along and ask to marry me and that I should be given to him."

The younger Thora answered: "You've certainly taken good care not to let go of the man who is now considered the best match in the country. And of course you wanted to choose first because you saw that that would make the choice harder for me. But it happens to be something much more difficult and improbable that appeals to me. I wish that Jora Bishop's-daughter would die and that Thorvald Gizursson would come here and ask to marry me."

"Let's stop this talk," said Thora the Elder, "and say nothing about it."

Then they walked home.

The ten winters that Archbishop Guttorm had permitted Thorvald and Jora to live together had now passed by, and Thorvald said that never had he loved her more than now, and that he did not know whether he could bring himself to part from her as he had promised the Archbishop. But that same year Jora died. The next spring both Thorvald and Jon had errands west in Borgarfjord. They rode together and spent the night at Thingvellir. And the next day, as they rode on toward the west, they talked a great deal about Gudmund's two daughters.

The two sisters used to sleep in the same bed, and Thora the Elder

always slept on the outside. When Thorvald and Jon came back from
the west, they again visited Thingvellir. Then Thora the Elder said
to her sister: "I'm going to put Thorvald and Jon in our bed tonight.
And since they're sure now to propose, I shall take the one who lies
in my place and you the one who lies next the wall." She knew that
Thorvald was in the habit of sleeping on the outside. And now both
of them preferred him.

"Why shouldn't you decide," said Thora the Younger, "how you
want to divide up the bed? Our fate will be as it is foreordained in
any case."

In the evening, when Thorvald and Jon went to bed, Jon asked:
"Thorvald, where would you rather sleep—on the outside or next
the wall?" Thorvald answered: "I always sleep on the outside, but
you choose now." "Then I'll sleep on the outside," said Jon, and
so it was. The next morning they made their proposals and the result
was that the elder Thora was married to Jon and the younger to
Thorvald.

Sighvat's Warning

1235

Sturla Þórðarson

Sturlunga saga

In 1235, after a pilgrimage to Rome and an extended visit to King Hakon
Hakonarson, Sturla Sighvatsson (1199-1238) returned to Iceland, resolved to subdue the rival chieftains and impose order on the country.
His father, Sighvat Sturluson, a brother of the great Snorri, who tries
in this scene to temper with irony his son's overweening ambition, died
fighting at his side in the battle of Örlygsstath in 1238. All the "servants"
suggested by Sighvat are of high rank, several of them members of the
proud Oddaverjar family, who were descended from King Magnus
Barefoot.

◄§In the spring Sturla went north to Eyjafjord to meet Sighvat,
his father, who received him kindly and had much to say about the
battle at Bae, albeit with a degree of sarcasm. He asked Sturla:
"Have you people been in yet another battle, my son?"

"We called it that," said Sturla.

"The shower must have been a short one," said Sighvat.

"It didn't seem too short to us," answered Sturla.

"You think you've risen pretty high now," said Sighvat, "that's plain to be seen."

"Why shouldn't it be?" answered Sturla smiling. "But I haven't said anything about it."

Then Sighvat said: "You'll be planning to set up an establishment for yourself, son, for I hear you've let Reykjaholt go. And now, of course, you look down on most of the estates. But where, then, will you find an abode that seems suitable to you?"

"I leave that entirely to you," said Sturla.

"There are only two that can be considered," said Sighvat, "if we leave out the episcopal sees: the one is Oddi, the other Mödruvellir in Hörgardal. These are the finest estates and will not seem at all too big for you."

"I like both of them very much," said Sturla, "but I don't suppose they're very easy to get hold of."

"It takes a lot to keep up an estate, son," continued Sighvat. "You'll need a steward and a housekeeper; they must be provident people and good managers. I know exactly whom you should have: your brother-in-law Halfdan of Keldur and your sister Steinvör. They would be excellent for these positions."

"You have certainly made a good choice," replied Sturla.

"But first and foremost you must have a shepherd," said Sighvat. "He should be small and light in the saddle, fond of women, and should lie for long hours on the wall of the sheepfold. I know just the man for that too: it's Björn Sæmundsson. Also I shall find attendants for you, who will follow you out and in; these will be your brothers Thord Krok and Markus."

Sturla said that would be very proper for his brothers.

"It takes a lot to keep up an estate, son," said Sighvat. "You will also need men who can look after the fishing and who know something about how to use a hammer, so that they can keep the boats and farm implements in repair. For this I recommend your relatives Bödvar of Stad and Thorleif of Gardar."

Sturla answered rather curtly, but allowed that they were both quite handy.

"Then, too, son," said Sighvat, "you will need people who know how to look after horses properly and can make the necessary plans for each journey. The men for this, as I see it, would be Lopt Bishop's-son and Bödvar of Bae."

"I can't expect all men to serve me," said Sturla, "and this is idle talk."

"There are only a few positions left," said Sighvat, "that really must be filled; but you must have men to bring you supplies, to go to the markets and to the ships, trustworthy and smart, who know how to keep men at work and can take charge of a journey. For this Gizur Thorvaldsson and Kolbein the Young would be suitable."

At this Sturla sprang up and went out. But when he came in again, Sighvat joked with him and they began to talk about something else. Sturla did not stay there long, however, but rode home to Saudafell.

When the conversation between Sighvat and Sturla was repeated to Lopt Bishop's-son, he said: "That's extremely funny and very much to the point; he has hit every one of them off to perfection." But when they told him that he and Bödvar were to look after the horses, he burst out: "The devil take their jibes! Bad luck to them, and I hope things will turn out otherwise than that everybody has to seek their favor."

The Death of Snorri Sturluson

September 22, 1241

Sturla Þórðarson

Sturlunga saga

THE great historian Snorri Sturluson was brutally murdered at the age of sixty-three by a party of assassins under the leadership of his former son-in-law, Gizur Thorvaldsson, a son of Thorvald Gizursson and Thora the Younger.

⊷ KOLBEIN the Young and Gizur met at that time on the Keel and laid plans which were later carried out. That summer Kol the Rich was killed by Arni, who was called "the Bitter." He then fled to Gizur, who took him in. When Gizur came down from the Keel, he summoned men to him, among them the brothers Klæng and Orm, Lopt Bishop's-son, and Arni the Untrusty. He now made known the letters that Eyvind and Arni had brought back with them from Norway. It was there stated that Gizur was either to send Snorri abroad whether he was willing to go or not; or else put him to death, because he had sailed to Iceland in defiance of the King's ban. King Hakon declared Snorri a traitor to him. Gizur said he would on no account disregard the King's letter but added that he knew Snorri would not go abroad willingly; and that he would therefore go [to Reykjaholt] and take Snorri by force.

Orm refused to have any part in this decision and rode home to Breidabolstad. Gizur collected troops and sent the brothers Arni the Bitter and Svart west to spy in Borgarfjord; but he himself rode on ahead with seventy men, leaving Lopt Bishop's-son in command of the force which followed. Klæng rode after troops to Kjalarnes and then up into the district [Borgarfjord].

Gizur came to Reykjaholt in the night after St. Mauritius's Day. They broke into the building in which Snorri was sleeping, but he sprang up and ran out of the house and into the small buildings close by. There he met Arnbjörn the priest and spoke with him. They decided that Snorri should go down into the cellar which was underneath the storeroom there. Gizur and his men now began to look for Snorri in the buildings. Then Gizur met Arnbjörn the priest and asked where Snorri was. He said he did not know. Gizur said it would be impossible to come to terms if he did not find him. The priest said he might be found if he were granted pardon.

Then they discovered where Snorri was, and Markus Mördsson, Simon Knot, Arni the Bitter, Thorstein Gudinason, and Thorarin Asgrimsson went into the cellar. Simon ordered Arni to strike him down. "Don't strike," said Snorri. "Strike," said Simon. "Don't strike," said Snorri. Thereupon Arni dealt him a mortal wound, and both he and Thorstein killed him.

The Fire at Flugumyri

October 22, 1253

Sturla Þórðarson

Sturlunga saga

Introduction and translation by W. P. Ker.

THE scenes of *Sturlunga* come into rivalry with the best of those in the heroic Sagas. No one will ever be able to say, much less to convince any one else, whether the burning of Njal's house or the burning of Flugumyri is the better told or the more impressive. There is no comparison between the personages in the two stories. But in pure art of language and in the certainty of its effect the story of Flugumyri is not less notable

than the story of Bergthorsknoll. It may be repeated here, to stand as the
last words of the great Icelandic school; the school which went out and
had no successor till all its methods were invented again, independently,
by the great novelists, after ages of fumbling and helpless experiments,
after all the weariness of pedantic chronicles and the inflation of heroic
romance.

Sturla had given his daughter Ingibjorg in marriage to Hall, son of
Gizur, and had come to the wedding at Flugumyri, Gizur's house at the
foot of the hills of Skagafjord, with steep slopes behind and the broad
open valley in front, a place with no exceptional defences, no fortress.
It was here, just after the bridal, and after the bride's father had gone
away, that Gizur's enemy, Eyjolf, came upon him, as he had threatened
openly in men's hearing. Sturla, who had left the house just before, tells
the story with the details that came to him from the eye-witnesses, with
exact particular descriptions. But there is no drag in the story, and nothing mean in the style, whatever may have been the brutal reality. It is,
once again, the great scene of Epic poetry repeated, the defence of a
man's life and of his own people against surrounding enemies; it is the
drama of Gunnar or of Njal played out again at the very end of the
Northern heroic age, and the prose history is quick to recognize the
claims upon it.

This is the end of the wedding at Flugumyri, in October of the year
1253, as told by Sturla:

EYJOLF saw that the attack was beginning to flag, and grew afraid
that the countryside might be raised upon them; so they brought up
the fire. John of Bakki had a tar-pin with him; they took the sheepskins from the frames that stood outside there, and tarred them and
set them on fire. Some took hay and stuffed it into the windows and
put fire to it; and soon there was a great smoke in the house and a
choking heat. Gizur lay down in the hall by one of the rows of pillars,
and kept his nose on the floor. Groa his wife was near him. Thorbjorn
Neb was lying there too, and he and Gizur had their heads close together. Thorbjorn could hear Gizur praying to God in many ways
and fervently, and thought he had never before heard praying like it.
As for himself, he could not have opened his mouth for the smoke.
After that Gizur stood up and Groa supported him, and he went to the
south porch. He was much distressed by the smoke and heat, and
thought to make his way out rather than be choked inside. Gizur
Glad was standing at the door, talking to Kolbein Grön, and Kolbein
was offering him quarter, for there was a pact between them, that if
ever it came to that, they should give quarter to one another, which-
ever of them had it in his power. Gizur stood behind Gizur Glad, his

namesake while they were talking, and got some coolness the while. Gizur Glad said to Kolbein, "I will take quarter for myself, if I may bring out another man along with me." Kolbein agreed to this at once, excepting only Gizur and his sons.

Then Ingibjorg, Sturla's daughter, came to Groa at the door; she was in her nightgown, and barefoot. She was then in her fourteenth year, and tall and comely to see. Her silver belt had tangled round her feet as she came from her bedroom. There was on it a purse with many gold rings of hers in it; she had it there with her. Groa was very glad to see her, and said that there should be one lot for both of them, whatever might befall.

When Gizur had got himself cooled a little, he gave up his thought of dashing out of the house. He was in linen clothes, with a mail-coat over them, and a steel cap on his head, and his sword *Corselet-biter* in his hand. Groa was in her nightgown only. Gizur went to Groa and took two gold rings out of his girdle-pocket and put them into her hand, because he thought that she would live through it, but not he himself. One ring had belonged to Bishop Magnus his uncle, and the other to his father Thorvald.

"I wish my friends to have the good of these," he says, "if things go as I would have them."

Gizur saw that Groa took their parting much to heart.

Then he felt his way through the house, and with him went Gudmund the Headstrong, his kinsman, who did not wish to lose sight of him. They came to the doors of the ladies' room; and Gizur was going to make his way out there. Then he heard outside the voices of men cursing and swearing, and turned back from there.

Now in the meantime Groa and Ingibjorg had gone to the door. Groa asked for freedom for Ingibjorg. Kolbein heard that, her kinsman, and asked Ingibjorg to come out to him. She would not, unless she got leave to take some one out along with her. Kolbein said that was too much to ask. Groa besought her to go.

"I have to look after the lad Thorlak, my sister's son," says she.

Thorlak was a boy of ten, the son of Thorleif the Noisy. He had jumped out of the house before this, and his linen clothes were all ablaze when he came down to the ground: he got safe to the church. Some men say that Thorstein Genja pushed Groa back into the fire; she was found in the porch afterwards. Kolbein dashed into the fire for Ingibjorg, and carried her out to the church.

Then the house began to blaze up. A little after, Hall Gizur's son
[the bridegroom] came to the south door, and Arni the Bitter, his
henchman, with him. They were both very hard put to it, and distressed by the heat. There was a board across the doorway, halfway
up. Hall did not stop to look, but jumped straight out over the hatch.
He had a sword in one hand, and no weapon besides. Einar Thorgrimsson was posted near where he leapt out, and hewed at his head
with a sword, and that was his death-wound. As he fell, another man
cut at his right leg below the knee and slashed it nearly off. Thorleif
the monk from Thverá, the brewer, had got out before, and was in
the yard; he took a sheepskin and put it under Hall when Einar and
the others went away; then he rolled all together, Hall and the sheepskin, along to the church when they were not looking. Hall was
lightly clad, and the cold struck deep into his wounds. The monk was
barefoot, and his feet were frostbitten, but he brought himself and
Hall to the church at last.

Arni leapt out straight after Hall; he struck his foot on the hatch
(he was turning old) and fell as he came out. They asked who that
might be, coming in such a hurry.

"Arni the Bitter is here," says he; "and I will not ask for quarter.
I see one lying not far away makes me like it well enough if I travel
the same road with him."

Then said Kolbein: "Is there no man here remembers Snorri
Sturluson?"

They both had a stroke at him, Kolbein and Ari Ingimund's son,
and more of them besides hewed at him, and he came by his death
there.

Then the hall fell in, beginning from the north side into the loft
above the hall. Now all the buildings began to flare up, except that the
guest-house did not burn, nor the ladies' room, nor the dairy.

Now to go back to Gizur: he made his way through the house to the
dairy, with Gudmund, his kinsman, after him. Gizur asked him to go
away, and said that one man might find a way of escape, if fate would
have it so, that would not do for two. Then Parson John Haldorsson
came up; and Gizur asked them both to leave him. He took off his
coat of mail and his morion, but kept his sword in his hand. Parson
John and Gudmund made their way from the dairy to the south door,
and got quarter. Gizur went into the dairy and found a curd-tub
standing on stocks; there he thrust the sword into the curds down

over the hilts. He saw close by a vat sunk in the earth with whey in it, and the curd-tub stood over it and nearly hid the sunken vat altogether. There was room for Gizur to get into it, and he sat down in the whey in his linen clothes and nothing else, and the whey came up to his breast. It was cold in the whey. He had not been long there when he heard voices, and their talk went thus, that three men were meant to have the hewing of him; each man his stroke, and no hurry about it, so as to see how he took it. The three appointed were Hrani and Kolbein and Ari. And now they came into the dairy with a light, and searched about everywhere. They came to the vat that Gizur was in, and thrust into it three or four times with spears. Then there was a wrangle among them; some said there was something in the vat, and others said no. Gizur kept his hand over his belly, moving gently, so that they might be as long as possible in finding out that there was anything there. He had grazes on his hands, and all down to his knees skin wounds, little and many. Gizur said afterwards that before they came in he was shaking with cold, so that it rippled in the vat, but after they came in he did not shiver at all. They made two searches through the dairy, and the second time was like the first. After that they went out and made ready to ride away. Those men that still had life in them were spared, to wit, Gudmund Falkason, Thord the Deacon, and Olaf, who was afterwards called Guest, whose life Einar Thorgrimsson had attempted before. By that time it was dawn.

Sturla the Historian

1263

Sturla Þórðarson

Sturlunga saga

Introduction and translation by W. P. Ker.

In the year 1262 came the submission of Iceland to Norway, "the end of an auld sang." In 1263 Sturla was ruined, to all appearances. He had been dragged into trouble by an ill-conditioned son of his, and was beaten by his adversary, Hrafn Oddsson, and had to leave Iceland. He resolved to go to Norway to try for the favour of the king. Hacon by this time had set out on his great expedition to Scotland, but the young King Magnus, who had been already crowned, was at home with his queen, the

Danish lady Ingiborg. This was the beginning of Sturla's Norwegian historical work, and this is the story of his visit to King Magnus.

⊷§Sturla sailed for Norway from Eyre [in the South of Iceland]; he had scarcely any supplies with him. They had a good voyage and took the land at Bergen; Magnus the king was there; as also was Gaut of Mel. Sturla went at once to find Gaut. Gaut was pleased and said: "Art thou Sturla the Icelander?" "That is so," said Sturla. Gaut said, "You are welcome at my table like the other Sturlungs." "No house would be better for me, as far as I can see," said Sturla. So he went to stay with Gaut and told him clearly the whole story of his coming to Norway; and Gaut, on the other hand, told him how he had been evil spoken of with Magnus the king, and still more with Hacon. A little after Gaut and Sturla went to King Magnus. Gaut paid his respects to the king, and he took it well; Sturla did the same, but he made no answer. He said: "Tell me, Gaut, who is this man that goes along with you?" Gaut said: "This man is Sturla, Thord's son, the poet, and he is come to throw himself on your grace; and I think him, Sir, to be a wise man." The king said: "We think of him that he would not have come here of his own accord; he must put it to the proof when he meets my father." Gaut said: "Even so, for I think he has poems to offer to you and your father." "It is not likely that I will have him put to death," said King Magnus, "but he shall not come into my service." Then they went away, and when they came to their lodging Gaut said to Sturla: "The king seemed very slow to take you up, but he has put you out of danger; there must have been much evil-speaking against you." Sturla says: "I have no doubt of that, nay, I seem to make out clearly that Hrafn has been spreading slanders; all kinds of things were mixed up together in Iceland, small and great, truth and lies."

The next day Gaut went down to the king's house. When he came back and met Sturla he said: "Now you are provided for, since the king wishes you to come with him when he sails for the South." Sturla answered: "Shall not the king decide? But I have no great mind to go from here."

Then he got ready to sail away with the king, and his name was put on the list. He went on board before many men had come; he had a sleeping bag and a travelling chest, and took his place on the fore-deck. A little later the king came on to the quay, and a company of men with him. Sturla rose and bowed, and bade the king "hail," but the king answered nothing, and went aft along the ship to the quarter-deck. They sailed that day to go south along the coast. But in the evening when men unpacked their provisions Sturla sat still, and no one invited him to mess. Then a servant of the king's came and asked Sturla if he had any meat and drink. Sturla said "No." Then the king's servant went to the king and spoke with him, out of hearing: and then went forward to Sturla and said: "You shall go to mess with Thorir Mouth and Erlend Maw." They took him into their mess, but rather stiffly. When men were turning in to sleep, a sailor of the king's asked who should tell them stories. There was little answer. Then said he: "Sturla the Icelander, will you tell stories?" "As you will," said Sturla. So he told them the story of Huld, better and fuller than any one there had ever heard it told before. Then many men pushed forward to the fore-deck, wanting to hear as clearly as might be, and there was a great crowd. The queen asked: "What is that crowd on deck there?" A man answered: "The men are listening to the story that the Icelander tells." "What story is that?" said she. He answered: "It is about a great troll-wife, and it is a good story and well told." The king bade her pay no heed to that, and go to sleep. She says, "I think this Icelander must be a good fellow, and less to blame than he is reported." The king was silent.

So the night passed, and the next morning there was no wind for them, and the king's ship lay in the same place. Later in the day, when men sat at their drink, the king sent dishes from his table to Sturla. Sturla's messmates were pleased with this: "You bring better luck than we thought, if this sort of thing goes on." After dinner the queen sent for Sturla and asked him to come to her and bring the troll-wife story along with him. So Sturla went aft to the quarter-deck, and greeted the king and queen. The king answered little, the queen well and cheerfully. She asked him to tell the same story he had told overnight. He did so, for a great part of the day. When he had finished the queen thanked him, and many others besides, and made him out in their minds to be a learned man and sensible. But the king said nothing; only he smiled a little. Sturla thought he saw that the king's whole frame of mind was brighter than the day before. So he said to the king that he had made a poem about him, and another about his father: "I would gladly get a hearing for them." The queen said: "Let him recite his poem; I am told that he is the best of poets, and his poem will be excellent." The king bade him say on, if he would, and repeat the poem he professed to have made about him. Sturla chanted it to the end. The queen said: "To my mind that is a good poem." The king said to her: "Can you follow the poem clearly?" "I would be fain to have you think so, Sir," said the queen. The king said: "I have learned that Sturla is good at verses." Sturla took his leave of the king and queen and went to his place. There was no sailing for the king all that day. In the evening before he went to bed he sent for Sturla. And when he came he greeted the king and said: "What will you have me to do, Sir?" The king called for a silver goblet of wine, and drank some and gave it to Sturla and said: "A health to a friend in wine!" (*Vín skal til vinar drekka*). Sturla said: "God be praised for it!" "Even so," says the king; "and now I wish you to say the poem you have made about my father." Sturla repeated it: and when it was finished men praised it much, and most of all the queen. The king said: "To my thinking, you are a better reciter than the Pope."

Icelandic Recipes

Fourteenth century

MS Royal Irish Academy 23 D 43

THE Icelandic sagas do not contain much information about cooking, but modern English books of travel praise the farmers' wives of Iceland for their imaginative culinary arts. Here are recipes for almond butter and for cured venison found in Dublin in an old Icelandic manuscript.

ALMOND BUTTER

One shall take almond meats and add water and make a milk in a pot and heat it over the coals. And one shall add afterwards well-crushed saffron and salt and vinegar so that it is clearly noticeable and boil until it is thoroughly thickened. Then one shall put it in a clean pot and hang it up until all the juice is run out. After that take out what is left and make a butter thereof.

CURED VENISON

One shall take cloves and mace, cardemom, pepper, cinnamon, ginger—an equal weight of each except cinnamon, of which there shall be just as much as of all the others, and as much baked bread as all that has been said above. And he shall cut it all together and grind it in strong vinegar; and put it in a cask. That is their salt and it is good for half a year.

When a man wants to use of this salt, he shall boil it in a pan over coals without flame. Then he shall take venison of hart or roe and carefully garnish with fat and roast it. And cut it well burned; and when the salt is cold then the meat shall be cut up therein with a little salt. Then it can lie for three weeks. So a man may long keep geese, ducks, and other game, if he cuts them thin. This is the best salt the gentry have.

Icelandic Medicines

Fourteenth century

MS Royal Irish Academy 23 D 43

IN spite of their vigorous life, Icelanders were sometimes sick and had their remedies. Here are the prescriptions for gold, onions, and burdock.

GOLD

Aurum is gold and is more fitly tempered in its nature than any other metal. And therefore it helps well the stomach which has a weakness and is very ill. Gold strengthens, too, him who has a cold and dry nature. Any sore treated with gold will not rot, where the gold was poured on and remains like a froth. It is good for eye trouble and draws a membrane from the eyes and dries their flow of water. Gold also strengthens the eyelids and the sinews that are within the eyelids.

ONION

Cepa is onion. It is good for them that have cold and wet natures, and it does good in the stomach, and gives good complexion. He who eats it fasting, on that day gets no pain. Onion gives sleep and purgation to him who eats it. Onion is good for dog's bite if it is crushed with honey or vinegar and is applied for four days. If one crushes salt and onion together, it is good for viper's bite. Onion's juice and woman's milk often drives away great earache. If one drinks onion's juice in water, it is good for him who suddenly loses his voice. If one draws onion's juice into his nose, it drives out harmful humors. If one mixes onion's juice and paunch fat of chickens, it is good to rub on shoes that cut. If one washes his teeth with it in the morning, he will not get toothache. If one eats onion and bread, it is good for a sore and swollen mouth. If one boils onion in butter or oil, it is good for dysentery. If one washes his bald head in onion's juice, hair will grow upon it. Onion is good in the mouth against evil smell, and does away with loathing of food. Onion's juice mixed with honey is good for dim eyes. If it is mixed with vinegar, it cleanses blotches if they are washed therewith.

BUR-DOCK

Lappacium, the bur-dock or haevindla. It is of four kinds and all have almost the same power, and they are all dry and hot. They strengthen the stomach and belch out of the stomach bad wind. If one eats the bur-kale, that binds the stomach. If one washes in warm juice of bur-dock, scabies and the itch will leave him. If one rinses his mouth with the juice, that is good for the uvula and for toothache. If one boils roots of bur-dock with wine or water and drinks it, that will drive stone from the bladder and is good for jaundice.

IV. NORWAY

Harald Fairhaired

King of Norway, 860-930

Snorri Sturluson

Heimskringla

NORWAY remained partitioned into small kingdoms long after Denmark and Sweden. Harald Fairhaired accomplished the difficult task of uniting all Norway, in answer, according to the chronicles, to the challenge of a spirited girl.

◆§KING Harald sent his men after a certain maiden called Gyda, the daughter of King Eric of Hordaland, and she was at fostering at Valldres with a rich bonder. Now the king would fain have her to his bed-mate, because she was a maiden exceeding fair, and withal somewhat high-minded. So when the messengers came there, they put forth their errand to the maiden, and she answered in this wise:

"I will not waste my maidenhood for the taking to husband of a king who has no more realm to rule over than a few Folks. Marvelous it seems to me," she says, "that there be no king minded to make Norway his own, and be sole lord thereof in such wise as Gorm of Denmark or Eric of Upsala have done."

Great words indeed seemed this answer to the messengers, and they ask her concerning her words, what wise this answer shall come to, and they say that Harald was a king so mighty, that the offer was right meet for her. But yet though she answered to their errand otherwise than they would, they see no way as at this time to have her away but if she herself were willing thereto, so they arrayed them for their departing, and when they were ready, men lead them out; then spake Gyda to the messengers:

"Give this my word to King Harald, that only so will I say yea to being his sole and lawful wife, if he will first do so much for my sake as to lay under him all Norway, and rule that realm as freely as King Eric rules the Swede-realm, or King Gorm Denmark; for only so meseems may he be called aright a King of the People."

The messengers fare back to King Harald and tell him of this word of the maiden, calling her overbold and witless, and saying withal that it would be but meet for the king to send after her with many men, for the doing of some shame to her. Then answered the king that the maid had spoken nought of ill, and done nought worthy of evil reward. Rather he bade her much thank for her word; "For she has brought to my mind that matter which it now seems to me wondrous I have not had in my mind heretofore."

And moreover he said: "This oath I make fast, and swear before that god who made me and rules over all things, that never more will I cut my hair nor comb it, till I have gotten to me all Norway, with the scat thereof and the dues, and all rule thereover, or else will I die rather."

The Battle of Hafrsfjord

872

Snorri Sturluson

Heimskringla

KING Harald Fairhaired won his final victory over the independent kings and jarls of Norway in the naval engagement of Hafrsfjord.

⤲§Now came tidings from the south that the men of Hordaland and Rogaland, they of Agdir and Thelmark, had arisen and gathered together with great plenty of weapons and ships and many men; and their captains were Eric, king of Hordaland, Sulki, king of Roga-land, and Earl Soti his brother, Kiotvi the Wealthy, king of Agdir, and Thorir Long-chin; from Thelmark came two brethren, Roald and Rig, and Hadd the Hardy to wit.

But when King Harald heard these tidings he gathered an host, and put forth his ships into the sea. Then he arrayed a great host, and fared south along the land, and gat many men from every folk-land. But when he was come south about the Stad, King Eric heard thereof; and he had by then gotten together all the folk he looked to have. So he fared south to meet the host that he wotted would come from the east to his helping; and the whole host of them met north of Jadar and made for Hafursfirth, where lay King Harald with his host awaiting them. There a great fight befell, and both long and hard it was; but such was the end thereof that King Harald had the victory, and King Eric fell there, and King Sulki, and Earl Soti his brother.

Thorir Long-chin had laid his ship against King Harald's; and a great bareserk was Thorir. Hard was the brunt before Thorir fell, when his ship was cleared utterly. Then fled away King Kiotvi to a certain holm where was good vantage for fighting. Then all their host fled away, some by ship, and some ran up country, and so inland south about Jadar.

* * *

After this battle King Harald found nought to withstand him in all Norway; for all his greatest foemen were fallen. But certain fled away from the land, and a many folk were these; for then were the waste lands peopled far and wide. Jamptland and Helsingland were peopled, though either of them indeed had been somewhat peopled by Northmen aforetime.

Amid this unpeace, whenas King Harald was fighting for the land in Norway, were the Outlands found and peopled, the Faroes and Iceland to wit; also was there much faring of Northmen to Shetland. And many mighty men of Norway fled as outlaws before King Harald, and fell to the warring of the West: in the winter they abode in the South-isles or the Orkneys, but a-summer harried in Norway, and wrought great scathe on the land.

Nevertheless there were many mighty men who did fealty to King Harald and became his men, and abode in the land along with him.

Olaf Tryggvason

September 9, 1000

Snorri Sturluson

Heimskringla

KING Olaf Tryggvason was the apostle of militant Christianity to West Scandinavia. During his short reign (995-1000) America was discovered, and Norway, the Orkneys, and the Western Isles, the Faeroes, Iceland, and Greenland accepted the Church of Rome. His dramatic end in the naval engagement of Svold between Olaf and the kings of Denmark and Sweden and Jarl Erik of Norway is as familiar to Norwegian school-children as the assassination of Julius Caesar or of Abraham Lincoln. This battle has been celebrated in poetry by Longfellow and in music by Grieg.

Now Einar Thambarskelvir was aboard the Worm aft in the main-hold; and he shot with the bow and was the hardest shooting of all men. Einar shot at Earl Eric, and the arrow smote the tiller-head above the head of the earl, and went in up to the shaft binding. The earl looked thereon and asked if they wist who shot; and even therewith came another arrow so nigh that it flew betwixt the earl's side and his arm, and so on into the staying board of the steersman, and the point stood out far beyond. Then spake the earl to a man whom some name Finn, but othersome say that he was of Finnish kin, and he was the greatest of bowmen; and he said, "Shoot me yonder big man in the strait hold."

So Finn shot, and the arrow came on Einar's bow even as he drew the third time, and the bow burst asunder in the midst. Then spake King Olaf: "What brake there so loud?"

Answereth Einar: "Norway, king, from thine hands."

"No such crash as that," said the king; "take my bow and shoot therewith." And he cast the bow to him. So Einar took the bow and drew it straightway, right over the arrowhead, and said: "Too weak, too weak, All-wielder's bow!" and cast the bow back. Then took he his shield and sword, and fought manfully.

King Olaf Tryggvison stood on the poop of the Worm, and shot full oft that day, whiles with the bow and whiles with javelins, and ever twain at once. Now looked he forward on the ship, and saw his men heave up sword and smite full fast, but saw withal that they bit but ill; so he cried out aloud: "Is it because ye raise your swords so dully, that I see that none of ye bite?"

So a man answered: "Our swords are dull and all to-sharded."

Then went the king down into the forehold, and unlocked the chest of the high-seat; and took thence many sharp swords and gave them to his men.

But as he stretched down his right hand men saw that the blood ran down from under his byrny sleeve; but none wist where he was wounded.

Now the most defence on the Worm and the most murderous to men was of those of the forehold and the forecastle, for in either place was the most chosen folk and the bulwark highest; but the folk began to fall first amidships. But now whenas but few men were on their feet about the mast, Earl Eric fell to boarding, and came up on to the Worm with fourteen men. Then came against him Hyrning, brother-in-law of King Olaf, with a company of men, and there befell the hardest battle; but such was the end of it that the earl drew back on to Iron-beak, and of those men who followed him, some fell and some were wounded. Hereof telleth Thord Kolbeinson:

"There was upraised the war-din
Around the gory Hropt's walls
Of the king's host: and there Hyrning,
Who turned the blue swords' edges,
Gat good word. Ere it dieth
Shall the high fells' hall be fallen."

And yet again was the battle of the sharpest, and many men fell aboard the Worm. But when the crew of the Worm waxed thin for the warding, then Earl Eric fell on again to come up on to her; and yet again was his meeting hard. But when the forecastle men of the Worm saw this, they went aft and turned against the earl to defend them, and dealt him a hard meeting. Nevertheless, whereas there was so much folk fallen aboard the Worm that the bulwarks were widely waste of men, the earl's men came aboard on every side, and all the folk that yet stood upon their feet for the warding of the Worm fell aback aft whereas the king was. So saith Haldor the Unchristened, telling how Earl Eric cheered on his men:

"Back shrank the folk with Olaf
Across the thwarts, when glad-heart
The earl cheered on his war-lads,
The doughty in the battle,
When they had locked the ship-boards
Around the King of Halland,
Bounteous of sea-flame. Tided
Sword-oath round that Wend-slayer."

Now Kolbiorn the Marshal went up on to the poop to the king, and much alike were they in raiment and weapons, and Kolbiorn also was the fairest and biggest of men. And now once more in the fore-hold was the battle full fierce; but, because so much folk of the earl was gotten aboard the Worm as the ship might well hold, and his ships also lay close all round about the Worm, and but a few folk were left for warding her against so great an host, now albeit those men were both strong and stout of heart, yet there in short space fell the more part of them. But King Olaf himself and Kolbiorn leapt overboard, either on his own board; but the earl's men had put forth small boats and slew such as leapt into the deep. So when the king himself leapt into the sea they would have laid hands on him and brought him to Earl Eric; but King Olaf threw up his shield over him, and sank down into the deep sea. But Kolbiorn the Marshal thrust his shield under him to guard him from the weapons thrust up at him from the boats that lay below, and in such wise he came into the sea that his shield was under him, so that he sank not so speedily, but that they laid hand on him and drew him up into a boat; and they deemed of him that he was the king. So he was led before the earl; and when the earl was ware that it was Kolbiorn and not King Olaf, then was peace given to Kolbiorn.

But even at this point of time leapt overboard from the Worm all King Olaf's men that were yet alive; and Hallfred sayeth that Thorkel Nosy the king's brother leapt overboard the last of all:

> "The waster of the arm-stone
> Saw the Crane floating empty,
> And either Adder: gladsome
> He reddened spear in the battle
> Ere the fight-daring, bold-heart
> Thorketil deft at swimming
> Fled from huge brunt of battle
> Offboard the wolf of tackle."

Now as is aforewrit Earl Sigvaldi had fallen into fellowship with King Olaf in Wendland, and had ten ships with him; but an eleventh there was whereon were the men of Astrid the king's daughter, wife of Earl Sigvaldi. But whenas King Olaf leaped overboard, then all the host cried the cry of victory, and therewith Earl Sigvaldi and his men dashed their oars into the water and rowed into the battle. Hereof telleth Haldor the Unchristened:

> "From wide away the Wend-ships
> Drew o'er the sea together,
> And Thridi's land's lean monsters
> On the folk yawned iron-throated.
> Swords'-din at sea betided,
> Wolf's fare the erne was tearing,
> There fought the lads' dear leader,
> And fled full many a war-host."

But the Wendland cutter whereon were Astrid's men rowed away
and back under Wendland; and the talk of many it was then and there
that King Olaf will have done off his byrny under water, and so
dived out under the long-ships and swum for the Wendland cutter,
and that Astrid's men brought him to land. And many are the tales
told thereafter by some men about King Olaf's farings. Nevertheless in this wise sayeth Hallfred:

> "I wot not one or the other,
> To call him dead or living,
> The soother of mews of clatter
> Of the sheen of Leyfi's sea-deer
> Since either tale folk tell me
> For true, and this is certain
> That wounded must the king be,
> And tidings of him fail us."

And howsoever it may have been, nevermore thenceforward came
Olaf Tryggvison back to his realm of Norway.

Asbjorn Seal's-Bane

c. 1025

Snorri Sturluson

Heimskringla

A prosperous Norwegian farmer had his troubles with Saint Olaf.

THERE was a famine in Halegoland far up on the coast of Norway. Yet Asbiorn of Throndness vowed he would have his three
great banquets that year, as usual. It was no easy matter to buy corn
even at high prices, for news came from the south that King Olaf
had forbidden people in the south of Norway to sell grain to any
who lived in the North-country.

Asbiorn was a young man, very rash and confident, as he had just
inherited his father's large estate. He laughed at the king's orders,
and decided to go south for grain. So he and twenty men put out in
his merchant ship, a splendid vessel with fine rigging and a sail
striped with a colored ribbon. Nothing is told of their journey until
they hove into Kormt Sound one evening, and lay to off Ogvaldsness.
That was the name of a great manor house belonging to the king. It

NORWAY   239

stood a little way up on the island of Kormt. A man named Thorir
Seal lived there and was steward of it for King Olaf. Thorir was a
mean, tricky sort of man of low birth, who had worked his way into
the king's favor by his strong will and quick wits.

Asbiorn lay off Ogvaldsness over night. At daybreak Thorir came
down to the ship, and some men with him.

"Who is captain of this handsome vessel?" he asked.

Asbiorn told who was.

"How far are you going and what is your errand?"

Asbiorn said he wished to buy corn. "Perhaps we can get some
here. I see your ricks are full. Then we shall not have to go further
south."

"O, you need not go any further," said Thorir, laughing sarcastically. "You may as well turn back, you can get no grain here, nor
further south, for King Olaf forbids selling to northerners. So go
back Halegolander; that will be best for you."

"In that case," Asbiorn replied, "I will only sail down to Jader and
visit my uncle Erling."

Thorir seemed suspicious. For many people thought that Erling
had plotted against King Olaf and was at heart his enemy.

But Thorir tried to appear friendly. He called after Asbiorn as he
sailed away, "A good voyage! Stop here again on your way back!"

Asbiorn said he would.

That evening they came to Jader, where his uncle Erling gave
Asbiorn a hearty welcome.

At first Erling said there was no way of selling corn, on account
of the king's order. But, next day, he called out his slaves, who did
not come under the king's laws, and let them sell Asbiorn all the
corn he wanted. By this clever trick he filled his ship, and headed
north.

As he had promised, he hove to again, off Ogvaldsness.

That night Thorir Seal heard about Asbiorn's coming, and this
also, that his ship was deep laden. Thorir summoned men to him during the night, so that he collected some sixty before day, and went to
find Asbiorn just as it began to dawn. They went straight to the ship.
By that time Asbiorn and his men were up and dressed, and Asbiorn
welcomed Thorir.

Thorir asked what cargo he had on board.

Asbiorn said it was corn and malt.

"Then Erling is up to his old tricks again, making a joke of all the king's commands!"

Thorir raved and talked furiously for a while. When he stopped for breath, Asbiorn said Erling's slaves had owned the corn.

Thorir replied snappishly that he did not care a straw for Erling's tricks. "Now Asbiorn, it's come to this, either you will go on shore, or we will put you overboard; for we are not going to have you in the way while we unload this ship."

Asbiorn saw he had not enough men to resist Thorir, so he and his crew went to land, and Thorir had the ship cleared of all its cargo.

When the ship was empty, Thorir walked down the deck and said, "These Halegolanders have a mighty good sail. Let's take the dirty sail from our old skow and give it to them; it will be good enough for them, sailing with an empty keel."

So the sails were exchanged, and with the ship rigged in this fashion, Asbiorn's people sailed away, and made north along the coast, and did not stop until they came home, early in winter; and the news of their journey spread far and wide. So now all the trouble of preparing feasts was taken from Asbiorn that winter.

That winter Asbiorn stayed close at home. He heard that people in Halegoland were joking about his expedition south for grain. At Christmas he did not go to the great family feast given by one of his uncles, and the uncle, jesting about the matter, said, "I wonder if Asbiorn thinks Seal-Thorir is laying for him on every island." This of course made Asbiorn very angry and eager to go to Ogvaldsness again and get his revenge on Thorir.

Now Asbiorn owned another ship, a long one, made for speed and fighting, a twenty-benched cutter, which stood in a large boat-shed. After Candlemass, in February, Asbiorn launched this ship, and summoned his friends to him and had nearly ninety men, all well armed. And when he was ready, and the wind fair, he sailed south along the land, going rather slowly. And when they got farther south, they kept as much as they could to sea, outside the chain of islands, instead of taking the regular highway between the islands and the mainland, where they would have met many ships. Nothing is told of their voyage until they hove in to Kormt, in the evening of Thursday after Easter. On the eastern side of Kormt were many dwellings, including Ogvaldsness, where Seal-Thorir lived, but the island was unpopulated in that part which lies toward the sea. On this western coast, where there were no dwellings, landed Asbiorn and his men. When they had set their tents, Asbiorn said, "Now you shall stay behind here and wait for me, while I go up on the island and spy out how things are, for we have heard nothing yet."

Asbiorn was dressed in rags like a tramp, with a slouch hat; he had a boat hook in his hand, and a sword girt under his clothing. He went up across the land and over the island, and when he came to a rising from which he could look at the buildings of Ogvaldsness and farther out over Kormt Sound, there he saw great numbers of people coming both by land and by sea, and all this crowd was making for the homestead of Ogvaldsness. Asbiorn thought this very strange. So he went to Ogvaldsness himself and to a place where serving-men were preparing meat. And immediately he heard from their talk that King Olaf had come to a feast and was now at the table with Thorir Seal.

Then Asbiorn turned to the great hall, the building in which the king was eating. And when he came into the porch men went in and out and no one paid any attention to him. Asbiorn stood outside the hall door, which was open, and looked in. As usual in such halls, there were two long narrow tables on each side of the room, running lengthwise, near the wall. These tables were put together for meal time, by laying boards on trestles and covering them with cloth. Men sat only on one side, on benches, along the wall, facing the room, in the middle of which smoldered a fire. Before them stewards laid the food. The middle board, along each wall, was raised higher than the others, and behind it stood an engraved chair, or high-seat, for men of note. In the high-seat on the left side of Thorir's hall the king was sitting and eating.

As Asbiorn stood looking in, the sun was setting and shone across the men's faces. Thorir had finished his dinner and was standing in front of the high-seat, talking glibly and earnestly to the king. The other men at the tables, whether they were done or not, stopped eating and listened intently to what Thorir was saying, and even the stewards stopped scurrying in with food.

Asbiorn listened too. He heard men asking Thorir about his dealings with Asbiorn last summer, and Thorir made a long tale of it, and it seemed to Asbiorn that he twisted the story. Then he heard a man ask, "How did Asbiorn behave himself while you were unloading his ship?"

"He bore up in a way," said Thorir, laughing, "and still not very well, while we were clearing the ship, but when we took the sail from him, then he wept."

The minute Asbiorn heard this, he drew his sword hard and quick, and sprang into the hall and instantly hacked at Thorir; the stroke came on the back of his neck, his head fell on the table before the king, and his trunk across the king's ankles, and the table cloths were all soaked with blood.

The king spoke, bade them take him and lead him out, and so it was done, and Asbiorn was seized and led out of the hall. And the table-service was taken, and the linen, and brought away, and Thorir's body carried off, and everything washed up which was bloody. The king seemed terribly angry, yet, as he always did, he controlled his speech.

There happened to be present a son of Erling of Jadar, named Skjalg, an own cousin to Asbiorn. He got up from his seat, went before the king and said, "Some atonement must be given you, king, for Asbiorn's crime. I will offer money that he may keep his life and limb, but you, king, do what else you like with him."

"Is it not a crime to be punished by death, Skjalg," said the king, "for a man to break the Easter-peace? And is this not another, that he murdered a man in the king's hall? And a third (which you and your father will think a small matter) that he used my feet for a chopping block?"

Skjalg answered, "It's a bad deed, king, if you are displeased; otherwise Asbiorn did a splendid piece of work. But even if you think this a great crime, I still hope, for all my services to you, to receive as great a favour. Many will say you would do well to grant me this."

"However much you are worth, Skjalg," said the king, "I shall not for your sake break the law or lay aside my kingly honour."

Then Skjalg turned away and out of the hall. Twelve men there had been with him and they all followed him, and many others went away with him.

Among those left behind was a very dear friend of Erling's family, a man named Thorarin Nefiolfson. Before he went away Skjalg spoke to this friend in private. "This is Thursday night," he said, "If you wish to keep my friendship, you must do everything in your power to prevent Asbiorn from being hanged before Sunday."

After that Skjalg and his men went away, and took a rowing-cutter, which he owned, and rowed south, all night, as hard as they could, and came at day-break to Jadar, where Skjalg's father lived, and went up to the homestead and into the loft in which his father slept. Skjalg ran against the door so hard that it split. The noise woke up Erling and the others inside. Erling was the quickest on foot, and grabbed his shield and sword, and rushed to the door and asked who came so fiercely.

Skjalg told him and bade open the door.

Said Erling, "I might have known it was you, playing the fool,—or perhaps you are pursued?"

Then the door was opened and Skjalg said, "Though you think I am acting the fool, father, your nephew Asbiorn doesn't think I'm hurrying too fast, now that he sits in chains north at Ogvaldsness; and the best thing you can do, father, is to go and rescue him."

Meanwhile, in the hall at Ogvaldsness, things had been put straight again. King Olaf sat down in his seat, and was very angry. He asked what had become of the murderer. They told him he was out on the porch and well watched. The king said, "Why is he not put to death?" Thorarin Nefiolfson answered, "My Lord, do you not call it murder at night?" The king replied, "Put him in fetters then, and hang him in the morning!"

So Asbiorn was fettered and locked up in a house through the night.

Next morning the king heard early prayers and then went to a council until it was time for high-mass. Afterwards he went to mass, and when he came from the service he spoke to Thorarin. "Will the sun perhaps be high enough now so that Asbiorn, your friend, can hang?"

Thorarin answered, bowing to the king: "Lord, today is Friday. You remember how, last Friday, the bishop said that the King who rules over all, he, too, suffered trials; and blessed is he who tries to do like him, rather than like those who put the Man to death. Now it is not long before tomorrow, and tomorrow is a working day."

The king looked him straight in the eyes and said, "You shall have what you wish so far, that he shall not be killed today; now you shall take him yourself and guard him; and remember this, that your life be the penalty if he gets away, no matter how."

After that, the king went about his affairs, and Thorarin to where Asbiorn sat in irons. Thorarin took off his fetters and brought him into a little room and had meat and drink fetched to him and told him what the king had laid upon Thorarin in case Asbiorn ran away. Asbiorn said Thorarin need not fear. So he sat beside him all day long and slept there at night.

On Saturday, the king arose and went to early-prayers. From these he walked to council, and a great throng of men were there who had many complaints to be settled by the king. So the king sat at council a great part of the day and went rather late to the high-mass; afterward he went to the mid-day meal, and when he had finished eating, he drank for a while, and the boards of the table were left on their trestles.

Then Thorarin Nefiolfson went to the priest who took care of the church and gave him two ounces of silver to ring in the holy-time, the minute the boards of the king's table were taken up. In those days it was the custom in Norway to begin holy-time, that is, the Sabbath, on Saturday evening, by ringing the church bells; and the usual time to ring was not for several hours after the king stopped eating.

Now when the king had drunk so long as he thought proper, the boards were taken up. Then the king spoke, saying that it was high time for the slaves to take the murderer and put him to death!

At that very instant the bell rang in the holy-time.

Thorarin went then to the king, and said, "That man will have reprieve, I suppose, during holy-day, even though he is a criminal?"

"Guard him, Thorarin!" said the king, sternly. "Don't let him get away!"

So the king went to church, to the three o'clock service, and Thorarin sat that day also beside Asbiorn.

Sunday morning the bishop came to Asbiorn, and shrived him, and gave him leave to go and hear high-mass. Thorarin went then to the king again and asked him to get new men to guard the murderer. "I wish now," said he, "to have nothing more to do with this affair."

The king thanked him for what he had already done and sent men to guard Asbiorn, whom they put again into fetters. And when people went to high-mass, Asbiorn was led to church, and he stood outside the church, together with those who guarded him. The king and all the people stood inside at the mass.

Now we must take up the story where we left it before, when Erling and Skjalg, his son, were planning together how to rescue Asbiorn. Through the urging of Skjalg and his brothers, it was decided to send out war-arrows and gather a band together; and soon a great company collected, and they went aboard ship, and when they were counted, there were nearly fifteen hundred men.

With this company they set out and came on Sunday to Ogvaldsness on Kormt and went with all the band up to the homestead and came there at the time when the gospel had been read. They went straight to the church-door and took Asbiorn and broke the fetters off him.

At this noise and clashing of weapons, all who were outside ran into the church, and those who were in the church turned and looked out, except the king alone; he watched the service and did not look around.

Erling's people drew up their band on either side of the path which led from the church to the great hall, and Erling and his sons stood next to the hall.

Now, as soon as all the service had been sung, the king went boldly straight out of the church. He was the first to come into the alley between Erling's lines, and his men followed, one after the other.

When he came to the door of the hall, Erling stepped in the way, and bowed before the king, and greeted him.

The king answered and bade God help him!

Then Erling began to speak. "I hear my nephew, Asbiorn, has been very foolish. I am sorry you are displeased. Now I have come to offer peace and as much ransom-money as you desire, and to get in return Asbiorn's life and limbs and liberty."

The king answered, "It looks as though you intend to have your own way. Why do you offer peace when you bring a whole army with you?"

Sharp words followed, and they became very angry, and Erling was as red as blood in the face.

Then Sigurd the Bishop came forward and said to the king, "Lord, I command you as a Christian to make the peace with Erling which he offers, that this man be safe in life and limb, but that you alone shall make all the peace-terms."

The king replied, "You shall have your way."

Then said the bishop, "Erling! give the king whatever money he desires, and let Asbiorn afterwards go in safety into the power of the king."

Erling got securities, and the king took them. Then Asbiorn went in safety and gave himself up to the king and kissed the king's hand. After that, Erling withdrew his company. There were no "good-byes." The king went into the hall, and Asbiorn went with him.

The king then let them know the terms of peace, saying, "Our agreement shall begin in this way, Asbiorn. There is a law that the man who kills a servant of the king shall himself undertake the same service, if it is the king's will. Now I desire you to take this office of steward which Seal-Thorir had, and rule over my manor here at Ogvaldsness."

Asbiorn said he would do as the king desired. "But first I ought to go home, to my estate, and set it in order."

The king said he was willing, and he left Ogvaldsness for another feast which was waiting him.

Asbiorn went then to find his ship, which he had left Thursday off the other side of the island. His companions had lain in hidden caves all the time that Asbiorn was away. They had news of all that happened to him and would not go home until they knew the outcome.

After that, Asbiorn sailed home and did not stop until he came north to his estate. Always afterwards he was called Asbiorn Seal's-bane, that is Asbiorn, the slayer of Seal.

When Asbiorn had been home a short time, an uncle came to see him and asked him about everything that happened on his journey. When Asbiorn had told the whole story, his uncle said,

"Then perhaps you think you have revenged the shame done you when you were robbed last autumn?"

"So I do," said Asbiorn, "what do you think, uncle?"

"That is soon said," he replied. "Your first journey south was most shameful and needed revenge; but this journey is the shame both of you and your relatives, if this is to be the end of it, that you are to become the king's slave, and no better than that vile fellow Thorir Seal. Now act like a man, stay here on your own farm, and we, your relations, will give you so much support, that you shall be perfectly safe."

Asbiorn thought this good advice, and before he and his uncle parted, this plan was settled, that Asbiorn should stay at home and not go to see the king, or into his service, and so he did and remained at home on his own farms.

Meanwhile the king had appointed a sheriff over Halegoland, the district in the north of Norway, in which Asbiorn lived. The sheriff's name was Asmund. Asmund learned about Asbiorn, and how he was disobeying the king's orders, and staying at home, instead of taking charge of the king's estate at Ogvaldsness. So, as sheriff of the king, he thought it his duty to punish Asbiorn, if he found the chance.

That summer Asmund started south to visit King Olaf. He went on a war-cutter, with nearly thirty men, and all well-weaponed, and took with him a very dear friend, a handsome young man named Karli, whom he wished to introduce to the king. Asmund and Karli were always together. On the voyage south they heard that Asbiorn Seal's-bane had also gone south in his merchant ship to the great fair at Vaga and was now likely to be on his way back. Asmund told Karli that he had never seen this Asbiorn and was very anxious to know what he looked like.

Asmund and Karli went on their way south, keeping close to land, and had a head wind, though a light one. They met many ships sailing back from Vaga, and asked secretly about Asbiorn's doings. They were told he would now be coming back.

Then the ships ran past each other, and Karli said, "There he sits —Seal's-bane—at the tiller, in a blue coat."

Asmund answered, "I shall get him a red coat."

And saying that, Asmund shot a spear at Asbiorn Seal's-bane, and it struck him in the middle, and flew through him, so that it stuck fast in the head-board, and Asbiorn fell dead from the tiller. After that both ships went their own way.

Asbiorn's crew brought the dead body north to his home at Throndness. Then Sigrid his mother sent for his uncle Thorir Hound, and he came when the body was laid out according to their custom. And when people were going away, after the funeral, Sigrid gave gifts to her friends and led Thorir to his ship.

Before they parted, she said, sarcastically, "So it is now, Thorir, that Asbiorn, my son, followed your loving advice. Now his life did not last long enough to reward you, as he should, and though I am less fit to do so than he would have been, still I will do my best. Here is a present that I will give you, which I hope will be very useful."

—It was a spear.—"This is the spear which passed through Asbiorn, my son, and the blood is still on it. You must remember that this spear fits the wound you saw on Asbiorn, your brother's son. Now it would be a manly deed for you, if you should so let this spear go out of your hand that it sticks in the breast of King Olaf the Thick. Now I plead this also," she said, "may you be a coward in the eyes of all the world if you do not avenge Asbiorn." Then she went back to the house.

Thorir Hound became so angry at her words that he could not answer at all. He paid no attention to the spear—whether he let go of it or not—nor to the gang-way, and would have fallen into the sea if men had not caught hold of him and steadied him, as he went aboard the ship. The spear was not a heavy one and its socket inlaid with gold.

Thorir and his people rowed away home.

And in the course of time Thorir carried out the revenge laid upon him by Asbiorn's mother. On a viking trip to foreign lands, he killed Karli with the very spear which had slain Asbiorn. Whether he used this same spear against King Olaf we do not know. But Thorir Hound was one of the leaders in the rebellion which Canute the Great, King of Denmark and England, stirred up against King Olaf; and in the final battle of Sticklestead when Olaf attacked him, Asbiorn's uncle thrust a spear into the king's stomach. This was one of the three wounds which caused the death of King Olaf.

Thormoth and Saint Olaf

July 29, 1030

Snorri Sturluson

Heimskringla

THORMOTH "the coal-brow skald" was an earnest poet and a fearless warrior. He followed the fortunes of Saint Olaf (1015-1030) until both were slain by the rebels on the battlefield of Sticklestead, northeast of Trondhjem. The anniversary is now "Saint Olav's Day" in the Norwegian calendar. Thormoth aroused the army by reciting an Icelandic version of the lost *Bjarkamál*, the poem paraphrased by Saxo, that described the Battle of Leire in Denmark, about 550, when King Hrolf Kraki, the Hrothulf of *Bēowulf*, was killed. In his dying minutes Thormoth continued to compose verses of his own.

IN the battle of Sticklestead, in which King Olaf died, was a poet named Thormoth, "the coal-brow skald." Thormoth was as good at fighting as at making verses about the battle.

At dawn, before the battle began, King Olaf called for Thormoth and told him to wake up the army with a song. Thormoth sat up and sang out very clear, so that he was heard throughout all the army. He sang a song called "The Old Lay of Biarki" of which this is the beginning:

> "Day is come up again,
> Cock's wings are flapping,
> Wake to your work again,
> Up from your napping!
>
> Not to your wine to-day,
> Women's sweet prattle,
> I to a harder play
> Wake you to battle!"

Then the host awoke. And when the song was done, men thanked him for it, and liked it very much, and thought it well chosen. The king also thanked him and took a gold ring weighing half a mark from his own arm and gave it to Thormoth.

Said Thormoth: "A good king we have, but it is just now hard to tell how long he will live, and it is my prayer, King Olaf, that we may never part, alive or dead."

Thormoth the Skald fought well in the battle under the banners of the king. After the king had fallen, Thormoth was so tired from fighting and weak from his wounds that he could only stand at one side and cheer on his comrades.

While standing there, he was struck by an arrow in the left side; he broke off the arrow-shaft, leaving the head in the wound, and went away from the battlefield to some houses and toward a big barn out of which came loud noises like weeping and groaning. Thormoth had a naked sword in his hand.

As he was going into the barn, he met a man coming out, who said, "They are carrying on like children in here, whining and howling. Maybe the king's men have fought bravely enough, but they bear their wounds like cowards."

Thormoth asked his name.

The man said his name was Kimbi.

Thormoth asked, "Were you in the battle?"

"I was," he said, "against the king, on the side which had the better."

"Are you badly wounded?" asked Thormoth.

"A little," said Kimbi. "Were you in the battle?"

"I was," Thormoth replied, "on the better side."

Kimbi saw that Thormoth had a gold ring on his arm; he said, "You must be one of the king's men; hand me your gold ring, and I will hide you; for our men will kill you if you come in their way."

Thormoth said, "Take the ring, if you can get it off; I have now lost more than that."

Kimbi reached forward his hand to take the ring. Thormoth swished his naked sword, and hewed off the hand. And it is said that Kimbi bore his own wound no better than the others whom he had sneered at.

After that Thormoth walked on till he came to a certain woman's cottage and went in.

The woman was a leech, and she was binding the wounds of a great many injured men inside her room. A fire burned on the middle of the floor, where she warmed water to bathe their cuts. But Thormoth sat down outside the door. One man went out, another in, those who were tending to the injured. One of them turned toward Thormoth, looked at him, and said:

"Why are you so pale? Are you hurt? Why don't you ask for attention?"

The skald recited some verses, telling about his wound. Then he got up, and went in to the fire, and stood by it some time.

After a while the leech said to him:

"You, man! go out and bring me the kindling wood, just outside, there, in front of the door."

He went out, brought in an armful, and threw it down on the floor.

Then the woman looked him in the face, and said:

"This man is mighty pale; what ails you?"

Thormoth answered in verses.

Then the woman said: "Let me see your wound, and I will attend to it."

Thormoth sat down, and pulled off his shirt. The leech glanced over all his cuts, and examined carefully the wound in his side; she felt where the iron stuck in, but she did not know just which way it had turned, inside.

She had there in a stone kettle a mixture of onions and strong-smelling herbs, ground up and boiled together, which she gave the wounded to eat, and found out in this way if a man had a stomach-wound, because she could smell the onions out of the wound which had gouged the stomach. She brought this dose to Thormoth, and ordered him to eat. He replied:

"Take it away! I haven't any onion-disease."

After that she took a pair of tongs and tried to pull out the iron, but it stuck fast, and would not budge. The flesh stood out a little, too, because the wound was swollen. Said Thormoth,

"You cut away the flesh around the arrow-head, so that it can be got at with the tongs; then give them to me, and let me tug."

She did as he suggested.

Then Thormoth drew the gold-ring off his hand and gave it to the leech and told her to do what she liked with it.

"It belonged to a good man," says he; "King Olaf gave me that ring this morning."

Then Thormoth took the tongs and jerked out the arrow-head. But there were hooks on it, and shreds of flesh from around his heart clung to the barbs, some red, some white. And when he saw that, he said:

"The king has fed us well; there's fat around my heart-roots."

Then he bent over backwards, and he was dead.

Harald Harthrathi in Byzantium

c. 1040

Snorri Sturluson

Heimskringla

KING Harald Sigurthsson "Hard-in-Counsel" (1046-1066) was an uncompromising warrior. In his youth he was many years in Russia, Byzantium, and the Near East. He fended off the allurements of the Greek ladies but married, on his way back in Kiev, a princess of Swedish descent and brought her home with a rich dowry.

◢§ AT that time there ruled over Greekland Queen Zoe the Rich, and with her Michael Katalaktus. And when Harald came to Micklegarth to see the queen, he took war-service there, and went forthwith that same autumn on board galleys with those warriors who fared out into Greekland's sea, and Harald held the company of his own men. Then was captain over the host the man who is named Gyrgir; he was kinsman of the queen.

But Harald had been for but a little while in the host when the Værings drew them much to him, and they would fare all together whenso were battles, and it came to this that Harald became captain over all the Værings. He and Gyrgir fared wide about the isles of Greekland, and wrought mighty deeds of war on the corsairs.

The Battle of Stamford Bridge

September 25, 1066

Snorri Sturluson

Heimskringla

KING Harald Sigurthsson invaded the east coast of England only a month before William the Conqueror landed in the south. The Norwegians were defeated by King Harold of England, who then hurried south to meet the Normans at Hastings, where he fell on October 14.

KING Harald Godwinson had come with an immense army, both of cavalry and infantry. Now King Harald Sigurdson rode around his array, to see how every part was drawn up. He was upon a black horse, and the horse stumbled under him, so that the king fell off. He got up in haste, and said, "A fall is lucky for a traveller."

The English king Harald said to the Northmen who were with him, "Do ye know the stout man who fell from his horse, with the blue kirtle and the beautiful helmet?"

"That is the king himself," said they.

The English king said, "A great man, and of stately appearance is he; but I think his luck has left him."

Twenty horsemen rode forward from the Thing-men's troops against the Northmen's array; and all of them, and likewise their horses, were clothed in armour.

One of the horsemen said, "Is Earl Toste in this army?"

The earl answered, "It is not to be denied that ye will find him here."

The horseman says, "Thy brother King Harald sends thee salutation, with the message that thou shalt have the whole of Northumberland; and rather than thou shouldst not submit to him, he will give thee the third part of his kingdom to rule over along with himself."

The earl replies, "This is something different from the enmity and scorn he offered last winter; and if this had been offered then it would have saved many a man's life who now is dead and it would have been better for the kingdom of England. But if I accept of this offer, what will he give King Harald Sigurdson for his trouble?"

The horseman replied, "He has also spoken of this; and will give him seven feet of English ground, or as much more as he may be taller than other men."

"Then," said the earl, "go now and tell King Harald to get ready for battle; for never shall the Northmen say with truth that Earl Toste left King Harald Sigurdson to join his enemy's troops, when he came to fight west here in England. We shall rather all take the resolution to die with honour, or to gain England by a victory."

Then the horsemen rode back.

* * *

Now the battle began. The Englishmen made a hot assault upon the Northmen, who sustained it bravely. It was no easy matter for the English to ride against the Northmen on account of their spears; therefore they rode in a circle around them. And the fight at first was but loose and light, as long as the Northmen kept their order of battle; for although the English rode hard against the Northmen, they gave way again immediately, as they could do nothing against them. Now when the Northmen thought they perceived that the enemy were making but weak assaults, they set after them, and would drive them into flight; but when they had broken their shield-rampart the Englishmen rode up from all sides, and threw arrows and spears on them. Now when King Harald Sigurdson saw this; he went into the fray where the greatest crash of weapons was; and there was a sharp conflict, in which many people fell on both sides. King Harald then was in a rage, and ran out in front of the array, and hewed down with both hands; so that neither helmet nor armour could withstand him, and all who were nearest gave way before him. It was then very near with the English that they had taken to flight.

* * *

King Harald Sigurdson was hit by an arrow in the windpipe, and that was his death-wound. He fell, and all who had advanced with him, except those who retired with the banner.

The Debate of the Kings
c. 1115
Snorri Sturluson
Heimskringla

THE brothers King Eystein (1103-1123) and King Sigurth (1103-1130) ruled Norway jointly. Sigurth "Jerusalem-farer" was much abroad in the crusades, while Eystein attended to domestic affairs. After Sigurth's return the brothers debated about their accomplishments.

KING Eystein and King Sigurd were both on a winter a-feasting in the Uplands, and each had there his own stead. But as there was but a short way betwixt the steads whereas the kings should take feast, then did men that rede, that they should both be together at the banquets, each at the other's stead, turn and turn about; and for the first time they were both together at a stead owned of King Eystein. Now in the evening, when men took to drinking, then was the ale nought good, and men were hushed. Then spake King Eystein: "Though men be hushed, it is more of ale-wont for men to make them glee; get we some ale-joyance, that will yet take root for the pastime of men. Brother Sigurd, that will seem to all men most meet that we heave up some gamesome talk."

King Sigurd answered somewhat shortly: "Be thou as talksome as it pleases thee, but let me hold my peace for thee."

Then spake King Eystein: "That ale-wont hath oft been, that men should match them with men, and so will I let it be here."

Then King Sigurd held his peace. "I see," said King Eystein, "that I must begin this joyance, and I shall take thee, brother, for my match; and this is my reason thereto, that we have both an equal name, equal land, and I make no difference between our kindred or our breeding."

Then answered King Sigurd: "Mindest thou not that I used to throw thee on thy back, when I would, and thou wert a year older?"

Said King Eystein: "I mind me no less, that thou never couldst play such game wherein was nimbleness."

Spake King Sigurd then: "Mindest thou how it fared in the swimming with us? I might have drowned thee if I had willed."

King Eystein answered: "I swam not shorter than thou, nor was I worse a diving-swimmer. I also knew how to fare on ice-bones, so that no one did I know who could champion me therein, but thou knewest it no more than a neat."

King Sigurd answered: "A more lordly sport and a more useful I deem it, to ken well the bow. I am minded to think that thou canst not draw my bow, though thou spurn thy foot therein."

Answered King Eystein: "As bow-strong as thou I am not; but less sundereth our straight shooting. And much better can I on snow-shoes than thou, and that has been called, time agone at least, a good sport."

King Sigurd said: "This deem I the lordlier matter by a great deal, that he, who shall be over-man over other men, be mickle in the flock, strong, and weapon-deft better than other men, and easy to see, and easy to ken whereas most are together."

King Eystein said: "That is no less a thing to be known by, that a man be fair, and such an one is easily kenned in a man-throng, and that also methinks lordly, for fairness fits the best array. Can I also law much better than thou, and on whatsoever we have to talk, I am much the more smooth-spoken."

King Sigurd said: "Maybe thou hast mastered more law-quibbles, for I had then other things to do; and no one taunts thee of smooth-speech; but this say a many, that thou art not right fast of word, and that little is to mark what thou mayst behight, that thou speakest according to them who may be near beside; and that is nought kingly."

King Eystein said: "Causeth it, that when men bear their cases before me, that think I of this first, so to make an end of each man's case as best may like him; but then comes oft the other, who has the case against the first; then often things are drawn in that make matters middling to the liking of both. Oft it is, that I promise what I am bidden; for that I will that all should fare fain from the finding of me. I see another choice, if I would have it, as thou dost, to promise ill to all, for I hear no one taunt thee for not keeping thy promises."

King Sigurd said: "That has been the talk of men, that the journey on which I fared out of the land was somewhat lordly; but thou sattest at home meanwhile, as a daughter of thy father."

King Eystein answers: "Now thou didst nip the boil. I should not have waked this talk, if I had known nought how to answer this.

Near to this, it seemed to me, that I dowered thee from home as my sister, ere thou wert boun for the journey."

King Sigurd said: "Thou must have heard it that I had battles right many in Serkland, which thou must have heard tell of, and that I won the victory in all, and many kind of precious things, the like whereof never before came hither to the land. I was thought of most worshipful there, whereas I met the noblest men; but I think that thou hast not yet cast off the home-laggard."

King Eystein said: "I have heard it, that thou hadst sundry battles in the outlands, but more profitable for our land was it that I was doing meantime. Five churches I reared from the groundsel, and I made a haven at Agdirness which erst was desert, though every man's way lay there when he fared north or south along the land; I made withal the tower in Sinholmsound, and the hall in Bergen, while thou wert brittling Bluemen for the fiend in Serkland. I deem that of little gain for our realm."

King Sigurd said: "I fared in this faring the longest out to Jordan, and swam over the river; but out on the bank there is a copse; and there in the copse I tied a knot, and spoke thereover words, that thou shouldst loose it, brother, or have else such-like spell-words as thereon were laid."

King Eystein said: "Nought will I loose that knot which thou didst tie for me; but I might have tied thee such a knot as much less wouldst thou have loosed, when thou sailedst in one ship amidst of my host, whenas thou camest into the land."

After that both held their peace, and were wroth either of them.

More things there were in the dealings of the brothers from which might be seen how each drew himself forward and his case, and how each would be greater than the other; yet peace held betwixt them, while both lived.

King Sverri's Speech at Bergen

1186

Karl Jónsson

Sverris saga

KING Sverri (1177-1202) was a social reformer and champion of the forgotten man. His New Deal, like the New Deal in China in the First

Century B.C., met with much opposition. This speech shows that the English merchants were more in favor in Norway than were the Germans.

❦ SHORTLY afterwards King Sverri held an Assembly in the town, at which he spoke, saying:

"We desire to thank the Englishmen who have come here, bringing wheat and honey, flour and cloth. We desire also to thank those who have brought here linen or flax, wax or caldrons. We desire next to make mention of those who have come from the Orkneys, Shetland, the Færeys or Iceland; all those who have brought here such things as make this land the richer, and we cannot do without. But there are Germans who have come here in great numbers, with large ships, intending to carry away butter and dried fish, of which the exportation much impoverishes the land; and they bring wine instead, which people strive to purchase, both my men, townsmen, and merchants. From that purchase much evil and no good has arisen, for many have lost life through it, and some their limbs; some carry marks of disfigurement to the end of their days; others suffer disgrace, being wounded or beaten. Overdrinking is the cause. To those Southmen I feel much ill-will for their voyage here; and if they would preserve their lives or property, let them depart hence; their business has become harmful to us and to our realm. Call to mind what overdrinking means, what it produces, what it destroys.

"First, to mention its least evil, whoever takes to overdrinking ceases to make money, and the price of overdrinking is the waste and loss of his wealth, until he who was blessed with wealth becomes poor and wretched and needy, if he does not forsake his ways.

"As to the second evil, overdrinking destroys the memory, and makes a man forget all that he is bound to keep in mind.

"In the third place, it makes a man lust to do all manner of unrighteous deeds; he is not afraid to lay hands wrongfully on money or women.   ·

"As a fourth evil, overdrinking incites a man to bear with nothing, word or deed, but to return far more evil than is deserved; and beyond that, it incites him to find means of slandering the innocent.

"Another evil follows overdrinking: a man strains his body to the utmost to endure labour, to keep awake until exhausted, to lose blood in every limb, and he will spill his blood till he is ill, and thus destroy all health. And when all wealth, health, and reason, too, are destroyed by overdrinking, it incites a man to destroy what is not yet lost, his soul. It incites him to neglect all right conduct and right ordinances, to lust after sins, to forget God and all that is right, and to remember nothing that He has done. Consider now, you men that overdrink: who will most likely seize the soul when your life and drinking-bouts come to an end at the same time. Call to mind how unlike is your conduct to what it should be, for a calm restraint should accompany all things.

"Warriors in time of peace should be gentle as lambs, but in war dauntless as lions; merchants and yeomen should go about their business, acquiring wealth justly, yet with toil, taking care of it wisely, and bestowing it with liberality. Those who are lowly should be grateful, and each one serve his master with good-will and according to his ability."

The King brought his speech to an end by bidding his men be well behaved and peaceful towards the townsmen, yeomen, and merchants.

This speech was highly approved by all wise men.

Ancient Norwegian Law
Twelfth century
Gulaþingslög

OLD Scandinavian civilization was built upon law. This selection about marriage is from the laws of the Gula Thing, an assembly on the west coast of Norway.

⸰§ Now, the next is this, that we must learn how we shall buy our wives with the mund in order that a child may be capable of inheriting property. A man shall pledge himself to pay the lowest mund [at least], which is twelve oras, and there shall be witnesses present, and let him have bridesmen and let her have brideswomen [at the wedding]. And in the morning after they have been together during the night, he shall give her such a [morning] gift as he has pledged to her; then the child that is born after that shall be capable of inheriting. The next is this, that a man may wish to arrange a marriage that calls for greater outlay; in that case the father shall himself betroth his daughter, if she is a maid; but the brother [shall betroth her] if the father is dead. If the father refuses to wed his daughter to the man who has betrothed her, he [the fiancé] shall give him a home summons and appoint a day on which he wishes to have his betrothed. But if the father refuses to let him have her, he shall make a formal demand for his betrothed and summon him [the father] before the thing for robbery; and it shall be the duty of the thingmen to declare him an outlaw. A maiden has by no means the right to decide whether she will fulfill the obligation. The man [who controls the marriage] shall keep an affianced woman twelve months for her betrothed. If leprosy appears on either side, the betrothal is annulled. If a man lies with his betrothed, he shall pay atonement to her rightful heir; after that he may have her as wife. A widow shall betroth herself but with the advice of kinsmen; then she may not break the contract. But if she has not had the advice of kinsmen, she may break it, but she shall pay three marks for breach of promise to the one who had affianced her. Every man shall have his betrothed if she is affianced to him by the one who has the right to give her in marriage; but if a man pledges a woman whose marriage is not in his control, he shall pay three marks to the man to whom he pledged her. If there are brothers, two or more, who have the right to give a sister in marriage, and if one of them betroths her to a man and the other wishes to annul [the contract], they shall determine by lot who shall have the decision. If the one who made the agreement wins the lot, it shall remain valid, otherwise not; and he shall pay three marks for breach of contract. If either one [of the betrothed] falls ill or is wounded, let them wait twelve months and then do one of two [things], either proceed according to contract in spite of the defect that has come into it, or annul the betrothal. The woman shall not be given in marriage [to another] before a twelve-month has passed unless [the earlier fiancé] is willing; nor shall he take another woman to wife sooner than that unless [the guardian] is willing. If a man refuses to wed his betrothed, he shall be served with a home summons and a day shall be appointed when he must take her; he shall then be summoned to make answer at the thing for having avoided his betrothed; and the thingmen shall declare him an outlaw and he shall be known as *fuðflogi*.[1] In the same way a day shall be appointed for a woman who has affianced herself to a man, in case she has failed to come on the day agreed upon to marry the man to whom she had pledged herself. If she refuses to come on the ap-

[1] One who flees from the female sex organ.

pointed day, she shall be summoned before the thing to answer for having fled from her betrothed; and she shall be outlawed at the thing, and she shall leave the land and shall be known as *flannfluga*.[2] If a hostile force invades the land, every man shall make provision for his betrothed, if she is offered to him before witnesses; but if he refuses and will not provide for her, he breaks the betrothal with that refusal. If a man's betrothed is carried off in a foray, it is his duty to go after her and to give three marks toward her ransom, her heir to supply what more is needed. If a man takes another man's betrothed and has her [as his own], both having consented to this, let him who had affianced her summon the one who has taken her to appear before a thing; and it shall be the duty of the thingmen to outlaw them both. But if the woman did not give her consent, she has nothing to answer for.

The Queen Hears the News

December, 1239

Sturla Þórðarson

Hákonar saga gamla Hákonarsonar

In December, 1239, a messenger came to King Hakon in Bergen with the bad news that his wife's father, the powerful Duke Skuli, had revolted and let himself be proclaimed king. Ibsen has made effective use of this dramatic scene in the third act of *The Pretenders*.

§There were few men with the king when he heard these tidings. He held his peace some time and then said:

"God be praised that I know what I shall have to do henceforth; for that which has now come out was long since purposed."

After that he went to the queen's lodging and bade them open the door. That was done, the king went into the lodging; there was a light burning. There slept some pages and the queen's waiting-maids. The king went up to the bed; but the queen stood in a silken sark, and threw over herself a red cloak with bands. She greeted the king. He took her greeting kindly. She took a silken cushion and bade the king sit down. He said he had no wish to sit down. She asked if the king had heard any new tidings.

---

[2] One who flees from the male sex organ.

"Small are the tidings," says he, "there are two kings in Norway at once."

She said: "One must be the rightful king, and that is you; and so may God grant and the saint king Olaf."

Then the king said that her father had let himself be given the title of king of the Eyra-Thing.

"It must be better than that," she says, "and do not, for God's sake, believe this so long as you can disavow it."

Then she burst out into tears, and could say no more. The king bade her be easy, and said she should not suffer for the undertaking of her father. A little after the king went away. But as soon as it was day the king went to mass. After that he called to him his councillors; Grim was then present, and told the tidings which he had brought. That course was taken that the arrow of war was sent out north and south from Bergen, and the whole levy summoned thither.

The End of King Hakon the Old

December 15, 1263

Sturla Þórðarson

Hákonar saga gamla Hákonarsonar

THE last undertaking of King Hakon the Old (1217-1263) was to command a naval expedition against Scotland. After the indecisive Battle of Largs in the Hebrides, he retired to the Orkneys, where he died. His son and successor King Magnus sold to Scotland all Norwegian rights there except the Orkneys and the Shetlands, which remained Norwegian territory for another two centuries.

⚜§KING Hacon came into Rognvalds-voe, and then a great part of the host had sailed to Norway, some with his leave, but some gave themselves leave to go home. King Hacon had at first given out when he came to the Isles, that he would sail to Norway. But because the weather began to harden, and there was no fair wind, he took that counsel to sit in the Orkneys that winter. Then he named near twenty ships to stay behind, but to the others he gave leave to sail home. King Hacon then sent letters by his men as to the ruling of the realm in Norway and other things. Behind with king Hacon were all the liegemen who had fared west, except Eilif of Naustdale, he had sailed east; but most of the best men were behind with the king.

After All Saints Day the king let his ship sail out to Middleland's haven; but he stayed that day in Rognvaldsey, and fared thence in to Kirkwall. After that each ship captain looked after his ship. Some were laid up in Middleland's haven, but some further in by Scapa-neck. King Hacon rode out to Middleland's haven on Saturday before Martinmas, that was on the eve of the mass. He was there very sick that night he was on board his ship. Next morning he let mass be sung for him on land. After that he settled about his ship, where she should be laid up, and bade men to bestow great pains in caring for the ship. After that he fared into Scapa-neck, and so to Kirkwall; he went to the bishop's house with all his train for whom he kept a table. They both had their boards in the hall, the king and the bishop, each of them for his men; but the king was up in his lodging, and took his meat always there. King Hacon then made out a list for his liegemen and the chiefs in his train of so much geldable land for their support to keep the bands that were with them, and in the same way with each crown estate in the Isles. Andrew clubfoot was to under-take to keep the king's own board, and to meet the outgoings for the bodyguard, guests, pages, and all his followers. When men had looked after their ships, each fared to the place that was allotted him for his quarters. These liegemen were in Kirkwall, Brynjolf John's son, Erling Alf's son, Rognvald ork, Erling of Bjarkey, John queen, Erlend the red, and many other ship captains; but the other liegemen and ship captains were in the country on those geldable lands which were allotted them.

The king had had during the summer great watchings and much care; he was often called up, and had little peace from his men. But when he came off the sea out of Middleland's haven from his ship, as was already told, then he soon took to his bed for sickness. The sickness did not take its course very violently at first. And when the king had lain some three weeks he grew rather better, and for some three days he was in that state that he walked the first day much about his lodging, and the next day into the bishop's chapel, and heard mass there; but the third day he walked to St. Magnus' church, and round the shrine of Saint Magnus the earl. That day he let a bath be made for him, and went into it, and let himself be shaved. Afterwards that same night the course of his sickness began to get heavier, and then he took to his bed the second time, and men thought then that his sickness began to be much worse. In the sickness he let Latin books be read to him at first. But then he thought it great trouble to think over what that (the Latin) meant. Then he let be read to him Norse books, night and day; first the Sagas of the saints; and when they were read out he let be read to him the tale of the kings from Halfdan the black, and so on of all the kings of Norway, one after the other. When king Hacon thought he felt that the course of the sickness got much worse, then he took counsel for the wages-gifts to his body-guard, and he commanded that a mark of burnt silver should be given to each man of the body-guard; but half a mark to the guests and dish-swains, and the rest of his serving-men. Then he let all the furniture of his table be weighed that was not gilt, and so ordered that where pure silver fell short, then his table-plate should be given, so that all might have what was their fair due. Then also were written those letters which he wished to send to king Magnus, with all those arrangements which he thought were most needful. King Hacon was annealed one night before Lucy's mass. The bishops were there present: Thorgils bishop of Stavanger, Gilbert bishop of Hammar, and Henry bishop of the Orkneys; and abbot Thorleif, and many other learned clerks. And ere he was anointed then those men kissed him who were by. The king was then still speech-hale. He was asked in the sickness by his trustiest men if it happened so hardly that his life were lost or that of king Magnus whether he had no other son behind him; or whether it was any good to seek in some other place where his off-spring might be. But he spoke strongly as to this, that he had no son to succeed him but king Magnus; and no daughters that men did not know of already. When the tale of the kings was read down to Sverrir, then he let them take to reading Sverrir's saga. Then it was read both night and day whenever he was awake.

The mass-day of St. Lucy the virgin was on a Thursday. But the Saturday after, late in the evening, the course of the king's sickness was so heavy on him that he lost his speech. Near midnight Sverrir's saga was read through. But just as midnight was past Almighty God called king Hacon from this world's life. That was the greatest grief to all those men that were by, and to many others who heard it afterwards. These liegemen were by when the king breathed his last: Brynjolf John's son, Erling Alf's son, John queen, Rognvald ork, and some serving-men who had been most about the king in the sickness. At once after the king's death the bishops and clerks were sent for. And as soon as they came they sang the mass for the dead.

After that all men went out of the chamber, save bishop Thorgils and Brynjolf John's son, and two other men. Then they washed the body, and shaved it; and showed it all the care that beseemed so noble a king as king Hacon had been. On Sunday the body was borne up into the upper hall. There was ready a bier with splendid furniture. The body was clad in noble robes and a garland set on his head, and everything was done as befitted so noble a prince and crowned king. The body was laid on a bier. Then all the bishops and priests who were then in the house and all the king's henchmen went thither. Then the candle-swains held torches, and then it was light all over the hall. Then the folk came in to see the body, and it seemed to all bright and comely, with a fair ruddiness on the face as of a living man. It was a great comfort to men for their great grief which had then come over men to see so fair a corse of a dead man and their own lord. Afterwards a solemn mass for the king's soul was sung, and the body-guard watched over the body that night. But on Monday the body of king Hacon was borne to Magnus' church, and there watched the second night. On Tuesday the body of king Hacon was laid in a coffin with such ceremony as is wont for a crowned king. He was buried in the choir in Magnus' church there on the steps before the shrine of Saint Magnus the earl. After that the stone was closed over it as it was before, and a pall was spread over it. Then a meeting of the body-guard was held, and that counsel was taken, that all the winter the main-guard should be kept over the king's grave. At Yule the bishop and Andrew clubfoot gave a feast according as king Hacon had settled it. Then too were good wages given to all men.

King Hacon had so settled it in his sickness that his body should be carried to Norway, and that he should be buried in Bergen with his fathers and other kinsmen. And as soon as high-winter was over and the sea began to be smooth, the big ship was brought out in which the king had sailed west, and fitted out with all speed. On Ash Wednesday the body of king Hacon was taken out of the earth. That was on the 3rd of the Nones of the month of March. Then all the body-guard went out with it across Scapa neck, and the body was carried out in a boat to the ship. These had most care over the ship, bishop Thorgils, Erling Alf's son, and Andrew clubfoot. There on board was the king's body-guard which had fared west. And when they were "boun," they put out to sea. They sailed out the first Saturday in Lent, and got hard and cross weather; and they made the land south in Sila-voe; and sent at once letters to king Magnus, and told him of those great tidings which had happened in their expedition. After that they went north to Bergen as soon as they had a chance. They came into Lax-voe the day before St. Benedict's mass. On the saint's day king Magnus rowed to meet them and bishop Peter. Then the ship was rowed up to the town off the king's house. The body was borne out of the ship up into the summer hall. But the morning after the body was borne out to Christ's Church. King Magnus walked along with it, and both the queens, the bishops, the clerks, henchmen, and all the townsfolk. After that the body of king Hacon was buried in the choir in Christ's Church. And king Magnus thanked God at the funeral with many fair words, and spoke a clever speech over the grave. There stood all the people with troubled heart. As Sturla sang:

> "Woden's companion
> To Bergen came
> Three nights before
> He was buried in Church.
> There stood many thanes
> Not lively with wet lids,
> Very sad o'er his grave,
> It tried the heart hard."

King Hacon was buried three nights before Lady Day. Then had passed from the birth and incarnation of our Lord Jesus Christ twelve hundred and sixty and three years, less three nights.

V. THE WESTERN ISLANDS
Queen Auth Leaves Ireland
892
Ari Þorgilsson
Landnámabók

MANY of the settlers in Iceland sailed direct from the west coast of Norway. Many others, however, sailed from Ireland and Scotland and the Celtic islands, which Norwegians had begun to colonize as early as the seventh century. Thus there was a large infusion of Celtic blood in the Icelanders. Both West-coast Norwegians and the Irish are famous for disputatious temperaments. It is easy, therefore, to explain the inquiring and contentious qualities of the Icelandic mind.

OLEIF the White was the name of a war-lord, he was the son of King Ingald, the son of Helgi, the son of Olaf, the son of Gudraud, the son of Halfdan Whiteleg, the King of the Uplanders. Olave the White harried in the West-viking, and conquered Dublin in Ireland, and Dublinshire, and was made King over it. He married Aud the Deep-minded, the daughter of Ketil Flatnose. Thorstein the Red was their son. Oleif fell in battle in Ireland, and Aud and Thorstein went thence to Sodor, or the Hebrides; there Thorstein married Thurid, the daughter of Eyvind the Easterner, and sister of Helgi the Lean; they had many children. Their son was named Olaf Feilan, and their daughters, Groa and Alof, Osk, and Thorhild, Thorgerd and Vigdis. Thorstein became a war-lord; he entered partnership with Sigurd the Mighty, the son of Eystein Glumra; they conquered Caithness, Sutherland, Ross and Murray, and more than half Scotland, and Thorstein became King thereover, until the Scots betrayed him, and he fell there in battle. Aud was then in Caithness, when she heard of the fall of Thorstein; she caused a merchant ship to be made in a wood, in secret, and when it was ready she held out to the Orkneys; there she gave in marriage Gro, the daughter of Thorstein the Red. She was the mother of Grelad, whom Thorfinn Skullcleaver had in marriage. After that Aud went to seek Iceland; she had with her in the ships twenty free men.

Queen Aud settles all the Dale-lands, A.D. 892.

There was a man named Koll, the son of Vedrar (Wether) Grim, the son of Asi a hersir; he had the management of the affairs of Aud, and was most honoured by her. Koll married Thorgerd, daughter of Thorstein the Red. A freedman of Aud's was named Erp; he was the son of Melldun, an Earl in Scotland, even he who fell before Earl Sigurd the Mighty. The mother of Erp was Myrgjol, the daughter of Gljomal, King of the Irish. Earl Sigurd took them (Erp and Myrgjol), captives in war, and enslaved them. Myrgjol was the hand-maid of the wife of the Earl, and served her faithfully; she was skilled in many arts; she took charge of a charmed child of the Earl's lady, whilst she was at the bath. After that Aud bought her for a great price, and promised her freedom if she would serve Thurid, the wife of Thorstein the Red, as she had served the Earl's lady. Myrgjol and Erp her son went to Iceland with Aud. Aud held first to the Faroe Islands and there gave in marriage Alof, the daughter of Thorstein the Red; thence are the Gotuskeggjar (the Gatebeards) descended. Afterwards she went to seek Iceland. She came to Veikarskeid, and there was shipwrecked. She went thence to Keelness to Helga Bjola, her brother, who offered her a lodging there with half of her companions, which she thinking a mean offer, said that he would always be a manikin. She then went west to Broadfirth, to her brother Bjorn, who, knowing the liberal and gen-erous character of his sister, went to meet her, accompanied by all his domestics, and asked her to stay with him, and also offered to provide for all her retinue. She accepted his offer. Afterwards in spring Aud went to seek a settlement (landaleit) up the Broadfirth, accompanied by her liegemen. They ate their Dogurd (day meal) in the south of Broadfirth, at the place which is now called Dogurdarness (Daymeal ness); afterwards they passed through Eyjasund (Island sound). They came ashore at that ness where Aud lost her comb, which they called from that circumstance Kambness (Combe Ness).

Queen Aud settled all the territory of the Dale lands to the inner firth from Daymeal-river to Skraumhlaups river. She dwelt at Hvamm, at the mouth of the Char river, there the place is called Aud's tofts. She had her prayer station at Cross-Knolls; there she caused them to raise crosses because she was baptized and was a true believer. Her kinsfolk had great faith in those Knolls. There they made a temple and there they sacrificed, and it was the firm belief of them that they should die into that mound, and Thord the Yeller was led thither before he took over his lordship of a Godi, as is related in his saga.

A Faeroëse Trader

Tenth century

Færeyinga saga

NORWEGIANS also settled in the Faeroe Islands, which are now a Danish dominion. They contributed their saga to literature, as well as their people's dancing ballads.

&§THERE was a man called Grim Kamban, he was the first who settled in the Faroes in the days of Harald Fairhair, when men fled from his tyranny, and some settled in the Faroes and lived there, and some went to other islands.

Aud, the very rich, came to the Faroes, and gave in marriage Olof the daughter of Thorstein the Red, and from her are come the highest family in the Faroes, who are called Göteskegg, who live on Austrey.

Thorbjorn was the name of a man, he was surnamed Göteskegg. He lived on Austrey in the Faroes, Gudrun was the name of his wife. They had two sons, the eldest named Thorlak, and Thrand the younger. They were promising men. Thorlak was both tall and strong and Thrand was the same when he was grown up, for the difference of age between the brothers was great. Thrand was red of hair, freckled of face, with fine features. Thorbjorn was a rich man and was already old at this time. Thorlak married in the islands but still lived with his father at Gata.

Soon after Thorlak married, Thorbjorn Göteskegg died, and was carried out and buried with all the ancient customs, for they were all heathen then in the Faroes. The sons divided the inheritance between them and both wished for the homestead at Gata, for it was the greatest treasure. They cast lots for it, and the lot fell to Thrand.

After the division, Thorlak asked Thrand to let him have the homestead and Thrand should have more of the money. But Thrand would have none of that. Then Thorlak went away and made himself a home on another of the islands. Thrand let out the land at Gata on lease, and took a large rent for it.

Thrand took passage on a ship, in the summer, but had not much merchandise with him, and went to Norway. He stayed there the winter and was always considered rather difficult of temper.

Harald Greycloak ruled at that time in Norway.

The summer after this Thrand went with merchants south to Denmark, and came during the summer to Haley. Haley is the place in all the north lands to which come the greatest crowd of men during the market time there. There ruled over Denmark Harald the king, Gorm's son, who was called Blue Tooth. Harald the king was at Haley that summer, and a great many men with him. Two men of the guard of Harald the king are named here, who were with him, one called Sigurd, the other Harek. These brothers often went to the market, for they wished to buy a gold ring, the largest, the best they could get. They came to a booth that was wonderfully well decked out. There sat a man who greeted them and asked what they would buy. They said they wished to buy a ring, both large and good. He said they would find a good choice there. They asked his name and he said he was called Holmgeir the Rich. He then brought out his goods and showed them a thick gold ring, which was the greatest treasure of all, but he set so high a price on it that they doubted if they had brought silver enough to give what he asked, and begged him to wait till next morning. He agreed to that. They went away, having arranged this, and so the night passed.

In the morning Sigurd went out of the booth, and Harek remained behind inside. A little later Sigurd came back to the tent door.

"Harek, friend," said he, "give me the purse at once in which is the silver with which we intend to buy the ring. For the market is open. And you stay here and mind the tent." Then Harek gave him the silver through the flap of the tent.

A little after Sigurd came to the tent to his brother and said: "Take the silver, for now the market is open." Harek replied: "I gave you the silver a little time ago." "No," said Sigurd, "I did not take it." They wrangled over this awhile, after which they told the king. The king guessed, as did other men, that some one must have stolen the money from them. Then the king forbade any one to go away. No ship was allowed to depart from Haley. This, most men thought a great nuisance, as it really was, to be obliged to stay over the market time. Then the Northmen had a meeting amongst themselves to take counsel. Thrand was at the meeting, and said: "Men have come here, and are very much at a loss what to do." They asked him if he had any advice to give. "That I have," he said. "Set forth your advice then," they said. "I do not do it for nothing," said he. They asked him what he wanted for it. He said: "Each of you shall give me a silver piece." They said that was too much. But they made a bargain that each man should give him half a silver piece there at once, and another half if the thing went through.

The next day the king had a meeting and said that no one should be free to go, so long as they did not know who had done this. Then up spoke a young man, with curly red hair and a rather freckled face and strongly marked features, and said: "Here are come men and rather at a loss what to do." The king's counsellors asked what advice he had to give. He replied: "It is my advice that every man who is come here shall lay down as much silver as the king shall ask, and when the money is collected in one place, the men shall be paid who have suffered this loss, and that which is left over the king shall have to his honour. And I know he will make good use of his share. For all this crowd of men and ships have to be here, yet not weather bound, to their great loss." This was agreed to at once by every one, for they said they would sooner pay money to the king's honour, than stay there at their own loss. This counsel was followed and when the money was got together there was a great sum. After that many ships sailed away.

The king summoned a Thing, and there they counted the money, and the brothers were paid for their loss out of it. Then the king spoke with his men as to what should be done with all the rest of the money. Then a man spoke and said: "What do you think the man worth who gave this advice?" They now saw that it was the same young man who had given the advice and who now stood there before the king. Then said Harald the king: "This money shall be divided into two parts. My men shall have one part. Then the other shall be divided into two. And this young man shall have one of these lots, I will look after the other." Thrand thanked the king with fair and flattering words. There was so much money in Thrand's lot that it could hardly be counted in marks. Harald the king then sailed away, and all the rest of the crowd who had been there.

Thrand went out to Norway with the Norwegian merchants with whom he had come; they paid him the money that he had asked. He bought a good merchant ship and laid on it the great quantity of goods that he had got on this voyage. He steered this ship to the Faroes and came there safe and sound, with all his goods, and set up house at Gata in the spring. And there was no lack of money.

Thrand was a very tall man, red of hair, red bearded, with freckled, strongly marked features. Difficult of temper, cunning, full of tricks. Overbearing and ill-natured with common people, but mealy-mouthed with greater men than himself. Speaking fair but thinking false.

The Battle of Clontarf
Dublin, 1014
Cogadh Gaedhel re Gallaibh
From the Old Irish

THE king of Leinster invited the Scandinavian jarls of the Orkneys, Hebrides, and Man to defeat Brian Boru and conquer Ireland. Their armies invaded Ireland, and many Icelanders with them. The Norse Sigtrygg and his Irish wife, daughter of Brian Boru, watched the engagement from the battlements of Dublin. This battle is described also in the Icelandic *Njáls saga*.

AND it appeared to the people of Ath Cliath, who were watching them from their battlements, that not more numerous would be the sheaves floating over a great company reaping a field of oats; even though two or three battalions were working at it, than the hair flying with the wind from them, cut away by heavy gleaming axes, and by bright flaming swords. Whereupon the son of Amhlaibh, who was on the battlements of his watch tower, watching them, said, "Well do the foreigners reap the field," said he, "many is the sheaf they let go from them." "It will be at the end of the day that will be seen," said Brian's daughter, namely, the wife of Amhlaibh's son.

However, now, they continued in battle array, and fighting from sunrise to evening. This is the same length of time as that which the tide takes to go, and to flood, and to fill. For it was at the full tide the foreigners came out to fight the battle in the morning, and the tide had come to the same place again at the close of the day, when the foreigners were defeated; and the tide had carried away their ships from them, so that they had not at the last any place to fly to, but into the sea; after the mail-coated foreigners had been all killed by the Dál Cais. An awful rout was made of the foreigners, and of the Laighin, so that they fled simultaneously; and they shouted their cries for mercy, and whoops of rout, and retreat, and running; but they could only fly to the sea, because they had no other place to retreat to, seeing they were cut off between it and the head of Dubh-gall's Bridge; and they were cut off between it and the wood on the other side. They retreated therefore to the sea, like a herd of cows in heat, from sun, and from gad-flies, and from insects; and they were pursued closely, rapidly, and lightly; and the foreigners were drowned in great numbers in the sea, and they lay in heaps and in hundreds, confounded, after parting with their bodily senses and understandings, under the powerful, stout, belabouring; and under the tremendous, hard-hearted pressure, with which the Dál Cais, and the men of Conacht, and as many as were also there of the nobles of Erinn, pursued them.

* * *

Then it was that Brian's daughter, namely, the wife of Amhlaibh's son said, "It appears to me," said she, "that the foreigners have gained their inheritance." "What meanest thou, O woman?" said Amhlaibh's son. "The foreigners are going into the sea, their natural inheritance," said she; "I wonder is it heat that is upon them; but they tarry not to be milked, if it is." The son of Amhlaibh became angered, and he gave her a blow.

* * *

While they were engaged in this conversation the attendant perceived a party of the foreigners approaching them. The Earl Brodar was there, and two warriors along with them. "There are people coming towards us here," said the attendant. "Woe is me, what manner of people are they?" said Brian. "A blue stark naked people," said the attendant. "Alas!" said Brian, "they are the foreigners of the armour, and it is not to do good to thee they come." While he was saying this, he arose and stepped off the cushion, and unsheathed his sword. Brodar passed him by and noticed him not. One of the three who were there, and who had been in Brian's service, said—"Cing, Cing," said he, "this is the king." "No, no, but Priest, Priest," said Brodar, "it is not he," says he, "but a noble priest." "By no means," said the soldier, "that is the great king, Brian." Brodar then turned round, and appeared with a bright, gleaming, trusty battle-axe in his hand, with the handle set in the middle of it. When Brian saw him he gazed at him, and gave him a stroke with his sword, and cut off his left leg at the knee, and his right leg at the foot. The foreigner dealt Brian a stroke which cleft his head utterly; and Brian killed the second man that was with Brodar, and they fell both mutually by each other.

There was not done in Erinn, since Christianity, excepting the beheading of Cormac Mac Cuilennain, any greater deed than this. In fact he was one of the three best that ever were born in Erinn; and one of the three men who most caused Erinn to prosper, namely, Lugh Lamha-fada, and Finn Mac Cumhaill, and Brian Mac Ceinneidigh. For it was he that released the men of Erinn, and its women, from the bondage and iniquity of the foreigners, and the pirates.

* * *

Moreover, there were killed in that battle together the greater part of the men of valour of the Gaill and the Gaedhil, of all the west of Europe. There was killed there, Brodar, son of Osli, Earl of Caer Ebroc, and along with him were killed a thousand plundering Danars, both Saxons and Lochlanns. There was killed there Sitriuc, the son of Ladar, Earl of Innsi Orc.

The Fatal Shirt

1128

Orkneyinga saga

IT happened in the days of the brothers Harald and Paul that they were to hold a Yule feast in Orphir at the house of Earl Harald and that he was to bear the expense for both of them that Yule. He was now there in the thick of his preparations and making a stir.

Those sisters were there, Frakok and Helga, the Earl's mother, and they sat in a little sitting-room sewing. Now Earl Harald went into the room, and the sisters were sitting on the cross-dais, and a newly sewn linen shirt lay between them, white as driven snow. The Earl took up the shirt and saw that it was embroidered in gold.

He said: "For whom is this precious thing?"

Frakok answered: "It is meant for thy brother Paul."

Harald said: "Why take such pains over a shirt for him? Thou dost not exert thyself so long in making me a fair garment."

The Earl had just risen, and was in a nightshirt and linen trousers and had thrown a cloak over his shoulders. He cast off the cloak and spread out the linen shirt. His mother caught at it and bade him not be envious because his brother had a fine garment. The Earl snatched it from her and prepared to put it on. Then Frakok pulled off her hood and tore her hair, and said that his life was at stake if he put on the shirt; then they both wept passionately.

None the less the Earl put it on, and let it drop down over him. But even as the garment clung about him a shiver thrilled through his flesh, instantly followed by exquisite pain. And with that the Earl took to bed and it was not long ere he breathed his last. This was a great grief to his friends.

Immediately after his death his brother Earl Paul took all the realm under him with the consent of all the bonder in the Orkneys. Earl Paul guessed that Frakok and her sister had meant for him the rich garment which Earl Harald had put on; and for this reason he had no desire to have them staying there in the Orkneys. They then went away with all their household, first to Caithness, and thence up into Sutherland, to the estates that Frakok owned there.

Runes of Man and Orkney

c. 1100

KIRK MICHAEL, ISLE OF MAN

MAEL-LOMCHON and the daughter of Dubh-Gael, whom Athils had to wife, raised this cross in memory of Mael-Muire, his foster-mother. It is better to leave a good fosterson than a bad son.

1152-3

ON THE STONES OF MAESHOWE, ORKNEY

The crusaders to Jerusalem broke open the Orkney grave-mound.

Out north is the great treasure hidden, which was left behind (after death); great treasure was hidden. Happy he who can find this great wealth!

These runes that man cut who is most skilled in rune-craft west over sea, with that axe which Gauk owned—Trandil's son from the south country.

Hildina

Date uncertain

A BALLAD OF THE SHETLAND ISLANDS

From the Norn

It was the Earl from Orkney,
   And counsel of his kin sought he,
Whether he should the maiden
   Free from her misery.

"If thou free the maid from her gleaming hall,
   O kinsman dear of mine,
Ever while the world shall last
   Thy glory still shall shine."

Home came the King,
   Home from the ship's levy
The lady Hildina she was gone,
   And only her stepmother there found he.

"Be he in whatever land,
   This will I prove true,
He shall be hanged from the highest tree
   That ever upward grew."

"If the Earl but come to Orkney,
   Saint Magnus will be his aid,
And in Orkney ever he will remain—
   Haste after him with speed."

The King he stood before his lady,
   And a box on her ear gave he,
And all adown her lily white cheeks
   The tears did flow truly.

The Earl he stood before Hildina,
   And a pat on her cheek gave he,—
"O which of us two wouldst thou have lie dead,
   Thy father dear or me?"

"I would rather see my father doomed,
   And all his company,

If so my own true lord and I
  May long rule in Orkney.

"Now do thou take in hand thy steed,
  And ride thou down to the strand;
And do thou greet my sire full blithely,
  And gladly will he clasp thy hand."

The King he now made answer—
  So sore displeased was he—
"In payment for my daughter
  What wilt thou give to me?"

"Thirty marks of the red gold,
  This to thee will I give,
And never shalt thou lack a son
  As long as I may live."

Now long stood the King,
  And long on the Earl gazed he:—
"O thou art worth a host of sons;
  Thy boon is granted thee."

VI. GREENLAND

The Settlement of Greenland
986
Ari Þorgilsson
Íslendingabók

GREENLAND was discovered by an Icelander named Gunnbjorn, but Eirik the Red was the first to colonize, in 986. There were two settlements, one on the south, the other on the west coast. These settlements lost contact with Europe in the fifteenth century and disappeared. In recent years many graves have been excavated. Greenland, after Australia the world's largest island, is now a Danish dominion.

⋙THE country which is called Greenland was discovered and settled from Iceland. Erik the Red was the name of a man from Breidafjord who went from here thither and took possession of land at the place which since has been called Eriksfjord. He gave a name to the country and called it Greenland, and said that people would desire to go thither, if the country had a good name. Both east and west in the country they found human habitations, fragments of skin boats and stone implements from which it was evident that the same kind of people had been there as inhabited Wineland and whom the Greenlanders called Skrellings. He began colonizing the country fourteen or fifteen winters before Christianity came to Iceland [985 or 986] according to what a man who himself had gone thither with Erik the Red told Thorkel Gellisson in Greenland.

A Polar Bear
c. 1000
Flóamanna saga

THIS episode of a small boy and a bear is taken from a saga describing the hardships of a shipload of emigrants to Greenland.

⋙ AND when the winter was wearing on, there came men to trade with Thorgisl and Thorstan, and there were many people in the outbower or store-house where the wares were lying, and there was the boy Thorfin. He spake to his father: "There is such a beautiful dog come outside here, father; I never saw such an one before; he is so big."

Says Thorgisl, "Never mind it; do not go out." But the boy ran out. It was the bear come there, and it had walked down off the glacier. It caught up the boy and he called out. Thorgisl ran out straightway, and he had his sword Earth-house-loom drawn in his hand. The bear was playing with the boy. Thorgisl hewed at it between the lugs with all his might and anger, and clove the whole skull of the beast, and it fell down dead. Thorgisl took up the boy; he was little hurt.

Daily Life in Greenland

1245

Konungs Skuggsjá

THIS dialogue about living conditions in medieval Greenland is taken from the Norwegian book of instruction entitled *The King's Mirror*.

Father. There still remains another species which the Greenlanders count among the whales, but which, it seems to me, ought rather to be classed with the seals. These are called walrus and grow to a length of fourteen ells or fifteen at the very highest. In shape this fish resembles the seal both as to hair, head, skin, and the webbed feet behind; it also has the swimming feet in front like the seal. Its flesh like that of other seals must not be eaten on fast days. Its appearance is distinguished from that of other seals in that it has, in addition to the other small teeth, two large and long tusks, which are placed in the front part of the upper jaw and sometimes grow to a length of nearly an ell and a half. Its hide is thick and good to make ropes of; it can be cut into leather strips of such strength that sixty or more men may pull at one rope without breaking it. The seals that we have just discussed are called fish because they find their food in the sea and subsist upon other fishes. They may be freely eaten, though not like the whales, for whale flesh may be eaten on fast days like other fish food, while these fishes may be eaten only on the days when flesh food is allowed. Now I know of nothing else in the waters of Greenland which seems worth mentioning or reporting,—only those things that we have just discussed.

Son. These things must seem wonderful to all who may hear of them,—both what is told about the fishes and that about the monsters which are said to exist in those waters. Now I understand that this ocean must be more tempestuous than all other seas; and therefore I think it strange that it is covered with ice both in winter and in summer, more than all other seas are. I am also curious to know why men should be so eager to fare thither, where there are such great perils to beware of, and what one can look for in that country which can be turned to use or pleasure. With your permission I also wish to ask what the people who inhabit those lands live upon; what the character of the country is, whether it is ice-clad like the ocean or free from ice even though the sea be frozen; and whether corn grows in that country as in other lands. I should also like to know whether you regard it as mainland or as an island, and whether there are any beasts or such other things in that country as there are in other lands.

Father. The answer to your query as to what people go to seek in that country and why they fare thither through such great perils is to be sought in man's threefold nature. One motive is fame and rivalry, for it is in the nature of man to seek places where great dangers may be met, and thus to win fame. A second motive is curiosity, for it is also in man's nature to wish to see and experience the things that he has heard about, and thus to learn whether the facts are as told or not. The third is desire for gain; for men seek wealth wherever they have heard that gain is to be gotten, though, on the other hand, there may be great dangers too. But in Greenland it is this way, as you probably know, that whatever comes from other lands is high in price, for this land lies so distant from other countries that men seldom visit it. And everything that is needed to improve the land must be purchased abroad, both iron and all the timber used in building houses. In return for their wares the merchants bring back the following products: buckskin, or hides, sealskins, and rope of the kind that we talked about earlier which is called "leather rope" and is cut from the fish called walrus, and also the teeth of the walrus.

As to whether any sort of grain can grow there, my belief is that the country draws but little profit from that source. And yet there are men among those who are counted the wealthiest and most prominent who have tried to sow grain as an experiment; but the great majority in that country do not know what bread is, having never seen it. You have also asked about the extent of the land and whether it is mainland or an island; but I believe that few know the size of the land, though all believe that it is continental and connected with some mainland, inasmuch as it evidently contains a number of such animals as are known to live on the mainland but rarely on islands. Hares and wolves are very plentiful and there are multitudes of reindeer. It seems to be generally held, however, that these animals do not inhabit islands, except where men have brought them in; and everybody seems to feel sure that no one has brought them to Greenland, but that they must have run thither from other mainlands. There are bears, too, in that region; they are white, and people think they are native to the country, for they differ very much in their habits from the black bears that roam the forests. These kill horses, cattle, and other beasts to feed upon; but the white bear of Greenland wanders most of the time about on the ice in the sea, hunting seals and whales and feeding upon them. It is also as skillful a swimmer as any seal or whale.

In reply to your question whether the land thaws out or remains icebound like the sea, I can state definitely that only a small part of the land thaws out, while all the rest remains under the ice. But nobody knows whether the land is large or small, because all the mountain ranges and all the valleys are covered with ice, and no opening has been found anywhere. But it is quite evident that there are such openings, either along the shore or in the valleys that lie between the mountains, through which beasts can find a way; for they could not run thither from other lands, unless they should find open roads through the ice and the soil thawed out. Men have often tried to go up into the country and climb the highest mountains in various places to look about and learn whether any land could be found that was free from ice and habitable. But nowhere have they found such a place, except what is now occupied, which is a little strip along the water's edge.

There is much marble in those parts that are inhabited; it is variously colored, both red and blue and streaked with green. There are also many large hawks in the land, which in other countries would be counted very precious,—white falcons, and they are more numerous there than in any other country; but the natives do not know how to make any use of them.

Son. You stated earlier in your talk that no grain grows in that country; therefore I now want to ask you what the people who inhabit the land live on, how large the population is, what sort of food they have, and whether they have accepted Christianity.

Father. The people in that country are few, for only a small part is sufficiently free from ice to be habitable; but the people are all Christians and have churches and priests. If the land lay near to some other country it might be reckoned a third of a bishopric; but the Greenlanders now have their own bishop, as no other arrangement is possible on account of the great distance from other people. You ask what the inhabitants live on in that country since they sow no grain; but men can live on other food than bread. It is reported that the pasturage is good and that there are large and fine farms in Greenland. The farmers raise cattle and sheep in large numbers and make butter and cheese in great quantities. The people subsist chiefly on these foods and on beef; but they also eat the flesh of various kinds of game, such as reindeer, whales, seals, and bears. That is what men live on in that country.

The Northernmost Runes

Latitude 72° 55′

c. 1300

A runic inscription found on a stone on Kingiktorsoak Island in Baffin's Bay, west of Greenland.

§ ERLING Sighvatsson and Bjarni Thordarson and Eindrithi Jonsson on Saturday before Rogation Day [April 25th] piled these cairns and cleared.

VII. VINLAND THE GOOD

THE earliest written record of the discovery of the American mainland by the Northmen is that of Adam of Bremen about 1070. The two Icelandic sagas that describe the various attempts to plant colonies there in the years after 1000, when Leif the son of Eirik the Red first landed, are so different in details that they have been, like the Four Gospels, the subject of volumes of controversy and commentary. It is clear that Leif Eiriksson went at least as far south as the sandy beaches of Cape Cod, while other colonists survived for a few years on rocky coasts farther north.

Adam of Bremen

Descriptio insularum aquilonis

Written c. 1070

From the Latin

◄§ THERE are, moreover, many other islands in the ocean, not the least of which is Greenland, located far out in the ocean. . . . To this island they say that one can sail from the coast of the Normans [*i.e.,* Norway] in from five to seven days. . . . Moreover, he [the King of Denmark] reported that there was still another island found by many in that ocean, called *Vinland,* because there vines grow without cultivation, producing the best wine. For we have found out that, in addition, crops abound there even without planting, not from fabulous report but by the sure information of the Danes.

Bjarni Herjulfsson Sights the Mainland

986

Grænlendinga þáttr

◄§ BJARNI was a young, promising, and successful merchant. He owned his own ship and traded in foreign lands. He used to spend every second winter with his father, Herjulf, in Iceland, but the last winter that Bjarni was in Norway Herjulf prepared to go to Greenland with Eric the Red. Upon the ship with Herjulf was a Christian man from the Hebrides. He composed the *Hafgerðinga Drápa,* which contains this stave:

"My voyage to the Meek One,
Monk-heart-searcher [Christ], I commit now;
The Lord of Heaven shall hold the hawk's seat [the hand]
Over me forever!"

Herjulf settled in Herjulfness in Greenland and was a very distinguished man. When Bjarni came to Eyrar in Iceland in the summer, he learned that his father had already gone in the spring to settle in Greenland.

Bjarni now determined not to unload his ship, and when his men asked him what he was going to do, he answered that he intended as usual to spend the winter with his father, and "I will," he said, "go to Greenland with my ship, if you are willing to go with me." They all said that they were ready to do as he advised, whereupon he said: "Unwise may our voyage appear, since none of us have been in the Greenland Sea before." Nevertheless, they sailed out on the sea as soon as they were ready, and sailed for three days, until the land disappeared under the water; but then they got a calm and thereafter they got northerly winds and fogs. They did not know where they were, and so it went on for many days. Finally, they saw the sun again, and they could tell the directions; they hoisted their sail and sailed that day, before they saw land. Bjarni did not think that this land was Greenland; they sailed close up to the land and saw that it had no mountains, and that it was covered with woods and had low hills. They left the land on their port side, and let the sheet turn towards the land. After that (siðan) they sailed two days, before they saw a second land. Bjarni did not believe this land to be Greenland either, since there were said to be great glaciers in Greenland. They soon approached this land and saw that it was flat and wooded. Then they were becalmed, and the crew thought it most advisable to land, but Bjarni refused. The men pretended that they lacked both fuel and water. Bjarni said: "You do not lack any of these things"; but he was blamed for this by his men. They hoisted the sail, turned the stern from the shore, and sailed out on the open sea with a southwesterly wind for three days. Then they saw a third land, and this land was high, covered with mountains and glaciers. The men asked if Bjarni would land here, but he said that he would not, "for this land does not appear to me to be good to live in." Hence they did not lower their sail, but kept going along the coast, and saw that it was an island.

They turned again the stern to the land, and sailed out on the sea with the same wind; but the wind increased in strength, and Bjarni ordered that the sail should be shortened, and they should not sail harder than their ship and rigging could stand. They now sailed on for four days, when they sighted a distant land. The man asked Bjarni if he thought this was Greenland or not. Bjarni said: "This is most like Greenland, according to what I have been told of it, and here we will steer to the land." They did so, and landed in the evening on a headland (*ness*) where there was a boat. On this headland lived Bjarni's father, Herjulf; from whom it was given the name Herjulf-ness. Bjarni went now to his father, gave up sailing, and remained with his father during the latter's lifetime, and lived there afterwards.

Leif Eiriksson Discovers America

1000

Snorri Sturluson

Ólafs saga Tryggvasonar

◆§ THAT same summer the King [Olaf Tryggvason] sent Gizur and Hjalti to Iceland, as has already been written. At that time he also sent Leif Ericsson to Greenland to preach Christianity there. The King sent with him a priest and some other holy men to baptize the people there, and to teach them the true faith. Leif went to Greenland that same summer. He took on the sea [on board his vessel] a ship's crew, who were at that time in great distress and were lying on a completely broken wreck, and on that same voyage he found Vinland the Good. He arrived in Greenland late in the summer, and went home to Brat-tahlid to his father Eric. People afterwards called him Leif the Lucky, but his father Eric said that Leif's having rescued a ship's crew and restored the men to life might be balanced against the fact that he had brought the impostor (*skemanninn*), as he called the priest, to Greenland. Nevertheless, through Leif's advice and persuasion, Eric was baptized, and all of the people of Greenland.

Leif Explores the Coast

After 1000

Grænlendinga þáttr

⋘ THERE was now much talk of explorations. Leif, a son of Eric the Red, from Brattahlid, went to Bjarni Herjulfsson, bought his ship, and hired a crew for it, so that they were in all thirty-five men. Leif vainly attempted to make his father join the expedition. On the expedition was a German, by name Tyrker. After having fitted out the ship for the voyage, they sailed out on the sea, and found first the land which Bjarni had seen last. They sailed to the land, anchored, put out the boat, and went ashore. No grass grew there, and great glaciers were seen inland, while the coast between the glaciers and the sea looked like one large, flat stone, and this land did not seem to them to have any value. Then said Leif: "Now it has gone better with us than with Bjarni, who came here and did not go ashore; now I will give this land a name and call it Helluland."

After that they went on board the ship, sailed out on the sea, and found another land. They sailed again to the land, anchored, put out the boat, and went ashore. This land was flat and covered with woods, and there were extensive white sands, wherever they went, and the beach was not steep. Then said Leif: "This land shall be named according to its nature and it shall be called Markland." After that they went as soon as possible to the ship, and sailed out on the open sea with a northeast wind, and were on the sea two days before they saw land. It was fine weather. They looked round and noticed that there was dew on the grass. This dew was found to have a very sweet taste. After that they went on board the ship and sailed into the sound between the island and a cape which stretched northward from the coast, and steered westward past the cape. The water was so shallow there that the ship ran aground and stood dry at ebb-tide; the sea was then visible only at a great distance. But Leif and his men were so anxious to get ashore that they did not care to wait till the water rose again under their ship, and they ran ashore at once where a river flowed out from a lake. At next high tide they took the boat, pulled to the ship, and took it up through the river into the lake, anchored, and carried their leather bags ashore. They first built wooden huts (sheds), but later they decided to prepare to remain there during the winter, and they built then large houses.

Salmon, larger than they had seen before, were plentiful in the river and the lake. The land seemed to them so good that there would be no need of storing fodder for the cattle for the winter; there came no frost in the winters and the grass withered but little. Day and night were there more nearly of equal length than is the case in Greenland and Iceland; the sun had there *eyktarstaðr* and *dagmálastaðr* on the shortest day of the year. When they had built the house, Leif said to his men: "Now I will divide our party into two halves and explore the land; and one half of the men shall remain at the house, while the other half shall examine the country, but shall not go farther than to let them be back in the evening, and they must never part from one another." They did so for some time, and Leif was alternately one day with the exploring party, the other day at the house. Leif was a fine, strong man, of impressive personality, and moreover intelligent and wise.

It was found one night that one of their men was missing, and that was Tyrker Southman. Leif was much troubled by this, for Tyrker had been for a long time with him and his father, and had been very fond of Leif in his childhood. Leif now reprimanded his men severely, and prepared to go in search of him with twelve men. But when they were only a short distance from the house, they were met by Tyrker, whom they received with great joy. Leif saw at once that his foster-father was queer. Tyrker had a high forehead and restless eyes; he was freckled in the face and small of stature, but adept in all sorts of handicraft. Then Leif said to him: "Why were you so late, foster-father, and why did you part from the others?" Then at first he spoke in German for a long time, and rolled his eyes, and twisted his mouth when they did not understand what he said. After some time he spoke in the Norse tongue: "I did not go much farther, and yet I have discovered something new; I found *vínvið* and *vínber*." "Can this be true, foster-father?" said Leif. "Certainly, this is true," said he, "for I was born where there is no lack of either *vínvið* or *vínber*." They now slept that night, but in the morning Leif said to his men: "We will now divide our labors, and each day we will either gather *vínber* or cut *vínvið* and fell trees, so as to obtain a cargo of these for my ship." This advice was followed. It is said that their after-boat was filled with *vínber*. A cargo was now cut for the ship, and when the spring came, they made ready and sailed away, and Leif

gave the land a name in accordance with its products, and called it
Vinland.

Then they sailed out on the sea, and had a fair wind, until they
sighted Greenland and the mountains below the glaciers.

Thorfinn Karlsefni Plants a Colony

After 1000

Eiríks saga rauða

◄§ KARLSEFNI, together with Snorri and Bjarni and their people,
went southward along the coast. They sailed for a long time, and came
at last to a river which flowed down from the land into a lake and
then into the sea. There were great beaches (*eyrar*) before the mouth
of the river, and the river could not be entered except at high tide.
Karlsefni and his men sailed into the mouth of the river and called
the place Hóp. They found there on the shore self-sown wheat-fields
on the low land, but vines (*vínviðr*) where the ground was high.
Every brook there was full of fish. They dug pits on the beach at the
edge of the high tide, and when the tide fell there were halibut in
the pits. There were great numbers of animals of all kinds in the
woods. They remained there half a month and enjoyed themselves
without anything happening. They had brought their livestock with
them. One morning early they observed a great number of skin-boats,
and saw that staves (or rods) were brandished, and it sounded like
the wind whistling in stacks of straw, and the staves were swung with
the sun. Karlsefni thought this might be a sign of peace and ordered
his men to display a white shield. These people rowed up to them,
went ashore, and looked at the newcomers with surprise. They were
swarthy men of a savage appearance and had scraggly (*illt*) hair on
their heads. They had big eyes and broad cheeks. They tarried there
for a while, wondering at the people they saw before them, and after
that they rowed away southward around the cape.

Karlsefni and his followers built their houses (*búðir*) above the
lake. Some of their dwellings (*skálar*) were near the lake, others
farther away. They remained there that winter. No snow came and all
of their livestock lived by grazing.

At the beginning of spring, early one morning, they observed a
number of skin-boats rowed from the south round the headland, so

many that it looked as if coal had been strewn at the mouth of the harbor. Then again staves were swung on each boat. Karlsefni and his men raised their shields, and when they got together they began to barter, and these people preferred red cloth; in exchange they gave peltries and pure gray (squirrel?) skins. They also desired to buy swords and spears, but this was forbidden by Karlsefni and Snorri. For a pure gray skin the Skrælings received one span of red cloth, which they tied around their heads. So their trade went on for a time. Then the cloth began to get scarce, and the Norsemen cut it in small pieces not wider than a finger, and yet the Skrælings gave as much for it as before, or even more.

It happened that Karlsefni's bull ran out from the woods, bellowing loudly. This frightened the Skrælings; they ran to their boats and rowed away southward along the shore; after this nothing was seen of them for three whole weeks. But at the end of that time, a great number of Skræling boats came from the south, a dense stream of them; the staves were now swung against the direction of the sun (*withershins*); and the Skrælings all yelled loudly. Karlsefni and his men displayed a red shield. The Skrælings ran out of their boats, and a fight ensued. There was a fierce shower of missiles, for the Skrælings had war-slings (*valslöngur*). The Skrælings raised up on a pole a very large ball-shaped body, somewhat like a sheep's belly and bluish of color; this they hurled from the pole up on the land above Karlsefni's people, and it made a terrific sound where it fell. (According to *AM* 557, it appears that several poles with balls attached to them were thrown.) This frightened Karlsefni and all his men so much that they fled, and they made their escape up along the river-bank, for it seemed to them that the Skrælings were rushing towards them from all sides; they did not halt till they came to some jutting rocks, where they offered a stout resistance. It is now told how Freydis came out, and, seeing that the men were fleeing, upbraided them for their cowardice. She tried to follow them, but, being at that time pregnant, she could not run so fast; still she went after them into the woods. The Skrælings pursued her. On her way she found the dead body of Thorbrand Snorrason with a flat stone in his head and his naked sword lying beside him; she took it up and prepared to defend herself. The Skrælings then reached her, whereupon she pulled out her breast from under her clothing, and struck it with the naked

sword. At this the Skrælings were frightened and ran to their boats
and rowed away. Karlsefni and his companions praised her valor. . . .

* * *

The third winter they were in Straumfiord. Then the men split
up into factions, the women being the cause; for the unmarried men
tried to seize the married women, whence great trouble arose. There
Snorri, Karlsefni's son, was born the first fall, and he was three
winters old when they went away. When they sailed from Vinland,
they got a southerly wind, and so came to Markland, where they
found five Skrælings, of whom one was bearded, two were women,
and two were children. The Norsemen caught the boys, but the
others escaped and sank into the ground. They took the two boys
with them, taught them the language, and baptized them. They called
their mother Vethilldi (*AM* 557: Vætilldi) and their father Uvæge.
They said that the Skrælings were ruled by kings, of whom one was
called Avalldanía (*AM* 557: Avaldamon) and the other Valldidida.
They stated that they had no houses; the people lived in caves or holes.
They said there was a land on the other side, opposite their land,
which was inhabited by people who wore white garments, and who
carried poles before them to which pieces of cloth were attached, and
they shouted loudly; people think that this must have been Hvitra-
mannaland (White-men's Land), or Great-Ireland. (*AM* 557: Now
they arrived in Greenland, and remained with Eric the Red during
the winter.)

VIII. DENMARK

A Danish March on Rome

101 B.C.

Strabo

From the Greek

In the second century before Christ the fertile Danish peninsula of Jutland became inundated and overpopulated and, in a great migration, many of four of its peoples—Himbrer, Teutoner, Ambroner, and Charuder—moved south. Their place-names are still found on the map of Jutland. The Teutoner and Ambroner were defeated by Roman armies under Consul Marius at Aix-Les-Bains near the Rhone in 102 B.C. The Himbrer came through the Brenner Pass to the plains of the Po and were defeated by Marius near Vercelli, July 30, 101 B.C. The following extravagant description is one of the many accounts of this invasion in ancient Latin and Greek authors.

◆§ It is reported that the Cimbri had a peculiar custom. They were accompanied in their expeditions by their wives; these were followed by hoary-headed priestesses, clad in white, with cloaks of carbasus fastened on with clasps, girt with brazen girdles, and bare-footed. These individuals, bearing drawn swords, went to meet the captives throughout the camp, and, having crowned them, led them to a brazen vessel containing about twenty amphoræ, and placed on a raised platform, which one of the priestesses having ascended, and holding the prisoner above the vessel, cut his throat; then, from the manner in which the blood flowed into the vessel, some drew certain divinations; while others, having opened the corpse, and inspected the entrails, prophesied victory to their army. In battle too they beat skins stretched on the wicker sides of chariots, which produces a stunning noise.

A Roman Fleet Visits Jutland

C. A.D. 5

Caesar Augustus

Res gestae divi Augusti

From the Latin and Greek of the inscriptions at Angora, Appolonia, and Antioch

◆§ My fleet sailed along the ocean from the mouth of the Rhine as far towards the east as the borders of the Cimbri, whither no

Roman before that time had penetrated either by land or sea. The Cimbri and the Charydes and the Semnones and other German peoples of the same region through their envoys petitioned for my friendship and that of the Roman people.

Hygelac Invades Merovingia

c. 525

Gregory of Tours

From the Latin

LATIN chronicles confirm the historical fact of one of the incidents of *Bēowulf*. A treatise *On Monsters and Prodigies* records Hygelac's nationality more precisely than does Gregory of Tours: *rex Huiglaucus qui imperavit Getis.*

⋧ AFTER these events, the Danes with their king Chlochilaicus made for Gaul by sea with a naval expedition. After disembarking, they devastated one district of the kingdom of Theuderic and took prisoners, and having loaded the ships with captives and other spoils, were of a mind to return home to their own country. Their king remained on shore, intending himself to follow when the ships should have reached the open sea. When the news was brought to Theuderic that his territory had been laid waste by foreigners, he sent his son Theudebert into those regions with a strong army and great supply of war-gear. After killing the king, he defeated the enemy in a naval battle, and recovered all the booty stolen from the land.

Runes of Gallehus and Glavendrup

THE GOLDEN HORN OF GALLEHUS

c. 425

I, Hlewagastir the Holting, made this horn.

THE STONE OF GLAVENDRUP

c. 910

⋧ RAGNHILD raised this stone in memory of Alli, priest in Salve, the revered servant of the temple. Alli's sons raised this monument in memory of their father, and his wife in memory of her husband;

but Soti cut these runes in memory of his lord. May Thor hallow these runes. He shall expiate his guilt, who throws down this stone or removes it elsewhere.

The Jellinge Stones

THE OLDER JELLINGE STONE

c. 935

Gorm the king raised this stone in memory of Thyra his wife, Denmark's defence.

THE LATER JELLINGE STONE

c. 980

HARALD the king ordered this memorial to be raised in honour of Gorm his father and Thyra his mother, the Harald who won all Denmark and Norway and made the Danes Christians.

Valdemar and Tove

1157

Danmarks gamle folkeviser

From the Danish

ALREADY in the sixteenth century the Danes were transcribing the folk ballads that they sang while dancing. In the nineteenth century the popular ballads were collected from oral and written tradition by the scholar Svend Grundtvig. This collection, with its many variants and notes comparing the themes with the ballads of other lands, is the world's most comprehensive body of national folk songs. Following the Danish method, Professor Francis J. Child of Harvard University edited the English and Scottish popular ballads. These are the two great ballad collections. There are editions of the ballads of Sweden, Norway, the Faeroes, and Iceland, but incomplete. The Faeroe ballads are collected and edited in manuscript in The Royal Library of Copenhagen, but still await publication. Dance ballads came to England from France and were transmitted by sailors and traders to Norway, whence this custom was distributed over Scandinavia.

The ballad selected here describes an amour of King Valdemar the Great (1157-1182) and one of his boyhood playmates.

Gay went the dance in King Valdemar's hall,
(By my troth)
There danced the Queen with her ladies all.
King Valdemar needs must love them both.

There danced the Queen with ladies fair,
There danced Tove with waving hair.

"Harken now, Tove, my play-fellow sweet,
Gird up thy silk skirts around thy feet."

"Small praise from me the King would gain
If I might not trail a silken train."

"Tove, my play-fellow, tell thou me
How first the King got his will of thee."

"Askest thou, I will tell thee why,
Because the King was stronger than I.

"I was but a maiden small
Dwelling in my father's hall.

"So little and fair by the gate stood I,
The King and all his merry men they came a-riding by.

"By one, by two, his knights he sent,
But never for their commands I went.

"The King he came himself with all his merry men,
And I, Tovelille, must follow then."

"Tove, my play-fellow, tell thou me
What morning-gift did he give to thee?"

"He gave me a casket of golden sheen,
Better was never in Denmark seen.

"Nine rings he gave me of red, red gold
That Sweden's Queen did have and hold.

"He clad me in silk and scarlet gay,
Thou and all thy maidens ne'er go in such array."

Up spake the Queen in anger wild:
" 'Twas enough, I vow, for a peasant's child!

"By God the Lord, if I breathe and live,
Less by half to thee shall he give!"

The Queen she wrapped her in cloak of vair,
To speak with King Valdemar did she fare.

"Now answer what I ask of thee,
Why lovest thou Tove more than me?"

"For this Tovelille to me is so dear,
Because she hath two sons that serve my person near.

"When Flensborg Town I first rode by
Christopher bore my banner so high.

"When first I rode to Holsterland
Knud bore my banner in his right hand."

Winters twain were gone and past
Ere the Queen got her will at last.

All on holy Christmas Day
Tove went in kirk to pray.

Tovelille fared forth in the street
Golden silk and samite floated round her feet.

Forth from her window the Queen did spy,
She saw proud Tovelille passing by.

The Queen she spake to her ladies three:
"Now bid proud Tovelille hither to me!"

Tove wrapped her in cloak of vair,
To seek the Queen she did repair.

"Lithe now and listen, Tove, to me,
I would fain seek the bath tonight with thee."

"Ne'er of the bath can I have my fill,
I'll do thy bidding with right good-will!"

The Queen she spake to her pages three:
"Take heed that the bath is hot for me.

"Heat it hot, and heat it red!
There shall Tovelille lie dead."

Tovelille she went in before,
The Queen herself she locked the door.   •

"Here is no water, here is no lye,
Let me out for the sake of God on high!"

Christopher went riding by,
He heard his mother wail and cry.

He struck the door a blow so stout
That bolt and nail came leaping out.

In rue and wrath he burst the door,
His mother from the bath he bore.

He bore her into the garden green,
But she was dead ere day was seen.

The Dannebrog Falls from Heaven

June 15, 1219

Peder Olsen

From the Latin

It is generally believed that the Danish flag, a white cross on a red field, was presented from the Pope to King Valdemar the Victorious for his crusade against the pagan Estonians in 1219 when he won the Battle of Tallinn ("the Danes' city"). Legend is more picturesque. The following account, dating from the Reformation, is based on earlier tradition.

When the Christian Danes in Estonia were warring against the infidel Estonians in a place called Tallinn and were nearly worn out, they prayed devoutly for divine aid, and were immediately permitted to receive, fallen from the sky, a banner with a white cross imprinted on the cloth. They also heard a voice from the heavens saying that, if the banner were raised high in the air, they would surely crush their enemies and win a complete victory. And thus it came to pass. That banner is usually called by the familiar name, "Danebroge."

IX. SWEDEN

The Rök Stone

c. 835

Runic Inscription

THE longest of the four thousand runic inscriptions for
is cut on a large granite slab that now stands by the ro
churchyard of Rök in East Götland. To-day it provide
tourists. The stone is still somewhat of a mystery whic
treatises have attempted to solve. The names inscribed
unknown to history. Part of the inscription is in Old Verse. Some lines
are in cypher, and some seem to have religious symbolism. According to
the present interpretation the father reminds the youth of his and coming
generations of past examples of justice, in the hope that someone may be
enboldened to avenge his slain son.

᪆ AFTER Væmoth stand these runes, but Varin his father carved
them after his death-doomed son.

I tell to youth what were the two spoils that were taken twelve
times as booty, both together, from one man after another.

This I tell, as the second, who nine generations ago invaded our
coast with his Hreith-Goths and died with them for his aggression.

Thiaurik the brave viking chief was lord over the Hreith-Sea
shore. Now, equipped, he sits on his steed, his shield strapped, prince
of the Maerings.

Sibi, guard of the sanctuary, begot offspring at the age of ninety.

I tell to youth this, who of Inguld's kin was avenged through a
woman's sacrifice.

I tell to youth for whom an heir is born.

To avenge a young hero he is born.

That is still the intention.

He knew how to slay the giant.

That is still the intention.

Good may come of it.

This I tell, as the twelfth, where the Valkyrie's horse shall find
feed on the battlefield where twenty kings lie.

This I tell, as the thirteenth, who were the kings who dwelt on
Sjælland for four winters, known by four names, sons of four brothers.

They were Valki and his four brothers, sons of Rathulf, Hraithulf and his four brothers, sons of Rugulf, Haisl and his four brothers, sons of Haruth, Kunmund and his four brothers, sons of Björn.

Now I am fostering a youth who may himself decide who requires revenge.

I say to youth: be bold.

Swedish Ambassadors

May 18, 839

Galinda Prudentius

Annales Bertilini

From the Latin

IN the year 839 there came to the emperor Louis the Pious Greek ambassadors, sent by the Byzantine emperor Theophilos, who brought with them a letter, together with costly presents. The emperor received them most honorably at Ingelheim on the eighteenth of May. Together with them, he sent some persons who said that they—that is to say their nation—were called *Rhos,* and whom their own king, called *Khan,* had sent to him for friendship's sake, as they asserted.

Now Theophilos begged Louis in the said letter that they might travel under his protection through the whole of his empire, as he would not allow them to return by the same way they had come, because they were obliged to pass through rough and barbarous tribes of the utmost ferocity. But, inquiring more exactly the reason of their coming, *Louis learned that they were of Swedish nationality,* and supposing that they had come rather as spies than in search of friendship, he resolved to detain them near him until he could discover whether their intentions were honest or not.

Emperor Louis informed Emperor Theophilos through the mediation of his ambassadors and by a letter that out of regard for him he had graciously received the men. If they were found to be honest they would have the opportunity to return in safety to their native land, and be sent back with sufficient protection. Otherwise, they would be conducted by the ambassadors of Louis back again to Theophilos, who then could decide "what to do with the Swedes."

Swedes Establish the State of Russia

860-862

The Russian Primary Chronicle

From the Slavic

SWEDES founded the Russian Empire and gave their name to Russia. When Danes and Norwegians were planting colonies in Western Europe, and even in Sicily and the American mainland, the Swedes were trading along the Russian rivers and sending their fleets across the Black Sea in unsuccessful attacks on Constantinople. Swedes served the Greek emperors as mercenaries in the Varangian Guard. The Slavs called the Swedes *Russes*, a word apparently adopted from the Finnish name for the Swedes, "The Rowers"; Greeks and Arabs also called them *Russes* and, at a later time, *Varangians*. Byzantine annals record both the Swedish and Slavic names of the cataracts of the Dnjeper River. Sweden is rich in finds of old Greek and Arabic coins.

At the invitation of Slavic tribes, the Swedes organized the Russian state with a capital first at Novgorod and later at Kiev.

◆§ THE tributaries of the Varangians drove them back beyond the sea and, refusing them further tribute, set out to govern themselves. There was no law among them, but tribe rose against tribe. Discord thus ensued among them, and they began to war one against another. They said to themselves, "Let us seek a prince who may rule over us, and judge us according to the law." They accordingly went overseas to the Varangian Russes: these particular Varangians were known as Russes, just as some are called Swedes, and others Normans, Angles, and Gotlanders, for they were thus named. The Chuds, the Slavs, and the Krivichians then said to the people of Rus, "Our whole land is great and rich, but there is no order in it. Come to rule and reign over us." They thus selected three brothers, with their kinsfolk, who took with them all the Russes and migrated. The oldest, Rurik, located himself in Novgorod; the second, Sineus, at Byelo ozero; and the third, Truvor, in Izborsk. On account of these Varangians, the district of Novgorod became known as the land of Rus. The present inhabitants of Novgorod are descended from the Varangian race, but aforetime they were Slavs.

Swedes on the Volga

922

Ibn Faḍlān

From the Arabic

THE following Arabic account of the Swedes on the Volga, written by an ambassador sent out by Al-Muktadir, caliph of Bagdad, is preserved in the *Geographical Dictionary* of Yākūt.

I SAW how the Northmen had arrived with their wares, and pitched their camp beside the Volga. Never did I see people so gigantic; they are tall as palm trees; and florid and ruddy of complexion. They wear neither camisoles nor *chaftans,* but the men among them wear a garment of rough cloth, which is thrown over one side, so that one hand remains free. Every one carries an axe, a dagger, and a sword, and without these weapons they are never seen. Their swords are broad, with wavy lines, and of Frankish make. From the tip of the finger-nails to the neck, each man of them is tattooed with pictures of trees, living beings, and other things. The women carry, fastened to their breast, a little case of iron, copper, silver, or gold, according to the wealth and resources of their husbands. Fastened to the case they wear a ring, and upon that a dagger, all attached to their breast. About their necks they wear gold and silver chains.

* * *

I was told that the least of what they do for their chiefs when they die, is to consume them with fire. When I was finally informed of the death of one of their magnates, I sought to witness what befell. First they laid him in his grave—over which a roof was erected—for the space of ten days, until they had completed the cutting and sewing of his clothes. In the case of a poor man, however, they merely build for him a boat, in which they place him, and consume it with fire. At the death of a rich man, they bring together his goods, and divide them into three parts. The first of these is for his family; the second is expended for the garments they make; and with the third they purchase strong drink, against the day when the girl resigns herself to death, and is burned with her master. To the use of wine they abandon themselves in mad fashion, drinking it day and night; and not seldom does one die with the cup in his hand.

When the day was now come that the dead man and the girl were to be committed to the flames, I went to the river in which his ship lay, but found that it had already been drawn ashore. Four corner-blocks of birch and other woods had been placed in position for it, while around were stationed large wooden figures in the semblance of human beings. Thereupon the ship was brought up, and placed on the timbers above mentioned. In the mean time the people began to walk to and fro, uttering words which I did not understand. The dead man, meanwhile, lay at a distance in his grave, from which they had not yet removed him. Next they brought a couch, placed it in the ship, and covered it with Greek cloth of gold, wadded and quilted, with pillows of the same material. There came an old crone, whom they call the angel of death, and spread the articles mentioned on the couch. It was she who attended to the sewing of the garments, and to all the equipment; it was she, also, who was to slay the girl.

* * *

They now clothed him in drawers, leggings, boots, and a *kurtak* and *chaftan* of cloth of gold, with golden buttons, placing on his head a cap made of cloth of gold, trimmed with sable. Then they carried him into a tent placed in the ship, seated him on the wadded and quilted covering, supported him with the pillows, and, bringing strong drink, fruits, and basil, placed them all beside him. Then they brought a dog, which they cut in two, and threw into the ship; laid all his weapons beside him; and led up two horses, which they chased until they were dripping with sweat, whereupon they cut them in pieces with their swords, and threw the flesh into the ship. Two oxen were then brought forward, cut in pieces, and flung into the ship. Finally they brought a cock and a hen, killed them, and threw them in also.

* * *

The pile was soon aflame, then the ship, finally the tent, the man, and the girl, and everything else in the ship. A terrible storm began to blow up, and thus intensified the flames, and gave wings to the blaze.

At my side stood one of the Northmen, and I heard him talking with the interpreter, who stood near him. I asked the interpreter what the Northman had said, and received this answer: "You Arabs," he said, "must be a stupid set! You take him who is to you the most revered and beloved of men, and cast him into the ground, to be devoured by creeping things and worms. We, on the other hand, burn him in a twinkling, so that he instantly, without a moment's delay, enters into Paradise." At this he burst out into uncontrollable laughter, and then continued: "It is the love of the Master [God] that causes the wind to blow and snatch him away in an instant." And, in very truth, before an hour had passed, ship, wood, and girl had, with the man, turned to ashes.

Thereupon they heaped over the place where the ship had stood something like a rounded hill, and, erecting on the centre of it a large birchen post, wrote on it the name of the deceased, along with that of the king of the Northmen. Having done this, they left the spot.

A Swedish Princess at the Byzantine Court

September 9, 957

Constantine VII Porphyrogenitos

Ceremonies

From the Greek

SWEDEN faces east as well as west, and Swedes have always cherished the refinements of eastern civilizations. Swedish archeologists have unearthed the magnificent prehistoric potteries of China. The Town Hall of Stockholm is a symbol of the glory of cosmopolitan architecture.

It is hard to realize that, for a thousand years after the fall of Rome, "the glory that was Greece and the grandeur that was Rome" were maintained in the city of Byzantium. This was "The Great City" of Old Scandinavian literature. From the seventh century onward Swedes journeyed the East Way to Constantinople as tourists, as merchants, as soldiers. The present selection describes the reception of Olga, Swedish princess of Kiev, at the court of the Greek emperor.

⋙ ON Wednesday, September 9, 957, there was a reception on the occasion of the arrival of Her Highness the Princess Olga of Russia. The princess herself entered the palace accompanied by her female relatives of princely blood and rank and by her high ranking suite. The princess led the procession, the rest followed according to rank, one behind the other. Princess Olga stopped there where the secretary-of-state usually examines the credentials of the ambassadors. After her the delegates and the negotiators of the princes of Russia entered; they remained underneath the banners. The ceremony followed according to the prescribed rules.

Then again the princess came out, and went first through the orchard, then into the dining hall of the chamberlains, that is to say the hall in which the canopy stands and where the magistrates are promoted. Then she went through the gallery and the "hand-of-gold" or vestibule of the Emperor, where she sat down.

When, in the meantime, according to custom, the Emperor returned to the Great Palace, a new reception took place in the following manner. In the Hall of Receptions of Justinian there was a dais covered with a purple carpet, and on it stood the great throne of Emperor Theophilos and, next to it, a royal golden chair. Farther down, outside the two banners, stood the musicians who carried the silver instruments of the two countries while the bearers of the wind instruments stood outside.

When the princess was called by the Emperor, she proceeded through the arch and through the interior corridors of the court of the Emperor. The Empress sat on the aforementioned throne, and her daughter-in-law and all the court came in. The various orders were introduced by the chief of the Emperor's eunuchs, aided by the ushers. The orders followed each other according to the following gradation: First, the ladies-in-waiting; second, the wives of the magistrates; third, the wives of the patricians; fourth, the wives of the officers of the first body-guard; fifth, the wives of the rest of the first body-guard; sixth, the wives of body-guard officers; seventh, the wives of the body-guard, grooms, and officers.

After all these had assembled, the Russian princess came in, introduced by the chief of the eunuchs and the ushers. She walked at the head of her suite, her women relatives and selected maids-of-honor following according to protocol. Then the chief of the eunuchs in the name of the Emperor whispered something into the ear of the princess; whereupon she left again and sat down on the bench.

Then the Empress, rising from her throne, went through the Lausiakon, the Tripitonos, and the New Salon into her bed chamber. After this the princess also entered the Hall of Justinian, and the Lausiakon and Tripitonos into the New Salon, where she rested for a short time. In the meantime the Emperor had come to the bed chamber of the Empress. There he sat down with his wife and with their sons born in the purple. Then the princess was asked by the

Emperor to enter from the New Salon. On the invitation of the Emperor she sat down and talked to him just as she pleased.

That same day a solemn banquet was served in the Hall of Justinian. The Empress was seated there on the aforementioned throne, with her daughter-in-law next to her. Princess Olga stood aside at first until the other women of royal blood, introduced by the steward, had paid solemn reverence to the Empress. After this the princess herself expressed her respect, by a certain inclination of her head, and then she sat down where she had stood, at a table that had been placed a short distance from the seat of the Empress. She sat, according to custom, with the close friends of the Empress and her daughter-in-law. At this banquet there were present the musicians of the Church of the Apostles and of Saint Sophia, who sang songs in praise of the royal family. Also actors of every kind performed.

At the same time another meal was being served in the Golden Dining Hall in which all the male relatives and negotiators of Princess Olga took part. They received presents after the dinner. An uncle of the princess received thirty silver coins, eight of her close friends and councillors twenty coins each, twenty deputies twelve, forty-three negotiators twelve, Father Gregorius eight, both interpreters twelve, the men of Prince Svyatoslav five each, six men of the deputies three each, the interpreter of the princess fifteen silver coins.

As soon as the Emperor had left the banquet, desserts were served in the dining room on a small table of gold which usually stands in the chest called The Pentapyrgion. Sweets and cakes were served on dishes adorned with gems and enamel. There was sitting the Emperor Constantinos himself, the Emperor Romanus, the porphyrogenite sons, the Emperor's daughter-in-law, and the Princess Olga. Five hundred silver coins in a gold case set with gems were given to Princess Olga. Six of her intimate women friends received twenty coins each, eighteen of her maids-of-honor each received eight silver pieces.

On Sunday, October 18, another feast took place in the Golden Dining Hall where the male Russians dined with the Emperor, and another in the Five-domed Salon of Saint Paul, where the Empress with her porphyrogenite sons, her daughter-in-law, and Princess Olga dined together. On that occasion the princess received a gift of two hundred silver coins, her uncle twenty, her father confessor Gregorius eight, sixteen of her female relatives twelve each, eighteen of her

maids-of-honor six each, twenty-two envoys twelve each, forty-four
negotiators six each, and both interpreters each ten silver coins.

The Gripsholm Stone

c. 1041

Runic Inscription

SOME twenty-five runic inscriptions have been found in Sweden com-
memorating men who accompanied Ingvar the Far-traveler on his expedition across Russia to the Caspian Sea. Ingvar died in 1041. There is a late
romantic Icelandic saga about him. Part of the Gripsholm inscription
is in Old Verse (*fornyrðislag*).

TOLA had this stone raised for her son Harald, Ingvar's brother:

> They fared bravely
> Afar after gold
> And in the East Way
> Fed the eagles;
> Died in the South Way
> In Saracen Land.

The Lion of the Piraeus

c. 1050

Runic Inscription

THESE runes are carved on the marble lion now in Venice, removed in
1687 from Greece where it had stood in the harbor of Piraeus at the
entrance to the road to Athens. The lion is of white marble, more than
life size, ten feet high, and is a magnificent example of classical Greek
sculpture. The runes are clearly Swedish and may have been inscribed by
soldiers of the Varangian guard from Byzantium. The inscription includes a decorative scroll and four lines in verse.

> They hacked him down
> In the midst of his host,

but in this harbor the men hewed runes after Horse, a good land-
holder from the bay. The Swedes put this on the lion. He travelled
with wisdom, won gold in his journeys.

> Ten warriors wrought the runes,
> Writ them in rich scroll.

Aeskil and Thorlef and others had them well cut, they who lived in
Roslagen . . . . son of . . . . . . cut these runes. Ulv and . . . .
colored them . . . . . . He won gold in his journeys.

Worship at Uppsala

c. 1070

Adam of Bremen

Gesta Hammaburgensis Ecclesiae Pontificum

From the Latin

THE old religion persisted in Sweden a century after the other Scandinavian countries had adopted Christianity. This is due to the inherent calm-
ness and conservatism of the Swedes who, even when they became
protestants, retained the apostolic succession. Only at Uppsala do we read
of a professional Othinic priesthood instead of lay leaders who conducted the rites and maintained the temples. For the following account
of Swedish ritual we are indebted to the same Bremen monk who gave us
the earliest written account of the discovery of America.

AT this point I shall say a few words about the religious beliefs
of the Swedes. That nation has a magnificent temple, which is called
Upsala, located not far from the city of Sigtuna. In this temple,
built entirely of gold, the people worship the statues of three gods.
These images are arranged so that Thor, the most powerful, has his
throne in the middle of the group of three. On either side of him sit
Othin and Freyr. Their provinces are as follows: "Thor," they say,
"rules the heavens; he is the god of thunder and lightning, wind and
rain, fair weather and the produce of the fields. The second god,
Othin (i.e., Madness), is the god of war, and he provides man with
courage in the face of his enemies. The third god is Freyr, who
bestows peace and pleasure upon mortals." Indeed they depict him as
having a large phallus. Othin they represent armed just as our people
usually portray Mars, and Thor with his scepter seems to be the
counterpart of Jupiter. They also worship deified human beings upon
whom they bestow immortality because of their outstanding deeds.

To all their gods they have assigned priests to offer up the sacrifices
of the people. If pestilence and famine threaten, a libation is made
to the image of Thor; if war is imminent, one is made to Othin; if a

marriage is to be performed, to Freyr. A general festival for all
the provinces of Sweden is customarily held at Upsala every nine
years. Participation in this festival is required of everyone. Kings
and their subjects, collectively and individually, send their gifts to
Upsala; and—a thing more cruel than any punishment—those who
have already adopted Christianity buy themselves off from these
ceremonies. The sacrifice is as follows : of every kind of male creature,
nine victims are offered. By the blood of these creatures it is the
custom to appease the gods. Their bodies, moreover, are hanged in a
grove which is adjacent to the temple. This grove is so sacred to the
people that the separate trees in it are believed to be holy because of
the death or putrefaction of the sacrificial victims. There even dogs
and horses hang beside human beings. A certain Christian told me that
he had seen seventy-two of their bodies hanging up together. The in-
cantations, however, which are usually sung in the performance of a
libation of this kind are numerous and disgraceful, and it is better
not to speak of them.

Scholia

Near that temple is a very large tree with widespread branches
which are always green both in winter and summer. What kind of
tree it is nobody knows. There is also a spring there where the pagans
are accustomed to perform sacrifices and to immerse a human being
alive. As long as his body is not found, the request of the people will
be fulfilled.

A golden chain encircles that temple and hangs over the gables
of the building. Those who approach see its gleam from afar off
because the shrine, which is itself located on a plain, is encircled by
mountains so situated as to give the effect of a theater.

For nine days feasts and sacrifices of this kind are celebrated.
Every day they sacrifice one human being in addition to other animals,
so that in nine days there are 72 victims which are sacrificed. This
sacrifice takes place about the time of the vernal equinox.

The Life of Saint Eric

King of Sweden, 1150-1160

Gudz martire Sancto Erico

From the Old Swedish

§WE shall here with the Grace of God record a few words concerning God's holy martyr, Saint Eric, who formerly was king of Sweden. By birth and extraction he certainly was not only of royal race but had descended from other chiefs of Sweden. Since the kingdom was without a ruler, and he was cherished by all the leaders of the land as well as the people, they chose him as their king, with the good will of the country folk, and he was worthily placed in the royal seat at Uppsala. After he came to power he honored God greatly; he altered his life in three [principal] ways, not so much because of the power which he had acquired, but for reason of deep reflection; and perfected his life nobly until he ended it in a glorious martyrdom. He followed the example of those good kings who were mentioned in the Old Law, first in the promotion of activities in the Holy Church and the increase of the worship of God; afterwards in the guidance and government of the common people, the support of wise men; and finally, in strongly combating the enemies of faith. Later, in Uppsala Church [Cathedral], which his royal ancestors had started and partially completed, he held dedication services. Afterwards he traveled about his whole kingdom, visited his people, and conducted himself in truly royal manner. He pronounced right judgments without [influence of personal] friendship or greed, and gave no unjust sentence because of fear or hatred. He followed the path which leads to heaven. He reconciled hostile men; he rescued poor men from [the power of] their overlords; and strengthened righteous men in the service of the Lord; but he would not endure unrighteous men in his kingdom, for he dealt justly with everyone. He was so loved by the people both for this and other good deeds, that all wanted to give him a third part of all departure tolls which according to the law of the land should go into the king's treasury. Then he is said to have answered them who made the offer: "I have enough of my own goods, and you keep what is yours, because those who come after you [your children] may have need of it." These were a wise man's words, and seldom do we now find anyone who, like him, is satisfied with his own possessions and does not covet his neighbors' goods.

For indeed it is just that he who would rule and judge others, should first judge himself and humble his spirit and direct his soul to God, as is written: "I mortify my body and dwell in the service of the Lord." For that reason the holy king was strong in vigil, ardent in prayer, patient in difficulties, generous in alms, and subdued his flesh with a prickly hairshirt; and he was dressed in this same hairshirt, as though in a byrnie of righteousness, at the time that he was slain, and it is to this very day preserved in Uppsala Church wet with his sacred blood. On a fast day or on any other sacred occasion he never entered the bed of his queen [Christina], but when natural desires threatened to master his flesh he extinguished the natural lusts by immersing himself in a tub of cold water, which he had ready for that purpose both in winter and summer.

After the church had been built, as we first indicated, and the kingdom well put in order, he gathered an army against unbelief and the enemies of his people, and took with him from Uppsala Church Saint Henry the Bishop and went to Finland and fought, and slew all those who would not accept righteousness and the true faith; for he had often offered them the faith and peace of God, but they were so hard of heart that they would in no wise be subdued except through a sharp hand. After he had won the victory, and was engaged in prayer, he implored the Lord, with flowing tears, for he had a soft heart. Then one of his attendants asked him why he wept, since he had won a victory over God's enemies, which might rather be a cause for rejoicing. He answered thus: "Truly I am happy and praise God for victory won, but I am full of sorrow [to think] that so many souls should have been lost this day who rather might have come into the heavenly kingdom." And then he called together the people who survived, made peace in the land, had the faith of God preached in the country, Christianized the people and built churches, and appointed as head [of religious affairs in Finland] Saint Henry, who later suffered martyrdom. Afterwards priests were assigned and other matters arranged that belonged to the worship of God. Thereupon he returned to Sweden with honorable victory.

In the tenth year of his reign as king, the ancient enemy [the devil] aroused against him a man by the name of Magnus, the son of the King of Denmark, who on his mother's side claimed the throne, which, however, was against the law, which forbids that foreigners should rule. He won over one of the nobles to his side, and together they planned his death, secretly collecting an army against the [Swedish] king at Östra Årus [now called Uppsala]. This happened on Maundy Thursday in the Church of the Holy Trinity, upon that hill which is named Mons Domini, and where the temple is built. While he was attending mass he was told that his enemies were near the town, and that it would be wise to meet them at once with his armed force. Then answered the king: "Leave me in peace and let me on such a holy festival hear the divine service to the end, for I hope that what remains of this service [on earth] will be heard elsewhere [in heaven]." After this had been said he committed himself into the hands and power of God, crossed himself, and passed out of the church, arming himself and his men first with the sign of the cross and then with weapons, though they were inferior in numbers, and met the inhuman foe in a manly way. When they clashed in arms, the majority took, with great ferocity, the side against the good friend of God. After he had been struck down and wound upon wound had been inflicted so that he was nearly dead, the grim foes became yet grimmer, scorned his glorious body, and cut off his head as [though he were one of a group] of foul prisoners. He committed his soul to God and left this earthly kingdom for that in heaven.

The first miracle to happen in the place where his blood was first shed was the bursting forth of a flowing spring, which can be seen to this day as a testimony of the event. After they [the enemies] were gone, and his holy body had been left in the place where he had fallen, some of his servants remaining behind took his body and carried it into the house of a poor widow. There was an old woman who had been blind for a long time, and after she had touched his body and her fingers had become wet with his blood, she touched her own eyes, and in that very moment recovered her sight and praised the Lord. Many other such miracles which God has worked through his sacred martyr, Saint Eric, are recorded elsewhere. He was killed, one thousand, one hundred and sixty years after the birth of Christ, on the fifteenth of June in the days of Pope Alexander III, regnante domino nostro Iesu Christo, cui est omnis honor ac gloria in secula seculorum. Amen.

The Law of the Westgoths

Thirteenth Century

Corpus juris Sueogotorum antiqui

From the Old Swedish

&§THE Svear [Swedes] have a right to accept and depose a king. He shall travel with safe-conduct from the upper country into Östergötland. Then he shall send messengers hither to the Thing of all Goths. Then the lawman [chief justice] shall appoint as hostages two men from the southern and two from the northern part of the land. Afterwards four other men of the land shall work with them. They shall meet at Junabäck [Juna Creek on the border between Västergötland and Småland]. The hostages from Östergötland shall follow thither and testify that he [the king] is a native, as their laws provide [and that he has been accepted by them as king].

Then the Thing of all the Goths shall provide a welcome for him. When he arrives at the Thing he shall swear loyalty to all Goths [and affirm] that he will not break any right laws of our land. Then shall the lawmen first proclaim him king, and then others whomsoever he may ask to do so. The king shall then restore liberty to three men, who have not committed a felony.

If a bishop is to be appointed, the king shall ask all the inhabitants of the land whom they wish to have. He must be the son of a freeholder. Then the king shall put a staff in his hand and give him a golden ring. Thereupon he shall be conducted into the church and placed in the bishop's chair. He shall then have full power without his consecration having yet taken place.

A lawman shall be the son of a freeholder. For this reason all freeholders shall have authority by the Grace of God. 1. The king "has the power vested in him to hold a court of justice at the Assembly, and so has the lawman." 2. It is always called the Thing of all Goths if a lawman is present. There people may establish [adopt] legal family lineage and proclaim reconciliations.

These are the rights of a minstrel.

If a traveling minstrel is beaten, it shall always be unpunished. If a player is wounded, [that is] he who wanders about with a rebeck or carries a fiddle and drum, then shall a wild heifer be taken and brought to the top of a hill. Her tail shall be shaved smooth and greased, and he shall be given newly greased shoes. Then the minstrel shall grasp the heifer by the tail, and someone shall strike [the heifer] hard with a sharp lash. If he is able to hold on, he shall have the good beast and enjoy it as dogs do grass. If he is not able to hold fast, he shall have and endure what he received, shame and injury. He may not expect more rights than a flogged bondwoman.

The defendant always has the right of witness [to free himself by oath], and the nearest of kin has the right of inheritance.

Deed for a Copper Mine

June 16, 1288

Stora Kopparberget

From the Latin

WE, Peter, by the grace of God Bishop of Västerås, send to all those who shall read this letter, our greeting in the name of the Saviour of the world. Owing to the uncertainty of our earthly life, even those proceedings which are carried out in a lawful manner are at times apt to be obscured by the darkness of oblivion. Therefore that which shall endure is confirmed for posterity by means of letters and testimonies. Led by these wise considerations, and with the counsel of those present, we wish openly to make known to all that to our nephew Nils Kristinesson we have assigned an eighth part of the copper mine named Tiskasjöberg in the parish of Torsång, which eighth part, as is known, was acquired by our care; and this in return for a loan which, conscious of our near relationship, we accepted from the same our nephew during our first year of office in our then many and various straits. Thereafter on the petition, on the counsel, and with the support of our chapter, we have made an assignment with the afore-mentioned Nils, by which the occupation or the right of possession of the above-mentioned eighth part shall revert to us and our church, and in its place he shall have, firstly, Fröslunda estate in the parish of Haraker with the mills situated thereon, and secondly, the land which our church possesses in Hasselbäck in the same parish with what lawfully appertains thereto, freely to occupy in perpetuity. All the rights, possessions and properties which lawfully belong to us, our church, and our chapter, on the above-mentioned Fröslunda estate, mills, arable land, meadows, pasture-land, fishing-waters, woods or paddocks, and other goods of any kind whatsoever appurtenant to the same estate, and in the same manner our right to the above-mentioned land at Hasselbäck, with all the particular possessions of the same, we transfer without reservation to the previously-mentioned Nils, our nephew, and his heirs, in our name and in that of the whole of our chapter. And so that in this matter no false statements can be made in the future, we have had this letter written, and seal it with the seal of our High and Exalted Lord, Magnus, King of the Swedes, and also no less with the seal of the Reverend Father, Lord Magnus, the appointed Archbishop of Uppsala church, and with the seals of our Reverend Brothers as follows, Bengt, Bishop of Linköping, Anund, Bishop of Strängnäs, and Johan, Bishop of Åbo. Hereto we also append our seal and that of our chapter, so that it may hereby be the more manifest, that both the above-mentioned assignment and the arrangement were made with the consent of our whole chapter. Given at Färingö on the sixteenth of June in the year of our Lord one thousand two hundred and eighty-eight.

The Legendary History of Gotland

Written c. 1350

Guta saga

From the Old Swedish

GOTLAND was first discovered by a man named Tjelvar. At that time Gotland was so enchanted that it sank by day and was above water by night. But that man was the first to bring fire to the land, and after that it never sank.

This Tjelvar had a son named Havdi, and Havdi's wife was called Vitastjärna [White Star]. Those two lived first on Gotland.

The first night that they slept together, she had a dream: that three serpents were intertwined in her bosom, and that these were crawling out of her breast. She told her dream to her husband Havdi. He interpreted it in the following manner:

"All is bound together with rings;
This land shall become inhabited,
And we shall have three sons."

He gave names to all of them before they were born:

"Gute shall have Gotland;
Grajper shall be the name of the second,
And Gunfjaun the third."

These afterwards divided Gotland into three parts, so that Grajper, the oldest, received the northern third; and Gute, the middle one; while Gunfjaun, the youngest, got the southernmost. From these three the number of inhabitants increased so rapidly for a long time that the country was not able to feed them all. Then it was decided by lot that every third person should leave the land, but that those exiled should be allowed to keep and carry away all that they owned above ground. Later they were unwilling to leave, and went to Torsborg and dwelt there. Afterwards their fellow-countrymen would not tolerate them there and drove them away.

The Gotlanders at the Court of the Greek Emperor

After a time they moved to Fårön [Sheep Island, in the Baltic] and settled there. But they were unable to support themselves in that place and so moved, again, to an island near Estland [Estonia] which is called Dagö, and stayed there and built a stronghold which may still be seen. But they were not able to support themselves there either, and so they proceeded to a river called Dyna and up through Russia. They traveled [later] so far [South] that they came to Greece. There they asked permission of the Greek king to stay during the waxing and waning of the moon. The King promised this, believing that it was not more than a month. When the month was up, he intended to send them away; but they answered that the waxing and waning of the moon was eternal, and that they had interpreted his promise in that sense.

At last their quarrel came to the attention of the Queen. She said: "My lord and king, you promised that they might live here during the waxing and the waning of the moon, and that is forever. You may not withdraw that promise." And so they continued to live there, and still do. Also, they still have something left of our language.

About Human Sacrifices

Before that time and for a long period thereafter, people believed in sacrificial groves and grave-mounds, in temples and sacred enclosures, and in heathen gods. They sacrificed their sons and daughters, and their cattle along with meat and drink [i.e., with feasting and drinking]. They did this because of their unbelief. At the greatest sacrificial feast, which embraced the whole land, there were human victims. Otherwise each third part of the island had its own sacrifices; but smaller assemblies had smaller offerings, with cattle, meat and drink. Some of these [taking part] were called "boiling companions" [*suþnautar*], since they did their boiling together.

Gotland Becomes a Part of the Swedish Domain

Many kings fought against Gotland while it was heathen, but the Gotlanders were always victorious and preserved their rights. Afterwards the Gotlanders sent many messengers to Sweden; but none of them was able to make peace until Ivar Stråben [Strawleg] from Alva Parish appeared. He was the first to make peace with the King of the Svear.

When the Gotlanders asked him to go as their messenger, he answered: "You know that I am now near doom and death. Therefore, if you want me to risk such danger, give me wergild to the value of three men—one for myself, the second for my born son, and the third for my wife." For he was a wise and learned man, as sagas about him testify. He made a lasting treaty with the King of the Svear. The tax of the Gotlanders was to be sixty marks of silver a year, of which the Swedish king would receive forty marks, and the Earl twenty marks. This law was made with the Council of the land before he left home.

And so the Gotlanders of their own free will accepted the King of the Svear, so that they might freely visit Sweden anywhere without paying toll or other charges. In the same way the Svear might visit Gotland without any grain-trade restrictions or other prohibitions. The King should give aid and protection to the Gotlanders, if they needed and asked for it. Both the King and the Earl shall send representatives to the Landsthing of the Gotlanders and there have their tribute collected. The messengers shall have the duty to proclaim peace to the Gotlanders, that they may visit all places across the sea that belong to the King at Uppsala; and similarly with those Svear who have the right to visit here with us.

X. OTHER POETRY

The Death Song of Egil the Son of Grim

948

Höfuðlausn

SHIPWRECKED on the English coast, Egil Skallagrimsson was captured
by Eirik Blood-Axe and his cruel Queen Gunnhild in Northumbria. He
saved his life by composing during the night a poem which he recited as
his ransom. This English version is an original poem by Henry Adams
Bellows inspired by Egil's ode. Literal translations of this ode as well
as Egil's other two great odes may be found in *The Skalds* by Lee M.
Hollander (The American-Scandinavian Foundation, 1945).

"THEN came Arinbjorn by night from Erik the Bloody Axe,
King of Northumberland, to the room where Egill lay, and said to
him that the King and Queen Gunnhild had willed that Egill should
be slain when morning came; and he counseled him, if yet he would
save his head, that he should wake through the night and make a
poem in praise of Erik, that perchance the King might still grant him
his life."

Egils Saga Skallagrimssonar.

* * *

I, Egill, rover of the North, am cast
Into your hands, and Erik's day at last
Has come. I know the waves I yet shall see
Tomorrow, ere I die, will beckon me
Homeward in vain. The storm that stripped my deck
Of men, and flung my ship, a broken wreck,
Upon your barren shore, has brought me here
To look upon this king the Southrons fear.
Go, tell your lord, Erik the Bloody Axe,
That Egill fain would sleep; the writhing backs
Of waves have borne me over long, and death,
That follows with the sun, yet grants this breath
Of quiet in the darkness. Say I rest
Contented, nought of tumult in my breast.
The sea I fought, and men, but will not fight
Against the gods, that wait for me tonight.

The day is his; darkness belongs to me.
Tell him that, dead or living, I am free;
His prison is my chosen resting-place.
Go, tell him that, and tell him that the face
Of Egill, doomed to die, has shown no fear.—
It was to see me weep he sent you here.
What should I know of sorrow? Deeds like these
Of mine shall ring across the northern seas
When Erik and his axe have been forgot
In the grey mists of Niflheim. Each man's lot
Is written, and the Norns will never heed
Weeping or threats. In death there is no need
For prayer, or hope, or fear. Say to your king
That, ere I sleep, I once again shall sing,
And fashion the last song that I shall make.
Tell him, when in a nightmare he shall wake,
Let him give ear, and there will come to him
The battle-song of Egill son of Grim.

Alone.—They say that round the dying stand
All who were known in life, by sea or land;
So did the sorrowing gods in pity throng
About Bald's bale-fire. Aye, there Bard the Strong
Watches me from the doorway,—him I slew
At that brave feast in Norway, when I knew
The mead-cup reeked with death. The chattering thralls
Bid to that mockery in Atley's halls
Fled shrieking when I clove their master's head
Down to the leering lips. And you, long dead,
Come once again to look upon me! Now
The fates have scored their rune upon my brow,
But you, who sought to slay me long ago,
Died by my hand, and I am glad.—

                                     I know
Yon face beside you.—Thorolf, brother mine,
Borne down by spears when, in the Saxon line,
We two made firm his crown for Athelstan
That mighty day at Vinheath. Never man
Had truer friend than you. I come at last

To feast with you in Valhall, but the past
Has cleared the debt I owed you. I have slain
The men who slew you, brother; none remain
On Middle-Earth to boast your death unpaid
By death. We two, together, unafraid,
Shall seek tomorrow Odin's golden door,
And speak as comrades with the mighty Thor.
More faces in the shadows,—men who sailed
With me from Kurland, when the darkness paled
To morning, and the flame glowed far astern,
The flame we kindled for a torch to burn
The hearts of them we hated.—Other men,
Comrades and foes in Iceland, from the glen,
The mountain and the plain they come, for I
Can never come to them. 'Tis good to die
Since death brings me so close to all mankind,
The living and the dead. I leave behind
No grief that vengeance will not burn away.
For, through the darkness, I can see a day
Not long to wait, that threatens with the gleam
Of ruddy sails; the flash of oars shall seem
The lightning of Thor's anger. In the shout
Of battle, and the tumult, and the rout,
Shall Erik once more hark to Egill's voice.
Few then shall be the Southrons who rejoice
That I am dead.
            At morn the gulls will fly
Northward to Iceland, and their shrilling cry
Shall wake the distant sleepers with the word
"Egill is slain!" even as the gods once heard
The Gjallarhorn. Oh birds, that were my friends,
Take up the song that forth your comrade sends;
It is the heart of Egill ye shall bear
Back to his home. This is the only prayer
I make to Odin, that in Iceland long
The cliffs shall echo Egill's dying song.

    Men of Iceland, mates of mine
    On field and furrowed sea,

Bold in battle, seamen brave,
Hewers of helms with me,
Mindful of mighty blows full many
We dealt in days gone by,
Grind and gird ye the swords again;
Doomed is Egill to die.
Fearless forth to his fate he goes,
Fearless he lived and free;
Need of a master never he knew,
At the call of a king to be.
Ever the song of the sea he sang,
Ever the song of the sword;
Hollow the hearts that heard his voice
In the land of the southern lord.

Hearken, Erik, give heed and hear,
For a dead man's words are wise;
Across the seas my song I send,
Forth on the wind it flies;
Egill's body you bear to the bale,
But him you cannot kill;
In a thousand hearts his home shall he have
And his sword shall stay not still.

Glad the greeting I gave the sea,
Glad did I greet the sun;
Wind and wave knew well my voice,
And the beaches where breakers run;
The biting blast was brother of mine,
My kin were the clouds on high;—
Are you fain to fight such mighty folk
That you dare to let me die?

Long have I lived, and light of heart,
Wealth have I won and fame;
High on my hearth burned the fire of home
When back from the battle I came.
Gladly I go to the land of the gods
Beyond the rainbow's rim,
For the rocks and ridges of Iceland ring
With the song of the son of Grim.

Now let the sun climb up the sky; I wait
The day that bears the shadow of my fate
Untroubled. I have fought, and bled, and won,
And seen the happy end of work begun
In doubt and danger;—aye, and I have made
A song that shall bear children. Unafraid
I listen for the summons of the horn
Of Heimdall.—Yonder, cloudless, breaks the morn.

The Eiríksmál

954

In 930, Harald Fairhaired, at the age of eighty, resigned as king of Norway in favor of his son Eirik Blood-Axe. Three years later, Harald died, and Eirik found himself unpopular. In 934 he left Norway to his youngest brother, Hakon the Good, and went to England where he became king of Northumbria. Olaf Cuaran, Norse king of Dublin, also claimed Northumbria, and in conflict with him Eirik was slain. Eirik's widow, Queen Gunnhild, retired to the Orkneys and had a poem composed in memory of her husband. The name of the skald is unknown.

"What dream is this?" said Othin, "a little before daylight I thought I was preparing Valhöll for a slain host. I was awakening the einherjar, and bidding them rise up and cover the benches and cleanse the beakers—I was bidding the Valkyries bring wine as if a prince was coming. I have hope of some noble heroes from the world; so my heart is glad.

"What uproar is that, Bragi, as if thousands were in motion—an exceeding great host approaching?" "All the timbers of the benches are creaking as if Balder were coming back to Othin's abode."

"Surely thou art talking folly, thou wise Bragi," replied Othin, "although thou knowest everything well. The noise betokens the approach of the hero Eric, who must be coming here into Othin's abode.

"Sigmundr and Sinfjötli! Arise quickly and go to meet the prince. If it be Eric, invite him in! I have now confident hope that it is he."

"Why dost thou hope for Eric rather than for other kings?" asked Sigmundr. "Because he has reddened his sword in many a land," replied Othin, "and carried a bloodstained blade."

"Why hast thou robbed him of victory when thou knewest him to

be valiant?" "Because it cannot be clearly known," replied Othin:—
"The grey wolf is gazing upon the abodes of the gods."

"Hail now to thee, Eric!" cried Sigmundr, "Welcome shalt thou
be here! Enter our hall, wise [prince]! One thing I would ask thee:
What heroes attend thee from the roar of battle?"

"There are five kings [here]," said Eric, "I will make known to
thee the names of all. I am the sixth myself."

The Loss of My Sons

961

Egill Skallagrímsson

Sonatorrek

AFTER the death of a second son, Bothvar, who was drowned, Egil
despaired of life and took to his bed, refusing food. He was persuaded by
his daughter, instead of dying, to celebrate his sons by composing a poem.
The circumstances are recorded in the selection "Father and Son."

Much doth it task me
My tongue to move,
Through my throat to utter
The breath of song.
Poesy, prize of Odin,
Promise now I may not,
A draught drawn not lightly
From deep thought's dwelling.

Forth it flows but hardly;
For within my breast
Heavy sobbing stifles
Hindered stream of song—
Blessèd boon to mortals
Brought from Odin's kin,
Goodly treasure, stolen
From Giant-land of yore.

He, who so blameless
Bore him in life,
O'erborne by billows
With boat was whelmed.

Sea-waves—flood that whilom
Welled from giant's wound—
Smite upon the grave-gate
Of my sire and son.

Dwindling now my kindred
Draw near to their end,
Ev'n as forest-saplings
Felled or tempest-strown.
Not gay or gladsome
Goes he who beareth
Body of kinsman
On funeral bier.

Of a father fallen
First I may tell;
Of a much-loved mother
Must mourn the loss.
Sad store hath memory
For minstrel skill,
A wood to bloom leafy
With words of song.

Most woful the breach,
Where the wave in-brake
On the fencèd hold
Of my father's kin.
Unfilled, as I wot,
And open doth stand
The gap of son rent
By the greedy surge.

Me Ran, the sea-queen,
Roughly hath shaken:
I stand of beloved ones
Stript and all bare.
Cut hath the billow
The cord of my kin,
Strand of mine own twisting
So stout and strong.

Sure, if sword could venge
Such cruel wrong,
Evil times would wait
Ægir, ocean-god.
That wind-giant's brother
Were I strong to slay,
'Gainst him and his sea-brood
Battling would I go.

But I in no wise
Boast, as I ween,
Strength that may strive
With the stout ships' bane.
For to eyes of all
Easy now 'tis seen
How the old man's lot
Helpless is and lone.

Me hath the main
Of much bereaved;
Dire is the tale,
The deaths of kin:

Since he, the shelter
And shield of my house,
Hied him from life
To heaven's glad realm.

Full surely I know,
In my son was waxing
The stuff and the strength
Of a stout-limbed wight:
Had he reached but ripeness
To raise his shield,
And Odin laid hand
On his liegeman true.

Willing he followed
His father's word,
Though all opposing
Should thwart my rede:
He in mine household
Mine honour upheld,
Of my power and rule
The prop and the stay.

Oft to my mind
My loss doth come,
How I brotherless bide
Bereaved and lone.
Thereon I bethink me,
When thickens the fight!
Thereon with much searching
My soul doth muse:

Who staunch stands by me
In stress of fight,
Shoulder to shoulder,
Side by side?
Such want doth weaken
In war's dread hour;
Weak-winged I fly,
Whom friends all fail.

"Son's place to his sire
(Saith a proverb true)
Another son born
Alone can fill."
Of kinsmen none
(Though ne'er so kind)
To brother can stand
In brother's stead.

O'er all our ice-fields,
Our northern snows,
Few now I find
Faithful and true.
Dark deeds men love,
Doom death to their kin,
A brother's body
Barter for gold.

Unpleasing to me
Our people's mood,
Each seeking his own
In selfish peace.
To the happier bees' home
Hath passed my son,
My good wife's child
To his glorious kin.

Odin, mighty monarch,
Of minstrel mead the lord,
On me a heavy hand
Harmful doth lay.
Gloomy in unrest
Ever I grieve,
Sinks my drooping brow,
Seat of sight and thought.

Fierce fire of sickness
First from my home
Swept off a son
With savage blow:

One who was heedful,
Harmless, I wot,
In deeds unblemished,
In words unblamed.

Still do I mind me,
When the Friend of men
High uplifted
To the home of gods
That sapling stout
Of his father's stem,
Of my true wife born
A branch so fair.

Once bare I goodwill
To the great spear-lord,
Him trusty and true
I trowed for friend:
Till the giver of conquest,
The car-borne god,
Broke faith and friendship,
False in my need.

Now victim and worship
To Vilir's brother,
The god once honoured,
I give no more.
Yet the friend of Mimir
On me hath bestowed
Some boot for bale,
If all boons I tell.

Yea he, the wolf-tamer,
The war-god skilful,
Gave poesy faultless
To fill my soul:
Gave wit to know well
Each wily trickster,
And force him to face me
As foeman in fight.

Hard am I beset;
Whom Hel, the sister
Of Odin's fell captive,
On Digra-ness waits.

Yet shall I gladly
With right good welcome
Dauntless in bearing
Her death-blow hide.

The Lay of Hakon

961

Eyvind Finnsson Skáldaspillir

Hákonarmál

EIRIK'S widow Gunnhild and her sons made war on King Hakon the Good, who finally fell in battle. He was celebrated by his skald and comrade-in-arms, the poet Eyvind "the Plagiarist."

Gautatýr sent forth   Gondul and Skogul
      to choose among kings' kinsmen:
who of Yngvi's offspring   should with Óthin dwell,
      and wend with him to Valholl.

They found Biorn's brother   his byrnie donning,
under standard standing   the stalwart leader—
were darts uplifted   and spearshafts lowered;
      up the strife then started.

Called on Hálogaland's heroes   and Horthaland's swordsmen
the Northmen's folkwarder,   ere he fared to battle:
a good host had he   of henchmen from Norway—
the Danes'-terror   donned his bronze-helm.

Threw down his war-weeds,   thrust off his byrnie
the great-hearted lord,   ere began the battle—
laughed with his liege-men;   his land would he shield now,
the gladsome hero   'neath gold-helm standing.

Cut then keenly   the king's broadsword
through foemen's war-weeds,   as though water it sundered.
Clashed then spear-blades,   cleft were war-shields;
did ring-decked war-swords   rattle on helmets.

Were targes trodden   by the Týr-of-shields,
by the hard-footed hilt-blade,   and heads eke of Northmen;

battle raged on the island,   athelings reddened
the shining shield-castles   with shedded life-blood.

Burned the wound-fires   in bloody gashes,
were the long-beards lifted   against the life of warriors—
the sea-of-wounds surged high   around the swords' edges,
ran the stream-of-arrows   on the strand of Storth-isle.

Reddened war-shields   rang 'gainst each other,
did Skogul's-stormblasts   scar red targes;
billowed blood-waves   in the blast-of-Óthin—
was many a man's son   mowed down in battle.

Sate then the liege-lords   with swords brandished,
with shields shattered   and shredded byrnies:
not happy in their hearts   was that host of men,
and to Valholl wended their way.

Spoke then Gondul,   on spearshaft leaning:
"groweth now the gods' following,
since Hákon hath been   with host so goodly
bidden home by holy gods."

Heard the war-lord   what the valkyries spoke of,
high-hearted, on horseback—
wisely they bore them,   sitting war-helmeted,
and with shields them sheltering.

Hákon said:

"Why didst' Geirskogul,   grudge us victory?
Yet worthy were we   that the gods granted it."

Skogul said:

" 'Tis owing to us   that the issue was won
and your foemen did flee.

Ride forth now shall we,"   said fierce Skogul,
"to the green homes of the godheads,—
there to tell Óthin   that the atheling will now
come to see him himself."

"Hermóth and Bragi!"   called out Hróptatýr:
"Go ye to greet the hero;

for a king cometh   who hath keenly foughten,
     to our halls hither."

Said the war-worker,   wending from battle—
     was his byrnie all bloody:
"Angry-minded   Óthin meseemeth.
     Be we heedful of his hate!"

"All einheriar   shall swear oaths to thee:
     share thou the æsir's ale,
thou enemy-of-earls!   Here within hast thou
     brethren eight," said Bragi.

"Our gear of war,"   said the goodly king,
     "we mean to keep in our might.
Helmet and hauberk   one should heed right well:
     'tis good to guard one's spear."

Then was it seen   how that sea-king had
     upheld the holy altars,
since Hákon all   did hail with welcome,
     both gods and heavenly hosts.

On a good day is born   that great-souled lord
     who hath a heart like his;
aye will his times   be told of on earth,
     and men will speak of his might.

Unfettered will fare   the Fenriswolf,
     and fall on the fields of men,
ere that there cometh   a kingly lord
     as good, to stand in his stead.

Cattle die   and kinsmen die,
     land and lieges are whelmed;
since Hákon   to the heathen gods fared
     many a host is harried.

The Song of the Norns

1014

Darraðarlióð

THE Valkyries here usurp the function of the Norns, weaving destiny. The origin of this poem is unknown, but it turns up in *Njáls saga* following the description of the Battle of Clontarf, near Dublin.

◆§ON Good Friday it happened in Caithness that a man called Dorroth went out of doors. He saw twelve persons ride toward a [stone] hut. There they were lost to his sight. When he came up to the hut and looked through a chink in the wall he saw that some women were inside and had set up a web. Heads of men served as weights, men's entrails formed the woof and weft, a sword did as a weaver's reed, and arrows as the rods. They sang this song: [follows the *Song of the Valkyries*]. Then they tore the web down and into pieces, and each one held on to what she had in her hands. Dorroth left the opening and went home; but the women mounted their horses and rode away—six to the south and six to the north.

Widely is flung, warning of slaughter,
the weaver's-beam's-web: 't is wet with blood;
is spread now, grey, the spear-thing before,
the woof-of-the-warriors which valkyries fill
with the red-warp-of- Randvér's-banesman.

Is this web woven and wound of entrails,
and heavy weighted with heads of slain;
are blood-bespattered spears the treadles,
iron-bound the beams, the battens, arrows:
let us weave with our swords this web of victory!

Goes Hild to weave, and Hiorthrimul,
Sangrith and Svipul, with swords brandished:
shields will be shattered, shafts will be splintered,
will the hound-of-helmets the hauberks bite.

Wind we, wind we the web-of-darts,
and follow the atheling after to war!
Will men behold shields hewn and bloody
where Gunn and Gondul have guarded the thane.

Wind we, wind we   such web-of-darts
as the young war-worker   waged afore-time!
Forth shall we fare   where the fray is thickest,
where friends and fellows   'gainst foemen battle!

Wind we, wind we   the web-of-darts
where float the flags   of unflinching men!
Let not the liege's   life be taken:
valkyries award   the weird of battle.

Will seafaring men   hold sway over lands,
who erstwhile dwelled   on outer nesses;
is doomed to die   a doughty king,
lies slain an earl   by swords e'en now.

Will Irish men eke   much ill abide:
't will not ever after   be out of men's minds.
Now the web is woven,   and weapons reddened—
in all lands will be heard   the heroes' fall.

Now awful is it   to be without,
as blood-red rack   races overhead;
is the welkin gory   with warriors' blood
as we valkyries   war-songs chanted.

Well have we chanted   charms full many
about the king's son: may it bode him well!
Let him learn them   who listens to us,
and speak these spells   to spearmen after.

Start we swiftly   with steeds unsaddled—
hence to battle   with brandished swords!

XI. ROMANCE

IN the fourteenth century European medieval romance superseded native themes in popularity in the North. King Hakon Hakonarson of Norway (1217-1263) had set a new standard of taste by sponsoring several romances of chivalry and Breton lays translated from Anglo-Norman into Norwegian. The Matter of Britain, The Matter of France, The Matter of the Orient are copiously represented in Icelandic versions. These were known as "Knights' Sagas," *riddarasögur,* whereas romances dealing with foreign lore the sources of which were not identified were called "Lying Sagas," *lygisögur.* But few of the latter have ever been printed. Scores of them are available in manuscript in the various Scandinavian libraries.

The Ballad of Tristram

Translated 1226

Tristrams kvæði

Tristan, the Anglo-Norman romance by Thomas, was translated into Norwegian in 1226 by order of King Hakon Hakonarson. Centuries earlier, the name of Tristan was preserved in Iceland, in nearly its original Pictish form, in Trostansfjord. Iceland also produced a rustic version of the Norwegian translation, as well as another romance containing the love theme of *Tristan*: The Saga of Harald Hringsbane. The most sympathetic interpretation in Iceland of this Pictish tragedy, however, is the ballad about Tristan's death, when Isolt the Fair, summoned from Cornwall to his bedside in Brittany, crossed the Channel but arrived too late.

> Tristram against the heathen hound
> > The battle set;
> Many a man got bloody wounds
> > When there they met.—
> *To the lovers it was shapen but to sunder.*
>
> Back was he borne upon a shield,
> > That brave young knight;
> Many a leech sought leave to heal
> > His body's blight.
>
> But all their leechcraft he refused
> > And swore a vow:

"Only Iseult, that lady fair,
    May heal me now!"

Tristram sends his messengers
    And three men leap:
"O go and tell Iseult the Fair
    My wounds are deep."

Tristram sends his messengers;
    Five take his plea:
"O go and tell Iseult the Fair
    To come to me."

"And bid her as I shall command
    Prepare her trip:
Let all the sails be dyed with blue
    Upon her ship."

His messengers to Cornwall came
    O'er waters dim:
"Young Tristram, lady, bids you come
    To visit him."

Then went Iseult into the hall
    And sought the king:
"O may I not to this knight, thy friend,
    Some healing bring?"

The king made answer in angry wise
    And stern did say:
"He spurns the healing of all the rest;
    He must be fey."

Iseult the Fair with softest speech
    Pled piteously;
Her arms about the monarch's neck
    Made earnest plea.

"I'd gladly let thee heal this knight
    Of his sore wound,
Could I but know thou wouldst return
    Both safe and sound."

"With God must rest my safe return,"
    The lady quoth.
"I may not in this journey now
    Forget my troth."

She cast on her a sable fur
    With sigh and tear;
Then went the jewelled lady out
    Upon the pier.

"I must as Tristram did command
    Prepare my trip,
And let the sails be all of blue
    Upon my ship."

They wound the sails as the lady bade
    To the masthead high;
To Tristram she will not fail to come,
    So like to die.

Iseult the Dark went from the hall,
    And said not true:
"Black are the sails upon the ship
    Instead of blue."

Into the hall Iseult the Dark
    Returned once more:
"Black are the sails upon the ship
    That nears the shore."

Tristram turned his face to the wall,
    And naught he spake.
Three miles away a man might hear
    That great heart break.

They brought the blue-sailed ship to shore
    On the cold black sand;
Retainers bore Iseult the Fair
    The first to land.

Long was the way they had to walk;
    The road was wide;

But ever she heard the sound of bells
  That clanged and cried.

Long was the way they had to walk;
  It marred the feet;
And ever she heard the sound of bells
  And chanting sweet.

Then said Iseult, the lady fair
  From o'er the foam:
"Tristram, alas, should not be dead
  When I come home."

Iseult came into the solemn church
  With a hundred men;
The priests were chanting their last farewell
  O'er his body then.

Iseult o'er his coffined body bent,
  Like a rose-bud bright;
The silent priests in the chancel stood
  By candle-light.

Iseult o'er his coffined body bent;
  Scarce seemed alive;
The silent priests in the chancel stood
  With candles five.

Many a heart in this weary world
  With woe is fed.
Iseult o'er his coffined body bent,
  And lay there dead.

The bitter soul of Iseult the Dark
  With grief was torn.
Two bodies then from the ivied church
  Were straightway borne.

Iseult the Dark in anger spoke,
  And took her troth:
"If I can help it, death shall fail
  To join them both!"

Hastily, quickly they were laid
     Beneath the mould;
To north and south of the church they lie
     Alone and cold.

And from their graves two birches grow
     That mutely strain
Across the roof of that dark church
     To meet, in vain.—
To them it was not shapen but to sunder.

A Lost Carolingian Romance

Translated in 1287

Karlamagnús saga ok kappa hans

THE epics about Charlemagne and his peers became even more popular
in Scandinavia than in England. Seven kings of Norway were christened
"Magnus." To this day Faeroe islanders dance a ballad about Roland
and Ronceval. Some of the tales of Carolingian epic of which the
French originals are now lost are preserved only in Icelandic translations.
The following selection consists of an introduction and two chapters from
a Norse translation of a lost English version.

⊷§ THE story that begins here is not such idle chatter as men make
for their amusement; rather, it is told truthfully, as will appear later.
Lord Bjarni Erlingsson of Bjarkö found this saga written down and
told in the English language in Scotland, when he was there in the
winter after the death of King Alexander. And after him Margaret,
daughter of the gracious Lord Erik, king of Norway, son of King
Magnus, got the kingdom, and the said Margaret was Alexander's
daughter's daughter. For this reason Lord Bjarni was sent west: to
steady and make firm the rule of the maid (Margaret). But that it
be the clearer to men and that they may have from it the more profit
and amusement, Lord Bjarni had it translated from the English
language into Norwegian. Men can find in it, too, how much it is
best to be faithful and steadfast to God, and what reward he gets
who is put to the proof through and through in the midst of frauds,
and how he ends up, though for a time he endures the Devil's temptations.

This story deals especially with this most courtly lady, who was the most steadfast at that time, and with the worst villain who has (ever) lived and who tempted her greatly, though there are many events after (the temptation).

CAP. I

This story begins about an excellent and powerful king who is named Hugon and also by another name called Duke of the valley which was called Munon. Many powerful men served this king— counts, barons, and knights, and other men of great importance. This King Hugon and most of his men were good Christians. There was a knight with the king who is named Milon, and the book says that he has received God's curse from priests and parsons and from all who wear the tonsure. This king was completely happy but for the fact that he was not married and had begotten no heir. At that time the gracious king, Lord Pippin, ruled over France; he had a daughter who was named Olive: she was favored and endowed with many good qualities, especially faithfulness and patience in the trials which her body endured, as will appear later in the story. Olive was reared as was fitting, in great state. This mighty King Hugon, with whom we began the story, heard of this lady, the excellent Olive; therefore, he dispatches messengers to King Pippin with the message asking for the hand of Lady Olive. And when they come before King Pippin, they declare to him their message, which he receives courteously and declares to the messengers that he wants King Hugon himself to come. The messengers return and tell the king this. And he straightway makes ready for his journey with a fitting retinue and rides in pomp to King Pippin, and he is welcomed there with all honor and esteem. King Hugon does not leave before he has become betrothed to Lady Olive, daughter of King Pippin. Then the duke rides and makes ready for his wedding-feast, and he is sparing in nothing, since his distinction was now greater than before. From his whole kingdom, wide as it was, he now invites a crowd and a multitude to this feast, and all men who were invited come at the time named.

CAP. II

Pippin, king of France, and his nobility come at the appointed time to the duke's castle; with them is Lady Olive. The duke rides now out to meet them with his distinguished lords; he greets King

Pippin very honorably and this excellent Lady Olive, who had come there then. All good men rejoiced who saw her countenance with (its) happy look; she greeted all fairly and blithely with courtly words, and therefore all men laid God's blessing on her. In King Pippin's retinue were also many other good men—many archbishops and suffragan bishops, counts and barons. This whole group of courtiers was treated honorably and provided for worthily, and now there was the best wedding feast in all respects. No man was humiliated or shamed, but all there were honored by great gifts. Many a gleeman had come there, and there one could see many clothes given and many a costly dish brought in: cranes and swans and peacocks, and many other kinds of delicious game; with it suitable drink was served in great golden beakers by courteous cupbearers; many tortes and other candles were to be seen there. And when men were most merry and evening was drawing on, Lady Olive was led to bed. Then young men struck up fair dance-tunes both in the hall and sleeping-room. Every one else went also to his chamber with great joy. That feast ended with great splendor; each man went home then to his dwelling, departing with great friendship. The king and queen dwelt but a little while together before they begot a son, and in due time she gave birth to a great and fine boy. All men, (both) within the king's bodyguard and without, were joyous of this begetting, and immediately the boy was carried to the church and baptized and called Landres by name. And when he came home to his mother, she was exceedingly glad and said: "Landres my son," says she, "now art thou come from baptism and signed to God; now do I give thee all my blessing." In that time people thought it good to bless their children for good luck. Thus several years now pass. . . .

Dinus the Proud and Philotemia the Fair

Imported c. 1300

Dínus saga drambláta

THE Icelandic "Lying Sagas" are packed with native folklore and picturesque episodes of Russian, Greek, and Oriental origin. Some of these sagas were doubtless translated directly out of Byzantine Greek either by Scandinavians in Byzantium or Greeks visiting the North. The Saga of Victor and Blaus relates that King Hakon Magnusson of Norway

(1270-1319) "took pleasure in good old sagas and had many turned into Norse from Greek."

The Saga of Dinus the Proud may be one of these. The scene is Africa, where Prince Dinus, after three years of study in Memphis, "the city in all the world most famous for its clerkdom," returned to Alexandria resolved "never to love a woman himself, until he found one his equal in cunning and wisdom." He met his match in Princess Philotemia of Ethiopia. The episode selected is the first of several contests of wits.

⋖§ ALTHOUGH the distance was great between Egypt and Blaland [Ethiopia], Dinus the proud and Philotemia the fair had heard of each other. One day Philotemia told her father that she wished to test Dinus. She sent as her messengers to Egypt two brothers, skilled in stratagems, named Patrix and Patrocianus, who had the trick of appearing old or middle-aged as they pleased. They were mounted on dromedaries with wings under their shoulders, the swiftest of beasts. The brothers reached Alexandria, stalled their steeds in hiding outside the city, and went to king Tolomeus, saying they were friars from India. They were well received, but stayed some time without seeing the prince. One day, they left the castle and stood below the balcony of the prince's hall. Two retainers of the prince, Ninus and Moranus, came out on the balcony. "What are you doing here?" asked Ninus. "The prince does not wish to see such men."

"We will do the prince no harm," Patrix replied: "we wish to sell this precious apple." They bribed their way into the hall, and the prince ate the apple. Then they hurried back to Blaspuaborg [Axum].

Dinus awoke in the night, after a little sleep, and called his counselor Grammaton, and told him he had fallen in love with Philotemia of Blaland. Accordingly Dinus and his knights saddled their horses and rode swiftly away in the dead of night and came to Blaspuaborg. They were hospitably received by king Maximianus, and seated at a banquet. The king saw that Dinus and his men were not eating, and asked the reason why.

"I did not come here to be fed," said Dinus. "I have so great a longing for your daughter that I shall die at once if I do not get to her bed. I ask your leave."

"I had not intended my daughter to be any man's paramour," the king replied, "but I would rather she slept with you one night than marry her to other princes. So I give her to you, and her maids."

Dinus and his men went to the princess's hall, and found the doors open, but no maidens. There were forty beds in the hall. It was all one glitter of splendor—gold, marble pillars, gems, busts, doves, songs, and odors. But when the men tried to seize the doves they flew straight out through the blank wall. The prince affected a calm demeanor.

"I call such things wondrous fair," he said, "but still not learning nor craft."

A little later the hall doors opened, and forty maidens came in, splendidly gowned. Philotemia's complexion was like the blood-red rose and the snow-white lily. The sun shone on them through windows adorned with crystal. The princess came to Dinus and threw her arms around his neck. Her maidens did the same to the prince's knights. They drank and played games until at sunset they prepared themselves for bed. Philotemia unrobed Dinus herself, and the other maidens did the same for their lovers. Then each took off her own outer garments, and stood in her kirtle before her bed. But just as they were going to bed, a din shook the hall, like the approach of a great cavalcade. Every one started. Again the din.

"What is it?" asked Dinus.

"I must tell you," said the princess. "My father Maximianus has forty knights who were sent to him from the ultimate darkness of Blaland. They are strong as trolls, big as giants, black as pitch. And their armor has this property, that they can ride through mountains and stone walls. The king has appointed them to guard this hall; they ride through the walls and kill all the men they find."

The maidens armed the knights in haste. A third time the din. Then forty knights came riding through the walls, liker to fiends than men. A stubborn combat followed. The walls seemed to expand, and allow them room. It was little use to chop off the feet or the hands of the enemy, for the limbs flew back to their places. At last, when the sun shone through the windows, the fiends leaped through the wall and disappeared, and Dinus and his men were left behind, wounded and weary. They climbed into their beds, expecting fond embraces, but the beds were empty. Yet they slept from weariness.

They awoke to a strange transformation. Beds and palace had vanished. They were lying naked on a plain, with oaks above them, and the oaks were all hacked, and the limbs were strewn over the grass, and it was evident to them that the knights they had been fighting all night were nothing but oaks. They saw their clothes lying near by, and dressed at once. All desire for women was gone out of them.

"We have been put to a great shame," said Grammaton.

"Gladly will I get me hence," cried Dinus, "if I may but find horse and weapons."

And lo!—their horses standing saddled in the wood a little way off!

Now they rode home, and behind them in the city arose a hue and cry. Some citizens struck their shields, some urged on their dogs, some shot arrows, and some shouted jeeringly: "There goes Dinus the proud. They are not so hot after women now, he and his fellows."

When they came to a forest, Dinus left his comrades, and slipped back alone into the city and the princess's palace. They were all away at drink in the king's hall. After spending a little while in the palace, he stole out and back to his men. They returned to Alexandria as they had departed, in the night, so that no one knew of their going, except those who were left to guard the hall. There they rested and healed their bruises.

Samson the Fair

Imported fourteenth century

Samsons saga fagra

"SAMSON the Fair" is apparently an Icelandic translation of an Anglo-Norman romance lost in England but transmitted to the North via Norway. Although it is a pleasant and restrained narrative, this saga has been neglected by historians of literature and has never been published in a scholarly edition or translated into English. For two reasons *Samson* is of special interest to students of English. Like *Grettis saga* and one or two other sagas, it contains a version of the Bear's-son folktale, the adventure of the hero who slays a monster dwelling under a waterfall, that we find in *Bēowulf*. Also, it includes an account of the chastity test of the magic mantle, familiar to readers of Arthurian romance.

According to the saga, King Arthur of England had a son named Samson the Fair. Samson fell in love with a hostage at the court, the beautiful Valentina, daughter of King Garlant of Ireland. On a visit to Brittany or Scotland she was enticed into a forest by the harping of a woman-stealer, Kvintalin, whose mother was a she-troll living under a waterfall. Samson slew the troll and eventually found Valentina. For punishment Kvintalin was sent to the Land of the Little Maids to steal the mantle that would serve as a test for chastity. His quest was successful, Valentina passed the test, Samson married her, and ruled happily over England.

THE WATERFALL

◄§ WHILE they were discussing this, Samson was standing at the edge of the fall, and the first thing he knew he was seized by both feet and pushed down into the water. He had to match his strength against a huge she-troll. They wrestled together hard and long, and were drawn downwards towards the bottom; it was a matter of life and death with him to get the upper hand of her when they got to the bottom, and just about then he reached through the water for his knife, which he carried in his belt, and which Valentina had given him. He plunged the knife into her belly so that all the entrails fell out. When he was freed from the clutches of the she-troll, he dived under the waterfall, and immediately perceived the mouth of a cave, but he was so weakened that he had to lie there a considerable time.

When he came to himself after this labor, he wrung out his clothes and went into the cave, and he thought that he might never come out. He went far along the cave, and he wondered greatly at the size and the shape of it, and presently he came to a side-cave, and found there women's gear, precious objects, gold and silver. There was a couch with remarkably beautiful hangings, and the bedclothes were of the same sort. In the cave he found the kirtle and mantle of the Princess Valentina, and her diadem and girdle. He took from these what he desired, and went to the end of the cave, and found at last a big door, which was let down in a cleft, but not locked, and when he got it open, with great effort, for it was heavy, he saw ahead of him a great and beautiful forest.

THE CHASTITY MANTLE

Now the story turns to Samson the Fair celebrating his bridal in Ruthuborg in Ireland. Invited to his wedding were his father King Arthur, Jarl Finnlaug, and many other notables. The morning that the bride was led in there came to the castle Kvintalin and the dwarf Grelant, along with their goods. After they had saluted the notables properly they produced their trophies and presented them to Samson. When he showed them to his table guests they were much impressed over their magic properties.

The mantle was put to test in many ways, and it was held to be true that few maidens were proved to be chaste there any more than in Giant Land. And it was the opinion of the wedding guests that broken pots are found in many a kitchen. Princess Valentina was the one who stood this ordeal, and men whispered to one another that she had Olympia to thank for this honor and not her own prudence.

Samson gave the bride the good mantle as his bench gift.

SELECTED READING

PUBLICATIONS OF THE AMERICAN-SCANDINAVIAN FOUNDATION,
116 EAST 64TH STREET, NEW YORK 21, N.Y.:

The Poetic Edda. Translated by Henry Adams Bellows.
The Prose Edda. Translated by Arthur Gilchrist Brodeur.
The King's Mirror. Translated by Laurence Marcellus Larson.
Four Icelandic Sagas. Translated by Gwyn Jones.
Vatnsdalers' Saga. Translated by Gwyn Jones.
The Saga of the Volsungs and the Saga of Ragnar Lodbrok. Translated by Margaret Schlauch.
Norse Mythology. By P. A. Munch. Revised by Magnus Olsen.
The Old Norse Sagas. By Halvdan Koht.
Romance in Iceland. By Margaret Schlauch.
Heroic Legends of Denmark. By Axel Olrik.
Ballad Criticism. By Sigurd Bernhard Hustvedt.
Viking Civilization. By Axel Olrik.
The Voyages of the Norsemen to America. By William Hovgaard.
The Skalds. Translated by Lee M. Hollander.

OTHER PUBLISHERS

Prolegomena to *Sturlunga Saga.* By Gudbrand Vigfusson. vol. 1. Oxford 1878.
The Viking Age. By P. B. Du Chaillu. London and New York 1889.
The Vikings in Western Christendom. By C. F. Keary. London 1891.
The Saga Library. Edited by William Morris and Eiríkr Magnússon. 6 vols. London 1891 fol.
The Saga of Hacon. Translated by G. W. Dasent. London 1894.
Saxo Grammaticus. (First nine books.) Translated by Oliver Elton. London 1894.
Hamlet in Iceland. By Israel Gollancz. London 1898.
Sverris Saga. Translated by J. Sephton. London 1899.
Stories from the Northern Sagas. Translated by A. F. Major and E. E. Speight. London 1905.
Origines Islandicae. Edited and translated by Gudbrand Vigfusson and F. York Powell. 2 vols. Oxford 1905.
The Origin of the English Nation. By H. M. Chadwick. Cambridge 1905.
The Religion of Ancient Scandinavia. By W. A. Craigie. London 1906.
Islandica. Edited by Halldór Hermannsson. Many volumes. Cornell University Press 1908 fol.
Epic and Romance. By W. P. Ker. London 1908.
The Icelandic Sagas. By W. A. Craigie. Cambridge 1913.
Kindred and Clan. By Bertha S. Phillpotts. Cambridge 1913.
History of the Norwegian People. By K. Gjerset. 2 vols. New York 1915.

The Saga of Grettir the Strong. Translated by George A. Hight. (Every-man's Library) London and New York 1915.

The Elder Edda and Ancient Scandinavian Drama. By Bertha S. Phill-potts. Cambridge 1920.

Social Scandinavia in the Viking Age. By Mary W. Williams. New York 1920.

Angevin Britain and Scandinavia. By H. G. Leach. Harvard University Press 1921.

History of Iceland. By K. Gjerset. New York 1924.

The Laxdæla Saga. Translated by Thorstein Veblen. New York 1925.

An Introduction to Old Norse. By E. V. Gordon. Oxford 1927 fol.

Beowulf and Epic Tradition. By W. W. Lawrence. Harvard University Press 1928.

A History of the Vikings. By T. D. Kendrick. New York 1930.

Egil's Saga. Translated by E. R. Eddison. Cambridge 1931.

Edda and Saga. By Bertha S. Phillpotts. London 1931.

Old Norse Poems (not in *The Skalds* or *The Poetic Edda*). Translated by Lee M. Hollander. Columbia University Press 1936.

The Art of Poetry in Iceland. By W. A. Craigie. Oxford 1937.

The Story of Burnt Njal. Translated by George W. Dasent. 2 vols. several editions.

SOURCES

I. THE GODS

NERTHUS. *Angevin Britain and Scandinavia.* By Henry Goddard Leach. Cambridge, Harvard University Press, 1921, pp. 4-5.

THE BEGINNING AND THE END. *The Poetic Edda.* Tr. Henry Adams Bellows. New York, The American-Scandinavian Foundation, 1923, pp. 3-26.

THE SAYINGS OF THE HIGH ONE. *The Poetic Edda.* Tr. Henry Adams Bellows. New York, The American-Scandinavian Foundation, 1923, pp. 29-60.

FREYR'S COURTSHIP. *The Poetic Edda.* Tr. Henry Adams Bellows. New York, The American-Scandinavian Foundation, 1923, pp. 107-120.

THOR GETS BACK HIS HAMMER. *The Elder Edda and Ancient Scandinavian Drama.* By Bertha S. Phillpotts. Cambridge, The University Press, 1920, pp. 66-71. (By permission of The Macmillan Company, New York.)

THOR'S EXPLOITS. *The Prose Edda.* By Snorri Sturluson. Tr. Arthur Gilchrist Brodeur. New York, The American-Scandinavian Foundation, 1916, pp. 68-70.

THE HORSE SLEIPNIR. *The Prose Edda.* By Snorri Sturluson. Tr. Arthur Gilchrist Brodeur. New York, The American-Scandinavian Foundation, 1916, pp. 53-55.

WOLVES OR SEAGULLS? *The Prose Edda.* By Snorri Sturluson. Tr. Arthur Gilchrist Brodeur. New York, The American-Scandinavian Foundation, 1916, pp. 36-38.

FREYR AND FREYJA. *The Prose Edda.* By Snorri Sturluson. Tr. Arthur Gilchrist Brodeur. New York, The American-Scandinavian Foundation, 1916, p. 38.

BALDR THE BEAUTIFUL. *The Prose Edda.* By Snorri Sturluson. Tr. Arthur Gilchrist Brodeur. New York, The American-Scandinavian Foundation, 1916, pp. 70-75.

II. LEGENDARY HEROES

THE LAY OF WAYLAND. *The Poetic Edda.* Tr. Henry Adams Bellows. New York, The American-Scandinavian Foundation, 1923, pp. 254-268.

FROTHI'S MEAL. *The Prose Edda.* By Snorri Sturluson. Tr. Arthur Gilchrist Brodeur. New York, The American-Scandinavian Foundation, 1916, pp. 161-169.

HELGI THRICE BORN. *The Poetic Edda.* Tr. Henry Adams Bellows. New York, The American-Scandinavian Foundation, 1923, pp. 269-331.

OFFA. *The First Nine Books of the Danish History of Saxo Grammaticus.* Tr. Oliver Elton. London, David Nutt, 1894, pp. 130-143.

TRAGEDY AT SIGERSTED. *The First Nine Books of the Danish History* of *Saxo Grammaticus.* Tr. Oliver Elton. London, David Nutt, 1894, pp. 280-285.

THE WAKING OF ANGANTYR. *Old Norse Poems.* Tr. Lee M. Hollander. New York, Columbia University Press, 1936, pp. 30-35.

THE ANGLIAN TRADITION. *The Oldest English Epic.* Tr. Francis B. Gummere. New York, The Macmillan Company, 1909, pp. 26, 36.
     Wīdsīð. Translation by H. G. Leach. For location of Heorot see Stephen J. Herben, Jr. in *Publications of the Modern Language Association,* Vol. L (1935), pp. 933-945.

KRAKI'S SEED. *The Prose Edda.* By Snorri Sturluson. Tr. Arthur Gilchrist Brodeur. New York, The American-Scandinavian Foundation, 1916, pp. 169-173.

BJARKI AND THE BEAST. *Beowulf.* By R. W. Chambers. Second edition. Cambridge, The University Press, 1932, pp. 142-146. (By permission of The Macmillan Company, New York.)

THE DESTRUCTION OF LEIRE. *Old Norse Poems.* Tr. Lee M. Hollander. New York, Columbia University Press, 1936, pp. 5-11.

"HERE THE SEA IS CALLED HAMLET'S CHURN." *Hamlet in Iceland.* By Israel Gollancz. London, David Nutt, 1898, p. xi.

HAMLET THE FOOL. *Hamlet in Iceland.* By Israel Gollancz. London, David Nutt, 1898, pp. 81-85.

HAMLET'S SHIELD. *The First Nine Books of the Danish History of Saxo Grammaticus.* Tr. Oliver Elton. London, David Nutt, 1894, pp. 122-123.

THE OTTER'S WERGILD. *The Prose Edda.* By Snorri Sturluson. Tr. Arthur Gilchrist Brodeur. New York, The American-Scandinavian Foundation, 1916, pp. 150-157.

SIGURTH IN FAEROËSE. *Sigurd the Dragon-Slayer. A Faroëse Ballad-Cycle.* Tr. E. M. Smith-Dampier. Oxford, Basil Blackwell, 1934, pp. 32, 63-66.

A VALKYRIE AWAKENS. *The Poetic Edda.* Tr. Henry Adams Bellows. New York, The American-Scandinavian Foundation, 1923, pp. 388-390.

BRYNHILD'S COMPLAINT. *The Saga of the Volsungs.* Tr. Margaret Schlauch. New York, The American-Scandinavian Foundation, 1930, pp. 129-141.

"HOME THEY BROUGHT HER WARRIOR DEAD." *The Poetic Edda.* Tr. Henry Adams Bellows. New York, The American-Scandinavian Foundation, 1923, pp. 412-419.

ATTILA THE HUN. *The Poetic Edda.* Tr. Henry Adams Bellows. New York, The American-Scandinavian Foundation, 1923, pp. 482-498.

THE LAST OF THE VOLSUNGS. *The Saga of the Volsungs.* Tr. Margaret Schlauch. New York, The American-Scandinavian Foundation, 1930, pp. 178-179.

THE LAST VOYAGE OF SIGURTH HRING. Translated by Donald W. Prakken and H. G. Leach from the Latin epitome of the lost *Skjöldunga saga* made by the Icelander Arngrímur Jónsson in 1596. *Sturlunga saga,* ed. G. Vigfusson, Oxford, Clarendon Press, 1878, I, p. xc, foot-note 1 ; *Skjöldunga saga,* ed. A. Olrik, *Aarböger for Nordisk Oldkyn-dighed og Historie.* Copenhagen 1894, p. 132.

III. ICELAND

INGOLF. *The Book of the Icelanders.* By Ari Thorgilsson. Tr. Halldór Hermannsson. (*Islandica* XX) Ithaca, Cornell University Library, 1930, p. 60.

THE THORSNESS SETTLEMENT. *Origines Islandicae.* Tr. Gudbrand Vig-fusson and F. York Powell. Oxford, The Clarendon Press, 1905, I, p. 257.

KING ATHELSTAN'S SILVER. *The Story of Egil Skallagrimsson.* Tr. W. C. Green. London, Elliot Stock, 1893, pp. 102-104, 196-197.

LAWSUIT AGAINST HRAFNKEL. *Four Icelandic Sagas.* Tr. Gwyn Jones. New York, The American-Scandinavian Foundation, 1935, pp. 44-51.

FARMS AND FENCES. *The Story of Viga Glum.* Tr. Sir Edmund Head. London, Williams and Norgate, 1866, pp. 27-30.

A POET FALLS IN LOVE. *The Life and Death of Cormac the Skald.* Tr. W. G. Collingwood and Jón Stefánsson. (Viking Club Translation Series. No. 1.) Ulverston, Wm. Holmes, 1902, pp. 33-38, 64-68.

For a recent discussion of the psychology of Cormac see "The Case of the Skald Kormak," by Lee M. Hollander in *Monatshefte für Deutschen Unterricht.* University of Wisconsin. Vol. XXXV (March, 1943), pp. 107-115.

FATHER AND SON. *Egil's Saga.* Tr. E. R. Eddison. Cambridge, The Uni-versity Press, 1930, pp. 186-194. (By permission of The Macmillan Company, New York.)

GISLI THE OUTLAW. From *The Saga of Gisli: Son of Sour.* Tr. Ralph B. Allen. New York, Harcourt, Brace and Company, Inc., copyright, 1936, pp. 130-138.

FRUSTRATED LOVERS. *Medieval Narrative.* Tr. Margaret Schlauch. New York, Prentice-Hall, Inc., 1928, pp. 38-42, 60-63, 69-72.

GUNNAR OF LITHEND. *The Story of Burnt Njal.* Tr. George Webbe Dasent. Edinburgh, Edmonston and Douglas, 1861, I, pp. 240-247.

CONVERSION OF ICELAND. *Origines Islandicae.* Tr. Gudbrand Vigfusson and F. York Powell. Oxford, The Clarendon Press, 1905, I, pp. 399, 400, 403.

THE TALE OF THORSTEIN STAFF-SMITTEN. *The Saga of Thorstein Staff-Blow.* Tr. Erik Wahlgren. *The University of Kansas City Re-view,* Spring 1945, pp. 213-217.

BONNET AND SWORD. From *The Laxdœla Saga.* Tr. Thorstein Veblen. New York, B. W. Huebsch, Inc. (By permission of The Viking Press, New York), copyright 1925, pp. 148-149, 158-163.

THE BURNING OF NJAL. *The Story of Burnt Njal.* Tr. George Webbe Dasent. Edinburgh, Edmonston and Douglas, 1861, II, pp. 172-181.

THE GHOST OF GLAM. Adapted by H. G. Leach from *Grettis saga*, chapters 32-35. *The American-Scandinavian Review*, New York 1945, pp. 244-250.

THE TROLLS OF THE WATERFALL. *The Saga of Grettir the Strong.* Tr. George Ainslie Hight. (Everyman's Library.) London, J. M. Dent; New York, E. P. Dutton & Co., 1914, pp. 170-177.

STUF'S SAGA. Translation by H. G. Leach edited by Benjamin H. J. Eiriksson from *Stúfs saga*, ed. Björn M. Ólsen, Filgir Árbók Háskóla Íslands. Reykjavík 1912, pp. 1-7.

AN ICELANDIC STORY-TELLER. Translation by H. G. Leach edited by Benjamin H. J. Eiriksson from *Morkinskinna*, ed. Finnur Jónsson. Copenhagen 1932, pp. 199-200.

BRAND THE OPEN-HANDED. Translation by H. G. Leach edited by Benjamin H. J. Eiriksson from *Morkinskinna*, ed. Finnur Jónsson. Copenhagen 1932, pp. 194-195.

AUTHUN AND HIS BEAR. Translated by Phillip M. Mitchell. See *Íslendinga þættir*, ed. Guðni Jónsson. Reykjavík 1935, pp. 1-10.

A CURE FOR LOVE-SICKNESS. Translation by H. G. Leach edited by Benjamin H. J. Eiriksson from *Morkinskinna*, ed. Finnur Jónsson. Copenhagen 1932, pp. 354-356.

JÓN LOPTSSON DEFIES THE HIERARCHY. Translation by H. G. Leach from *Biskupa sögur*. Copenhagen 1858, I, pp. 282-284.

SHIPWRECK. *Collected Essays of W. P. Ker.* Ed. Charles Whibley. London, Macmillan and Co., 1925, II, pp. 164-168.

THE TWO THORAS. Translated by J. B. C. Watkins from *Sturlunga saga*. Reykjavík 1909, II, pp. 23-26.

SIGHVAT'S WARNING. Translated by J. B. C. Watkins from *Sturlunga saga*. Reykjavík 1909, II, pp. 283-285.

THE DEATH OF SNORRI STURLUSON. Translated by J. B. C. Watkins from *Sturlunga saga*. Reykjavík 1909, II, pp. 349-351.

THE FIRE AT FLUGUMYRI. *Epic and Romance.* By W. P. Ker. London, Macmillan and Co., 1926, pp. 259-264.

STURLA THE HISTORIAN. *Sturla the Historian.* By W. P. Ker. *Collected Essays,* London, Macmillan and Co., 1925, II, pp. 182-186.

ICELANDIC RECIPES. *An Old Icelandic Medical Miscellany.* Tr. Henning Larsen. (Det Norske Videnskaps-Akademi.) Oslo 1931, pp. 214-215.

ICELANDIC MEDICINE. *An Old Icelandic Medical Miscellany.* Tr. Henning Larsen. (Det Norske Videnskaps-Akademi.) Oslo 1931, pp. 140, 154, 160.

IV. NORWAY

HARALD FAIRHAIRED. *The Stories of the Kings of Norway.* By Snorri Sturluson. Tr. William Morris and Eiríkr Magnússon. London, Bernard Quaritch, 1893, I, pp. 93-95.

THE BATTLE OF HAFRSFJORD. *The Stories of the Kings of Norway.* By

Snorri Sturluson. Tr. William Morris and Eiríkr Magnússon. London, Bernard Quaritch, 1893, I, pp. 111-113.

OLAF TRYGGVASON. *The Stories of the Kings of Norway.* By Snorri Sturluson. Tr. William Morris and Eiríkr Magnússon. London, Bernard Quaritch, 1893, I, pp. 371-376.

ASBIORN SEAL'S-BANE. Modernized by H. G. Leach from *Heimskringla* by Snorri Sturluson, ed. Finnur Jónsson. Copenhagen, G. E. C. Gad, 1911, pp. 288-302.

THORMOTH AND SAINT OLAF. Modernized by H. G. Leach from *Heimskringla* by Snorri Sturluson, ed. Finnur Jónsson. Copenhagen, G. E. C. Gad, 1911, pp. 389-390, 405-407.

HARALD HARTHRATHI IN BYZANTIUM. *The Stories of the Kings of Norway.* By Snorri Sturluson. Tr. William Morris and Eiríkr Magnússon. London, Bernard Quaritch, 1895, III, pp. 59-60.

THE BATTLE OF STAMFORD BRIDGE. *Heimskringla, The Norse King Sagas.* By Snorri Sturluson. Tr. Samuel Laing. (Everyman's) London, J. M. Dent & Sons Ltd.; New York, E. P. Dutton & Co., 1930, pp. 229-232.

THE DEBATE OF THE KINGS. *The Stories of the Kings of Norway.* By Snorri Sturluson. Tr. William Morris and Eiríkr Magnússon. London, Bernard Quaritch, 1895, III, pp. 279-283.

KING SVERRI'S SPEECH AT BERGEN. *The Saga of King Sverri of Norway.* (By Karl Jónsson.) Tr. John Sephton. London, David Nutt, 1899, pp. 129-131.

ANCIENT NORWEGIAN LAW. Reprinted from *The Earliest Norwegian Laws.* Tr. Laurence Marcellus Larson. New York, by permission of Columbia University Press, 1935, pp. 72-74.

THE QUEEN HEARS THE NEWS. *Icelandic Sagas.* Vol. IV, *The Saga of Hacon.* (By Sturla Þórðarson.) Tr. Sir G. W. Dasent. Rolls Series. By permission of the Controller of His Britannic Majesty's Stationery Office. London 1894, pp. 198-199.

THE END OF KING HAKON THE OLD. *Icelandic Sagas.* Vol. IV, *The Saga of Hacon.* (By Sturla Þórðarson.) Tr. Sir G. W. Dasent. Rolls Series. By permission of the Controller of His Britannic Majesty's Stationery Office. London 1894, pp. 364-370.

V. THE WESTERN ISLANDS

QUEEN AUTH LEAVES IRELAND. *The Book of the Settlement of Iceland.* By Ari the Learned (Thorgilsson). Tr. T. Ellwood. Kendal, T. Wilson, 1898, pp. 62-65.

A FAEROËSE TRADER. *The Saga of the Faroe Islanders.* Tr. Muriel A. C. Press. London, J. M. Dent & Sons Ltd., 1934, pp. 1-6.

THE BATTLE OF CLONTARF. *The War of the Gaedhil with the Gaill.* Tr. James Henthorn Todd. Rolls Series. By permission of the Controller of His Britannic Majesty's Stationery Office. London 1867, pp. 191-207.

The Fatal Shirt. *The Orkneyinga Saga.* Tr. Alexander Burt Taylor. Edinburgh and London, Oliver and Boyd, 1938, pp. 216-217.

Runes of Man and Orkney. *An Introduction to Old Norse.* By E. V. Gordon. Oxford, The Clarendon Press, 1927, pp. 164-165.

Hildina. *Stories and Ballads of the Far Past.* Tr. N. Kershaw. Cambridge, The University Press, 1921, pp. 217-219. (By permission of The Macmillan Company, New York.)

VI. GREENLAND

The Settlement of Greenland. *The Book of the Icelanders.* By Ari Thorgilsson. Tr. Halldór Hermannsson. (*Islandica* XX) Ithaca, Cornell University Library, 1930, p. 64.

A Polar Bear. *Origines Islandicae.* Tr. Gudbrand Vigfusson and F. York Powell. Oxford University Press, 1905, II, p. 659.

Daily Life in Greenland. *The King's Mirror.* Tr. Laurence Marcellus Larson. New York, The American-Scandinavian Foundation, 1917, pp. 140-145.

The Northernmost Runes. *An Introduction to Old Norse.* By E. V. Gordon. Oxford University Press, 1927, p. 166.

VII. VINLAND THE GOOD

Adam of Bremen. Translated by Richard Mott Gummere. See Adamus Bremensis, *"Descriptio insularum Aquilonis,"* chapters 36-38, appended to *Gesta Hammaburgensis Ecclesiae Pontificum.* Hanover 1876, pp. 185-186.

Bjarni Herjulfsson. *The Voyages of the Norsemen to America.* By William Hovgaard. New York, The American-Scandinavian Foundation, 1914, pp. 81-83.

Leif Ericsson Discovers America. *The Voyages of the Norsemen to America.* By William Hovgaard. New York, The American-Scandinavian Foundation, 1914, pp. 77-78.

Leif Explores the Coast. *The Voyages of the Norsemen to America.* By William Hovgaard. New York, The American-Scandinavian Foundation, 1914, pp. 84-87.

Thorfinn Karlsefni Plants a Colony. *The Voyages of the Norsemen to America.* By William Hovgaard. New York, The American-Scandinavian Foundation, 1914, pp. 106-112.

VIII. DENMARK

A Danish March on Rome. *The Geography of Strabo.* Tr. W. Falconer. London, George Bell & Sons, 1887, I, pp. 450-451.

A Roman Fleet Visits Jutland. *The Monumentum Ancyranum.* Ed. E. G. Hardy. Oxford, The Clarendon Press, 1923, p. 119. For facsimile see *Exploration archéologique de la Galatie.* Perrot, Guillaume et Delbet. Paris, Didot Frères, 1862-72. I, p. 253; II, plate 26. For bibliography see *Res gestae divi Augusti.* Ed. Jean Gagé. Paris 1935.

HYGELAC INVADES MEROVINGIA. *Beowulf and Epic Tradition.* By William Witherle Lawrence. Cambridge, Harvard University Press, 1928, pp. 92-93.

RUNES OF GALLEHUS AND GLAVENDRUP. *An Introduction to Old Norse.* By E. V. Gordon. Oxford, The Clarendon Press, 1927, pp. 166-168.

THE JELLINGE STONES. *Canute the Great.* By Laurence Marcellus Larson. New York, G. P. Putnam's Sons, 1912, pp. 6-7.

VALDEMAR AND TOVE. *A Book of Danish Ballads.* Tr. E. M. Smith-Dampier. New York, The American-Scandinavian Foundation, 1939, pp. 135-138.

THE DANNEBROG FALLS FROM HEAVEN. Translated by Donald W. Prakken and H. G. Leach from *Om Danebroges Oprindelse.* A. D. Jörgensen. *Historisk Tidsskrift* (Danish) IV, 5 (1875-1877), p. 423, and *Scriptores rerum Danicarum medii aevi.* Ed. Jacobus Langebek. Copenhagen 1834. I, p. 182; VIII, p. 499.

IX. SWEDEN

THE RÖK STONE. Translation by H. G. Leach from *Rökstenen.* By Otto von Friesen. Fornminneplatsen no. 23. Stockholm 1934, pp. 22-24. See also *Der Runenstein von Rök.* By Sophus Bugge, ed. Magnus Olsen. Stockholm 1910, pp. 314, Pl. I-IV. *Rökstenen.* By Otto v. Friesen. Stockholm 1920, pp. 147. Pl. I-IV. *An Introduction to Old Norse.* By E. V. Gordon. Oxford University Press, 1927, pp. 168-169, 240-242. *Rökstenens chiffergåtor.* By Sigurd Agrell. Humanistiska vetenskapssamfundet i Lund 1930, 120 pp.

SWEDISH AMBASSADORS. Edited by H. F. Abraham and H. G. Leach from *The Relations Between Ancient Russia and Scandinavia.* By Vilhelm Thomsen. Oxford and London, James Parker and Co., 1877, pp. 39-40.

SWEDES ESTABLISH THE RUSSIAN STATE. *The Russian Primary Chronicle.* Tr. S. H. Cross. Cambridge, Harvard University Press, 1930, pp. 144-145. Cf. *The Relations Between Ancient Russia and Scandinavia.* By Vilhelm Thomsen. Oxford and London, James Parker and Co., 1877. *Die Verbindungen zwischen Skandinavien und dem Ostbalticum in der jüngeren Eisenzeit.* By Birger Nerman. Stockholm, Akademiens Förlag, 1929, 185 pp.

SWEDES ON THE VOLGA. "Ibn Faḍlān's Account of Scandinavian Merchants on the Volga in 922." By Albert Stanburrough Cook. *The Journal of English and Germanic Philology,* XXII, Urbana, University of Illinois, 1923, pp. 56-63.

A SWEDISH PRINCESS AT THE BYZANTINE COURT. Translated by H. F. Abraham, George Melanos, and H. G. Leach from *Constantini Porphyrogeniti Imperatoris De Cerimoniis Aulae Byzantinae Libri Duo.* Ed. J. J. Reiske, vol. 1, lib. II, chap. 15, pp. 594-598. (*Corpus Scriptorum Historiae Byzantinae,* ed. B. G. Niebuhr, Bonn 1829.) For technical terms and charts see *Constantin VII Porphyrogente. Le Livre des Cérémonies.* By Albert Vogt. Paris 1935.

THE GRIPSHOLM STONE. Translated by H. G. Leach from *Södermanlands Runinskrifter,* ed. Erik Brate and Elias Wessén. Stockholm 1924-36. No. 179 (pp. 152-155).

THE LION OF THE PIRAEUS. Translated by H. G. Leach from text in *An Introduction to Old Norse.* By E. V. Gordon. Oxford University Press, 1927, pp. 171-172.

WORSHIP AT UPPSALA. Translated by Donald W. Prakken and H. G. Leach from Adamus Bremensis, *Gesta Hammaburgensis Ecclesiae Pontificum,* Lib. IV, 26-27, Scholia 134, 135, 137. Hanover 1876, pp. 174-176.

THE LIFE OF SAINT ERIC. Translated by Adolph Burnett Benson from text in *An Introduction to Old Norse.* By E. V. Gordon. Oxford University Press, 1927, pp. 152-155.

THE LAW OF THE WESTGOTHS. Translated by Adolph Burnett Benson from text in *An Introduction to Old Norse.* By E. V. Gordon. Oxford University Press, 1927, pp. 150-151.

DEED FOR A COPPER MINE. Unsigned translation by courtesy of Naboth Hedin from *Stora Kopparbergets Historie.* By Sven Tunberg. Uppsala, Almquist and Wicksell, 1922. Plate No. 1. See also *Stora Kopparberget under Medeltiden och Gustav Vasa.* By Tom Söderberg. Stockholm, Victor Petterson, 1932.

THE LEGENDARY HISTORY OF GOTLAND. Translated by Adolph Burnett Benson from text in *An Introduction to Old Norse.* By E. V. Gordon. Oxford University Press, 1927, pp. 156-158.

X. OTHER POEMS

THE DEATH-SONG OF EGIL THE SON OF GRIM. *Highland Light and Other Poems.* By Henry Adams Bellows. New York, The Macmillan Company, 1921, pp. 45-53.

THE EIRÍKSMÁL. *Anglo-Saxon and Norse Poems.* Tr. N. Kershaw. Cambridge, The University Press, 1922, pp. 97-99. (By permission of The Macmillan Company, New York.)

THE LOSS OF MY SONS. *Translations from the Icelandic.* By W. C. Green. London, Chatto and Windus, 1924, pp. 148-158.

THE LAY OF HAKON. Reprinted from *Old Norse Poems.* Tr. Lee M. Hollander. New York, by permission of Columbia University Press, 1936, pp. 68-71.

THE SONG OF THE NORNS. *Old Norse Poems.* Tr. Lee M. Hollander. New York, Columbia University Press, 1936, pp. 72-75.

XI. ROMANCE

THE BALLAD OF TRISTRAM. *The North American Book of Icelandic Verse.* Tr. Watson Kirkconnell. New York & Montreal, Louis Carrier & Alan Isles, Inc., 1930, pp. 93-98.

A Lost Carolingian Romance. Translated by H. M. Smyser in *Survivals in Old Norwegian*. Connecticut College Monograph No. 1. Baltimore, Waverly Press, Inc., 1941, pp. 3-5.

Dinus and Philotemia. Summary by H. G. Leach. *Angevin Britain and Scandinavia*. Cambridge, Harvard University Press, 1921, pp. 272-275.

Samson the Fair: the Waterfall. "Beowulf and the Saga of Samson the Fair." By William Witherle Lawrence in *Studies in English Philology . . . in Honor of Frederick Klæber*. Minneapolis, The University of Minnesota Press, 1929, pp. 175-176. See *Angevin Britain* by H. G. Leach. Cambridge, Harvard University Press, 1921 (index). *Beowulf* by R. W. Chambers. Cambridge, The University Press. 1932 (index).

Samson the Fair: The Chastity Mantle. Translated by H. G. Leach from *Samson Friði og Kvintalín kvennaþjófur*. Reykjavík 1905, pp. 43-44. Cf. *Samsons saga fagra* in Bjoerner's *Nordiska Kämpa Dater*. Stockholm, Joh. L. Horrn, 1737, chap. XXII.

Committee on Publications